1982

Inside the Iranian Revolution

Inside
the Iranian
Revolution

by JOHN D. STEMPEL

 Indiana University Press   Bloomington

Library of Congress Cataloging in Publication Data

Stempel, John D., 1938–
Inside the Iranian revolution.

Includes bibliographical references and index.
1. Iran—Politics and government—1941–1979. 2. Iran
—Politics and government—1979–   I. Title.
DS318.S78   955'.053   81–47564
ISBN 0–253–14200–8   AACR2
    1   2   3   4   5   85   84   83   82   81

To Nancy, my wife and editor,
in memory of
Dr. Akbar Bahadori,
executed May 10, 1979,
from both of us.

Contents

Preface

To write living history accurately and well is a difficult proposition. In a situation like Iran, where the revolutionary process is continuing, it is even more uncertain. The possibility for vast differences in perceptions is significant. Each participant or observer sees his own piece of the elephant; not enough time has elapsed to develop a thoroughly considered view of the beast as a complete animal. I both observed and participated in the events of that tumultuous period. My family and I arrived in Tehran in July 1975, when Iran was in the throes of the accelerated economic development process that had begun a year earlier. We witnessed the gradual disintegration of the Shah's political system. My wife and daughters were evacuated in December 1978; I left six months later, after watching the culmination of the revolution that would bring Khomeini to power, actively participating in the events surrounding the first seizure of the American embassy, and correctly forecasting the emerging dissension that now racks the revolutionary coalition. First as political officer, then as deputy chief of the political section, and finally as acting chief of the section, I would come to know personally many of the Iranians, particularly among the opposition, who would play important roles in the revolutionary drama.

My job was to report in detail on the emerging changes within Iran. I drafted many cables and memoranda explaining the positions of various groups and outlining their importance for U.S. policy. Though not a policy maker, I contributed directly to that process. Because this book is about those events and those people, many of whom are still involved in politics and thus potentially in danger, I have not documented specific insights and information derived from my contacts and friendships within Iran. Where possible, I have cited published works as information sources. No classified material was used in preparing this manuscript; the reconstruction of events is based entirely on my own experience and research. This included over 100 interviews with Iranians, other foreigners, and Americans both during and after the revolution. In addition to the interviews, my personal recollections were supplemented by notes jotted down in the course of my work, beginning shortly after my arrival in Tehran. The book was actually written during my tour as the Department of State's "diplomat in residence" at the United States Naval Academy from July 1979 to June 1981. While the State Department has approved publication of the manuscript, it should be emphasized that the views expressed are entirely the author's own. They do not necessarily reflect the opinion of the United States government.

My motive in writing the book was not to produce an "insider tells all" exposé, but to unravel the principal threads of the drama in order to help others understand the Iranian revolution and its aftermath. This story has the earmarks of a first-class adventure story—a supreme monarch driven from his throne, a fanatic elderly religious leader who takes over complete control, foreign involvement, the collapse of a nation's political system, and the unprecedented act of incarcerating diplomats not once but twice, the second time for more than 14 months.

From the standpoint of American policy, the Iranian experience of the past four years raises some troublesome questions. Did our intimate involvement with that country contribute to the turmoil? Was our policy making process adequate to cope with the broad current of social change? Did the U.S. suffer from an intelligence gap? An action gap? Both?

The answers to these questions have not only historical and human interest but considerable importance for how we organize ourselves to cope with and manage our external relations in the half-century to come, when the capacity of all political systems to cope with rapid social, economic, and political change will be constantly and severely tested. To survive, we will have to do more, better. The purpose of *Inside the Iranian Revolution* is to encourage us to do so.

Annapolis, Maryland   J.D.S.
June 1981

Acknowledgments

Years ago I labored over a doctoral dissertation. More recently I struggled through this, my first book. Both times I was particularly mindful of the assistance, both witting and unwitting, that I had received from others. For this book, first there is Nancy—wife, journalist, editor. While all the writing is mine, the editing is hers. She transformed a disorganized, pedantic manuscript into readable prose. She also typed the draft onto a computer and prepared the index. Our daughters, Amy and Jill, will always remember—and not too fondly—"the year Daddy wrote his book." They deserve a special thank you for just "hanging in there."

Iranians who befriended me over the years cannot be named lest they be subjected to "revolutionary excesses." To all the ones who cannot be identified—be they pro-monarchy or pro-revolution—my grateful thanks for your information, insights, and confidences. One gentleman, now in the United States, was especially valuable to me personally for over four years—Ahmad Jaffarbhoy, assistant to the American Embassy's political section.

Special tribute must also go to those State Department colleagues who assisted me. Some of them should be mentioned, including former ambassadors to Iran Richard Helms and William Sullivan; officers David Patterson, Stanley Escudero, George Lambrakis, Mark Johnson, Carl Clement, Wayne Miele, and Larry Semakis. Two directors of the Iranian Working Group, Henry Precht and Ralph Lindstrom, while we have disagreed frequently about things Iranian, contributed nonetheless. Peter Knecht, of the Bureau of Public Affairs, also gave valuable assistance on administrative matters.

Richard Preece and Clyde Mark of the Congressional Research Service facilitated my research, as did scholars Bill Lewis, Michael Ledeen, Richard Sales, and James Bill. Journalists Scott Armstrong and Andrew Whitley were similarly helpful. Feridoun Khajenouri, my teacher at the Foreign Service Institute in 1974–1975, improved my use of Farsi in the manuscript.

I am especially grateful for the support and encouragement I received while at the United States Naval Academy, where I was teaching full time while writing the book. Particularly significant was the backing offered by the Director of the United States and International Studies Division, Captain John Butterfield (himself in Iran as naval attaché at the U.S. Embassy from 1972 to 1975), and the chairman of the Political Science Department, Pope Atkins. Both urged me to undertake the project and they, along with other colleagues at the Academy, provided periodic, necessary morale boosts. Midshipmen Donald Loa and David DeJarnette helped me assemble a research bibliography. Sandra Erb taught both Nancy and me how to talk to the Navy Academy computer system so that it would not sass back.

Finally, a special thank you to those who helped me through the thicket of the publishing business—Frederick Praeger of Westview Press and the staff of Indiana University Press.

As with any book on a current public affairs issue, many people contributed to the factual accuracy and the understanding of shaded nuances. Errors and differences of opinion in either category are the responsibility of the author.

Inside the Iranian Revolution

Chapter One

★

The Context of Change

Genesis

Iran—or Persia, as it was called less than 50 years ago—has always been a geostrategic hotspot, located astride historic trade routes from Europe to Asia. It suffered through four major invasions from the time of Christ to the nineteenth century as armies fought to control its vital location. The most important of these was the Arab conquest in the seventh century, which brought Islam to Persia. Though Moslem, the Iranians are not Arabs, a distinction they share with their neighbors Turkey and Pakistan.

External pressure has always been an historic fact of life in Iran. During the last 150 years it has been Britain and Russia that have consistently locked horns there. Originally, the former sought to protect India and its interests in the Persian Gulf, and the latter wanted access to warm water ports as well as a position from which to protect its southern flank. Beginning in the 1850s, Iran's rulers tried to protect the country by balancing between the influence of the two great powers, but they were never very successful. During the final years of the Qajar dynasty, which ruled from 1787 until 1925, Britain and Russia intervened in the country's domestic affairs at will. In the most obvious example, in 1919, during the Bolshevik revolution, Soviet forces seized over 10,000 square miles of northwest Iran, successfully annexing about three-quarters of it to the southern Russia of today. As for the British, they bribed politicians continually, particularly in the early 1900s, trying to tempt the Qajar rulers into signing a treaty aligning Persia with England. The political pressure increased after oil prospecting began in southwest Persia in 1906.

The roots of Iran's revolution—the positioning of forces and the emergence of issues—go back to the rising discontent against the decadent Qajar shahs in the early years of the twentieth century. In 1906, the clergy and a small but powerful middle class imposed a constitution on Shah Muzaffar al-Din. It forced him to share power with a majles, or parliament, stimulating even greater religious influence in politics and encouraging continued social unrest. These events foreshadowed similar developments in later years, including the dissension culminating in the revolutionary takeover in February 1979.

When World War I began the perennial protagonists, Britain and Russia, started out as allies against Germany. Then the Communists took power in the Soviet Union after 1917 and the situation changed. With the two nations competing again, the internal confusion and foreign meddling reached greater heights. Intending to restore order with decisive action, a Persian general, Reza Khan, organized his brigade into the army's most effective unit. On February 21, 1921, Reza Khan led about 2,000 of his troops into Tehran, with himself the quintessential man on horseback come to prop up a decaying regime. There was only sporadic resistance from the gendarmerie (the national police), which was quickly overcome, and none from the rest of the army.

Reza Khan was welcomed by the anti-Qajar politicians, and his power expanded steadily. First he was named minister of war (1921–1923), then prime minister (1923–1925). Ahmad Shah did not rule, enjoying instead a luxurious lifestyle while living permanently in Europe and keeping out of politics at home. Thus Reza Khan exercised considerably more power than he might otherwise have been able to. The prime minister gathered around him younger men committed, as he was, to modernizing Iran and freeing it from foreign domination. By 1925 the prestige and power of Reza Khan had grown to the point that the politicians who had allied themselves with him pushed bills through parliament abolishing the Qajar dynasty and establishing Reza Khan (renamed Reza Pahlavi) and his heirs as the ruling family in Persia. There was no effective opposition to the change, not even from Ahmad Shah.

One of the first acts of the new shah was to encourage the use of the name "Iran" rather than the traditional "Persia," which had become identified with Qajar weakness. In 1935 the name was changed officially. The modernization of Iranian society started during Reza Shah's rule, with the imposition of effective government and the expanded control of the central administration. Even the most powerful independent tribal groups either accepted Reza Shah's rule or were defeated in a series of pitched battles.[1]

In a tremendous burst of economic expansion, railroad lines were extended across the country, factories were constructed, and state corporations were organized in basic industries. Socially, Reza Shah began to challenge the iron grip of religious leaders over the people's lives and habits. In 1936 he forbade women to wear the chador, a head-to-foot black veil covering everything but the face. That same year, in an effort to improve advanced education, he established Tehran University, Iran's first institution of higher learning. He also encouraged students to attend schools in the West. The number who did quadrupled immediately to about 1,000 per year. For the first time, Iranians who went abroad were allowed to study disciplines other than medicine.

The politically active elite participated in this first thrust at Western development in Iran, but there was no doubt that Reza Shah was boss. Though authoritarian in the best tradition of Persian kingship, he was astute enough to engage the loyalties of those who had to do the work of building. Nevertheless, the political process remained undeveloped, though the wealthy landowners — the "Thousand Families" — continued to dominate the Majles and religious leaders were bought off or crushed. Until the abrupt end of his reign in 1941, Reza Shah was the dominant force in Iranian politics, a true modernizing monarch using his prestige and his power to change society. His hierarchical, frequently arbitrary authoritarian power, exercised with considerable political skill, built up the country's strength and military might.

One of Reza Shah's primary goals had been to make Iran more independent of Britain and the Soviet Union. Prior to World War II he succeeded in juggling favors between these two countries, using Germany, France, and the United States as useful allies in reducing the leverage of England and Russia. Actually, the U.S. role was marginal, providing only small amounts of technical and expert assistance. In the late 1930s, however, Reza Shah decided renascent Germany under Hitler would be the best counterweight to Anglo-Soviet influence. Trade with Germany increased, a substantial number of German technicians arrived, and Nazi influence grew. While this made the British uneasy, it did not bother the Russians until the German invasion of the Soviet Union in June 1941. By late summer, both England and the U.S.S.R. needed access to Iran in order to ship vital war supplies from Britain through Iran's Persian Gulf ports to southern Russia. Fearing the growing German presence would thwart their plans, the two countries dispatched a joint Anglo-Soviet demarche, demanding that Iran send the Germans packing. When Reza Shah failed to respond positively, the Soviet Union and Britain invaded the country on August 25. The Iranian military abruptly collapsed. Only the navy actually resisted. The country was partitioned into zones of occupation, with the Soviets in charge of the northern half of Iran, the British the southern, and Tehran split between them. The next Anglo-Soviet move was to force Reza Shah to abdicate in favor of his 22-year-old son. Though he had greatly strengthened Iran, Reza Shah was not strong enough to prevent being deposed and was sent into exile on the Indian Ocean island of Mauritius on December 18, 1941. He died in Johannesburg, South Africa, on July 26, 1944.

Throughout World War II, the country's destiny was controlled by foreigners; Mohammad Reza Pahlavi (hereafter referred to as "the Shah") and the traditional political elites were allowed to play only a minimal role in the affairs of their own nation. After World War II, under prompting from key advisors, such as the Foroughi brothers and Ahmad Qavam, the Shah persuaded the United States to expand its role in Iran and force the termination of the allied occupation. The British left as scheduled in March 1946, but the Soviets refused to withdraw from Azarbaijan, Iran's northernmost province.[2] The U.S. assisted in forcing out the Russians in May 1946 by taking an uncompromising attitude within the United Nations. This act signalled the beginning of extremely close ties between Iran and the United States, which were to last until the expulsion of the Shah in January 1979.

Politically, the United States remained Iran's most important ally for over 35 years, while the country went through drastic social and economic change. U.S. dominance during this period is significant to the revolutionary evolution of Iran. Traditionally, the country's experience with allies, felt throughout society in different ways by different groups, has been that of a nation being acted upon by powerful external forces. The attitudes this has engendered in several generations of officials—including the hostility of students and religious groups and the way the foreign influence has affected domestic politics—help explain why current Iranian behavior is so at variance from Western expectations.

Feelings of inferiority, deep resentment, and prudent obsequiousness to the strong (the exception to this last point would be the seizure of American hostages in November 1979) are reflected in Iranian attitudes toward both powerful nations and their own rulers. The country's leaders have always kept a watchful eye on the activities of other nations that might affect their own destinies. Such wariness continued even into the mid-1970s, when Iran was no longer a weak country. Increased oil production at prices 400 percent higher than in 1970 had suddenly given Shah Mohammad Reza Pahlavi the leeway to exercise influence on his own. Though his nation's oil policy was clearly radically influencing international economics, Iranians still suspected that other countries were meddling in their domestic affairs. The issue of foreign involvement would remain explosive, culminating in the takeover of the American embassy in Tehran by young Iranian militants.

The Development of a Strong Leader

Shah Mohammad Reza Pahlavi was a weak personality until the early 1960s. Unfortunately events conspired to ensure that even when he developed into a strong leader, he still would be identified as dependent upon the West, specifically the United States.

Much has been written about the period from 1950 to 1953 when Mohammad Mossadeq was prime minister and the Shah was forced to leave the country for a short period and then, with covert U.S. assistance, returned to power at the head of a victorious coalition.[3] The events of 1953 have become so encrusted in legend that obtaining the complete truth may never be possible. Yet two points emerge which help in understanding subsequent political attitudes. First, whatever U.S. involvement actually was, it became an article of faith throughout Iran that the American participation had been critically important, and that therefore the Shah was a U.S. "puppet." Second, there actually were powerful forces within the country in 1953 who supported monarchical rule. Large and influential sectors of the population wanted the Shah to return, either because of dissatisfaction with Mossadeq's policies, which had left the economy weak and disorganized, or because of apprehension that Mossadeq was preparing the country for a communist (Tudeh Party) takeover. Today Iran's revolutionary liturgy denies this second point.

The events of 1953 influenced the Shah for the rest of his life, though by the late 1950s both his own situation and that of his country had improved dramatically. Specifically, from 1955 to 1963 the Shah purified the army, purging 300 to 400 officers who were Tudeh Party sympathizers. He created SAVAK, Iran's combination F.B.I.-C.I.A., to gather foreign and domestic intelligence and, increasingly, to repress dissent and to monitor and control opposition groups. Iran also continued its economic development, with U.S. assistance.

By 1963 the Shah was ready to make radical changes in the economy. His plan, first called the White Revolution, then expanded and called the Shah-People Revolution, was announced on January 9, 1963, and approved by national referendum on January 28. It called for intensive land reform, nationalization and development of forest and pasture lands, sale of government factories to finance land reform, electoral reform (including women's suffrage), a workers' profit-sharing plan, and formation of a "literacy corps" of teachers for rural areas. The results, however, were not completely positive. Discontent had been spurred by charges of electoral fraud in the fall of 1962. It was exacerbated by the clergy's hatred of the land reform program because it took so much income-producing property away from Islamic organizations controlled by the mosques.

During the first six months of 1963, while the Shah's programs were just starting to gain popular appeal, fundamentalist clerics rallied the masses, claiming the changes attacked Islam and were meant to enslave the people, not to free them. Riots, sparked by the religious harangues, began on June 5, 1963. They lasted for two to three days in Tehran and other major cities. Up to this point the revolt was a model of revolutionary activity to come in 1978. But this time the riots did not lead to the overthrow of the monarchy because Prime Minister Asadollah Alam was convinced, on behalf of the Shah, that he should use harsh measures and call in overwhelming military force to put down the unrest. Estimates of casualties ranged from official government figures of 86 killed, 100 to 200 injured, to opposition claims of several hundred killed, 1,500 wounded. In 1978 dissident sources were claiming 5,000 to 15,000 died in 1963. The most important development from this anti-Shah uprising, aside from the fact that it failed, was the beginning of collaboration between the two types of opposition—the secular forces and the religious groups. Fifteen years later this close cooperation had expanded and gained in strength. Without it Mohammad Reza Pahlavi would not have been overthrown.

Beginning in 1963 the Shah clearly dominated politics until his rapid decline in 1978–1979. In the parliamentary elections in September 1963 there were strict controls on candidate eligibility. Dissidents were not allowed to run for office. However, a group of reformers acceptable to the Shah and headed by Hassan Ali Mansur prepared a list of candidates who swept the field. Mansur became prime minister the following year and eventually was murdered by religious fanatics, but not before turning his group into the Iran Novin (New Iran) Party. Iran Novin remained the leading party until March 1975, when the Shah, heeding advice from a new generation of "establishment" reformers, created the Rastakhiz Party (Resurgence Party of the People of Iran). Until that time a second political group legally remained in existence, the Mardom

Party. But for all practical purposes 1963 marked the end of parliamentary party politics as practiced in the West and the beginning of a "royal dictatorship." Now a strong personality dominated the consitutional political process.

Persian politics from 1963 to 1977 was fairly simple. The Shah controlled everything, institutionalizing decision making around the throne. The government was run by technocratic ministers rather than politicians; the parliament was pliant, and political dissidence was controlled by SAVAK and the military. Opposition from within the system ceased to be significant in terms of policy making, decision making, and the allocation of resources for development. The executive arm of government functioned under the Shah and Prime Minister Amir Abbas Hoveyda, who took over in 1965, after Mansur was assassinated. With one important exception, the political scene remained quiescent until 1977, when those opposed to the Shah began generating public support for their position. The exception was the organization of an underground guerrilla movement in 1969–1970, leading to terrorist attacks on SAVAK personnel and eventually on other government and police officials as well. This overt, violent challenge to the regime forced SAVAK to become repressive; later, the drastic measures it imposed would be a major issue raised by the dissidents. The important point, however, is that the organizational base from which the regime could be challenged had been established well before revolutionary incidents started in 1977.[4]

From 1963 to 1977 the system decayed in terms of actual political participation, since the Shah centralized effective power within himself and his chosen ministers. He insisted that doing it this way freed the government from political pressures that threatened to impede the country's development. At the same time, the monarch gained confidence—others called this new assurance megalomania—as his Shah-People Revolution increased general prosperity and his political support. With his self image as well as others' perceptions of him improving as he was praised for the reform program, the Shah began to assert himself in the foreign policy sphere, differing occasionally with his ally, the United States. While he remained close to the U.S., the era of tutelage was over.

American-Iranian diplomatic interchanges from 1967 to 1975 show the two countries often disagreed within their basic relationship of shared mutual interests. Moreover, Iran prevailed in a surprising number of these disputes, particularly concerning the amount and types of American weapons the Shah wanted to buy during his extensive purchases of arms.[5] Eventually, he felt strong enough to break with the United States on a major issue. Although there had been discussions between the Shah and leaders of the Arab oil-producing states as early as 1970, in 1973 the Shah was the first significant head of state to advocate publicly that OPEC raise the price of oil sharply. Iran's monarch had achieved independence from foreign influence, but he remained insecure. His imperial arrogance disguised a massive case of personal uncertainty.

The extra income made available to the government from the huge oil price hike enabled the Shah to accelerate development. The resulting economic, social, and cultural changes within the country ultimately accelerated the breakup of the Pahlavi political system and the eventual destruction of the monarchy. Specifically, efforts in late 1976 to control the country's double-digit inflation laid the foundation for political developments that undercut the strong philosophy and practice of kingship that the Shah had reinforced throughout the 1960s and 1970s.

The Economic Evolution

Within six months newly acquired oil revenues rocketed income from the sale of petroleum from an annual rate of $5 billion to $19 or $20 billion. In June 1974 the Plan and Budget Organization revised the Fifth Development Plan, jumping expenditures from $36.8 billion to $69.6 billion. Three factors are politically significant. First, arguments over how the money would be spent were private, involving only the Shah and ranking government officials. The public, especially important individuals not connected with the regime, were presented with the results. Second, the planning process itself had the look of a treasury raid, with ministries competing to see which one could suggest the largest number of exciting new projects. And third, the largest increase in spending went for military hardware and military housing.

The frenzied economic development policy from 1974 to 1978 had a certain rationale. In addition to improving the standard of living, the Shah felt his country had to build up its armed forces in order to protect Iran's oil shipping lines, filling the gap left by the departure of the British from the Persian Gulf in 1971. England had withdrawn her troops for financial reasons. The ruling Conservative Party did not feel it could any longer afford to keep up defense installations in Bahrain, Oman, and Abu Dhabi.

Starting in 1974 the effort to implement the rapid increase in development encouraged rising expectations—and rising inflation. As the bloated oil revenues circulated in the marketplace, the prices of all goods increased dramatically. According to official figures inflation reached the mid-teens in 1974 and probably averaged between 25 and 35 percent from 1975 to 1978. Prices soared, with the cost of urban housing leading the way. Renting an apartment in 1976 was 70 percent more expensive than in 1973, though prices did eventually abate to a still incredible 50 percent. The interaction of various economic factors was devastating. In 1975–1976 the rapid increase in purchases from abroad laid the foundation for delays of from 160 to 200 days for unloading goods in Iran's southern ports, the entry points for all but a small fraction of the country's imports. Thus construction projects were subject to interminable delays. Once the capacity of the ports improved, goods rotted on the docks because the internal transportation system could not distribute the cargo. Costs increased even more than expected, and wages were forced up as well. Economic dislocation became a major fact of life. In late 1976 an official in the Ministry of Finance described the situation.

> Our own bureaucracy was simply not equipped to handle greater flows of goods, and the vast increase in money available meant that more money found its way into officials' pockets. . . . Even so, corruption might have made the system go, except that those at the top began to get greedy and take the top layer of the cake.
>
> The government had no incentive to keep wages down—that merely created unrest. The P.B.O. [Plan and Budget Organization] was ready to accept a gradual increase in wages in all sectors. The word was quietly passed to allow workers to achieve their more reasonable wage demands.[6]

Constant reiteration by the Shah that he was building what he called "The Great Society" merely whetted appetites for a piece of the action. It is true that from 1974 to 1978 economic conditions improved, but for the majority there was no dramatic change. There was some "trickle-down" effect from the development, but not enough. Unofficial estimates place the percentage of those truly benefiting from the superheated economy at 15 to 20 percent, while the remaining 30 million Iranians looked on with growing envy, improving their lifestyle only slightly. The shortfall between expectation and results produced the political reaction that began to spell trouble for the government.[7]

For example, the revised Fifth Development Plan called for 1,050,000 housing units to be built within a five-year span, despite the fact that at no time, even during a major building boom, had housing starts topped 100,000, or about half the number necessary to reach Fifth Plan goals.

The pressure to construct more urban dwellings had increased after 1973 because the migration of the peasants to the cities had accelerated. Tehran's population jumped from 2.8 million in 1971 to about 5.9 million in 1979. Other cities had similar, if not as dramatic, growth. Moreover, in Tehran, Isfahan, and Shiraz the influx of foreign technicians and military advisors (a large majority of them American) increased the pressure on local services. The first riots in Tehran, in August 1977, protested a lack of housing; there was restrained uneasiness in other cities. Many Iranians concluded that the foreigners were responsible for most, if not all, urban problems, including high rents and impossible traffic jams.

The pressures of rapid development were aggravated by problems of allocation. The Plan and Budget Organization ceased to function effectively after 1974, as the intake of oil money and efforts to spend it simply flowed around and over planning parameters. Given the ever-increasing domestic problems, the allocation of a mere 21 percent of the Fifth Budget Plan to social services was less than prudent. Galloping inflation also took its toll. The impact on the lower classes—workers, urban migrants, farmers—was devastating. By early 1977, unrest was growing.

Efforts to ease the impact of inflation created difficulties for others. In the fall of 1975, the government began to wage a war against merchants who were flagrantly overcharging. Initially, it organized "price vigilantes" through the newly formed Resurgence Party. Approximately 8,000 individuals were singled out. Included were two of Iran's biggest industrialists, Habib Sabet and Habib Elghanian, both of whom had close connections to the Shah, specifically the Imperial Court. The fact that they were even charged with price fixing was seen as evidence that the Shah was serious about curbing corrupt business practices, at least initially. Sabet went into exile in Paris and Elghanian simply closed down his plastic products corporation. The ominous note to the whole proceedings was the fact that Sabet was a Bahai, which is a religious sect particularly abhorrent to Shia Islam, and Elghanian was a leading Jewish merchant.

The campaign against price fixing increased uncertainty within the business community, heretofore a staunch supporter of modernization. Among the bazaar merchants (old-line traders who had dominated the economy in traditional Iran), the government's actions were considered a threat to their survival, perhaps the first move in a scheme to break their power. This view was reinforced when the governor of Khorasan province had the old bazaar in Mashad destroyed. The rebuilt shopping area was an improvement (in Western eyes) over the old rabbit-warren, hole-in-the-wall series of stalls. But the rental monies were going to the government-controlled Vaqaf Foundation that maintained Mashad's Islamic shrine, the second most important in the country. It did not go unnoticed that the director of the foundation was Abdul Aziz Valian, the provincial governor.

Because of the gradual breakdown of the economic superstructure throughout 1976–1977, many of those who originally supported the boom were becoming alienated. Businessmen and small merchants saw the regime as an impediment to development, not as a facilitator of their plans. The bottlenecks at the ports encouraged firms to use bribes to get needed construction materials promptly. Loan rates for businessmen doubled. In fact, so many people wanted advances that money was not always available, particularly near the end of the financial quarter before oil revenues were paid in. Shortages meant prices went up much faster than wages. Price controls almost immediately spawned a thriving black market which always seemed to have ample supplies of goods. Even the newly franchised landowners suffered in the economic boom. Lacking strong support organizations—agricultural banks, cooperatives, extension services—the small farmer was left to his own devices to cope with shortages of seed and fertilizer and lack of capital at reasonable interest rates. Hence, another group originally considered a supporter of modernization became disenchanted.

These conditions encouraged restive behavior, but they do not by themselves explain the country's revolutionary upsurge. Economic dislocation is endemic in many countries, either because of lack of organization or because of specific government policies. But when economic problems interact with political behavior, major changes can occur. In the case of Iran, the historical involvement of other nations, most recently the United States, and the nature of the monarchical system provided the catalyst to transform economic troubles into drastic political change.

Social and Religious Attitudes in the Shah's Iran

The lack of solid political institutions and the dependence on one leader intensified certain attitudes, already reinforced by the economic problems accompanying the oil boom. The most striking political characteristics to prevail in pre-revolutionary politics—insecurity, cynicism, and "me-firstism"—still underlie behavior in Iran.[8] These feelings stem from a basic mistrust of others, plus a generally negative attitude toward fate.

It is reflected most obviously in two areas: the tension between old and new and the hostility toward authority on both personal and national levels. Since the mid-nineteenth century the Persian social-cultural milieu has been marked by tensions. In every generation, some groups and individuals have turned toward new ideas and modernization while others have retained traditional fundamentalist beliefs. Occasionally, disagreements about these two basic views have even erupted into armed conflict, as happened during the struggle to impose a constitution in 1906–1907. In other instances, differences between the Qajar shahs and the rest of Iran's aristocracy badly weakened the dynasty in the early twentieth century. More recently, a mounting problem has been the struggle between parents and their children who have studied abroad and have returned to Iran rejecting the old customs.

Overwhelming power and the willingness to use it are keys to Persian family life. Until the age of five or six, male children are allowed to do anything they wish. From that point on, however, (and for girls from the time of their birth), the male child is ruled by his parents in a highly controlled fashion. Offspring come to expect it, are uncomfortable without it, and frequently define themselves in relation to the authoritarian figure who rules their lives. This has been especially true of those children sent abroad for schooling. Dependence upon the father figure to finance their educations (over half of them had government scholarships) generated fear and shame at being controlled. There would be uncertainty and a different kind of fear when such control was absent, and they had to make their own decisions, even something as basic as what course of study to follow. The young people cannot cope with opposing problems. They seek freedom and hate to be restrained, yet they need guidance. Alternating attitudes of dependence and defiance are common. Psychologists who have treated Iranian adolescents report that such attitudes are typical in over 85 percent of the cases they have dealt with.

Ambivalent feelings of obedience and hostility toward authority are carried over into the political sphere. To understand the concept of being controlled by an all-powerful leader is to understand how Iranians view their government. The Shah's basic approach to ruling — positioning himself as the "father" supervising his "children" — appealed to deep-rooted instincts in the Iranian psychic makeup. Ayatollah Ruhollah Khomeini, far from being the antithesis of the

Shah, is merely his mirror image in clerical dress. The Ayatollah succeeded where the Shah failed because he more consistently and successfully played the role of a strong, authoritarian figure who would not compromise.

Major officials in the Shah's government were also victims of the love-hate relationship with the authority figure. Thus the more imperial the Shah became, the more ambivalent were their attitudes. Fereidoun Hoveyda (former Iranian ambassador to the United Nations and brother of ex-Prime Minister Amir Abbas Hoveyda) and Jahangir Amouzegar (brother of ex-Prime Minister Jamshid Amouzegar) illustrate this point very well in their recently published books. Younger, Western-educated Iranians also recognize this phenomenon, but as one noted, "We are powerless to do anything about it. It is part of our life, our culture, our behavior from childbirth." As a result of these feelings of helplessness and frustration, the country's political behavior since 1978—the tumult and demonstrations—resembles a regression to childhood. It "kicked out the once all-powerful father, the Shah, and held hostage the most powerful country in the world for its sins."

The concept of the politically neutral public servant, or even a spirit of civic welfare, has never existed in Iran. Any sense of collective good is focused on the family and the religious community. Whether this attitude is reinforced by the Moslem religion or caused by it is arguable. Nevertheless, Persians tend to think of politics (and business as well) in terms of self and family first, clan or tribal group next. The health of the nation comes third. While Iranians, in a burst of patriotism, wholeheartedly support the war effort against Iraq, the protracted conflict has intensified major food and fuel shortages. Within a few months patriotic oratory had been tempered by disillusioned commentary.

Iran's strong religious beliefs have always had both a negative and a positive influence on the country's political attitudes. The tendency of most Moslems to take a fatalistic view of life—an event occurs because "God wills it"—was neatly woven into the Shah's philosophy of government, which regarded the leader as active (the all-powerful father) and the people as passive (the obedient children). As the political system came under pressure, feelings of resignation coupled with alienation became even more commonplace.

The mosque leadership and the Pahlavis, both father and son, lived uneasily at arm's length for the better part of this century. Occasionally they closed ranks, as in 1953, when the clergy supported restoration of the monarchy against the communist threat. More often they were distant to each other. This is entirely consistent with past experience. In all previous dynasties, the mosque has been at the philosophic opposite pole to the government. The country's history is replete with examples of religious attacks on any monarch perceived as corrupt or inept, so Khomeini's challenge is not inconsistent with past attempts to overthrow secular authority. It differs from previous efforts because of its call to the faithful to recognize an eminent religious figure as superior to a monarch.

There is another side to the religious influence. If the Shia clergy has traditionally acted as a watchdog on the monarchy, the secular government (particularly the military) has not hesitated to move against the clergy when it has been perceived as too powerful or too corrupt. Just as the Islamic leadership attacked the shahs in the eighteenth and nineteenth centuries, strong secular (usually military) figures manipulated the clergy and enforced political obedience.

By 1976 the economic boom had expanded the size of the middle class, but at the same time many of these people became more aware of what was wrong with the Shah's way of doing things. Feelings of cynicism spread as they realized that, at best, they had a very small stake in their political destiny. When the monarchy came under a severe challenge that required a show of loyalty under fire, thousands of the newly affluent expressed their sentiments in 1978–1979 by buying airplane tickets and leaving Iran. They chose not to remain and fight for the regime that had made them prosperous, convinced that events were accelerating beyond their control. Even those who could not afford to become expatriates—shopowners and small businessmen—watched during the riots in October and November 1978 as their stores were being destroyed. On one street, two demonstrators trashed and burned 15 shops while over 100 owners and clerks stood numbly by, their assets and jobs going up in flames. They simply opted out.

What the combination of these deeply ingrained social and religious attitudes portend for Khomeini's rule as Iran's economy disintegrates completely will be examined later. However, "rule by mullah" in Iran is by no means a foregone conclusion. Indeed historical evidence would imply just the opposite. The progressive destruction of the Shah's authority and the inability of succeeding governments to deal with the economic and social problems that created the context in which the revolution took place show that, politically, Iran remains weak and fractionalized. Because of typical Iranian political behavior, the reestablishment of stable legitimate authority will not be an easy task no matter who the leader is.[9]

Overture to Revolution

Do conditions such as economic dislocation, love-hate ties to authority, and a growing opposition's addiction to violence lead inevitably to revolution? Had social forces been set in motion which could not be stopped short of revolution? Did the Shah, imbued with the hubris of his modernizing monarchy, try like Icarus, to fly too close to the sun?

The emergence of a strong leader in a society that values power is testimony to the validity of the proposition that strength means legitimacy. The ideology of the monarchy was based on personal, patrimonial rule and the Shah's own version of nationalism, which included rapid modernization at any cost. Unlike the Japanese emperor, the German kaiser, and Hitler, the Shah never was able to gain acceptance for himself as the exclusive repository of nationalist legitimacy, largely because of his continued association with the United States and the circumstances under which he returned to the throne in 1953. His dismissal of Mossadeq conformed to the letter of the constitution, but his manipulation of the political system in the years since 1953 encouraged his countrymen to disdain politics.

After the riots in 1963 had been suppressed, for many years the Shah was able to overcome this political indifference with his modernization program. Disparate groups were drawn into alliance with, or at least acceptance of, the regime. Ironically, the government benefited from the efforts of the fundamentalist clergy to paint the new reforms as the work of the devil. As improvements reached the people, they ignored their religious leaders and supported the regime in ways they never had before. Peasants were committed to land reform. Middle-class modernizers were drawn toward the promise of a better life. Workers had a stake in the growth of industry. Even many of the clerics were neutralized after receiving personal "grants" or subsidies for their mosques and religious schools. Because a majority of the country had been drawn into the framework of the modernizing economy, dissidents who objected to the country's development kept quiet, were exiled, or forced to flee.

Starting in 1976, the gradually increasing economic disarray was a hardship, but not as bad as had been suffered in earlier times and not as severe as what other countries currently endure elsewhere in the world. The difference is that the effects of rampant inflation, import-export transport dislocations, wage-price problems, and the gradual breakdown of the system regulating development had political consequences as well. Precisely because the principal goal was to bring a better life to all the people, the gradual economic breakdown, which became a full-fledged recession in 1977, opened the way to question first the efficacy of the ruler, then the legitimacy of the ruling arrangement. The Shah failed to democratize or increasingly institutionalize the political system, which was therefore simply incapable of coping with economic and social change on the scale taking place in the Iran of the mid-1970s. But this is true only up to a point. The system could not handle the political impact of economic and social disarray, but the real reasons why the revolution occurred are basically political ones. The stresses in the economic system contributed to the development of an unstable situation, but they were not the direct cause of the revolution.

Frequently, external factors can be cited as a principal reason for the emergence of a revolutionary situation. In Iran's case, this is not true. It was not pressure from either the East or the West that promoted the oil-financed boom. That had been the Shah's decision. Iran was not pushed into superheated modernization, though it can be argued that diverting a major portion of the oil funds for military hardware, technical assistance, and other "unproductive" expenditures was forced upon the Shah by the need to build up security in the wake of Britain's departure from the Persian Gulf. Even so, that problem did not justify the type and scope of arms purchases that actually were made. That buildup was the concept and policy of the ruler of Iran who, for the first time in just over 30 years as king, was freed from any constraints on his desires for development.

To a degree not present in any other country that has gone through a revolutionary experience, the situation in Iran developed because of inefficiencies and defects in a modernizing monarchy committed to improvement as fast as possible. The economic dislocation caused by the development spurt heightened an already existing sense of alienation and encouraged a strong sense of deprivation among the urban masses. It provided fertile ground for the growth of specific interest groups uncompromisingly opposed to the Shah's regime. The political evolution of Iran's revolution is the story of the emergence of an oppostion despite the regime's efforts first to preempt and then to counter it.

Chapter Two

★

Political Evolution:
The Establishment

In the aftermath of the revolution, it is easy to gloss over the fact that there had been a workable political system in Iran. It all fell apart between 1974 and 1978, at first gradually, then dramatically, when the government became unable to meet the demands made on it. Throughout the 1960s the Shah's regime grew steadily more authoritarian. Increasingly, one man dominated all the important personal and political networks controlling the modernization process. No other institution —not even parliament or the courts—retained any independent influence.

Economic and social ferment generated a revolutionary situation leading to extreme actions—demonstrations, attacks against police, and general disobedience. By the end of 1976 and throughout 1977, clusters of unemployed workers would gather in the cities to protest lack of jobs. Street crime—theft, assault, disorderly conduct—multiplied to the point where it became an issue in the press. Demonstrations at the larger universities had increased from an average of one a month to one a week by the end of 1977. The results were a progressive and not immediately obvious disintegration of the Shah's governing mechanisms and the emergence of viable opposition groups for the first time in 15 years. Starting in 1977 the Shah sought to counteract the discontent by liberalizing his political system, even though in the intervening years he had relied more heavily on SAVAK and military force than on his own political skill when maneuvering among the dissident factions. It was true the monarch was encouraging political participation, but only within the framework of the single party he had created in 1975, the Resurgence Party.

Though professing to liberalize, the Shah would not let real power devolve into the hands of the Resurgence Party. Many Iranians, and particularly the fundamentalist clergy, reacted strongly against the stresses created by their ruler's rapid modernization program. For example, in 1977, the Shah insisted that the government include a new post, Minister of State for Women's Affairs, to recognize the enhanced role of females in Iran since the late 1930s. Mahnaz Afkhami, who was already in charge of the semi-official Iranian Women's Organization and a prominent, extremely competent friend of the Shah's twin sister, was given the job. Yet in deference to Moslem sensitivity to women working outside the home, and therefore mixing freely with men, this was the first post abolished when the cabinet was overhauled in August 1978. The country's middle and lower classes were ripe for recruitment by the opposition rather than eagerly supporting the monarchy, as they had been doing for years past. Using their newfound strength, the dissident groups were able to join together, organize, and develop military wings, the Mujahidin and Fedayeen guerrilla movements.

The nature of the Shah's system depended entirely on the personality of Iran's monarch. Since no post-1963 political leaders could challenge him or protect him from his excesses of zeal, when he began to have doubts about what he should do—a personality change caused to some degree by his cancer medicine—there were no others to take up the slack. Thus, as revolutionary unrest increased, Iran's political establishment could not play a role commensurate with its pre-1978 strength and political savvy.

The Pahlavi System

From 1963 and throughout 1978, the Shah succeeded in making himself the principal—indeed the only—policy and decision maker of any consequence in Iran. Such dominance excluded the possibility that government institutions might permit others to participate actively in either executive or parliamentary affairs. Iran's political elites were dependent on a system of royal patrimony—favors from the throne—for their positions, exacerbating long-held and deep-seated feelings of insecurity. The Shah had achieved their dependence by an extraordinary combination of political skill and a determination to control his country absolutely. The entire 37-year history of his reign can be understood best in terms of his continuous efforts to reinforce his position after accepting the shaky throne he received from his father in 1941. Another consideration was the Shah's own personal sense of divine mission. He continually spoke of God being on his side, and apparently believed that was so until the day he died.[1]

In a political system dominated by personalities, Iran's monarch became the ranking figure by deliberately overshadowing the elites he depended upon to make the country run. Abbas Khalatbari, foreign minister from 1972–1979, often told foreign ambassadors that he "was merely a messenger; his majesty makes all the major decisions and most of the minor ones."[2] Amir Abbas Hoveyda, prime minister from 1965 to 1977, and Jamshid Amouzegar, the "super-technocrat" of Iranian government for ten years and prime minister from 1977 to 1978, were also excluded from any decision making involving the religious groups, SAVAK, and military security.

There was no such thing as an institutional base from which a member of the elite could stake out an independent position and still participate in active political life. No groups from 1965 to 1978 had their own separate power bases within Iranian society. This was not true for earlier prime ministers. Two in particular argued for their policies: Dr. Ali Amini, who was dismissed in 1962 after 14 months for disagreeing with the Shah, and Hassan Ali Mansur, who was assassinated in 1965 by religious fanatics. Though the Shah made conscious efforts to coopt potential leaders interested in government and politics, by 1970 those who did not openly question the regime participated; those who did, either withdrew or were forced out. Many former opposition leaders had been living quietly in Iran for years, overtly uninvolved in politics. Others remained outside Iran, often in self-imposed exile. (The most obvious examples of the latter case would be Sadeq Ghotbzadeh and Abol Hassan Bani-Sadr.)

Such obvious control greatly contributed to political cynicism, particularly when those brought into high government positions had previously been strong critics of the regime. For instance, by 1977 the Ministry of the Interior included 8 of 12 office directors who had been members of the anti-regime Iranian Students Association while studying abroad a decade earlier. Even several ex-communists, like former Minister of Commerce Fereidoun Mahdavi and a secretary-general of the Resurgence Party, Mohammad Baheri, had been appointed to senior government positions. Frequently this gave rise to questions regarding the depth of their commitment in either incarnation. At one point, in 1977, Baheri was suspected of shaping the Resurgence Party in the mold of the Tudeh (Communist) organization, even though he had been a member only briefly while a university student and later renounced communism.

Dividing responsibility among individuals but focusing control in himself helped the Shah consolidate power, but it had several unfortunate side effects. For one thing, it required that decisions about all major programs and control of them be split between competitors so that centralization could occur only at the top. Oil policy, for example, was worked out between the Shah and Jamshid Amouzegar during most of the 1970s. The National Iranian Oil Company played only a subsidiary role, largely through its extremely competent international director, Dr. Parviz Mina. Such division of responsibility created tension and distrust among officials who remained at arm's length from their colleagues because they were already insecure, cynical, and suspicious. These feelings extended to the working levels of the government bureaucracy as well, because younger officials were identified with their bosses and promoted on this relationship rather than on the basis of their abilities. Personalization rather than institutionalization became the hallmark of royal rule.

Managing political life in this way certainly reduced challenges to the monarch's supremacy, but it also stultified the system. With all major decisions made by the Shah alone, the needs of a developing economy requiring decentralized policy and decision making conflicted with political style. Any such problems always were resolved in favor of the Shah's method of centralized policy, not in favor of the smooth functioning of the economic system. By 1972 imperial policy and decision making inhibited the growth of a complex developed economy and this added to emerging commercial and industrial problems. As stress increased, particularly from 1976 to 1978, added cynicism further weakened loyalty to the regime.

The ultimate problem with such authoritarian control is that the performance of the entire political structure becomes overly dependent upon the personality of the monarch-father figure. In the Shah's case, this meant serious danger when a crisis arose, for he might not be able to fulfill his role as the omnipotent leader and there would be few others, if any, to take charge in his place. Never the strongest or most stable of world leaders, until the Mossadeq crisis in 1953, the Shah was a playboy who took little interest in government. He depended upon older advisors, many of whom had worked for his father, and upon foreign diplomats, including a succession of astute American ambassadors. The change in the Shah from playboy to effective monarch began in the mid-1950s when he ousted then prime minister General Fazlollah Zahedi because he was becoming too powerful. It was more or less complete by 1963 when he shook off "guidance" from the Americans that he liberalize his regime and began instead his own reform program, the White Revolution. Though the Shah retained his links to the United States and even expanded them in the early 1970s, based largely on his personal affinity for President Richard Nixon and Secretary of State Henry Kissinger, U.S. influence was clearly on the wane. By 1976 Ambassador Richard Helms, a strong personality himself, could reply to suggestions that the United States "tell" Iran's monarch to liberalize his system with the comment, "The first time I try to tell the Shah what to do on such matters will be the last time I see him." This was in marked contrast to an earlier time when the Shah was receptive to American advice. It also suggests a monarch stronger and more confident than he actually was as the leadership crisis in Tehran intensified.

The Shah's relationship with his own people was complex. Never loved, he was respected by many, if not most, until the gradual unraveling of the Iranian political system. Even though those close to him shared love-hate feelings toward their father figure, they had concluded that the Shah was necessary for the stability of the country. As late as September and October 1978, many opposition leaders believed that the presence of the Shah as a constitutional monarch (not as an active ruler) was necessary to protect Iran's unity from foreign depredations. One prominent dissident figure suggested that the continuation of the monarchy would provide the necessary umbrella under which the country's political system would have a chance to develop in liberal democratic fashion.

The Shah's personal style was arrogantly distant. He never attempted to become a popular king, appealing directly to "the people" on specific issues. An elitist, he despaired of democracy and, like General De Gaulle, frequently confused the first person pronoun with the nation. Yet despite his imperious manner, there were significant personal influences on the Shah. The Empress Farah played an increasing role behind the scenes in the 1970s, particularly on social issues. Her "coming out" was the Ramsar Educational Conference in August 1975, at which she discreetly disagreed with the Shah on educational policy and the treatment of "ungrateful" students who benefited from free educations yet criticized the regime. As for the rest of the royal family, only the Shah's twin sister, Princess Ashraf, involved herself in politics. Always a stronger personality than her brother, she deserves as much credit as General Zahedi for bringing the Shah back from exile in 1953. Although she modestly denies such influence publicly, Ashraf had the Shah's ear on matters of importance to her. Court confidants believe her brother ordered her in the early 1970s to stop interfering in internal affairs, under penalty of exile. The 60 or so others in the extended royal family kept out of government affairs, enjoying the good life. Many enhanced their incomes through blatantly corrupt practices such as accepting kickbacks for steering all kinds of contracts through the labyrinth of the Persian bureaucracy. One reason for the Shah's tolerance of corruption within the family had been his desire to channel their interests in directions other than politics. By 1977–1978, this problem had become one of the principal issues the opposition would use against the regime.

There was another set of personal advisors who remained important to the Shah. Though older than he, they had been educated with the monarch, growing up with him, attending the same European schools, and assisting him for most of his rule. They held various posts at various times, but always remained influential. Nasratollah Moinian, director of the Special Bureau; Hossein Fardust, director of the Imperial Inspectorate; and General Nematollah Nassiri, head of SAVAK for over 15 years, were able to deal with the Shah without the trappings and the full formality of the king-subject relationship. They were his "kitchen cabinet." To these could be added political figures who had stood by him for a long time—Asadollah Alam, court minister for ten years; Amir Abbas Hoveyda, prime minister for 12 years; and Manuchehr Eqbal, former prime minister and chairman of the National Iranian Oil Company until the revolution.

One of the least appreciated aspects of Iran's slide into chaos is the degree to which the Shah gradually lost touch with his country through the illness, death, or defection of virtually all these key aides. By the time political problems were obvious in 1978, Alam was dead of cancer. Moinian had been ill off-and-on for years. Eqbal, who along with Alam had helped the Shah weather the Khomeini crisis in 1963, would die of a heart attack in August, and Hoveyda was dismissed in September because he disagreed with the Shah on how the emerging revolutionary situation should be handled. Perhaps the most fascinating of all is the case of Hossein Fardust, who as chief of the Imperial Inspectorate had access to every nook and cranny in government and society. Fardust was not on the Shah's plane with other loyalists when it left Tehran January 16, 1979. Instead, he remained in Iran to become a controlling figure in SAVAMA, the Khomeini regime's successor to SAVAK.

The Shah built up his web of personal loyalties through the years by moving officials around and by manipulating the symbols of monarchy. The coronation pageant in 1967 and the 2,500th anniversary celebration of the Iranian monarchy in 1971, plus the required constant use of royal pictures in the press, were evidence of the lengths to which the Shah went to establish himself as a symbol of nationalism. In spite of these efforts, he never fully escaped his earlier identification with America, starting in 1953. As his personal power diminished in 1978 more and more Westernized Iranians (but not the typical villager) came to see the trappings of monarchy—the constant adulation, the special relationship with God—as anachronistic. This increased the sense of alienation. Worse, since 1963, there had been no significant challenge to his regime, so the Shah's political skills were allowed to atrophy. He came to depend on coercion and control. After being called "King of Kings" and "Light of the Aryans" for so many years, he began to believe his own mystique. As one astute Iranian political figure put it, "He never should have started reading his own press clippings." By the mid-1970s, he was lecturing his Western allies on the effect of permissiveness on democratic societies, extolling the virtues of order in Iran as contrasted to unruly student demonstrations in the U.S., France, and Germany.

The Security Organizations

There were four principal aspects of the Shah's system of political control: his cabinet; the security services (SAVAK) for establishing order and ferreting out threats to the monarchy; the Pahlavi Foundation, an omnipresent nonprofit organization which distributed money for the purpose of tying peoples' loyalty to the regime; and the military. Their tasks were to carry out the modernization program, to ensure political loyalty, and to protect against violent threats to the regime.[3]

The amended constitution of 1906 provided for a parliament and a religious council that would review laws for conformity with Islamic legal standards. The first religious council of elders was allowed to lapse under Reza Shah and was never reconstituted. Seventy years later, this disregard of the country's first attempt to include the clergy in the government would be used by religious leaders to undermine Pahlavi rule. Parliament, after an active, semi-independent period in the 1940s and early 1950s, became a rubber stamp for the regime until mid-1978, when a number of deputies revolted against Resurgence Party discipline. Then parliament became increasingly free, even fractious, until it was disbanded during the revolution five months later. Although it was the focus for some popular attention, as an institution the parliament played a secondary role in the revolutionary upheaval. The important elements of the Shah's system bore only a sporadic relationship to the constitution in a formal sense, and often performed their most important service in an extra-constitutional capacity.

SAVAK, for example, a combination F.B.I.-C.I.A., was considered to be an effective, ubiquitous force until its failure to diagnose and damp down the Tabriz riots on February 19 and 20, 1978. Like other covert intelligence organizations, it deliberately set out to cultivate the image of being all-powerful. For 15 years after its creation in 1957 SAVAK worked closely with the C.I.A. and Israel's Mossad, two organizations which helped set it up. When there was an outbreak of political restlessness in his country in 1961 and 1962 the Shah feared it had been inspired by exhortations emanating from the administration of President Kennedy for him to increase political freedom. Therefore the monarch decided SAVAK should keep closer track of what the Americans and other friendly powers were doing in his country, and at the same time he reduced the amount of foreign involvement with his intelligence agency. Until 1970 SAVAK would meet the needs of the regime without creating the backlash that would spread like wildfire later over its treatment of political prisoners.

Liaison work between SAVAK and the C.I.A. continued until the overthrow of the Shah, because it was helpful to both sides with respect to the common threat of the Soviet Union. But American influence kept decreasing since Washington, and particularly the Carter administration, articulated greater concern for civil rights and political liberalization of the regime than encroaching communism. Thus when SAVAK began dealing with an incipient guerrilla insurgency in the early 1970s, the discreet tempering presence of U.S. personnel working closely with it was not there to press for restrained alternatives to the brutal tortures inflicted upon many captured terrorists. Eventually, General Nematollah Nassiri, who had controlled SAVAK since 1963 (and who as a young colonel had delivered to Mossadeq the order dismissing him as prime minister) was packed off as ambassador to Pakistan in May 1978 in an effort to appease the dissidents, who criticized SAVAK methods incessantly.

Until the Shah instituted his liberalization policy in mid-1977, the security services conducted unrestrained operations against guerrilla terrorist organizations, forcing such groups to struggle for their survival. In conjunction with the military, SAVAK successfully ran down Iran's first guerrilla band in 1971, and closed out 1976 by breaking up a substantial part of the Fedayeen movement. Most stories of SAVAK torture, which were to become the symbol of regime brutality, date from the years when the country was first faced with an active guerrilla insurgency. Opposition forces, particularly those engaged in violence, were subjected to intimidation, ranging from detention without trial to intensive interrogation, torture, and extensive jail terms. When SAVAK records fell into the hands of Iranian revolutionaries, the Bazargan government was able to show visitors 50 to 60 photographs and dossiers of political prisoners who had been tortured and killed. Many Iranian families had at least one relative who encountered difficulty, however slight, with SAVAK. Moreover, those most affected by harsh treatment from SAVAK violence were precisely the ones who were to become the mainstays of the revolutionary government's security forces.

SAVAK's scope and effectiveness has undergone some reanalysis in the wake of the Shah's collapse. Through mid-1977 the organization performed with at least minimal competence because there was no effective challenge to its authority. When the Shah tacitly changed the ground rules in the spring of 1977 to permit those opposed to the regime to participate in political activity, SAVAK found itself unable to cope. Others believe the efficiency of the secret police began to tail off in the early 1970s because its leader, General Nassiri, did not really keep pace with political developments and the methods needed to control them. SAVAK was never a first-rate intelligence and covert action organization because its training program was not adequate to meet the demands placed on it by counterinsurgency. The security agency was also unable to cope with the sophisticated public relations techniques—press releases and television interviews—used in the mid-1970s by dissident organizations abroad to publicize the regime's excesses.

Estimates of SAVAK personnel range from 7,000 to 10,000 full-time employees plus "stringers," or informers, totaling another 20,000 to 30,000, to a high estimate of 100,000. One measure of SAVAK's failure is that in spite of all that manpower, insurgent groups were able to maintain the bare minimum level of organization necessary to survive. Though SAVAK successfully hounded the guerrillas, a nucleus of terrorists remained, and political assassination became relatively common. Between 1971 and 1978, over 300 police, military, and government employees and approximately 10 foreigners were gunned down in the streets.

Consistent with the Shah's policy of divide and rule, however, SAVAK was not the only organization entrusted with intelligence responsibilities. There was also an extensive military intelligence, including one for each of the three branches of the armed forces. In fact, the director of military intelligence, General Nasser Moghaddam, succeeded Nassiri in 1978 as head of SAVAK. Coordination among the various intelligence groups was, of course, conducted through the

Shah, or in rare cases by General Fardust as head of the Imperial Inspectorate.

The Imperial Inspectorate was a remarkable, little-known, and even less-understood organization. Since its inception in 1963, it had the authority to enforce cooperation from every ministry and governmental organization in the country, including SAVAK. The chief of the Imperial Inspectorate reported only to the Shah—never to the prime minister or the parliament—after monitoring activities of high-ranking officials and stating whether they were complying with the monarch's policies. Whatever action it recommended always was carried out by someone else, usually SAVAK or a regular ministry such as Interior. The Imperial Inspectorate could go anywhere and arrange for anything to be done in a flexible, informal style. Despite its power and influence, it never drew publicity like SAVAK and the military. The Special Bureau headed by Nasratollah Moinian was a similar organization, but never as influential. It worked on Moinian's special projects, but it had no independent power.

In addition to the Imperial Inspectorate and regular intelligence organizations, there were special groups to combat terrorism. The counterterrorism committees were created in the mid-1970s to bring the growth of insurgent forces under control. Police, military, SAVAK, and on occasion, Imperial Inspectorate officials were members. These committees, established in all major cities, were responsible for tracking down and eliminating or bringing to trial the guerrilla groups trying to establish themselves in the country. Originally, existence of these committees was kept secret, in an effort to prevent assassinations. Since the special groups often organized counter-guerrilla attacks against individual cells, any government member who could be identified was liable to be killed.

The counterterrorism committees further stifled initiative among both government bureaucrats and private citizens. A "police state" mentality developed in Iran, particularly after 1970. While Iran was by no means a totalitarian state—"sloppy authoritarian" would be a closer description—SAVAK's efforts to build itself a reputation of omnipotence and the quiet way in which the Imperial Inspectorate operated significantly increased cautious behavior. There have been arguments that this effort to control Iranian life has been much overrated because it was not visible, but the essence of the technique was its indirectness. An individual would be told to do something by his boss; the lower ranking bureaucrat might disagree, showing why X would be better than Y. If the individual persisted, a hint would be dropped that the ministerial security officer wanted Y done, not X. If he continued to balk, the government employee would be "interviewed," perhaps eventually fired.

All ministries, parastatal organizations, universities, and anyone tied to politics felt the pressure of the security forces. In one two-month period in 1977, the weight of this unseen power was confirmed by virtually every office director or senior official of government—some 23 individuals in all. They had received calls, some of them very elliptical, from SAVAK or "security" officers about matters under their jurisdictions. In addition, newspapermen and editorial writers knew their work was censored. Copy editors could individually identify the Ministry of Information—actually SAVAK—officials, based on how they rewrote the day's stories. (Ironically the same procedure would be informally reinstituted by the revolutionary government in May 1979, and made more official in August.) Over 30 professors teaching at universities in Tehran, Isfahan, and Shiraz told of incidents of interference by SAVAK agents in either their teaching or writing. Some Tehran University professors made a game out of trying to identify the SAVAK-employed students who reported on class work. Such information was eventually to become the basis for a number of executions after the revolutionary takeover.[4]

Two measures of efficiency can be applied to a security system. One is whether it engenders cooperation, either through a willingness to help or through fear. The second is the degree to which it can find out what it wants to know in spite of resistance from those opposed to the government; in other words, its ability to penetrate opposition groups. Through 1977 SAVAK and the military intelligence units were more successful in obtaining cooperation than they were in penetrating the dissident movement. On the surface, Iran's intelligence organizations appear to have failed their ultimate test—to protect the regime against its opponents. The story is more complex than this, however, and has a great deal to do with unfolding events during the revolutionary period in 1978. SAVAK knew about many, if not most, of the secular leaders of the revolutionary forces; was less informed about the Mujahidin and Fedayeen, the dissidents' paramilitary wings; and knew very little about the religious leadership. The tragedy is that the Shah never used this information to break up the revolutionary coalition because he was uncertain whether to crush the opposition or to compromise with it.

Military Politics

The Shah's control of the military was not only to defend Iran from external threat but to reinforce the regime's domestic power as well. His father had insured that the Shah receive training in the armed forces. After his undergraduate schooling in Switzerland, his advanced education was provided by Iran's West Point, the Military College. From the beginning of his reign, the army was a particular concern to him. Always, the monarch retained an intense interest in the details of military preparedness, especially officer loyalty.

As a result of Iran's military collapse in the face of the Anglo-Soviet invasion of 1941 that ended with the abdication of his father, the young king and his advisors were faced with the prospect of rebuilding the shattered military services. This began immediately, during the occupation of Iran by Russia and Britain during World War II. An important component of the rebuilding was the establishment in 1943 of advisory missions to the gendarmerie and the army, staffed by U.S. military officers and men.

Communist infiltration of the military in the early post-war years was substantial, but the vast majority of the army remained loyal to the Shah, particularly after several hundred Tudeh sympathizers were purged. It was the personal loyalty of the senior officer corps to their monarch that was to become the bedrock of the new military system. The Shah spent much of his time getting to know the highest ranking officers of all three services—army, navy, air force. Certainly he was interested in their attitudes, but he also genuinely wanted to know all he could about his armed services. The monarch himself would personally select officers for the rank of general. Not surprisingly, the military would play a key role in the efforts of General Zahedi to return the Shah to power in 1953, when Prime Minister Mossadeq was ousted.

Two factors combined to weaken the fiber of the Iranian military with the same type of malaise that the vastly increased oil revenues precipitated in the economic arena. One was that stepped-up income freed Iran from previous fiscal limitations on military growth. The second was the Shah's growing belief after 1971 that Iran would have to play a more active role in the security of the region, because the British had withdrawn their military from the Persian Gulf. The necessity to build up the armed forces rapidly was perceived just as the financial wherewithal to do it became available. Major expansion was inevitable. Substantial military aid from the United States had enabled the Shah to modernize his armed forces throughout the late 1950s and 1960s. Now the Shah could pay for weapons and training himself. He was interested in both quantity and quality. Manpower went up by 50 percent from 1973 to early 1977, but the acquisition of ships and high performance aircraft strained to the limit the still meager technological resources and skilled manpower available to the military. This increased the stress on the civilian economy, which was competing for the same resources and manpower. Certainly it added to the country's inflation rate and placed an almost insurmountable burden on a military bureaucracy which had not yet fully assimilated modern managerial techniques.

The Shah deliberately developed the officer corps as a caste apart. Officers were strongly discouraged from contacts with foreigners, especially military attaches with the embassies in Tehran. Though only those below the rank of colonel were required to get permission to talk with foreign diplomats, in practice only those specially chosen for liaison functions dealt with non-Iranians. There had to be one major exception—the various technical missions. U.S. advisory teams to military forces, especially missile units and air force squadrons based outside Tehran, and British officers assigned to the armored training program (their Chieftains were Iran's battle tanks) enjoyed limited social exchanges with their counterparts. Presumably, Russians involved in transport programs (that country supplied trucks and jeeps) were able to do so as well.

Such informal contact had one important political fallout—it reinforced the Shah's natural suspicions that foreigners, particularly the British and the Americans, could collude independently with the military. This was not an unreasonable assumption. Some 11,000 officers were trained in the United States from 1950 to 1974, and approximately 2,000 more in England. Military intelligence and the Imperial Inspectorate spent inordinate amounts of time checking out the possibility that foreign officers were subverting assistance programs to the Iranian armed forces. The question of military officials' contacts with non-Iranians would become particularly acute in early 1979 when American General Robert Huyser came to Tehran for about five weeks.

Although all the military were privileged, some were more privileged than others. The Imperial Guard, an elite force of approximately 8,000 specially chosen officers and men, safeguarded the Shah's personal security and internal security around Tehran. Those in the Imperial Guard received 20 percent better pay and benefits than the regular forces, though even the pay and benefits for the latter were as much as 50 percent higher than that in neighboring countries. By 1977 a second lieutenant in the army drew a base salary of $221 per month, plus ample allowances. His Imperial Guard counterpart earned $270, plus slightly better additional benefits. In contrast, a second lieutenant in the Turkish army earned approximately $100 base pay, with allowances about half of what the Iranians received. Moreover, successful career officers generally received post-retirement appointments to a state corporation like the National Iranian Oil Company, or to the Senate, where the Shah could name 30 choices. Officers who deviated from favoring the regime were not promoted. In some cases they were dismissed outright. Such longtime special consideration for his ranking military helps explain why the armed forces remained a relatively passive factor during the political turmoil of 1978. Their loyalty was to the Shah.

Finally, the Iranian command structure was decentralized, inefficient, and not well adapted to either rapid modernization or potential combat. The officers themselves considered the way their command arrangements were set up to be ridiculous. Politically, however, the Shah regarded such decentralization as necessary in order to prevent officer cabals from threatening the regime. The three services were not linked in a command structure. The supreme commander's staff, the Iranian equivalent of the U.S. Joint Chiefs of Staff, had nowhere near the same power to coordinate activities as similar groups elsewhere. Each service commander always had individual audiences with the Shah; even the chief of the supreme commander's staff had little authority to coordinate. The situation was complicated by nepotism. General Mohammad Khatemi, the Shah's brother-in-law, commanded the air force until he was killed in a glider-kite accident in September 1975. Princess Ashraf's son, Captain Shahriyar Shafiq (assassinated on a Paris street December 7, 1979), was deputy head of the Indian Ocean squadron and clearly marked as the future head of the Iranian navy.

The titular heads of the military forces, minister of war General Reza Azimi and chief of the supreme commander's staff General Gholam Reza Azhari (who became prime minister November 6, 1978, for six weeks only), were not strong figures, and like many in the regime's upper echelons, were basically faithful executors of policy determined by the Shah, not independent contributors. Other younger officers such as commander of the air force (after Khatemi's death) General Amir Hussein Rabii, ground forces chief General Gholam Ali Oveissi (one of the few high-ranking military men to escape death during the revolution), and commander of the Imperial Guard General Ali Badrii (killed by his own men at the climax of the revolution), were much more attuned to political considerations and played greater roles in the unfolding revolution than their nominal superiors.

As Iran approached chaos in 1978, the same internal strains and problems of control and competence affected the military as they did the civilian sector. Only about one-third of the armed forces were career enlistees. The rest were civilians who had been drafted for 18 months to two years. Political agitation by the opposition began to affect the steadfastness of military units in the summer of 1978, and accelerated following the imposition of martial law throughout most of Iran in September of that year. While there were efforts by some commands and individually committed officers to combat the subversion, the overwhelming feeling of both the Shah and his ranking officers was that the armed forces were immune to the kinds of blandishments that the revolutionary forces were using on the rest of the population. The military was considered an automatic pillar of the regime. This assumption inhibited even the meager efforts which were undertaken by the army on behalf of the Shah just prior to the revolutionary takeover. Like the other organizations so much a part of the Shah's system of control, the armed forces were wholly dependent upon the leadership of their monarch in order to act effectively. In revolutionary circumstances, the very techniques used to ensure loyalty worked against military effectiveness.

Managing Political Participation

The Shah refined his style of governing throughout the 1960s and 1970s. Organizations and patterns already mentioned were the principal elements in a system which focused on controlling the politics of development and preventing interference in the modernization process, now well underway. However, from 1963 to 1978, the Shah experimented. A two-party system was established in 1957. The Mellioun Party, which later evolved into the Iran Novin Party, was pro-government; the Mardom Party was the "loyal" opposition. That structure remained in place until March 1975, when the Resurgence Party of the People of Iran was established, with the Shah's blessing. The other parties were invited to disband and join the new group, which they did, ending the two-party system.

The Shah did this because he believed that bringing everyone into the one party would enable him to increase public participation in government without losing control of the process and endangering the policy of rapid modernization. Political activity had become the exclusive province of the Shah, his small circle of advisors, and a supporting elite of some 300 to 400 individuals. There were no independent institutions through which even this limited group could express their differences, much less offer opponents of the Shah any prospect of being heard. In keeping with the monarch's concept of the people as passive partici- pants in the policy and decision making process, the political parties were considered merely a way of organizing opinion, not an institution of government. Although the Shah had adopted an intensely autocratic style, the presence of political parties was intended to modify it, but only gradually. In several interviews between 1975 and 1977, the Shah spoke of a time when his son might ascend the throne and need a more institutionalized system of politics. Privately, he spoke of building un- derpinnings for the eventual transfer of power to the crown prince. This was to occur in 10 to 12 years, about 1990, if all went well.

One of the Shah's motives for seeking change was reinforced by several small groups within the elite who came to him privately to ex- press their concern. Beginning in 1973 they were convinced that Iran had to modernize politically as well as economically if it were to survive and prosper. They pressed the Shah to create a one-party system in order to organize political life within a framework that would not threaten the stability of the country. Such an arrangement would allow both the elite and the masses to become involved in a controlled rela- tionship whereby to be in opposition would no longer automatically be synonomous with treason. Participation would mean the citizenry could practice responsible politics and provide the institutional frame- work for strengthening the "constitutional" side of Iran's constitutional monarchy. Apparently the Shah also agreed that this was so over the winter of 1974–1975.

Two other more immediate considerations probably influenced him to opt for a single-party structure despite his earlier commitment to a two-party system. One was concern that Prime Minister Hoveyda was becoming too powerful in his dual capacity as both secretary-general of the Iran Novin Party and prime minister. Creation of the Resurgence Party theoretically placed the Shah above politics as the omnipotent leader, neither subject to its control nor responsible for its failure. It was supposed to institutionalize a buffer between the monarch and popular discontent. As a broad national party, its leadership clearly would be subordinate to the Shah, whereas the Iran Novin party had become the personal tool of Prime Minister Hoveyda.

The other reason for dismantling the two-party system was the gen- eral perception that it had not been providing alternatives. At least dis- banding the two parties would remove the hypocrisy that choices were available. It was generally believed that if both parties were to compete in the June 1975 parliamentary elections, the result would be an overwhelming Iran Novin victory followed by public charges of corruption and dishonesty that would further discredit the political structure.

Despite these factors, the prime motivation to make the change to a single party was to create an organization which could propagandize the masses in the same way Iran's elite had learned to accept the regime. While the concept had a certain logic, it was not well thought out at the highest level. Also, beyond creating a single-party system, the Shah did not appear to have any long-range strategy for developing the new arrangement. He had no idea how to mesh the fresh organization with existing practices. Yet the structure in place was designed for control, not participation and bargaining. Moreover, given the impact of the Shah's authoritarian style of government, greater popular participation in politics would most likely also bring calls for changing the system. However, according to one of the authors of the proposed new concept, the Resurgence Party was designed to be a mechanism of controlled participation based on the assumption that people would be satisfied with minimal political activity and would not want to make major changes.

The structure of the new party provided for the Shah to be above the political infighting, but did not render unnecessary the mechanisms of control used previously. The only way the former political conditions could be eliminated would have been to include the opposition — members of Mossadeq's National Front, the Liberation Movement of Iran, and some other smaller groups, like the Pan Iran Party — all of whom had refused to participate in approved party politics since the mid-1960s. Major issues connected with the formation of a single party and how it would be managed were either never addressed or were dealt with only in a haphazard way. The result was that liberalizing controls — easing up on SAVAK repression of the opposition and officially taking a more tolerant attitude toward public criticism — began before any kind of institutional base was in place to shape the emerging participatory politics without either losing command of the changes or destroying the effectiveness of the participation scheme by retightening controls, or both.

Undoubtedly, the Shah thought problems could be worked out on an ad hoc basis, with the army as the final guardian of the system. When the pressure of potential revolution increased, however, the monarch vacillated, acting much less strongly than his own political skills would have suggested. Certainly there were extenuating circumstances, but one very important reason for this was the fact that the Shah had no real idea how the various elements — the Resurgence Party, the opposition groups, and the government bureaucracies—would evolve into a more constitutional government. He never offered a real rationale for what he was trying to do. Leading party figures have expressed similar confusion about what was expected of them and what was the ultimate objective of the Resurgence Party. Therefore each official developed his own list of priorities. Naturally a certain amount of activity for personal advancement at cross purposes with political development took place. Without a firm idea of where he was headed, by 1978 the Shah was reduced to improvisation and on-the-spot justifications for his actions. After he left Iran, the monarch continued to express mystification over how it all happened, focusing on individual incidents, specific problems, and the role of foreign influence.

The Shah's desultory behavior in 1978 was exacerbated by his lymphomatous cancer and the medicines used to treat it. Those who knew the monarch best believe his health had deteriorated significantly. Although his condition probably was first diagnosed in 1974, the existence of his illness was successfully concealed from everyone, including his countrymen. Rumors about the Shah's health had started circulating in late 1976, but they were discounted. The nagging suspicion that there really might be a severe medical problem was voiced in Tehran about April 1978, but such stories still were given little credence.

Even if the impact of the illness and treatments was not a factor until 1977, it severely reduced the Shah's ability to cope with an evolving problem that went to the very roots of his regime. It also underlined the extreme vulnerability of a political system so heavily dependent on one man's perception, intelligence, and skill. The Shah already had maneuvered Iran through several crises during the course of his rule. Partly because of this, and especially since 1963, the political talents of other leaders had atrophied. Both the establishment and the opposition alike had come to rely on the Shah as the principal—if not the only—independent actor on the political stage. No wonder the dissidents charged that the Resurgence Party was merely a new trick to sustain royal absolutism. Thus the monarch's inability in 1978 and 1979 to meet what would prove to be the toughest challenge yet to his regime left Iran fragmented, facing the chaos of unbridled change and collapse.

The Resurgence Party

The Resurgence Party was intended to be the vehicle for mobilizing the middle and lower classes.[5] Party chapters (kanouns), the basic organizational units, had 50 to 175 members and were supposed to provide a focus for the transmission of ideas upward to district, provincial, and national levels of the organization. Significantly, the kanouns, like the party structure itself, were organized from the top down. The first 35 kanouns in Fars province, for example, were established by men openly encouraged to do so by the governor general of that province, Nasser Esfahani, or by party officials in Tehran. The role of the Resurgence Party as a conduit for the middle class to move from private life to participation in government is obvious in the statistics. In June 1976, 18 of 21 provincial chairmen had not been active in political organizations before, and 19 of 20 were businessmen. A year later, 21 of 24 provincial chairmen still listed their main occupation as business.

The Resurgence Party was organized by a group of the politically active Western educated technocrats who joined with old-line politicians who strongly supported the Shah. Little or no effort was made to encourage dissident politicians or disaffected university professors to participate. All were invited to join the party, but no special effort was made to win the collaboration of the hard core opposition. The Shah left no doubt how he felt when he said that the Resurgence Party was for all Iranians who accepted the monarchy, the constitution, and the Shah-People Revolution of 1963. He pointedly excluded those who did not support the fundamentals of the regime, noting that they could either stay in Iran or leave, but if they chose to remain then they could have no say in the government. People were encouraged to join the party in a normal fashion, but rumors abounded that those who did not sign up could find it difficult to travel outside Iran or to keep a government job. The regime made the party the basic means of access to political rewards. Though there was little outright coercion—party membership, even based on government figures, never was more than 60 percent of the eligible population—subtler pressure put the message across quite well. Indeed, membership eventually did become mandatory for anyone involved in the government. Nonmembers were branded as supporters of the opposition. Thus those opposed to the party were automatically defined as being anti-regime as well.

Although little information is now available on Resurgence Party membership, in 1976 and 1977 a significant number of educated Iranians were interested in the party. Some of the kanouns became centers where younger professionals and university faculty members could debate and discuss political participation. In Tehran, approximately 600 members of several university faculties were actively involved in party affairs. Many middle-class Iranians were willing to give the party a chance, for various reasons. But the most obvious one was a desire to have an impact on their political destinies.

Unfortunately, the party never was allowed to develop independently of the government, nor did it ever provide sufficient political rewards to enough of its members to take advantage of its early promise. In an effort to organize and structure debate, two "wings" were formed—the Progressive Liberals headed first by Minister of the Interior Jamshid Amouzegar and later by Director of the Plan and Budget Organization Abdul Magid Magidi; and the Constructive Liberals under Minister of Finance Houshang Ansari. In 1978 a third force, the Independent Study Group, led by former Tehran University Chancellor Houshang Nahavandi, joined the fray just before the complete dissolution of the party machinery. The wings had no independent power, and in the summer of 1976, when it appeared that serious differences might develop between them, the Shah himself stepped in. There could be no direct competition between the wings within parliament, he said, and they would have to remain under overall party discipline. With the Shah ruling out conflict, the wings, which had worked hard to build themselves up during the summer of 1976, quickly lost their allure for the budding middle-class politicians. Their only real function after the autumn of 1976 was to serve as a platform for individual speakers, usually the wing leaders, on an occasional issue.

Links between the government and the party and the party and parliament were never clearly defined. At the top, 10 cabinet officials were to join 15 elected officials to be the political bureau of the Resurgence Party. There were also 55 members of the executive board, some of them also in the cabinet. Both groups coordinated party policy involving pending legislation. In practice, however, the party had little visible impact on bills being presented, though sometimes they were able to modify the new laws.

The government always retained control over party machinery. For the first 18 months, for example, the jobs of prime minister and secretary-general of the party were combined. Prime Minister Hoveyda remained secretary-general from the time the party was established until October 1976, when Jamshid Amouzegar replaced him. When Amouzegar was named prime minister in August 1977, he was succeeded as head of the Resurgence Party by then Deputy Court Minister Mohammad Baheri. After Baheri voiced his differences with the government, his independence became a problem. Amouzegar convinced the Shah to recombine the prime ministership and secretary-generalship in January 1978. When Amouzegar took over the second time, the Resurgence Party never challenged the government or debated important issues—an oil pricing policy, the defense budget, internal security, and control of the press and assembly—on its own. In fact, the only time it ever tried to stake out an independent position was in the fall of 1977 during Baheri's tenure as secretary-general, when he defended those protesting inadequate housing after the three days of riots in Tehran in mid-August. Baheri gave two other speeches a few months later which suggested he was about to carve out independent Resurgence Party stands on housing and inflation. The result was renewed interest in the party. Then the Shah dismissed Baheri in mid-December. When the party congress convened January 2 through 4 and chose Prime Minister Amouzegar as secretary-general, even the most optimistic participants in Resurgence Party affairs backed away. By firing Baheri and replacing him with Amouzegar, the Shah torpedoed the last shred of Resurgence Party legitimacy. Five days later, the first of the serious religious riots which began the revolutionary spiral took place in Qom. During the steadily increasing turmoil of 1978, the Resurgence Party played no role at all in Iranian politics.

This need not have been the case. In the provinces, the Resurgence Party had taken hold. The more astute provincial governors had not tried to compete with it. Instead they organized it as a pressure group to lobby both the party and parliament in Tehran, pressing for a greater share of the country's resources. At least two major development projects in Fars province were approved during 1976 and 1977 as a result, and Isfahan had similar good fortune. Countrywide, the kanouns also so successfully educated citizens in political participation that in 1977 Prime Minister Hoveyda was subjected to blistering criticism on at least five occasions when speaking before party chapters in south Tehran.

For dedicated party members, the ultimate betrayal was to participate in good faith and then learn that it was to have little effect. Late in 1977 the Shah announced that active membership in the Resurgence Party was neither a way to get ahead in a government job (or a way to get the job in the first place) nor was the party to act as a pressure group on behalf of specific policies. Members were to be merely watchdogs. The chief of the party's executive board, Ahmad Qoreishi, and other senior officials were stunned to learn that this interpretation would be included in the manifesto to be approved by the Resurgence Party congress in January.

Where the party was able to function as it should, advocating programs and grooming potential political leaders, as it did in about half the provinces, it was modestly successful.[6] The crux of the problem was the Shah's unwillingness to share any of his authoritative policy and decision making power with either the Resurgence Party or the party and parliament combined. Their experience with the Resurgence

Party whetted the appetites of those who participated but, for obvious reasons, becoming involved never was a viable option for dedicated dissidents. Though membership statistics remained high—between five and six million throughout 1977—enthusiasm gradually dwindled even for those who were committed to the party. After January 1978 membership became truly nominal for all but a few functionaries, despite the hopes and prospects of two years earlier.

Some politicians believed that one wing of the Resurgence Party might survive and form a majority in the 1979 parliamentary elections. However, by mid-summer 1978 the Shah and his government, including Resurgence Party leaders, were prepared to see it cease to be the sole legal party as part of a compromise arrangement with the opposition and to allow free and open political activity. But it was much too late. In August, incoming Prime Minister Sharif-Emami indicated his administration would terminate the one-party system. The Resurgence Party was formally disbanded on September 30. There were modest efforts by the two wing leaders to form separate political organizations, but these died aborning as unrest continued to grow. With the demise of the "official" party, supporters of the government were left with no institutional basis for supporting the Shah's efforts to achieve a compromise solution as the country became increasingly more unsettled. By this time, the initiative had shifted to the loose network of opposition groups which had been gaining strength throughout 1978. The continuing story of political evolution in Iran is largely theirs.

Chapter Three

★

_____

Political Evolution:
The Opposition

Opposition to authority has been part of Persian tradition since earliest times, but especially since the Arab conquest of Iran in the seventh century. Attacks against the regime of Mohammad Reza Pahlavi have come in waves, linked to historical events. In the early 1950s, the Tudeh Party and the National Front were the principal challengers. National Front Prime Minister Mohammad Mossadeq masterminded a coalition which almost ousted the monarch, but its power was destroyed in 1953 by the coup which brought the Shah back to the throne. The Tudeh Party was outlawed and went underground, resurfacing during and after the revolutionary takeover in 1979.

At the time of the events in 1953, many religious leaders, bazaar merchants, university students, and intellectuals stood by their monarch long enough for him to regain power. By 1963, however, the Shah's reform programs had adversely affected the clergy, who retaliated by instigating riots in several cities which severely challenged the regime before they were finally repressed in June. The threat to the monarchy starting in 1977 came from exactly the same source, strengthened by the addition of secular supporters from the bazaars and universities who had become disillusioned with "progress." These groups consolidated, transforming their dissident coalition into a revolutionary mass movement and finally into an armed insurrection.

Until 1977 the opposition had consisted of many factions tied together only by their distaste for the Shah and the way he was changing Iran. Dissident leaders had fought among themselves for years. Insignificant splinter parties and minor movements had proliferated, with their leaders criticizing each other with as much vitriol as they reserved for the Shah. While the clergy had been alienated since 1963, they had not been particularly active in politics, except to complain vigorously about what they believed to be the Shah's turning the country away from Islam as Iran modernized. It was only later, as the revolutionary situation developed throughout 1978, that all the factions gradually coalesced around Ayatollah Ruhollah Khomeini and created the network of organizations influenced by a small group of politicized radical clerics.[1]

Even as a young man, and as a virtually unknown clergyman, Khomeini had opposed the Pahlavi dynasty. He considered Reza Shah responsible for the death of his father, a mullah killed by government troops in a demonstration years earlier. Also, in October 1977 one of the Ayatollah's sons was killed in an automobile accident near Baghdad. It has never been proved that it was a trap set by SAVAK, but Khomeini and those around him believed that it was. Naturally this only reinforced the Ayatollah's hatred of the regime. His followers played on the twin emotions of sorrow and martyrdom to strengthen Khomeini's prestige. Effective manipulation of propaganda on this and other themes enabled dissident organizations to rally mass support— something they had been unable to do from 1963 to 1967—and to press successfully for the destruction of civil and military authority.

Their victory was not foreordained, revolutionary rhetoric to the contrary. The triumph of the opposition and the eventual emergence of the Islamic movement as the dominant force evolved because of diligent development of effective organization, good tactical choices made in terms of reaching attainable goals, and bad or ineffective decisions made by the Shah and his government. This dynamic interplay between the opposition and legitimate authority, which caused the progressive disintegration of that authority's power, is not fully understood, yet it lies at the heart of Iran's revolutionary story.

The Reasons for Discontent

Until 1977 internal opposition to the Shah remained fragmented. The modest guerrilla movements of the early 1970s had been determinedly hunted down and neutralized by SAVAK. The result was that the old-line opposition became demoralized and nearly depoliticized. Many former Mossadeq supporters took academic positions, sniping at the regime from the sidelines, yet still vulnerable to government pressure. No counter-elite developed from within, except in the guerrilla movement. The mosques, for example, operated within fairly narrow confines, especially between 1972 and 1976 when the government security forces were at their most brutal. Restrictions were placed on public speeches at religious schools, and four were closed intermittently because they were known as centers of opposition activity. This situation began to change in 1977 when the Shah liberalized the political process to a limited degree, permitting increased organizational activity and allowing dissidents to appeal to the public for support.

Generalized discontent has always been part of the Iranian political system, but these feelings began to intensify in 1977 because of the burgeoning economic and social problems exacerbated by the accelerating development process. Iran's Institute of Communication Studies outlined the growth of unrest in early 1978 and identified separate problems. The main themes sparking dissatisfaction among workers and farmers were economic—unemployment, inflation, and a lack in some areas of the country of basic social amenities like schools, electricity, and plumbing. As the government announced more programs for health, social care, and free education, the gap between its performance and reality became obvious to the average citizen, inclining him to pay more attention to those individuals who opposed the government. Increasing numbers of young professionals, intellectuals, and students were bothered by the Shah's authoritarian style and the lack of political freedom. From 1956 to 1976 the development program increased the size of this modernized-but-disaffected group from 6 to 13 percent of the population.[2] More importantly, representatives of this emerging class had begun to play significant roles managing the increasingly complex economy.

Two other changes in the political situation affected all classes of society, though in slightly different ways. First was the noticeable expansion of Iran's foreign interests under the Shah, including his decision to assist counterinsurgency in Oman and to advocate a Persian Gulf security pact. Of particular interest to dedicated Moslems was the monarch's second policy. Being pragmatic, the Shah had continued regular oil shipments to Israel after the 1973 Arab oil embargo, the only Middle Eastern country to do so. It was a particularly sensitive issue for the guerrillas, who had been receiving paramilitary training from various Palestinian factions since 1969. Arab radicals frequently made it clear that their assistance was predicated on "a more appropraite attitude" toward Israel and the United States, the latter because it supported the Jewish state. They insisted upon greater solidarity with their Islamic brethren when the revolution would be victorious.

The Israeli policy had an adverse impact on an important aspect of the Shah's political posture—his special relationship with the United States. Even those Iranians inclined to agree with the monarch on other issues saw the helpful policy toward Israel as another example of his dependence upon, and subservience to, the U.S. Furthermore, as a result of the oil boom and the arrival of foreign technical advisors, plus the expanded purchases of sophisticated weaponry, the American presence in Iran was growing. This presence also was a major reason why general willingness to listen to the dissidents increased. While U.S. involvement was considered to be good by those who benefited, the steadily expanding numbers of Americans and their families moving into the country to assist with development projects, especially military related ones, proved to be yet more "evidence" that the Shah was not truly a nationalist, and that problems in Iran were a direct result of this infusion of foreigners. This attitude is entirely congruent with Iran's traditional xenophobia. For centuries Persians have blamed their troubles on outside invaders such as the Mongols or the Arabs, or on intervention by foreign powers such as Britain and the Soviet Union.

Using these themes, the opposition built up its organizations and refined ideologies, appealing to the masses and constructing a political movement ultimately powerful enough to force the Shah to leave his country.

The Religious Opposition

THE CLERICS

Historically, Shia Islam has held that secular government is intrinsically corrupt, at best a necessary evil that will be done away with when the Mahdi, the Twelfth Imam, returns to establish God's justice on earth. The sect developed out of the Persian reaction to the Arab conquest. Iranians were willing to adopt Islam (and no longer be Zoroastrians), but they could not accept Arab domination. Hence the creation of Shiism. While several details distinguish Sunnis from Shias, the principal difference between them stems from a disagreement over the line of succession. The Sunnis believe that, after the Fourth Imam, subsequent caliphs did not have to be blood relatives of Islam's founder, Mohammad. The Shias, on the other hand, insist that Mohammad was succeeded by his son-in-law, Ali, and by direct male descendent after Ali down to the Twelfth Imam, who mysteriously disappeared in the year A. D. 939 and who eventually will return to earth to resume leadership of all Moslems, both Shiites and Sunnis. There are those—still only a few—who would elevate Khomeini to this position.

Shia Islam's lack of a formal hierarchical structure and formal leadership worked to the advantage of the clergy vis-à-vis the Shah from 1963 to 1977. In this branch of Islam there is no formal overarching structure of ordination or authority, thus the monarch could not attack a well-defined organization. Starting in the mid-1960s the government "adopted" a number of clergy, and used its influence in various ways to divide their allegiance and insure at least a minumum of accommodation with the regime. The Shah was not above using force to get his way. A number of mullahs and ayatollahs were jailed for various lengths of time because of their anti-government activities.

Individuals become mullahs after substantial training at one of the dozen or so religious schools. After years of teaching or preaching, some become hojatollahs. After more years of acquiring a following and becoming known as true Islamic scholars, a few are accepted as ayatollahs. A man of particular learning and distinction might in time become recognized as a grand ayatollah, or the deputy to Shia Islam's Twelfth Imam, missing since the tenth century. After his revolutionary victory, Ayatollah Khomeini was recognized by his followers as the preeminent cleric, or deputy to the Imam ("moaven-e-Imam", or "Imam" as the short form). The last "super" ayatollah before Khomeini, Ayatollah Hakim, died in 1975.

Several other ayatollahs have at least as much claim to religious (as opposed to religious-political) eminence as Khomeini. Ayatollah Kazem Shariatmadari, from Tabriz, was Iran's leading ayatollah during Khomeini's exile, and still commands predominant support in his home area in northwestern Iran, Azarbaijan province. In political terms, Shariatmadari even today probably could count on the loyalty of the people in the northwest if there was an open clash. Another outstanding figure both ecclesiastically and politically was Tehran's Ayatollah Mahmoud Taleqani, who died at age 84 in September 1979. Until his death, he was the only prominent revolutionary to publicly challenge Khomeini, when his two sons were "mistakenly" arrested by Revolutionary Guards.[3]

Iranian ayatollahs always have been a source of doctrine on issues of social as well as religious significance. The Shiite Islamic leadership has condemned the excesses of the Shah's modernization campaign from the time of land reform in 1963 to the present. But even when his father was shah, there had been serious clashes between the monarchy and the clergy. In 1936, for example, Reza Shah abolished the wearing of the chador (the black veil covering women from head to foot), though its use was restored in 1941 as part of a compromise to encourage the clergy to support the new shah, his son. As education outside the religious schools increased starting in the 1950s, the role of the mullahs was pushed aside. Then, in the 1960s, judicial reforms reduced the clerical role in marriage, divorce, and other family matters. The state gained management control of the shrine foundations in Mashad, Isfahan, and elsewhere in 1963, depriving the mosques of resources. These funds were only partially restored (perhaps 30 to 40 percent) through government subsidies for educational scholarships and construction costs. Eventually government modernizers began portraying Islamic leaders as political reactionaries only interested in their lands and funds.

Much of the clergy was also corruptible. After the takeover of SAVAK in February 1979, during the height of the revolution, a number of records were confiscated, indicating that the secret police had at least slight contact with over 1,200 religious leaders. Very few were full-time collaborators, but they had compromised themselves at one time or other. The radical clergy used these records to distinguish themselves from other clerics who were willing to go along with the Shah at least to some degree.

Although Ayatollah Khomeini was one of the organizers of the uprising in 1963 against the Shah, the Moslem leadership played a relatively minor role that year in organizing the general public politically, though it was effective in turning people into the streets for demonstrations. The alliance between the mosques and the city bazaars began in 1963 and ripened in the intervening years to 1977. During those 15 years the balance of power between Islam and nationalism within the opposition shifted to favoring the ecclesiastical forces. The religious movement, through the mosques, provided the only secure organizational base from which to challenge the regime in language the peasants and poor urban workers could understand. Most important of all, the religious opposition offered a charismatic leader to symbolize its unity against the Shah—Ayatollah Ruhollah Khomeini.

A very significant aspect of the development of the revolutionary movement was the steadily increasing participation of Iran's Shiite Islamic organization. There are approximately 80,000 to 90,000 mosques and 180,000 to 200,000 clerics in a population of 35 million. By mid-1977 the growing need of the opposition to communicate gave the religious structure a special importance. The swiftest and most reliable way to pass a message to leaders in another city was through the "mosque network" organized by the senior clergy. Simultaneous demonstrations in various cities during 1978 were coordinated this way, either by messenger or by phone calls between trusted contacts. For example, the staff of Hosseiniyeh Ershat, a religious educational center in Tehran, communicated with Ayatollah Shariatmadari in Tabriz almost daily throughout 1978. Also, clergy loyal to Khomeini were attached to the mosque in north Tehran supervised by Ayatollah Mohammad Beheshti. He would serve as the principal contact between Tehran and Paris when Ayatollah Khomeini moved to the French capital from Iraq in October 1978.

A unique feature of Iran's revolution is the degree to which communication took place outside established media channels. Tapes of Khomeini's sermons and speeches passed through the mosque network from his residence in Iraq to Qom, Iran's most holy city and the Ayatollah's home until his exile. From there, they were taken to other cities, where enterprising and friendly bazaar merchants duplicated tapes and sold them to the faithful. Beginning in 1976 the mosque network eliminated the middleman and delivered the cassettes and pamphlets which spread revolutionary doctrine directly to the sympathetic mullahs. They in turn passed it to the people in the mosques. Much of this activity went unnoticed until it was fully organized in late 1977. Strangely, there were no successful attempts on the part of the government to interfere with this network on a sustained basis. In a few sporadic cases local distributors were arrested, but this would only enrage the faithful and increase sympathy for revolutionary efforts.

The mosques also were the principal agents mobilizing the bazaar merchants, or "bazaaris." In any Islamic society, the bazaar is not only an organization of small businessmen, but also a web of social communication. In Tehran, for example, there are six miles of covered walkways connecting over 1,000 shops, all of whose owners remain in contact. Before the Shah's industrialization program gained headway, the bazaaris were the most influential businessmen in the country. Since the mid-1960s they had been eclipsed by the new entrepreneurs— bankers, manufacturers, and export-importers. The bazaars and the mosques, however, have always cooperated with each other. The money of these merchants financed the theological schools, and up to 80 percent of the clergy's operating expenses.

Bazaar merchants not only provide funds but also organizational talent. Their men have always helped organize the major Islamic religious processions, and their skills in bringing out crowds had been a significant factor in the near-success of the 1963 riots. As the number of demonstrations increased throughout 1978, bazaaris and religious leaders honed to a fine point their talent for organizing crowds. This combination managed the earlier demonstrations and marches which led to the beginning of the end for the Shah—the showdown in Tehran at Jaleh Square on September 8, 1978. Continuing a winning combination, they encouraged the million plus marchers in Tehran three months later on Tassua and Ashura, December 10 and 11.[4]

The religious leadership also benefited from its contacts with the Islamic guerrillas. The Mujahidin provided security for the demonstrations and some protection for the bazaaris as well. They muscled reluctant merchants when many became disillusioned with the increasingly violent trend the revolutionary movement was taking in September and October 1978. The bazaaris organized whatever the clergy wanted done; the Mujahidin enforced it.

After the success of the Islamic revolution in February 1979, this same group of clergymen, bazaar merchants, and Mujahidin transformed themselves into the Islamic Republican Party. Under the leadership of Ayatollah Beheshti, he and other senior clerics in cabinet or Revolutionary Council positions—Hojatollah Hashemi Rafsanjani and Ayatollahs Mahdavi-Kani, Hussein Ali Montazeri, and Mousavi-Ardebili Mofateh—surfaced as the radical political leadership. Their party is dominated by men who believe in hard-line anti-modernist ideology closely linked to the views of Ayatollah Khomeini and Ali Shariati. The latter, an Islamic theoretician who died in June 1977, blended Marxian socialism and Shiism into a call for radical social and political action. He preached that this would bring about a more communalist, egalitarian society consistent with Islamic principles.

KHOMEINI, THE CHARISMATIC AYATOLLAH

The religious opposition served as the organizational base for the person who would evolve into the symbol of the Islamic revolution— Ayatollah Ruhollah Khomeini. Born May 6, 1900, he was a little-known figure in the West even after he became prominent in Islamic circles in the early 1960s. Because of his obsession with foreign influence in Iran, he challenged the legitimacy of the desire of parliament (the Shah) to pass a law conferring diplomatic immunity on American military and technical assistance personnel. The bill passed. Khomeini was banished in 1964; he went to Turkey first, then settled in Najaf, Iraq, in 1965. Consistently anti-government, the Ayatollah lectured and wrote on diverse subjects throughout his exile, but his favorite theme was to blame outsiders for all the modernizing changes that he thought were reducing Islamic prestige:

> The influence of Islamic law in the Moslem Society has diminished; the nation has been afflicted with division, weakness, and degeneration; the

rules of Islam have been obstructed and the situation changed. The colonialists have used all this as an easy opportunity, brought foreign laws to which God has given no power, spread their poisoned cultures and thought and disseminated them among the Moslems, and we have lost the formations of the proper government.[5]

By "proper government" Khomeini means rule by eminent Shiite Islamic figures. "The presence of the qualities of the religious ruler in any individual will qualify him to rule the people." Although he is a shrewd politician who has deliberately obscured his basic ideas in public statements, Khomeini always sought the destruction of the Pahlavis. As a consequence, his political philosophy has always stressed the imposition of clerical control over secular power. His statements on the cassettes were clear on this point as early as 1977, and it is both implicit and explicit in his writings. He says government derives its legitimacy from God, and proper government requires a radical Islamic reconstruction of society. This doctrine is particularly appealing to the urban dispossessed, and complements the Islamic communalism of the Shiite Marxian socialist, Ali Shariati. Such an ideology is particularly challenging to a regime like the Shah's, criticized for its authoritarianism, corruption, and brutality.

While the religious devotion of many of the Ayatollah's followers is not as deep as Khomeini's own, there is no doubt that Islamic fervor has been a most important tool of the revolution. It has been the guiding principle for the faithful, particularly the young Islamic militants who were to become the backbone of the Revolutionary Guards and neighborhood committees after the takeover. Khomeini's vision of life is a radical reinterpretation of the Islamic social norms of nearly 1,300 years ago. This reversion to A.D. 700 did not become immediately obvious after the revolution, since initially only sporadic attempts were made to enforce many social restrictions. That changed in 1980, when death by stoning, for example, became a common mode of execution for women accused of adultery.

Several aspects of Khomeini's doctrine deserve closer attention. First is his own conception of himself as a moral leader above politics. At no time has he sought public office, yet he regards himself as the supreme figure of the Islamic revolution, to whom obedience and devotion naturally flow because of his religious qualities. When questioned by the renowned Italian journalist Oriana Fallaci, he answered:

Iran is not in my hands. Iran is in the hands of the people, because it was the people who handed the country over to the person who is their ser-

vant, and who want only what is good for them. They yell [at demonstra-
tions] like this because they love me, and they love me because they feel
that I care for their good, that is, to apply the commandments of Islam.
Islam is justice.[6]

People obey Khomeini, in short, because they think he does what is
best for them. If things go wrong, it is because of the plots of foreigners. If censorship must be imposed, for instance, it is because communists or the "rotten brains" of the West want to corrupt Islamic
society.

The adulation forced on Khomeini by the urban crowds of Tehran
(mostly males between the ages of 13 to 35) is likened to religious fervor. What makes Khomeini different from other politicians is that he
uses this fervor to channel the government along lines he finds worth-
while. His age and health have prevented him from playing an especially active political role, but then to do so is neither his style nor his
desire in any case. Since the revolutionary takeover the Ayatollah has
become a master at weaving among competing groups. He has refused
consistently to choose between President Bani-Sadr and the religious
leadership led by Ayatollah Beheshti. Both sides are forced to beg for
his favor; neither can ever be sure of his steady support.

The Ayatollah's authoritarianism stems from his belief that he em-
bodies the correct Islamic way. One does not have to accept the opinion
of others when one is God's own spokesman. This has created some
heartburn among his fellow ayatollahs and laid the groundwork for a
potential schism among the religious leaders. Both before and after the
revolutionary takeover, Khomeini has been particularly astute, backing
those clergy who agree with him at the expense of older, more established clerics, but the potential for religious division remains. In return,
those who share his views have elevated Khomeini to a position of
supremacy among his fellow ayatollahs.

The process began in October 1978 when Khomeini moved from
Najaf, Iraq to the small village of Neuphle-de-Chateau near Paris. From
there he and his close associates (Ibrahim Yazdi, Abol Hassan Bani-
Sadr, and Sadeq Ghotbzadeh) placed themselves at the forefront of the
revolution by orchestrating a well-crafted media campaign. Western
journalists and, more importantly, ranking opposition politicians such
as National Front leader Karim Sanjabi and the Liberation Movement's
Mehdi Bazargan, came to pay their respects. Khomeini's consistent refusal to compromise with the Shah or to accept the continued existence
of the Pahlavi dynasty under any circumstances distinguished him from

virtually all other politicians and senior clerics. By successfully maintaining this position until the Shah fled, he automatically established himself as the dominant figure of the revolution and was able to stamp Iran with his ideological and organizational imprimatur. Though Khomeini was to dominate, it is important to remember that choice and circumstance as well as stubbornness permitted the Ayatollah's inflexibility to win out.

The Secular Opposition

THE LIBERATION MOVEMENT OF IRAN

By 1977 most of Khomeini's secular allies of 1963 had organized themselves both at home and abroad into the Liberation Movement of Iran. The Liberation Movement developed an organizational capacity in those years with the help of many Iranian students and other political activists who established cells in western Europe and the United States. Its internal structure in Iran was closely linked to the mosque network of the Islamic faithful. The Liberation Movement organized the demonstrations for the various fundamentalist supporters of the Islamic movement, particularly throughout 1978. Their leader, Mehdi Bazargan (who would become Khomeini's first prime minister), combined nationalism with Islamic ideology. Around him were older men who had worked with the National Front under Mossadeq, but who broke away in 1963 to form closer links with the clergy. Until the revolutionary takeover, the second echelon of the Liberation Movement consisted of men in their 40s and 50s committed to democratic government and the division between mosque and state. When the revolutionary constitution was drafted in the summer of 1979, the Islamic Republic which emerged was closer to Khomeini's conception of a theocratic structure than to Bazargan's more liberal views. The prime minister definitely was the junior partner in the revolutionary coalition and the Ayatollah had become the senior partner.

Even so, Bazargan and the Liberation Movement have remained close to Khomeini, convinced that Iran needs an Islamic ideology to counter communism and to promote a viable national identity. This has meant remaining subordinate to the Ayatollah, as Bazargan himself acknowledged in an interview shortly before he resigned as prime minister in protest after the American hostages were taken in November 1979. However, Bazargan remained a member of the Revolutionary Council.

Bazargan was a major figure on the Committee for the Defense of Human Rights and Freedom, which consistently attacked the Shah's regime for civil rights violations. As the first prime minister in the revolutionary government, he disavowed the tribunals and immediate executions as well as the repressive censorship carried out in the name of the revolutionary committees. He accurately represents the views of many educated Iranians who believe that Islamic evolution and Western culture are not necessarily incompatible, as the Moslem ideologues insist. In the revolutionary turmoil in the autumn of 1978, it was the Liberation Movement that reassured uneasy urban dwellers and bazaar merchants that a government without the Shah would not go to extremes. The Ayatollah's secular ally played a critical role, encouraging many in the emerging middle class who were disillusioned with the Shah but suspicious of Khomeini to withdraw their support from the monarch. Without the soothing words of the Liberation Movement it is doubtful that the denouement of the overthrow would have been as free of violence as it was. By November 1979, particularly after the taking of the American hostages and Bazargan's resignation as prime minister, many middle-class Iranians would be disgusted with Khomeini as well. Out of fear they kept silent; many have left Iran.

There is also another problem. The ranking members of the Liberation Movement have no taste for the radical economics of President Bani-Sadr. It was the president who spearheaded the movement to nationalize the banks along Islamic lines. A service charge has replaced interest payments on loans, and borrowing of any kind is based on need, not ability to repay. However, even with these disagreements, there has yet to be an open break between the Liberation Movement and the group of Islamic fundamentalists surrounding Ayatollah Beheshti who jealously "protect" Khomeini.

THE NATIONAL FRONT

The National Front was revived in late 1977, the successor to the National Front of Mossadeq's time. After living quietly in Iran for years, several former members of the opposition decided to become politically active again. Emerging first among equals was Karim Sanjabi, an elderly lawyer who had served in a minor position in Mossadeq's government, as had Bazargan. Prominent in the renaissance of the National Front were Shapour Bakhtiar, who later broke with the opposition to become the Shah's last prime minister; Hedayatollah Matin-Daftari, grandson of Mossadeq; and Dariush Forouhar, former leader of the Pan Iran Party, who would become one of the spokesmen for the reconstituted National Front.

The National Front, more than the Liberation Movement, tried to operate as openly as possible. In the summer and fall of 1977 its members played a major role in expanded dissident activity, speaking before various groups, organizing "readings" with dissident overtones, and advocating major governmental reform, including the abolition of SAVAK, totally free parliamentary elections, and a more independent foreign policy between East and West. In public speeches National Front politicians paid appropriate obeisance to religious leaders, especially Ayatollah Khomeini, but they dealt principally with secular issues. For example, Forouhar, speaking to the merchants in the Tehran bazaar on October 25, 1977, commented:

> For over two centuries our country has been under the direct and indirect domination of foreign imperialist powers which have made a toy of our national life and values through all sorts of plots and designs and the creation of foreign inspired and affiliated dictatorship, corrupt governments . . . and cultural devastation.
>
> On the other hand, the traditional Bazaar has never been a mere center of trade, but a leading national institution of cultural and political life, too. . . .
>
> By stressing the role of the religious leaders and the bazaar, I do not intend to overlook other main social groups, such as the peasants and workers, as the backbones of these forces, as well as the intelligentsia.
>
> The conspicuous failure of the claimed revolution [the Shah-People Revolution] and reforms, and the untiring resistance of the national forces against the endless violations of the people's rights led to the staging of a new show—the setting up of a single political party which is a self-speaking symbol of dictatorship.[7]

By the time this speech was delivered such statements were beginning to find a ready audience among those people increasingly upset with the country's economic and social conditions.

The National Front was largely Tehran-based. Though it had supporters in other cities, it did not have close links with the religious movement nor did it participate as completely as the Liberation Movement in the political-religious mosque network. It was, however, one of the most vocal of the dissident organizations. Its leader, Karim Sanjabi, would become Prime Minister Bazargan's first foreign minister, from February to April, 1979. Significantly, Sanjabi resigned his post because he was upset about the ever-increasing religious control of the government and because he wanted to work toward building up the strength of the National Front throughout the country. As a group with acceptable revolutionary credentials, but not one formally associated with the Khomeini government, the National Front has had some success in attracting young professionals who cannot accept the Islamic potpourri but do not seek military rule or a return to the monarchy.

Unlike the Liberation Movement, the National Front never maintained ties with the guerrillas, nor does it have a military arm of its own. When authority collapsed in February 1979, it had no paramilitary organization to move into the breach when the armed forces disintegrated. In the post-revolutionary period the National Front was a recognized force, but by the end of 1979 that was no longer so. Because of its insignificant military capability, the National Front now plays a minor role politically.

THE GUERRILLA GROUPS

Understanding how the participants in the Iranian guerrilla movement are organized can be difficult. Divisions have never been clear cut, and new factions have emerged since the revolutionary victory. Two principal groups are recognized—the Islamic fundamentalists linked to the Mujahidin, or People's Strugglers; and the Fedayeen, or People's Sacrifice Guerrillas (occasionally called the Cheriks). In response to SAVAK pressure, guerrilla activity for years had been very decentralized and compartmentalized. For security reasons there was only loose coordination between various cells of the same organization. Thus different leaders emphasized different aspects of the ideological and military struggle.

There are hints that on occasion mosque money financed Fedayeen groups in exchange for their training religious recruits in military skills and insurgency techniques. Members of both the Mujahidin and the Fedayeen received assistance from the Palestine Liberation Organization (Yasser Arafat was the first foreign leader to visit Iran after the revolution) and probably from Colonel Qadaffi in Libya as well. Though pre-takeover estimates suggest there never were more than 300 guerrillas operating in Iran at any one time, subsequent information indicates that at least 400 to 600 individuals received military and organizational training from 1966 until the onset of the Iranian revolution.

After the revolutionary takeover at least four separate Mujahidin factions could be identified, totaling approximately 3,000 members. All supported the Islamic government. The members of one group were part of the original organization, imbued with leftist ideology and enthusiastic about the concept of people's democracy as espoused by Arab radicals. Another element consists of right wing Islamic militants who are fanatically fundamentalist in their religious and social ideology and fiercely loyal to Khomeini himself. The third faction is composed of several different groups, including displaced peasants living in the large cities, lower-class urban workers, and traditional small businessmen. Their ideological loyalties are somewhat varied but they are emotionally committed to Khomeini. The final group calls itself "The Students Following the Imam's Line." They are university students or ex-students who subscribe to various Mujahidin (and possibly even Fedayeen) doctrines. After setting up their organization in the spring of 1979, they would take over the U.S. embassy on November 4, 1979, aided by other Mujahidin units and a contingent of Fedayeen.[8] Originally, much of the funding for all these fundamentalist groups came from religious sources funneled through Khomeini's headquarters in Iraq. After the revolution, each faction became self-supporting through voluntary contributions, "liberation" of the assets of former supporters of the monarchy, and extortions from businessmen and ordinary citizens seeking favor, be they licenses to operate stores or visas to leave the country.

There were three divisions with about 1,000 members within the Fedayeen movement at the time of the revolutionary takeover; a pro-Tudeh group, somewhat weaker than the others, which deemphasizes its Communist ties and argues that the Soviets were less supportive of the Shah than the Chinese; the Jazani group, named after a slain guerrilla, which has concentrated on mobilizing students and professionals; and the Ahmadzadeh-Pouyan, named after two other insurgents killed fighting the Shah's security forces. All three wings of the Fedayeen are based on student recruitment and, unlike the Mujahidin, do not cater to either the working class or the poor. All are anti-Khomeini but pro-revolution.

Both the Mujahidin and the Fedayeen deliberately restricted their contacts with the nonviolent political movements such as the Liberation Movement and the National Front. This was done to maintain the secrecy of their membership. Pre-revolutionary takeover policy was coordinated by designated representatives of the more moderate opposition factions who occasionally met with them and frequently communicated with Mujahidin and Fedayeen contact men by phone.

In the wake of the complete breakdown of the Iranian military and the disintegration of the police and security forces in February 1979, the guerrillas became the only reliable, acceptable armed force controlled by the revolutionary movement. Mujahidin and Fedayeen cooperation would continue until the first takeover of the U.S. embassy on February 14, 1979. However, that event signaled the beginning of a mini-civil war between Mujahidin and Fedayeen forces that would last for four nights. The Mujahidin won most of those skirmishes, severly crippling the Fedayeen for several months. The Fedayeen began to rebuild its organization immediately and by the time the hostages were taken in November 1979 it was again strong enough to threaten the Mujahidin. Although the situation between the two groups has improved, it never has been good; there is an uneasy truce. Some of the Mujahidin reorganized themselves into the Revolutionary Guards in April 1979. The Revolutionary Guards (also known as the Pasdaran) would grow to include 7,000 men within two months after they were established. They are the only military force (albeit semi-trained) fully loyal to Khomeini and the radical religious leadership.

THE TUDEH PARTY

The Tudeh (Masses) Party is the successor to Iran's original Communist Party, which was founded in the 1920s and destroyed by Reza Shah in the early 1930s. The party was recreated during the Anglo-Soviet occupation of Iran from 1941 to 1945 and attained a considerable following in labor union organizations in the mid and late 1940s. It opposed Mossadeq's government until late in 1952, when it decided to try and benefit from the general unrest. The de facto alliance between the Tudeh Party and the Mossadeq movement was a significant reason why many Iranians decided to support the coup that brought the Shah back to power in 1953. Though the party did not actively support Mossadeq in his crisis, and though its underground remnants aligned themselves with the National Front in the early 1960s, the older National Front leaders such as Bazargan and Bakhtiar retained a healthy suspicion of Tudeh Party motives and refused to work with it during the spiraling unrest in 1978 and 1979.

After the Shah banned nearly all political activity from 1963 until late in 1978, the Tudeh Party operated in exile in East Germany. Within Iran, activity resurfaced in 1977, when a few Tudeh Party "study groups" were formed at several of Tehran's universities. These were transformed into small action units when the political situation heated up in 1978. Ideologically, the party members had begun to cast a wider net. By 1976 they were calling for an alliance with bourgeois elements—peasants, shopkeepers, and even the clergy. Dr. Noureddin Kianouri, who replaced longtime leader Iraj Iskandari in January 1979, immediately called for Tudeh Party support of the religious opposition. He made a point of emphasizing that Ayatollah Khomeini's program was acceptable to his organization as a first step toward revolution. The party supported the Islamic government until August 1979, when debate over Iran's new constitution began in earnest. Since that time the Tudeh Party has taken a more evenhanded position between Khomeini and the Fedayeen. However, the Fedayeen distrust the motives of the Tudeh Party, considering it to be subservient to Moscow.

From a Marxist viewpoint, the Tudeh Party is a standard, pro-Soviet group and therefore something to be wary of, since the Marxism of the other leftist groups stems from radical Arab sources. For this reason the Tudeh Party played a distinctly minor role in revolutionary activity in 1977 and 1978, and was only marginally influential in the post-takeover summer and fall of 1979. As a repository of organizational skills, however, it has trained more people in basic propaganda, including Fedayeen recruits, than its numbers and ideological importance suggest. For example, several partisans released from prison during the revolution established The Democratic Union of Iranian People, a splinter group which organized several rallies in the spring of 1979. The party itself was a satellite rather than a leader during the revolutionary period, but it could easily play an important long-term role in Iranian politics eventually.

CENTRIST LIBERTARIANS

Starting in the 1960s Iran also had its share of liberal democrats who were not formally aligned to any of the previously mentioned organizations. The Toilers Party, the virtually one-man effort of Dr. Muzaffar Baqai, put forth a program based on human and civil rights and a social-democratic parliamentary system. The Radical Movement, established in 1963 by the lawyer Rahmatollah Moghadam-Maraghei, was anything but what its name implied. It represented middle-class professional men and advocated a European-style political system. Although one former Pan Iran leader, Daruish Forouhar, joined up with the reconstituted National Front in the spring of 1978, Majles deputy Mohsen Pezeshkpour and some others attempted to revive the Pan Iran Party, which had disappeared when it became part of the Resurgence Party. Six parliamentary deputies had rallied to its banner when Majles debates were opened up temporarily in August 1978, but the party played only a peripheral role in the revolutionary upheaval and its aftermath.

The most important of these small organizations was the Committee for the Defense of Human Rights and Freedom, often called simply, the "Committee for Human Rights." It included among its leaders representatives from the Liberation Movement (Mehdi Bazargan) and the National Front (Karim Sanjabi). There were also other prominent opposition figures active in professional groups, such as the Writers' Syndicate (Ali Ashgar Haj Seyed Javadi), the Lawyers' Guild (Hedayatollah Matin-Daftari) and the Radical Movement (Rahmatollah Moghadam-Maraghei). Formally organized in December 1977, the Committee for Human Rights coordinated the documentation of civil rights violations. It distributed a statement to that effect within Iran, copy to President Carter, in December 1977, just before the President's New Year's Eve and New Year's Day visit to Iran. By midsummer 1978 the committee had compiled over 200 case histories of human and civil rights violations during the Shah's regime. It also worked with organizations abroad, including the International Commission of Jurists and Amnesty International. During the first nine months of 1978, before political attitudes changed after the showdown on September 8 at Jaleh Square, it was the Committee for Human Rights which would inspire and encourage opposition factions to criticize the government.

The committee rallied the dissatisfied middle class to the side of the revolution. Many of its leaders became ministers in Prime Minister Bazargan's government, including its executive director, Nasser Minatchi (Information and National Guidance), Haj Seyed Javadi (Interior), and Bazargan himself. As the revolution unfolded, however, the ideas represented by this group lost out to the conceptions of the more fundamentalist religious leaders around the Ayatollah. Therefore, few of the committee's beliefs regarding civil and political rights are reflected in Iran's current Islamic constitution. Several of its founding members have fled Iran since July 1979, notably Matin-Daftari and Moghadam-Maraghei.

The Opposition Goes Public

Some general comments are in order about the impact of the opposition. Until 1977 these groups were not well organized and contributed little to the political situation, except as a potential opposition. Their rise to visibility (and eventual power) stemmed initially from the Shah's decision in early 1977 to liberalize his regime and to relax controls on the press, public assembly, and criticism of government policies by public officials. SAVAK was ordered to refrain from persecution and torture of dissidents as long as opposition activities were not aimed at mass uprising or violent insurrection. The effectiveness of the reconstituted National Front and the expanding religious groups and their secular ally, the Liberation Movement of Iran, date from mid-1977. Until that time opposition had been largely passive—sporadic and unorganized labor slowdowns, black market activities, and non-cooperation with authorities hunting down terrorists.

Beginning in June 1977 the opposition started to push its case more aggressively. As it did so, the clergy and the mosque network began to saturate the masses with the messages of the Ayatollah through cassettes and word-of-mouth communications. The secular organizations played more prominent public roles in the early challenges to the Shah, but they, too, came to depend upon the mosque network more and more.

An important feature of the opposition movement was its nearly universal unwillingness to consider compromise with the Shah after October or November 1977. Suspicion of the monarch and cynicism about his political tactics were so ingrained that not even those who rejected fundamentalist religious attitudes were willing to consider compromise. Before the revolutionary takeover the first goal of the secular as well as the religious opposition was the overthrow of the Shah. That aim, rather than the establishment of a different kind of government, remained so important that the diverse revolutionary coalition preserved itself intact, despite substantial internal differences, until after it came to full power in February 1979.

Finally, one foreign power had a noticeably positive psychological impact on the secular opposition, but considerably less on the radical clerics. The Carter administration, which took office in January 1977, made a point of supporting human rights abroad, especially the expansion of civil and political rights. Dissidents who had seen such rights shrink from 1971 to 1976 considered President Carter's election a hopeful sign. Curiously enough, this newly enunciated American posture also reinforced supporters of the Shah who had been arguing for more liberalization and more participation in governmental policy and decision making. Prime Minister Amouzegar and Resurgence Party Deputy Secretary-General Dariush Homayoun encouraged the monarch to invite various international organizations such as Amnesty International and the Red Cross to visit. When the International Commission of Jurists came, the Shah promised that the government would reform the military codes under which political prisoners were tried. This change was signed into law on November 7, 1977. There were other private discussions about further improving civil rights within the country between Iranian officials and representatives of some Western embassies, including the U.S. mission. However, fundamentalist religious leaders regarded these attempts at change as essentially a Western sham. Because they did not believe the United States and other countries were serious about human rights, they merely considered the issue to be one they could use against the Shah by pointing out the monarch's failures, thereby driving a wedge between his government and its Western allies.

Amnesty International and the International Commission of Jurists as well as Western leaders welcomed the modest improvements in civil rights and the greater freedom of expression. But their concern for increased political leeway encouraged the dissidents to press for even more and reinforced the feelings of those in the establishment seeking more relaxation of authoritarian control. The opposition continued to exploit its gains; the government's moves became uncertain and sporadic. Though more open meetings were allowed, the growing vocal castigation of the Shah's rule caused the monarch to reconsider. The interplay between criticism from abroad and establishment and opposition attitudes in Iran underlined the extraordinary degree to which Iranians from the Shah down were concerned about the opinions of certain foreign nations almost to the point of obsession. Much of this attitude can be traced to the history of relations between the United States and Iran since World War II.

Chapter Four

★

America in Iran, 1900–1977

Until World War II, U.S. involvement in Iran had been distinctly secondary to the interests of other foreign powers, particularly those of Britain and Russia. However, the United States did provide one of the heroes in the long struggle to limit the power of the Qajar shahs. In 1906 Howard Baskerville, a 26-year-old Princeton graduate, was killed in Tabriz while on a night patrol for the constitutionalist forces. He is buried near the American consulate there. By the time the new constitution was in place, other Americans in Iran had started to westernize higher education in that country. Dr. Samuel Jordan transformed his high school for boys into Alborz College and ran it from 1899 until his retirement in 1940. Until the revolutionaries took over in 1979 and immediately changed anything that smacked of foreign influence, Jordan Avenue was the name of one of Tehran's major traffic arteries. His successors were leaders in the education of women, too, developing Damavand College in Tehran into a well-regarded institution for females.

After the Anglo-Soviet invasion in August 1941, Iranians looked to America as a helpful neutral to whom the country could turn to help fend off incursions on its independence. From 1942, when the U.S. mission to the gendarmerie arrived, until the fall of the Shah in 1979, America became progressively more involved both economically and politically. President Truman's blunt rejection of the Soviet occupation of Azarbaijan after World War II was instrumental in forcing out Russian troops. The United States also became an important market for Iranian oil. In fact, the refusal of President Eisenhower to purchase its oil for 15 months, and thereby break the British economic squeeze, was probably more decisive than any C.I.A. involvement in forcing the downfall of Prime Minister Mossadeq. Starting in the early 1960s the

59

relationship between Iran and the United States intensified, until the ties were deeper and broader than that of any other nation. First the U.S. replaced Britain as Iran's protector against the Soviet Union, and then America encouraged Iran to be its principal regional ally.

Commitments to the country's economic and military development impelled the United States to protect the interests of the Shah, aggravating the negative feelings of an ever-increasing number of Persians. Neither the government in Washington nor other interested Americans, such as businessmen with Iranian connections, adequately recognized the changes wrought by this Westernization. In the period leading up to the revolution American long-term interests were sacrificed for short-term gains. Historically unused to this type of involvement abroad, the U.S. failed to recognize the danger signals; others were noticed but went unheeded.

Early Ties: The United States as the Friendly Balancer

The first Americans to live in Persia were missionaries who arrived early in the nineteenth century. By the 1850s tentative official efforts were made to establish an embassy, but it was not until 1883 that the U.S. diplomatic mission opened its doors. Russian and British interest in Persia perked up after the discovery of oil at Masjed-e-Suleiman one year before the Anglo-Russian Treaty of 1907. This document divided the country into spheres of influence, in order to eliminate the constant conflict between Russian desires to acquire a warm water port and Britain's need to protect her lifeline to India. The U.S. started becoming more involved because the government of Nader Shah considered the United States a source of assistance untainted by great power politics. Morgan Shuster arrived in 1911, with a mandate to reorganize the treasury. Following him was Arthur Millspaugh, director of finance from 1922 to 1927. At the request of the Shah, Millspaugh returned during World War II to supervise the country's fiscal operation. Both are remembered fondly for their contribution to Iran's financial and political independence, educating officials to deal with the modern world.[1]

Iran was declared eligible for American lend-lease March 10, 1942. About 30,000 U.S. troops arrived to protect and manage the lend-lease supply line from the Persian Gulf to the Soviet Union. They were not considered invaders, but a hopeful sign—perhaps guarantee—that British and Russian forces would not make their occupation permanent. At the Tehran Conference attended by Churchill, Roosevelt, and Stalin on December 1, 1943, the Shah pressed the Allied war leaders to sign the Declaration of Tehran. It required the U.S. to adhere to the Anglo-Soviet Treaty of Alliance, concluded nearly two years earlier, that called for British and Soviet troop withdrawals within six months after hostilities ceased.

At the behest of the young and inexperienced Shah and his advisors, American commitments developed into long-term assistance even as World War II continued. In August 1942, Secretary of State Cordell Hull announced that aiding the military "would be helpful in strengthening our position in Iran at the present time and in building a firm foundation for future relations."[2] GENMISH, an advisory mission to the gendarmerie, began in October 1942 under Colonel Norman Schwarzkopf; it was not withdrawn until March 1976 and then only because a new U.S. law prohibited aid to police forces of other countries, thus requiring the program be abandoned. ARMISH, a similar organization to assist the army, was established in 1943 and stopped functioning only when its headquarters was overrun on February 11, 1979, during the revolutionary takeover. The political elite agreed with the Shah that the buildup was essential so that the country would need neither Soviet nor British assistance to maintain order after the war.

Meanwhile, financial advisor Millspaugh outlined a 20-year aid program in response to President Roosevelt's suggestion that Iran might be a test case for a policy of stabilizing and developing stagnating regions. Though Millspaugh and the 50 Americans under him were forced to leave in 1946, after steadfastly disagreeing with the monarch over the prospective size of the army (the Shah wanted 108,000 men; Millspaugh argued for 30,000), the commitment to Iran's development continued. While the intent of the assistance was political, the means was economic.

Internal problems in Iran pushed the U.S. even closer to that country when the war ended. The catalyst was the Soviet threat to Iran's independence, and America's recognition of the fact that it had both a political and an economic stake in seeing that Iran was not sucked into the Soviet orbit. Communist forces calling themselves the Azarbaijan Democratic Party staged a revolt in 1945 and declared the independence of Azarbaijan, the province which borders the Soviet Union for over 200 miles. The U.S.S.R. supported this claim as well as that of the neighboring Republic of Mahabad, established at the same time by Iranian Kurds. British troops had left by March 2, 1946. The Soviet Union refused to withdraw and insisted Iran recognize the new pro-Soviet republics, especially Azarbaijan. Mahabad existed for only a few months in 1946 until Russian forces pulled out, allowing Iranian troops to move in and crush the revolutionaries. After several months of maneuvering, on May 7, 1946, the Russians also were forced to withdraw from Azarbaijan because the West, and particularly the U.S., pressured the Soviets through extended confrontation in the United Nations. Iranians have consistently praised the United States for this action. When added to the postwar economic assistance, it meant Persians had become highly pro-American.[3]

Although the United States dealt mostly with the Shah when planning and carrying out the economic and military assistance, Iran's monarch was not the political force in the late 1940s that he was to become two decades later. Men such as Prime Minister Ali Sohayli and parliamentary leader Qavan-as-Sultaneh wielded much more influence than their counterparts 10 and 20 years later. U.S. assistance was never equated with direct personal support of the Shah, as involvement in 1953 and especially from 1975 to 1979 would be.

Iran received $25.8 million in postwar relief money from 1946 to 1948, and an additional $16.5 million economic and $16.6 million military assistance from 1949 to 1952. The aid continued during Mossadeq's prime ministership, while the U.S. balanced between Britain and Iran over the delicate, emotionally charged issue of what to do about the Anglo-Iranian Oil Company. The crisis arose when Mossadeq nationalized the company in 1951 without paying compensation. The British managers and engineers shut down production and departed, leaving the country without any oil income. Though oil money did not play as important a role in the country's economic life as it does now, the abrupt halt severely unbalanced the economy. U.S. aid increased in 1952–1953, but not enough to bail out Mossadeq's sinking economic ship. Although the Iranians were able to get limited production going by the fall of 1952, many countries refused to buy. President Eisenhower made it clear that the United States would not purchase Iranian oil until Mossadeq had settled with the British. The crisis was resolved only after Mossadeq was ousted. In August 1954, a 25-year pact gave the British 40 percent of the shares in the newly formed consortium, Iranian Oil Participants, Ltd., and guaranteed $70 million compensation.

American Influence Expands

U.S. interest in keeping excessive Soviet influence out of Iran had been reflected in economic and military assistance rather than in a formal political alliance. Economic aid, particularly the presence of Point Four advisors after 1950 (the forerunner of USAID), had a very positive impact.[4] In 1953 however, internal politics deteriorated. Economic difficulties and Mossadeq's increasingly authoritarian style caused several coalition partners to break with him. By July Mossadeq was accepting more Tudeh Party support, and began to attack the monarchy publicly. When the Shah dismissed the prime minister on August 16 and replaced him with General Fazlollah Zahedi, Mossadeq refused to give up his post, announcing he would oust the monarch. Tudeh mobs took to the streets. Mossadeq had tolerated Tudeh Party activity in hopes of frightening Britain and the United States, but he had to order the demonstrations terminated. On August 19, during the lull, General Zahedi (the father of Ardeshir Zahedi, Iran's ambassador to the U.S. at the time of the revolution in 1979) regrouped loyal army units. Pro-Shah mobs from south Tehran, organized by loyal politicians with C.I.A. help, surged into the streets calling for support of the monarch. Mossadeq fled when the army seized his residence but turned himself in within a week. Loyalist control was assured. On August 22 the Shah returned to Iran, after fleeing with his wife to Rome for three weeks. After a brief trial, Mossadeq was banished to his estate about 50 miles southeast of Tehran, where he died quietly in 1966.

The role of the U.S. government in the restoration of the Shah to the Peacock Throne has been argued for years. Former C.I.A. official Kermit Roosevelt has stated he spent less than $60,000 organizing the loyalists to support the Shah, describing what the C.I.A. did as "a modest effort." Such an assessment jibes with what another American intelligence officer serving in Iran at the time refers to as "agency puffery about its success in 1953." On the other hand, critics of the C.I.A. claim Roosevelt's role was crucial, that he masterminded the putsch that overthrew Prime Minister Mossadeq.[5]

Two Iranians intimately involved in political security affairs at the time say there was minimal U.S. involvement. Another senior official believes, "Your C.I.A. played a role, yes, but far less than either our people or yours thought. If anything, the fact that the Americans were interested in establishing stable government gave psychological support to those key Iranians who were ready to act anyway." What Kermit Roosevelt did was to encourage forces already restive and prepared to participate. The opposition, especially the present revolutionary government, insists that Mossadeq would not have been overthrown if the C.I.A. had not "thwarted progressive government." However, with Tudeh mobs in the streets, the clergy, the landowners, and the army feared a Communist takeover. It was for that same reason that the Americans and the British had decided in June to abandon efforts to work out a settlement with Mossadeq. From 1950 to 1952 the United States had been sympathetic to the goals of Iranian liberals, but as the Mossadeq confrontation continued, the disintegration of his political support, the increasing economic hardships, and especially the growing communist threat all had tipped the scale toward an American interest in changing the direction in which the country was heading.

The events of 1953 have assumed a political importance well beyond their intrinsic significance. For his own purposes the Shah quietly circulated word of the support he had received from the Americans, strengthening their position within the country. To advertise a successful foreign alliance was completely in line with centuries of Persian political practice and no fuss was made about it at the time. Iranian liberals, including the same National Front that would criticize the U.S. in the 1970s, were quite happy to have had American support against the possibility of a Tudeh Party takeover. In fact, similar attitudes surfaced on a much lesser scale in April 1980, when Defense Minister Mustafa Chamran, concerned about the recent Soviet invasion of neighboring Afghanistan, announced that Iran expected U.S. help against any Soviet move into Persia.

The C.I.A. took discreet credit for its success in 1953, which it has lumped with the 1954 overthrow of the Arbenz regime in Guatemala as an example of useful covert action. The agency benefited because it could cite its own effectiveness, but these episodes also gave Washington policy makers an exaggerated sense of what could be accomplished through surreptitious means. Kermit Roosevelt has stressed that the American effort in Iran in 1953 succeeded because it was in line with the wishes of the vast majority of the people, not because of any alleged American cleverness. From a long-term perspective, stories about the event probably had almost as great a political impact as the incident itself. Though there would never be another such action, all Iranians believed there might be. This attitude significantly shaped Persian thinking during the time when revolutionary activity was most intensive, from September 1978 to the revolutionary takeover in February 1979, and has continued to influence the country's political behavior.

After Mossadeq, America once again concentrated on assisting Iran by economic means:

American Economic Assistance to Iran, 1953–1966
(millions of dollars)

1953–1957	1958	1959	1960	1961	1962	1963	1964	1965	1966
36.8	51.9	46.9	38.2	107.2	67.3	43.9	25.9	45.4	21.2

USAID, *Foreign Assistance and Assistance from International Organizations*, year series.

The aid supplied was significant, a major contribution to development. Moreover, the presence from 1950 to 1966 of 300 to 500 USAID personnel insured recognition of the American effort. It also gave access to grass roots information about conditions in the country, since over half the Americans were stationed outside Tehran. Similar details were much more difficult to obtain after Iranian USAID was terminated in 1966.

As the economic takeoff began, American trade also increased. In 1954, five U.S. corporations joined other oil companies to form the National Iranian Oil Company consortium. Though Iran would receive 50 percent of the profits, Standard Oil of New Jersey, Standard Oil of California, Texaco, Socony-Mobil, and Gulf Oil acquired a 40 percent share of the oil production in return for technical assistance operating the refinery at Abadan and further development of the oil fields. Suddenly the U.S. could substantially influence Iranian oil policy.

The shift toward greater political involvement continued, but in a more traditional state-to-state fashion. Since the Shah approved of Western initiatives in the Middle East, Iran joined the Baghdad Pact, a British-sponsored security alliance against the threat of communism, in November 1955. Secretary of State John Foster Dulles, remembering the instability of the Mossadeq era, had to be talked into the idea. The U.S. became much more positive toward a potential regional role for Iran after the Suez crisis in 1956, and increased its economic and military aid to countries in the region, including Iran. Iraq withdrew from the Baghdad Pact in March 1959, after its own revolution the year before, and began receiving military equipment from the Soviets immediately. Concerned about the aftershocks of the Iraqi revolution, Washington signed a mutual cooperation agreement with Iran which committed the United States to come to its aid if the country were attacked. American intentions were reinforced by President Eisenhower's visit to Tehran in December 1959.

About this time, however, Iran's internal problems were proliferating, difficulties similar to those that would crop up a decade later. Inflation and mismanagement were out of control. Economic expansion encouraged by U.S. aid had greatly increased the opportunities for corruption, causing soaring land values, high rents, and food shortages. The crippled rapid development led to the need to redress the imbalances and, like other developing countries, Iran sought more money from abroad—rather than retrenchment at home—as the way out. The government did not adopt an economic stabilization policy until 1960, and then only after the World Bank and the United States government threatened to withhold further financing.[6]

Remedies enacted to cope with the economic problems emboldened disenfranchised politicians. Operating under the auspices of a loose National Front organization, dissidents, unsatisfied with the two-party system created by the Shah two years earlier, charged corruption in the parliamentary elections held in July and August 1960. Protest became so acute that the Shah annulled the results and in December called for a reballoting. From January to March 1961 demonstrations protesting the new elections and the opening of the Majles would evolve into riots which would cost Prime Minister Jaffar Sharif-Emami his job. (This is the same Sharif-Emami who would become prime minister again for ten weeks, from August to November 1978, when the revolutionary turmoil was increasing daily.)

At this same time the Kennedy administration began pressing the Shah to institute domestic reforms. Ali Amini, the new prime minister, had been ambassador to the United States from 1956 to 1958 and had known then Senator John F. Kennedy well. Amini kept up his contact with the senator and other liberal Democrats who would serve in President Kennedy's administration two years later. There are those who feel the U.S. forced the monarch to appoint Amini prime minister. Until his overthrow, the monarch never hid the fact that during this period he regarded relations between Iran and the United States to be at their nadir. Certainly Amini's name was one of several possibilities the Shah mentioned to the U.S. ambassador, Julius Holmes, during this time of trouble, and certainly the Shah was not unaware of Amini's relationship with the American President. But to conclude that Washington insisted he be prime minister is unwarranted. In 1977 Amini would be criticized by the dissidents for still being "a tool of the Americans." His reputation as a cohort of the United States ruled him out of a position of prominence as the political situation kept changing in 1977 and 1978, but did not keep him from playing a backstage role in the last-ditch search for a political compromise in November and December 1978.[7] He left the country before the revolutionary government came to power, and now lives in Paris.

U.S. policy in the Kennedy era was based on the premise that those rulers who undertook to reform their societies would be the most durable. Thus the United States pressed the Shah to accede to domestic demands for greater social change, on the assumption that a progressive outlook would stabilize the society more than continued authoritarian control. Actually, the Kennedy administration and the Shah disagreed about many things. They included how large the army should be (the U.S. wanted it cut one-third), economic and social reform (the U.S. wanted a more liberal political system), and the elimination of bribery and graft (the Shah resisted enforcing an anti-corruption campaign because he didn't want to probe too deeply into the financial holdings of his relatives and other affluent supporters). Also, the Shah sought more military hardware to bring Iran up to par with Iraq, already benefiting from Soviet largesse, but the United States wanted to concentrate on economic development. The military aspects of the disagreements were resolved amicably when the Shah traded a one-third cut in army strength (from 270,000 to 180,000) in exchange for further assurances of U.S. protection against any outside threats for five years. While Washington continued to press for improvement in the other areas, they never would become major issues, and therefore their impact would just dwindle away, particularly after Kennedy's death.

After this tug-of-war with the United States, the Shah sought to improve relations with the Soviets. He initiated economic talks, and pledged that no foreign (i.e., American) missiles would be permitted on Iranian soil. The unrest within his country the previous two years had convinced the Shah that he needed to build a stronger political base in order to better resist pressure from his American allies. These thoughts, plus advice from Iranian liberals such as Abol Hassan Ebtehaj, Hassan Arsenjani, and Ali Mansur, are what precipitated the modernizing program, the Shah–People Revolution. The implementation of these reforms would provoke the most severe challenge to the regime since 1953. It encouraged the alliance between the secular and religious dissidents, culminating in riots from June 4 to 6, 1963, in Tehran, Qom, and Isfahan. Nevertheless, the Shah–People Revolution improved the official U.S. attitude toward Iran. With land reform and social alterations catching hold, the United States considered the Shah a reformist monarch leading his country away from feudalism. As a reward, during the Shah's visit to Washington in June 1964, President Johnson increased military credits, allowing Iran to arm itself against potential threats, particularly those posed by Iraq.

If involvement in the Shah's return to power in 1953 marked the first active American engagement in Iranian internal affairs, 1964 signifies another watershed. The United States began to concern itself less with Iran's domestic politics and more with its strength as an ally. In 1961 and 1962 the Kennedy administration had pressed the Shah to liberalize his rule. The Shah-People Revolution was the monarch's response, a way to get the country moving as well as to placate foreign critics who insisted social change was necessary. By 1964 Washington was convinced that the Shah's modernizing reforms were improving the standard of living for his countrymen. The U.S. was basically unconcerned about the internal turmoil the changes had induced. As a result, American interest shifted away from the political ramifications of the Shah's programs toward Iran's potential as a strong ally of the United States in the Persian Gulf area.

Losing Leverage

Beginning in 1965 world affairs intervened to change important aspects of the traditional American-Iranian relationship. The U.S. was increasingly caught up in Vietnam. It had fewer resources to commit worldwide and more need for support from its allies. As the U.S. balance of payments position worsened, Iran's increasing oil revenues based on rising production meant the Shah had money to pay for military hardware. Output rose from 1.6 million barrels per day in 1965 to 2.8 million in 1967 and 3.5 million in 1970. Except for a low period in 1971 (probably primarily due to the irregular scheduling of purchases around the end of the fiscal year), the percentage of military sales for cash and credit (as opposed to equipment and training given as aid) steadily increased until 1979.

In 1972 President Nixon had adopted a policy of selling the Shah whatever he wanted, a decision which opened the door to unbridled military expenditure. The U.S. actually had begun to push arms sales much earlier, in 1966 and 1967, when President Johnson pressed corporations like McDonnell Douglas and Boeing to sell more. The companies worked in tandem with the Pentagon, which sought to improve the U.S. balance of payments through such purchases. Reduced leverage on military spending paralleled a similar decline in the influence of the training Americans provided for the gendarmerie and SAVAK. Thus the kind of pressure President Kennedy had used in 1961 and 1962 to prevent a buildup of the military establishment and to encourage political change was greatly reduced. A subtle change had taken place in the historical American-Iranian military supply relationship—the U.S. began to need Iran more than Iran needed the United States.

U.S. Military Aid and Sales to Iran
(deliveries in millions of dollars)

Year	Grant	Cash/Credit Sales	Total
1965	49.1	–0–	49.1
1966	41.0	3.6	44.6
1967	10.6	38.8	49.4
1968	5.2	52.1	57.3
1969	3.1	94.8	97.9
1970	.5	127.7	128.2
1971	.3	79.3	79.6
1972	.2	214.8	215.0
1973	.2	245.2	245.4
1974	.2	648.6	648.8
1975	.1	1,006.1	1,006.2
1976	.05	1,924.9	1,924.9
1977	negligible	2,424.7	2,424.7
1978	negligible	1,907.3	1,907.3
1979	–0–	924.5	924.5

U.S. Department of Defense, *Foreign Military Sales and Military Assistance Facts,* year series.

First the troubles in Southeast Asia and then initial efforts to improve cooperation with the Soviet Union (detente) diverted American attention and resources from the developing world. So the Shah continued to take a more amiable attitude toward the Soviet Union. In 1965 Russia agreed to build a 1.2 million ton annual capacity steel mill in Isfahan in exchange for natural gas to be piped from the Khuzistan oil fields (where the gas was produced along with crude oil) directly to the Soviet Caucasus. That same year Iran signed its first major military agreement with the Soviet Union, for trucks, armored personnel carriers, and antiaircraft guns. This also was paid for by shipments of natural gas.

The steadily increasing oil revenues meant that the Johnson administration removed Iran from its list of less developed countries in 1967. Now Iran could receive U.S. Export-Import Bank financing for the additional arms it wished to acquire. Six years before the real oil boom began, the country's cash and credit position was excellent, and the Shah made use of it. He approached the United States to buy F-4's, the most advanced jets in the American arsenal, and received them with the understanding that he would not turn elsewhere for weapons, particularly the Soviet Union. The initial order was for one squadron of 16 planes. The number doubled in 1968. The executive branch justified these sales to Congress by saying they helped Iran remain stable and provided a moderating American influence over the Shah's military policy.[8]

The changing U.S. position in the world had an important bureau-cratic impact, imposing an unstated constraint on policy. Beginning in 1967 and continuing through the mid-1970s, the American official pres-ence abroad was deliberately reduced through a series of administrative exercises with unusual names—BALPA, OPRED, OPRED II. The cumulative effect was a 20 percent decrease in personnel operating under the auspices of American embassies. In Iran this was amplified by the withdrawal of the USAID mission in 1967 and the phasing out of the Peace Corps and the gendarmerie mission, both deactivated in 1976. The U.S. military presence, ARMISH-MAAG (the combined Army Mission-Military Advisory Assistance Group), decreased as well:

U.S. Personnel Assigned to ARMISH-MAAG

Year	Military	Civilian	Total
1967	446	21	467
1968	417	30	447
1969	402	26	428
1970	319	27	346
1971	250	22	272
1972	250	22	272
1973	192	16	208
1974	192	16	208
1975	191	18	209
1976	191	18	209
1977	191	18	209

U.S. *Military Sales to Iran*, staff report of the Subcommittee on Foreign Assistance of the Committee on Foreign Rela-tions, U.S. Senate, year series.

Again, the broad pool of U.S. officials which for years had been pro-viding helpful information and especially informal insights had been se-verely cut back.

More importantly, the embassy's reporting capacity had also been sharply reduced. On April 30, 1963, 21 political officers were assigned to the mission. By May 1973 this had dropped to six, where it remained until the revolution.[9] The abolished slots belonged to junior diplomats specifically designated as contact officers. Desk duties took up an in-creasing percentage of time for those remaining. Regardless of the quality of the back-to-Washington reporting, there was greatly reduced capacity to get the kind of in-depth information required for accurate policy analysis. The problem is a general one with broad implications, but Iran is an outstanding example of false economy through sharp per-sonnel reductions overseas. It also points out how difficult it is for the foreign affairs bureaucracy to staff field posts in accordance with their rapidly changing importance. It took several years to strip down the political staff, yet Iran's move toward revolution occurred so quickly that there was little time to reverse the trend. In June 1978 all a foreign service inspection team reviewing embassy personnel assignments suggested was that there be an additional political-military affairs officer.

The embassy economic affairs section fared little better. In 1963 there were nine economic officers. In 1973 there were eight, but three of these were completely tied up in commercial work, aiding American businessmen representing firms eager to cash in on the rapidly expanding Iranian market. The work of the embassy commercial office had expanded five times within four years. In fact, in the post-1973 boom, all the economic officers were also involved in commercial work, drawn into the maelstrom created by the geometrically expanding U.S. business presence and the rapidly increasing U.S. military sales. The problem was compounded by the fact that two of the economic officers had specialized knowledge, and spent most of their time covering either oil or science affairs.

The diminished reporting presence contributed to decisions to spend less time on dissident contacts, particularly since the opposition was much less active from 1965 to 1977. Given fewer resources, the heads of the embassy political and economic sections targeted what they considered to be more important—the government's development program. Moreover, the possibility for broad gauge analyses was greatly reduced. There simply was no time. As the opposition began to revive in 1977, embassy officers resumed reporting on it, but trade-offs had to be made. The makeup of Iranian society was becoming more and more complex, but no corresponding increase in manpower arrived until November 1978. American Embassy Tehran had been pared to the bone by the successive personnel reductions. It was restaffed only briefly and temporarily when the final phase of the revolution was already underway, much too late to have a useful impact on events

The U.S. Dilemma: Political Intimacy but Limited Influence

Iran's growing influence in its relationship with the United States in particular and the world in general corresponded to a period of American retrenchment. The Nixon administration's Guam Doctrine, enunciated in June 1969, seemed made to order for further American-Iranian intimacy. In essence, it said that the U.S. would no longer be a world policeman. It would participate in the defense and development of allies and friends, but would not do it all; American troops would be used abroad only in special cases. The United States would rely on other nations to defend Western interests by encouraging them to defend themselves. Iran seemed made to order to be a regional partner. Unlike other heads of state, the Shah had established a moderate foreign policy, including evenhandedness toward Israel during the 1967 Arab-Israeli conflict. Iran's economic upsurge and strong central leadership appeared to indicate internal stability in a region clearly headed for rough times since the British planned to withdraw from the Persian Gulf in 1971. Also, Iran had supported the United States in the United Nations and remained sympathetic toward American policy in Vietnam.

Besides, the Shah himself was interested in a greater regional role, particularly since he already had concluded that his country would have to begin fending for itself more than it had in the past. He figured that if he were to become more powerful then he could keep Soviet-American rivalry out of the Persian Gulf when the British left. For that reason, he favored ending the homeporting in Bahrain of the tiny U.S. Middle East Force, consisting of two ships. The Shah believed that if no foreign vessels were in the Persian Gulf permanently, he could prevent a Soviet naval deployment to the Gulf after the British left. As it happened, American ships would remain in Bahrain through 1977. Moreover, though not stationed there, even today U.S. navy craft tie up in Bahrain for extended periods. Soviet ships traverse the Gulf, but never have homeported there.

A policy review in 1969 by the National Security Council on the effect of the British departure from the Persian Gulf rejected keeping a direct American presence in the Gulf other than the two ships in Bahrain, opting instead for regional cooperation based on the "twin pillars" of Iran and Saudi Arabia. Additional arms sales to "forward defense countries" were endorsed, since fulfilling the Guam Doctrine required sending increased military hardware to selected countries. Deliveries to Iran multiplied.[10]

A corresponding growth in U.S. commercial activity began in 1971 and accelerated sharply after 1973. American trading and investment were enhanced by military sales as well as by other contracts, such as American Bell International's $10 billion project to revitalize Iran's telephone system. By 1977 the U.S. share of the nonmilitary import market was 15.9 percent, or $2.2 billion. If military goods and services are included, total U.S. receipts from Iran were approximately $6.4 billion.[11]

U.S. Military Sales to Iran
(in millions of dollars)

Year	Orders	Deliveries
1969	235.8	94.8
1970	134.9	127.7
1971	363.9	78.6
1972	472.6	214.8
1973	2,171.3	248.4
1974	4,325.3	648.6
1975	2,447.1	1,006.1
1976	1,794.4	1,927.9
1977	5,713.8	2,433.0
1978	2,586.9	1,792.9

U.S. Department of Defense Security Assistance Agency, *Military Assistance Program Data*, fiscal year series.

Official acknowledgment of the cozy relationship developing between the United States and Iran started with President Nixon's state visit to Tehran in May 1972. The timing of his arrival was important. The British had withdrawn from the Persian Gulf six months earlier. This had been swiftly followed by the Iranian military occupation of three tiny, uninhabited islands in the Gulf, Abu Musa and the Greater and Lesser Tumbs, ostensibly for security reasons. Iran was emerging as a regional power to be reckoned with, and the Shah wanted sophisticated weaponry. While in Tehran, Nixon told him he would be able to purchase either F-14 or F-15 fighter-bombers, planes then coming into production. The President also said future decisions on conventional weapon acquisitions would be up to the Iranian government, without serious questioning from the United States. This instruction was confirmed by a memorandum from the National Security Council to the departments and agencies involved. Secretary of Defense James Schlesinger raised the issues of how the U.S. could protect the security of highly sensitive American equipment sold to other nations and whether providing technical support would require large numbers of American military physically present, training Iranians to use and repair their new gear. His questions were ignored.

No one, least of all the Nixon administration, expected a fourfold increase in oil prices the following year. Who could foresee what this phenomenal addition to the public treasury would do to Iranian arms requests? For whatever reason, though probably because of confusion in government generated by the Watergate scandal, there was no further study of the impact of U.S. arms policy with respect to Iran until early 1975. By that time Iranian military purchases were in full swing and the number of Americans in Iran was steadily growing.

Number of Americans in Iran, as of June 30

Year	U.S. Employees	U.S. Dependents	Other Americans	Total
1972	299	1,128	7,660	9,087
1973	434	1,502	8,062	9,998
1974	227	1,376	10,600	12,203
1975	295	1,867	16,972	19,134
1976	334	1,818	20,382	22,534
1977	545	1,539	40,061	42,145
1978	566	1,347	52,028	53,941
1978, Dec.	*150	*81	27,210	27,441

*Special flights to evacuate American dependents and non-essential government personnel from revolution-torn Iran began December 8.

U.S. Department of State, *Americans Abroad*, year series.

The number of government employees nearly doubled from 1972 to 1978. Over half of these were U.S. military personnel under contract to Iran as members of Technical Assistance Field Teams (TAFTs) to train its armed forces. Though linked to the official community through ARMISH-MAAG, they were under the operational control of the Iranian military. Most TAFTs were stationed at bases or field units outside Tehran. This isolation from civilian communities meant that these Americans, unlike the USAID officers a decade earlier, did not report to the embassy, even on an informal basis, news about any growing discontent they might have been aware of in their respective areas.

More significant was the sharp rise in private citizens, nearly a 600 percent increase from 1972 to 1978. Anti-American sentiments burgeoned between 1975 and 1978, as more families arrived every day. Accelerating the number of complex development programs using non-indigenous technical personnel aggravated Iranian xenophobia. Despite the presence of many foreigners from other nations working on similar projects, people on the street began to consider all Westerners U.S. citizens. By 1978 just over half the number of foreigners living in Iran were Americans, and 85 percent of them were in Tehran.

Iranians linked the arrival of the Americans to the new policies of the Shah, and rumblings about unnecessary military spending grew louder. In March 1976 an informal survey of 50 government officials and involved private citizens revealed serious reservations about the need for the additional hardware and the adequacy of the training to run the equipment.[12] These politically aware Iranians were convinced that the Shah's decision to speed up development actually increased the country's economic dependence on other nations because of the expanding requirement for foreign technical assistance.

Beginning in 1973 the Center for Management Studies, an Iranian clone of the Harvard Business School, identified an additional problem endemic to all industrializing countries—the lack of middle and senior level managers. State corporations in the Industrial Reconstruction and Development Organization (which controlled 80 percent of the government firms) were short 12 percent of their middle and upper level staff. By 1977 this figure had grown to 38 percent, despite intensive executive recruiting in both Iran and abroad. The shortage of skilled talent at higher levels was a boon to the emerging middle class. From 1973 to 1978 it turned its attention from politics to making money.

The pent-up anger of the unskilled and the unemployed intensified, particularly during the economic recession in 1977. Though initially the expanding economy had drained off some of the resentment, these families had benefited little, as waves of foreigners flaunting their prosperity invaded Tehran and other cities. Starting in 1976 the popularity of the Americans dropped drastically, reinforcing the discomfort of some of the elite, who saw the development process going awry but could do nothing about it. The establishment blamed the U.S. for encouraging the Shah's imperial pipe dreams. "In the old days, you had more control," one said. "You could rein in his wilder dreams, but now you are tied to him, tied to this process which is so frustrating." They saw only too clearly that the United States was symbiotically involved with Iran's development—and thus with Iran's problems.

The expanding U.S. presence created potential problems for America, too. As early as 1974 Ambassador Richard Helms was concerned about it, but he had little leverage because most of the growth was in the private sector. Neither the U.S. embassy nor Washington could control the pressures to expand American exports, especially after 1973. Arms salesmen would quote the administration's Guam Doctrine. Private corporations wanted to obtain lucrative contracts; 15 American banks had set up offices in Tehran by 1974. The rush to make money was on. Moreover, in 1973 and 1974 the the executive branch of the U.S. government was beleaguered by Watergate and in no position to exercise firm control in an area where it had no legislative authority and had collaborated in creating the problem.

There never would be a joint mechanism established for reviewing major arms purchases between the two countries. In earlier times fiscal constraints were enough to give the United States control over the growth of Iranian military power. The situation began to change in 1972, when the President said Iran could have what it wanted, and the Shah took Nixon at his word. Certainly the Majles did not have the power to restrain its monarch. If U.S. officials had attempted to do so, it would have implied that they were undercutting their own president. By the time the administration had changed in 1974, and again in 1976, any cutback in programs already underway would have created the impression that the U.S. was withdrawing its support of the Shah and encouraging his enemies.

Not surprisingly, by 1976 rumors were rampant of corruption in the arms purchase program. Investigations confirmed many of the allegations and approximately two dozen military men and civilians were incarcerated. Throughout the spring, charges were also filed against two senior officials in the state-run Iran Trading Company and the director of civil aviation; all were convicted. That summer, Rear Admiral Abbas Atai and ten other naval officers were found guilty of embezzlement and sent to prison. Accusations of bribery in order to land lucrative contracts included unusual arrangements for hiring "consultants," some of whom had U.S. government connections. Eventually the Department of Defense was forced to assign an official representative to Tehran to sort out problems connected with procurement and contracting arrangements. Eric Von Marbod stayed 18 months, until the summer of 1978, successfully reducing most purchasing problems to manageable levels and straightening out most of the shady financial practices.

Growing involvement also made America vulnerable in other ways. U.S. citizens became guerrilla targets, and maintaining the security of the official community became a major worry for the Iranian government. Four U.S. military officers were assassinated between 1973 and 1976, plus an Iranian employee of the embassy mistakenly identified as an American diplomat. In August 1976, three civilian employees of Rockwell International, a firm working on government projects involving communications and defense, were gunned down while driving to work.

Americans had become part of the problem—not part of the solution—especially in the eyes of Iranians alienated from their own political-economic system. The growing intimacy caused even those in the establishment to link America with the Shah's deficiencies rather than to see the U.S. as a contributor to Iran's progress. By 1977 the monarch appeared to be so closely tied to the United States that he was working for American aims, rather than Iranian goals. Those who saw the military buildup as unnecessary asked why it was being done. The opposition answer was that "the puppet Shah is slavishly carrying out the whims of American imperialism." The monarch's regional ambitions were no longer considered to be in the country's best interest, especially when economic dislocation began to cost his people money and jobs. While many recognized that U.S. technology and trained personnel had accelerated development, the direction it was taking made them increasingly sympathetic to opposition rhetoric.

America's role in the economic expansion also changed the opinions of the various dissident groups. As the number of embassy officers decreased and contacts with politically attuned Iranians became fewer, opposition leaders concluded that the U.S. was dealing with the Shah exclusively and wanted little to do with them. One moderate dissident stated in 1979, "We believed you had decided to put all your eggs in one basket, that you were no longer interested in democracy." This was especially true of the discontented young, who had no memory of the successful American push for reform in the early 1960s. For religious leaders, the rampant materialism of the new Iran was equated with the United States. The Shah didn't help matters when he tried to minimize contacts between mullahs and diplomats. He directed SAVAK to harass Islamic figures who talked with foreigners and encouraged embassies to avoid listening to these "malcontents." Their enforced isolation strengthened the feeling of the mullahs that U.S. influence was destroying traditional Iran. Farsi-speaking Americans, especially the half dozen in the embassy, were aware of this change in religious attitudes, but it was not until the opposition revived itself in 1977 that there could be more satisfactory contacts, as much because of opposition suspicions as because of any formal limitations.

Many Iranians also accepted the story developed by Dan Rather of CBS and former U.S. Ambassador to Saudi Arabia James Akins (1973–1975). In the fall of 1979 Akins confirmed on a "Sixty Minutes" program what he had been espousing informally for several years. He said that Henry Kissinger engineered the first oil price rise, or at least allowed it to happen, so that the Shah could spend more money on American weapons.[13] Anyone who believes Akins misunderstands the international oil market. By 1973 demand dictated a hefty price hike, and the real argument was merely over the amount. Given Arab sensibilities enraged over the role of the West in the Yom Kippur War a few months earlier, consumer needs which far outstripped available supply, and the Shah's desire, as well as that of other oil producing countries, for more national income, an increase to something near the level in 1974 was inevitable. The Shah had been one of the OPEC moderates; when he switched to favoring a large increase, the price of Arabian crude oil went from $2.50 a barrel in November 1973 to $10 a barrel by

March 1974. It is difficult to see how any pressure on the part of the United States to stop the process would have been effective. The first U.S. priority was to minimize the price hike if possible, but if it was not possible, to concentrate more on mitigating the economic aftereffects.

Two other considerations became important when President Carter took office in January 1977. The first was Carter's highly touted emphasis on human rights, which gave heart to dissidents on the one hand and made Iranian government officials uneasy on the other. The opposition hoped the policy would be the precursor of greater American interest in Iranian politics, as in 1960–1963. The Shah feared American meddling to the detriment of his programs. The other problem was arms procurement. As soon as he took office, President Carter stated that he planned to limit the sale of military equipment to all foreign countries to a total amount less than that sold in previous years. While this had no immediate effect on shipments to Iran, the Shah was concerned that he might be squeezed by the new ceiling within a year or two. On the surface, Washington's new human rights and arms sales policies were not significant, but the psychological impact on the monarch's self-confidence and his image of modernization was considerable.

On the Eve of the Revolutionary Period

By the mid-1970s there were visible differences between Iranian feelings about their monarch and the official U.S. conception. America regarded Iran as a key ally, focusing its attention on the Shah and modernization rather than on the political scene in general. Until the Shah began liberalizing in 1977, American views of Iranian reality were not seriously warped. On the other hand, an ever-increasing number of Iranians perceived their monarch to be a puppet sacrificing his country to the needs of Western security by overemphasizing a military buildup and by pressing development to the point of hardship. By 1977 many Iranian government officials could not see why the United States was condoning a catastrophic plan careening their country toward profound economic distress. Pronouncements out of Washington focused on the modernization successes—the rising per capita income and the establishment of new industry—not on the internal unhappiness these economic changes were generating. The U.S. appeared to favor all-out commitment to Iran rather than the earlier relationship which had balanced development with reform.

Negative signs, some unintentional, further confused the atmosphere. Uncertainty reinforced endemic suspicion of American motives, especially among those who did not fully understand the broad changes in U.S. foreign policy which had reduced American desire and capability to be greatly involved abroad. The most important of these signals was a six-month delay in the arrival of a new ambassador to replace Richard Helms. Helms had been in Tehran four years, until his resignation on November 2, 1976, and final departure in late December. The appointment of an ambassador by the fledgling Carter administration provided an opportunity to indicate policy intent through what type of person was chosen. Because the neophyte government was stressing two very sensitive subjects, human rights and arms sales limitations, who was selected was especially important to the dissidents. Since Iran had just recently achieved the status of an alliance partner rather than a poor relation, it was extremely disconcerting to the Shah that the President waited several months before sending William Sullivan, who arrived in June 1977. The unexplained delay did not allay Iranian uneasiness.

Sullivan's previous record communicated a mixed message. From the American standpoint, he seemed to be the ideal choice, a top professional ambassador in the career foreign service with an excellent record in hot spots — Vietnam, Washington, Laos, and the Philippines, the last two appointments as ambassador. From the Shah's point of view as well, Sullivan was an excellent nominee. He was the first American ambassador who was younger than the monarch, and a solid selection to ratify the new cooperative relationship rather than the teacher-pupil ties of former years. To the opposition, however, Sullivan appeared to be a hard-line proconsul, one who had been deeply involved in U.S. "interventions" in Asia of the type the dissidents feared could occur in Iran. Some lower level State Department officials in the newly established Division of Human Rights shared these views, and inadvertently communicated them to both official and dissident Iranians. Sullivan himself realized the Carter administration was uncertain about him, and he was particularly careful to maintain an appropriate emphasis on human rights in his contacts with the government and particularly the Shah. Moreover, he felt responsible for making the monarch understand what the new administration was about. Unfortunately, clarification of American intentions was not forthcoming from Washington, since there were distinct policy differences. Some officials were determined to complete the buildup of a loyal regional ally; others wished to bear down harder on Iranian human rights violations.

America did not realize what was happening in Iran. The U.S. had become identified by more and more Iranians as a major contributor to the deficiencies in the Shah's programs and the worsening economic situation. Both the establishment and the opposition began giving the embassy a wider berth, confused by conflicting signals. The new ambassador was an unknown quantity, speaking for a president whose policy emphasis still was not explicit six months after his inauguration. Although the U.S. had already lost its old leverage, there was scant effort made to increase the embassy staff proportionate to Iran's new political and economic importance. The situation was not like 1953 and 1963, when the official mission was larger and had better contacts much closer to the grass roots.

Until 1953 the United States was a relatively minor factor in Iranian politics. By 1963 America was first among equals, but by no means dominant. By 1977 the U.S. position was such that it was no surprise when other nations began engaging in periodic sniping at both the United States and the Shah. Commercial competition among the Americans, French, British, West Germans, Japanese, and South Koreans was intense. On several occasions, in order to harmonize military equipment or to insure compatible technology, the Shah tipped the balance in favor of an American supplicant. Certainly the French, probably the British, and perhaps other nations did not mind giving the Shah grief and complicating American policy. They saw the U.S. position inextricably intertwined with that of the Shah, to the detriment of their own countries.

By midsummer 1977 it was clear to most Iranians, but not to Washington (suffering more than usual from fragmentation of policy coordination), that the U.S. had become chained to the Shah in negative ways.[14] Both the establishment and the opposition considered the possibility of American political intervention as highly likely, though even the thought of such a possibility would have appalled Jimmy Carter. A new American ambassador was settling in and assessing his tasks. In the opinion of foreign diplomats in Tehran, the Shah was going through an uncomfortable time, but was unassailable. Thus America entered the revolutionary period, but neither the United States nor Iran realized what lay just ahead.

Chapter Five

The Emerging Confrontation

April 1977–June 1978

Iran's revolutionary storm gathered gradually through the spring and into the fall of 1977. Starting in May the economic dislocation precipitated by the intensified development of the previous four years turned into a major recession. Government efforts to halt the runaway inflation by tightening credit caused construction and business expansion to level off, increasing unemployment without halting the rise in comsumer prices. Unskilled peasants who had migrated to the cities were unable to get work or thrown off the jobs they had managed to find. Salaries did not keep pace with the cost of living in the cities, and even the heretofore relatively prosperous middle class began to feel the pinch. By June many civil servants and younger professional men were paying 50 to 60 percent of their salaries for housing.

Stimulated by these adverse economic conditions, dissidents had a reason to become more active. More and more former opposition politicians organized their followers, along with many new ones drawn from the groups now most affected by the economic slump. Leaders of the non-religious opposition, Dariush Forouhar and Karim Sanjabi, spoke out against runaway inflation, especially spiraling house rents and the rising cost of food. At the same time the clergy increasingly criticized the modernization process, particularly the Westernization of Islamic society that went with it. Both groups found a ready audience—bazaar merchants smarting from the government's price-fixing campaign, student idealists chafing under repression of campus activities, and the urban unemployed finding only poverty after coming to the cities to seek their fortunes.

Beginning in May 1977 dissident activity became even more public.

81

A group of 54 lawyers issued a manifesto critical of judicial changes the Shah was in the process of instituting which they thought increased the monarch's power to manipulate the legal system. Then a noted historian, Ibrahim Khajenouri, wrote an open letter to the leadership of the Resurgence Party, criticizing them for failing to encourage meaningful political activity and neglecting to improve ties between the government and the people. Another manifesto, this one promulgated by the National Front, called upon the Shah to stop violating the constitution and to turn Iran from a dictatorship into a constitutional government. In July many writers and intellectuals sent letters to the throne, distributing copies to the press. All dealt with the subject of ending one-man rule, press censorship, and police brutality. Only Khajenouri's letter was mentioned by the media, but a lively underground traffic in mimeographed flyers quickly developed.

The Shah was ready to make small gestures in favor of the opposition, but the dissidents just couldn't bring themselves to trust their ruler no matter what he did. For instance, during May and June 1977 the Iranian government invited the International Red Cross to inspect the prisons, and the Shah held private talks in Tehran on human and civil rights with the head of Amnesty International and representatives of the International Commision of Jurists. The monarch promised his visitors to upgrade prison conditions, eliminate torture by security forces, improve military court procedures to strengthen the judicial rights of defendants, and permit greater freedom of press and assembly. The opposition had won its point on all counts. The government was on the defensive, a signal to the dissidents that they could upgrade and intensify their disruptive activities.[1]

The Maturing of the Reactivated Opposition

Except for the sporadic public manifestations by agitating intellectuals, there was no significant visible activity by organized opposition groups until August and September 1977. Most dissidents were still operating very tentatively, testing what appeared to be a new, less oppressive approach to the opposition. Then, in August, the Shah changed prime ministers. The governmental shakeup which followed appeared to be an additional sign that things were, indeed, opening up politically.

By late spring, the terminal cancer of Court Minister Asadollah Alam had progressed to the point where he informed the Shah he would have to give up his post. Throughout the summer the monarch contemplated what the new government arrangements should be. By July senior politicians had concluded that either Prime Minister Hoveyda or National Iranian Oil Company director Manuchehr Eqbal was a likely candidate to replace Alam. When chronic electric power shortages (caused by light rainfall in areas with hydroelectric dams) began to afflict Iran's cities, the Shah used this as an excuse to kick Hoveyda upstairs to Alam's job as court minister and to appoint a whole new government. On August 7 the monarch chose as prime minister the secretary-general of the Resurgence Party, Jamshid Amouzegar. Installed along with him was a new cabinet emphasizing younger, more competent officials. The naming of Amouzegar to the prime ministership was not a surprise. It had been generally assumed Hoveyda's replacement would be either Amouzegar or Finance Minister Houshang Ansari, best known for advocating the "high growth" option in terms of Iran's development despite the political costs. Since the ranking member of the single political party had won the highest post in the land, the makeup of the new government appeared to signal increasing liberalization. One Iranian journalist wrote that in choosing Amouzegar, the Shah wished to indicate that the Resurgence Party could serve as a route for political advancement. At the same time, divesting the new prime minister of his post as secretary-general was supposed to foreshadow greater independence for the Resurgence Party, since it would permit the secretary-general and the party to advocate policies without regard for the government "line."[2]

Unfortunately, as good as these changes were, they still did not provide any legal way for the opposition, now gathering its forces, to participate in the governmental process. The Shah still insisted that all political activity had to be conducted within the framework of the Resurgence Party. This was an unacceptable demand for even the moderate dissidents and, above all, the very few radicals who had consistently argued for strict constitutional limits on the Shah or for an end to the monarchy.

The chief problem was that Prime Minister Amouzegar was more interested in economics than in politics. One initial policy shift alienated the Islamic leadership completely, since it terminated, presumably with the Shah's approval, all payments to the clergy and religious schools for grants and scholarships. It was absolutely the wrong moment to make the change. Though it was a shortsighted move, it was entirely consistent with Amouzegar's technocratic philosophy of government. That fall the prime minister told several observers who expressed concern over rumblings from within the mosques that "the reactionary mullahs are finished; Iran has moved beyond them." It never occurred to many officials that religious leaders who knew so little about the modern world could mobilize the population against a system which had brought Iran so much. This attitude neglected important facts. By 1977 many Iranians were dissatisfied with the defective political-economic system. Wage increases and government contracts were not being distributed equally because of corruption, general laxity, and inefficiency, and too many citizens felt only the coercive effects of the regime, none of its benefits.

Given new faces in government and a few sympathetic noises about human rights—by late summer the government had submitted a military court reform bill to parliament—the secular opposition was willing to give the Amouzegar government at least a tentative chance to "show some improvement, be responsive to us, and above all, to offer more political freedom." Such an approach was not shared by either the clergy or the more radical dissidents, especially the guerrilla movements, since they had already concluded that ultimately force would be required in order to change the system. A good deal of suspicion persisted that the Shah was merely trying to trick his opponents. This attitude was reinforced by two developments in August. One was the arrest and secret trial of an ayatollah from Tehran, Mahmoud Taleqani, on charges of subversive activity. Though he was sentenced to ten years in prison, he would be set free 15 months later when the Shah ordered the release of several hundred political prisoners. It was several days before his family and colleagues uncovered what had happened. This act was in direct violation of the Shah's promise to open up such trials to public view.

The second, more ominous event occurred during the week of August 21, when the government tore down some houses of squatters in southeastern Tehran. On the first day a bulldozer was brought in and five of these rural immigrants were killed resisting destruction of their homes. The following day approximately 1,000 squatters and dissidents gathered. After heavy fighting with the police, about 12 lay dead and more than 100 were injured. The third day tens of thousands of people, including representatives of at least two Fedayeen guerrilla groups, attacked several police posts. The army had to be brought in to quell the disturbance. Some backstairs negotiating between the ministries of Housing and Interior and the squatters defused the situation, but the specter of violent revolt had been raised.

The housing riots and the arrest of Taleqani caused the opposition to pause and take stock. The guerrilla groups wanted to press on with an escalating campaign of violence. The National Front and the Liberation Movement, on the other hand, were inclined to take a wait-and-see attitude, fearing a hostile U.S. reaction to any overt violence directed against the Shah. They did not trust the monarch's stated intention to liberalize on his own initiative, but they did feel that he could be pushed into granting more freedoms and easing police suppression of political activity.

Then, in April 1978, the U.S. offered to sell early warning aircraft (AWACS) to Iran to cement a joint intelligence program. The Shah's quick acceptance confirmed the worst fears of the opposition that the monarch's pronouncements about liberalization were more propaganda than reality, that the United States would support the Shah whether or not he changed his style of rule. The AWACS sale symbolized the kind of military purchase that made a good opposition issue. It appeared to offer few benefits to Iran but many to the United States, since the planes were designed to provide intelligence on Russian force dispositions. Moreover, the more radical dissidents believed that stationing these planes in Iran gave the U.S. a greater stake in preserving the Shah's regime.[3] The American congressional controversy over the offer did not prevent it; instead, it convinced the dissidents that U.S. ties to the monarch were absolutely solid. (Ironically, the sale would be cancelled in the fall of 1978, as political upheaval expanded.)

In August and September the top leadership in both the religious and secular opposition met several times, in Iran and elsewhere, though mostly in Europe. Decisions taken at these gatherings shaped the challenge to the Shah for the next year, until September 1978. The Mujahidin and the Fedayeen groups agreed to rein in their violent inclinations and let the more moderate elements step up their peaceful political provocation. This would give the Fedayeen time to build up their internal organization, particularly important since it had been badly damaged by Iranian government counterterrorist forces in the previous 12 months. Thus moderates such as Sanjabi, Bakhtiar, and Forouhar of the National Front and representatives of the lawyers and writers groups were the winners at these meetings. Now they could strive to bring the opposition into some legal relationship with the government, either through open competition for parliamentary seats or perhaps an eventual deal directly with the Shah, without having to cope with terrorist activity. The guerrilla forces, however, were formally linked to the revolutionary movement as a nascent security wing. The compromise strategy allowed everyone to continue developing their individual organizations while bringing the Moslem clergy into the revolutionary movement as part of the consultation process, a much closer connection than in 1963.

Many moderates thought the Shah was too powerful to dislodge directly. Others believed retaining him as a constitutional monarch was important in order to maintain effective national unity. Only the far left and very reactionary clerics (unknown, younger men) wished to rule out compromise at this time. Even Khomeini's supporters living in Iran, including Ayatollahs Mohammad Behesti and Mahdavi-Kani (who would be hard-liners in the post-revolutionary takeover) were willing to work within the system as far as possible while they sought to overturn it, if only to conserve resources and minimize the danger to themselves and their followers.

Throughout September and October 1977 this strategy worked. Public meetings sponsored by the dissidents grew larger. The challenge to the government, at first very subtle, became more overt and direct. It began in early October when students in Tehran called for the return from exile of Ayatollah Khomeini. A week later severe disturbances interrupted classes at Tehran University, Aryamehr Technical College, and Tehran Polytechnic College. At the same time meetings organized in the bazaars throughout the country demanded the return to constitutional government, freedom of press and speech, and an end to SAVAK brutality. In November, 56 prominent Iranians, including some former government figures, distributed flyers calling for the disbanding of the secret police and the punishment of those who violate individual rights.

The monarch's vist to Washington on November 15 and 16 provided an occasion to test the effectiveness of the opposition. In the U.S. capital, pro- and anti-Shah demonstrators clashed, with 11 arrested and 92 rioters and 29 policemen injured. Simultaneously, student meetings at several universities in Tehran and elsewhere called for the Shah "to put President Carter's human rights program into effect in Iran immediately." Demonstrations continued throughout the month of November, providing excellent practice for budding political organizers. Government reaction was spotty. Sometimes meetings were just broken up; sometimes a few arrests were made. During university uprisings, on several occasions college administrators urged judicial officials to release students rather than to provoke further polarization and confrontation. Such leniency encouraged opposition organizers, and student membership in dissident groups grew weekly. Many young intellectuals who would not support a specific anti-government faction were quite willing to demonstrate for more academic freedom and liberalized free speech and assembly. Beginning in October 1977 government efforts to ease restrictions on students and faculty were considered to be concessions to the dissidents, thereby reinforcing the opposition's appeals for support. Always the government tried concession *after* it was challenged. As a result, student rebels grew bolder.

University demonstrations continued on a regular, rhythmic basis from November 1977 until the Shah's overthrow 14 months later, determined by the organizational needs of the student movement and government attempts to control the centers of higher learning. As confrontation escalated, more students were arrested—30 to 40 in February 1978, 65 in April, and 23 at the small university in Babol in May. In none of these cases was the organizational structure of dissident activity at the universities demolished, or even significantly dented. Key leaders remained free.

The problem was that security forces were hampered by the complex instructions governing how they should handle dissent. Except in the case of direct violence, no heavy-handed force was to be used. The exact rules varied according to the time, place, and severity of the incident. For example, on April 21, 1978, security forces severely beat up a number of students gathered in the hills above Tehran. Many innocent hikers were roughed up as well. The week following, two demonstrations at Aryamehr University were not even cut short. A large majority of college students in Tehran were becoming polarized into two groups—Islamic fundamentalists who were Mujahidin sympathizers, or Marxists. The former accounted for 40 percent of the student population, the latter about 35 percent, and the silent, scared, pro-government remnant about 20 to 25 percent. This last group never actively organized itself. By the time of the revolutionary takeover, no students would openly support the monarchy.

During the rest of 1977 the more moderate opposition forces attempted to coordinate their activities. For the first time, the mosque network proved its effectiveness to the opposition, allowing the Liberation Movement to transmit instructions and messages to its followers. As a result, ordinary citizens were becoming aware of another information source, one not tied to the government. This communications web was an important means of developing trained cadres in each city that could get news to the masses quickly. These core groups interpreted events for their followers and others who cared to listen, creating an effective alternative to the political propaganda disseminated by the government-controlled media. Now the regime's monopoly on the legitimate communications network ceased to be a severely limiting factor for the opposition.

Two other events in the fall of 1977 hardened dissident attitudes and altered others besides members of the various opposition groups to the fact that political unrest was spreading. The first was a mini-contretemps triggered by a report which appeared in both English and Persian language newspapers in Iran the week of October 22. This story outlined alleged remarks by former U.S. Ambassador to Iran (1965–1969) Armin Meyer at a conference in Washington. It said that former Prime Minister Ali Amini had been the "American candidate" for prime minister of Iran in 1961. About a week later, Amini wrote a letter to the press denying his involvement in any such U.S. scheme, and former Ambassador Meyer denied he had been quoted correctly. On November 2 the Resurgence Party newspaper berated Amini for attempting to defend himself. The origin of the first attack on Amini was not clear, but its object obviously was to discredit him. Several U.S. government officials believed the slur on the former prime minister, coming just before the Shah's visit to Washington, was a signal from the monarch to President Carter that the same pressure tactic used by Kennedy in 1961 to loosen up the political system could not succeed in 1978. On the other hand, seasoned opposition politicians like Mehdi Bazargan reasoned that the monarch's need to express Iran's displeasure meant that the Shah was in fact feeling pressure from Washington on civil rights. Though no specific mention of this incident was made during the discussions the Shah and Carter had together, the President acknowledged that they had talked about human rights along with "almost every conceivable subject" during the Shah's visit.[4]

The second event would turn the moderates away from serious talk of compromise with their ruler and head them toward more confrontational demonstrations. On the evening of November 22 approximately 1,000 dissidents gathered just outside Tehran on the Karaj Road, at the garden home of a prominent bazaar merchant, Hossein Golzar, to hear a number of speakers talk about forming a unified anti-government coalition. Present were most of the prominent non-clerical leaders as well as several religious figures. After the meeting had been underway for several minutes, buses arrived carrying just over 200 men, who lined up in rows and marched through the garden beating up the guests. No one was killed, but about 100 were injured, including opposition leaders Forouhar and Matin-Daftari, who remained in the hospital overnight. The government claimed, and the press dutifully printed, that the men who broke up the gathering were "factory workers returning from work who were outraged by the expression of anti-national sentiments." The opposition believed they were either SAVAK agents or Resurgence Party thugs hired for the occasion, and pointed to the fact that the day involved was a work holiday, when no factories were open. At least some official sanction had been given—city buses were used, and police, notified in advance to protect the meeting, failed to arrive.

This "legal mugging" had an impact out of proportion to the fact of the event largely because it helped destroy the hope of moderate dissidents that there could be evolution to an acceptable political society. When this incident was followed two days later by the beating and near-rape of two prominent university professors—one male and one female—after an evening political rally, all opposition groups began to worry more about protecting themselves. Security became a priority item. The National Front stopped publicizing its movements and armed selected members. It also decided to "go public" with its demands, calling for the nationalization of major industries, greater independence of the judiciary, freedom of speech and assembly, and development of a foreign policy that focused on national interests rather than foreign alliances. In a press conference on its position paper, the organization's spokesman bluntly stated that there were too many Americans in the country. His last demands called for the elimination of the Israeli connection, including cessation of oil shipments to the Jewish state, as well as to South Africa.

Following the attack on the moderates at the meeting on November 22, opposition activity went underground for two weeks. Then, in December, 29 prominent Iranian dissidents wrote a letter to United Nations Secretary-General Kurt Waldheim, with a copy to President Carter, requesting international help to restore human and civil rights to Iran. It was a planned campaign. Anti-Shah organizers were focusing on President Carter's New Year's Eve and New Year's Day visit to Tehran. The appeal to the U.N. was publicized within Tehran just prior to Carter's arrival, and opposition supporters in the United States encouraged the President to recognize that Iranian dissidents were seeking the same human rights goals the President had been proclaiming. Three days before Carter came to Tehran a bomb went off in the Iran-American Society language center near Tehran University. Whether the explosion was set off by leftists, by Resurgence Party toughs, or by SAVAK agents was never proved. The damage was minimal, but it expressed growing hostile feelings against the United States. A day later the center for the American Friends of the Middle East was trashed by a group which entered and left quickly. The opposition claimed both these assaults were government sponsored and designed to frighten the United States into unqualified support for the Shah. Official spokesmen stated both incidents were the work of "Islamic Marxists," a blanket term used to describe the religious opposition.

The Carter visit itself was considered by all parties to be a clear reaffirmation of U.S.-Iran ties and particularly of the strong friendship between President Carter and the Shah. Rejecting suggestions that he balance his public expressions of support for the monarch with some recognition of the efforts of the opposition in favor of human rights, the President referred to his "close personal friendship" and offered "warm personal greetings" to the Shah and his people. He said Iran's ruler was "very deeply concerned about human rights," especially in terms of minority religions and women. Without mentioning the controversy over political and civil rights, he praised Iran under the Shah's leadership as "an island of stability . . . a great tribute to the respect, admiration, and love of your people for you."[5]

The opposition was severely disappointed. It thought the United States was betraying its own heritage of freedom and its past concern for independence in Iran in favor of the need for good regional security against Soviet threats. Carter's speech would be used to show that the United States as well as the Shah was the enemy, a theme that would surface more directly in seven months' time. Iran's press billed the visit as a triumphal expression of American-Iranian collaboration and closeness. There was a certain smugness in the official statements which dismayed many, even those in the establishment, who had looked to the U.S. to exercise a moderating influence on the Shah.

The Militant Opposition Asserts Itself

Immediately following the Carter stopover, one of those incidents occurred which do not seem overridingly important at the time, but which trigger a chain of events that eventually race out of control. On January 5 the Persian newspaper *Ettela'at* published an article titled "Iran and the Red and Black Colonialism," which attacked Ayatollah Khomeini as "an agent of Britain and of Indian descent." It labeled him the instigator of the "anti-national" riots of June 5, 1963. While the text appears only mildly abusive by Western standards, it was reportedly written by Minister of Information Dariush Homayoun at the Shah's insistence. It created a storm in Shiite religious circles, especially in Qom, the theological capital of Iran. The situation in Qom had been getting more tense since the previous autumn anyway, because the police had quelled several disturbances with particular roughness. A spirit of confrontation had been building ever since, and by January security forces were reluctant to enter parts of the city at night.

On January 7, demonstrations protesting the newspaper article and attacking the government began in Qom. The following day a serious riot took place near the main mosque and opposition sources claimed several were killed and 120 injured. Two days later approximately 5,000 people left the same mosque after hearing a strong anti-government sermon to march toward Ayatollah Shariatmadari's home. The police were ordered to break up the demonstration. When clubs failed to do so, the officer in charge ordered his men to fire their weapons. According to the official Pars News Agency account, several people were hit; 6 died, including a child. Opposition leaders claimed 30 were killed and over 200 injured. More importantly, two mullahs were among the dead and their blood-soaked turbans were posted above the entry gate to the main mosque. Police, aided by security forces, eventually restored order, but as one observer said, "It was a deadly truce."

In the wake of the Carter visit and faced with the bloodshed in Qom, the religious opposition moved into high gear. This was the first direct, public attack on clerics and it had taken place in Iran's holiest city. It touched the mosque network at its center. Word about the events in Qom went to all corners of Iran immediately by telephone and by messenger, with the usual Persian hyperbole affecting the details. American diplomats posted in Shiraz, Isfahan, and Tabriz reported that the death toll rose geometrically as the distance from Qom increased arithmetically.

What had happened in Qom offered the first real test of official media credibility versus the mosque network. Whose casualty figures should be accepted? Government officials believed, or professed to believe, Pars News Agency reports; the opposition quoted its own sources. An opinion survey in Tehran within a week of the incident indicated that 60 percent of the 100 non-government employees asked thought the casualty toll was nearer to the opposition claims than to the official figures. Yet in this case, the government statistics, eventually corrected to 9 killed and 150 injured, were closer to an unbiased count of 12 killed and 160 wounded obtained privately by U.S. diplomats from non-political medical sources.

Demonstrations began again almost immediately. There were anti-government riots in Ahwaz, where the bazaar closed for a time and two mullahs were sent to Qom for "internal exile," a form of legal banishment. The port city of Khorramshar, the refinery town of Abadan, and several smaller communities in southern Iran were targets as well. The Qom riots promoted unity against the regime in the name of the "fallen martyrs," giving the mullahs a rallying cry to use with the masses. Clergy across the country became more vocal and began telling the urban and rural poor "to prepare for the challenge of martyrdom in defense of Islam against the godless Shah." The Palestinian organization Al-Fatah, already annoyed by the reciprocal Shah-Carter visits, took advantage of the growing unrest to urge its erstwhile allies, the Mujahidin and the Fedayeen, into more anti-government activity. Galvanized by the "government violence" in Qom, and encouraged by the Al-Fatah, the guerrilla movements began preparing to attack. A national cycle of demonstration-reaction that would continue in ever-increasing frequency until the Shah's overthrow was about to begin.

What had happened in Qom showed quite impressively that the dissident movement was now well enough organized and strong enough to effectively challenge the government. Within a month press kits about the three days of riots had been compiled by the opposition and were available to visiting foreign correspondents.

For the government, Qom demonstrated that minor political problems were rapidly becoming big ones and, most graphically, that the police were inadequately trained for riot control. A Japanese diplomat remarked at the time that "the Tokyo riot police could handle any disturbance in this country with their duty squad." He was not to change his mind until very late in 1978.

In terms of the urban middle class, Qom began the destruction of the myth that the Pahlavi regime was invincible. For the first time, many enlightened loyalists began to think about the possibility of an alternative to the kind of authoritarian government Iran had always had in the past. In early 1978 the middle class did not question the policy of modernization, but many hesitantly discussed the possibility of reforming, improving, or "purifying" the governmental structure. They were seriously concerned about the country's future, fears reflected almost immediately by lengthening visa lines at the American embassy.

Only minor disturbances marred the domestic scene throughout the rest of January and into February. Then, according to Shiite custom, fortieth-day ceremonies mourning the "martyrs" at Qom were scheduled for February 18. There were peaceful commemorative parades in 15 of 16 cities. The one exception was Tabriz. What happened in that city that day would make Tabriz a benchmark on Iran's road to revolution.

The provincial government had closed down three mosques on the day of the ceremonies. About 10:00 A.M. a crowd gathered, demanding entry into the bazaar mosque. According to one story, the violence started when a police major shot a student in the chest during an argument. Some officials maintain that mourners had guns beneath their robes and deliberately provoked a demonstration. Whatever the cause, rioting broke out. The shooting and burning spread to the rest of the city. This was the first conflagration to mobilize the masses of youth and urban poor for economic as well as religious reasons. The recession had hit Tabriz particularly hard, and unemployment was higher there than elsewhere. Tabriz is also a more traditional city. The pattern of violence—destruction of banks, restaurants, liquor stores, hairdressing establishments, and government buildings, all symbols of modern Iran—strongly suggests both efficient leadership and a very conservative religious orientation among the rioters. Michael Metrinko, the U.S. consul in Tabriz and an eyewitness to these events, reported that hotel bars were attacked with vigor, and liquor dumped. Moderate revolutionaries would have confiscated the stock, not destroyed it. Private clubs and recreation centers for civil servants and teachers were vandalized as well, and then gutted on the grounds that such organizations were "immoral."

More unnerving was the complete breakdown of law and order. The rioting began about 10:15 and continued all day. By early afternoon, authorities were compelled to order army troops from nearby garrisons at Maraghei and Ajahshar to restore order. Demonstrations involving 50,000 people continued a second day, marking the first open, sustained clash between the army and civilians since 1963. Updated official figures show 26 or 27 killed and 262 wounded. Opposition leaders in Tehran claimed 300 killed and between 500 to 700 injured. The government again blamed "Islamic Marxists" and "foreign elements," though there is no proof of outside interference.

Army troops were not withdrawn until February 23, and a government investigating team was dispatched almost immediately. It learned that Tabriz officials had been totally unaware of preparations for mass participation in the fortieth-day ceremonies. The result was a wholesale purge of provincial and city officials for inefficiency and gross neglect. Longtime Shah loyalist and governor of East Azarbaijan province, Manuchehr Azmudeh, was fired as were the SAVAK province chief and his senior commander in Tabriz. The new governor was Major General Jaafar Shafiqat, who had headed the government investigation. This eased tensions, even though Shafiqat used a heavy hand to reestablish control. He tightened security, but at the same time he also reached an understanding with local religious leaders loyal to Ayatollah Shariatmadari (Tabriz is Shariatmadari's hometown) to avoid further bloodshed. There would be no more trouble in that city for nine months.[6]

But elsewhere throughout the country, from February until June, anti-regime organizers stepped up the pressure and the number of public disturbances proliferated. Minor demonstrations and commemorative services 40 days later became standard fare until April, when the 40-day cycle was broken by more frequent random outbursts.

At the fortieth-day ceremonies on March 30 for the Tabriz dead there were scattered incidents, but only in Babol, where some buildings were burned and 31 students arrested, was there any serious trouble. About the same time inmates in Tehran's Qasr Prison began a hunger strike to support their demands for better treatment. A number of political prisoners were in Qasr, and the coordination between the strikers and the opposition leaders calling for their freedom was worked out by the Committee for Human Rights. This cooperation indicated the two groups had worked out a well-organized propaganda campaign, something the dissidents eventually confirmed to reporters and diplomats.

In April there was at least one serious disturbance reported every day. Homes of two National Front leaders in Tehran were bombed and heavily damaged, and prominent opposition lawyer Karim Lahidji was physically attacked. Rezayeh, Varamin, Isfahan, Yazd, and Arak, cities which had not yet experienced violence, did see it on April 3 and 4. On April 10, at his home in Qom, there was a sit-in to support Ayatollah Shariatmadari.

The government-controlled press would state that in most of the violent incidents two or three persons had been killed, sometimes five or six. The newspapers tried to obtain accurate figures and were not censored when reporting them. This was not so much because the Shah was easing up, but because the government wanted news of the growing chaos to frighten people into supporting its efforts to maintain order. On April 17 and 18, the Resurgence Party held counterdemonstrations backing the monarchy in about 20 cities. Many of those who participated were government officials and security officers, but they did so willingly, in a carnival atmosphere.

The following month, on May 9, five persons were killed in disturbances at Qom. On May 11 serious rioting took place in Mashad and dissident mullahs charged the governor of Khorasan province with excessive violence. The American-born director of the Iran-American Society in Mashad was threatened, and foreign travel to any place within the province was discouraged. Armored cars and other heavy equipment were deployed in Tehran for the first time on May 11. This was followed within two weeks by a huge demonstration at Tehran University. Two professors and a dormitory supervisor were badly beaten.

Student unrest had first become obvious on March 5, when those attending Tehran University called for the return of Ayatollah Khomeini on the upcoming fifteenth anniversary of his arrest and exile, June 5, 1963. Other schools took up the rallying cry. By mid-April all major universities throughout the country were in constant turmoil. Classes simply ceased to meet. In May student unrest began spreading to the smaller colleges in Tehran and the provinces. Azarbadigan University in Tabriz was closed on May 9 after the dean of the faculty was attacked by students. Classes were suspended at Isfahan University at the same time. Fourteen persons were injured in a riot near Pahlavi University in Shiraz, though classes continued on a hit-and-miss basis.

The days surrounding Khomeini's fifteenth anniversary on June 5 were tense throughout the country, but especially in Tehran. The police and the army were on full alert. That day, 80 percent of the student body at Aryamehr University in Tehran were expelled, and SAVAK, with some army units as backup, forced the closing of the Tehran bazaar. In the face of this strong show of force by the government, opposition leaders backed off from direct confrontation.

The Government's Desultory Response

After the fact, the responses of the Shah and his government to the events of mid-1977 to mid-1978 are puzzling. While opposition leaders were gradually escalating their challenge, direct government action (anything other than mere riot control) aimed at dealing with the emerging political problem is difficult to identify. Throughout 1977, and until the Qom riots of January 9, 1978, neither the Shah nor the government even recognized there was a problem. The monarch and most of his advisors oozed confidence about basic conditions in the country. The Shah and the political elite believed their position of power was unassailable.

Iran's monarch was relatively unconcerned about the increasing unrest because he was proceeding with liberalization, and he thought this would induce the opposition to participate in politics on terms acceptable to him. For instance, legislation to reform military court procedures had been submitted to parliament, and was approved in October 1977. It provided for civilian defendants before military courts on security charges to have defense counsel and full access to the charges against them, both rights which had been denied previously. The Shah can take credit for reforming the court system; it was done at his initiative, and the Ministry of Justice was most receptive to the change. The ministry had been trying unsuccessfully for years to establish the judiciary's independence from political pressure. In another example of reform, the Shah responded to appeals from international groups such as the Red Cross and Amnesty International and began to release political prisoners. As part of the traditional royal pardon on his birthday, October 25, the monarch made a public show of freeing 131 such offenders. On several other occasions until the end of 1978, a total of approximately 1,500 political prisoners were released.[7]

The principal reason why the government, in the name of the Shah, did not immediately attempt to curtail the unrest was that Prime Minister Amouzegar and his cabinet, like their predecessors, had very little to do with security affairs. That aspect of the regime was always handled by the monarch, directly through SAVAK and the military. However, on at least two occasions in late 1977 and early 1978 the prime minister raised questions with the Shah about the increasing instability within the country. He was thanked for his opinions and told that the monarch himself would handle the problem of controlling political dissent.[8]

Despite the Shah's confidence, Amouzegar's misgivings reflected the mood of the country. Every Iranian knew that the security services were not truly under the control of the government officials supervising them, but actually doing the Shah's bidding. Throughout the years of Hoveyda's prime ministership, Persians had become conditioned to think of the government as only the administrative arm of the monarchy, with its power to act limited to whatever the Shah allowed it to do. They had no reason to think the situation would change under Amouzegar. Thus SAVAK was considered by everyone, from the lowest paid civil servant to the highest ranking parliamentarian, to be beyond the law. Iranians searched proclamations from the throne and news about the activities of SAVAK for clues to the behavior expected of them much more than they listened to the pronouncements of parliament or the prime minister. Thus they were surprised when the unrest kept spreading and yet the Shah did not order SAVAK to quash the trouble and round up the miscreants. When Qom exploded, the regime did little more than transfer the city's SAVAK chief, Brigadier General Reza Razmi, to Abadan. The firmest reaction to public disorder had been the firing of selected provincial and city officials after the Tabriz riots. Parliament remained unsatisfied, and some deputies wanted to force action. On March 15, in response to the demonstrations in Tabriz, Majles deputy Ahmad Bani-Ahmad proposed a censure motion against the government, the first such challenge in nearly two decades. The cabinet took the motion under study, but never had a chance to report back to parliament because the issue was rapidly overtaken by events.

Under pressure from the Majles, the government could do little but stall. The Resurgence Party might have been able to ease the threat if it could have acted as a mediator between the regime and the dissenting parliamentarians. But it could not do so because its own relationship with the government remained awkward. In December the Shah had finally acceded to Amouzegar's wishes and placed the Resurgence Party under the prime minister's control. However, this action would prove to be a major mistake. It destroyed the party's credibility as an institution and left the government with no serious political base on which to build support during the escalating crisis of 1978.

The month before, in November, on his own initiative, Mohammad Baheri, secretary-general of the Resurgence Party, had shifted the party's focus from mass participation to training party cadres to carry out political action. This major change of direction caused confusion, which was compounded when Amouzegar replaced Baheri and carried out wholesale personnel replacements. With two major upheavals in less than two months to cope with, the organizational structure of the party collapsed. All that remained of the national leadership were about 50 Amouzegar loyalists at party headquarters in Tehran. In a few individual Resurgence Party units in Tehran and other large cities some of the emerging middle class tried independently to continue using the party to advance themselves, but these efforts were never adequately channeled to support the government and the Shah.

Certain people in power and others with established reputations tried to warn their ruler that he must share some of his authority if the country was to remain strong and develop a stable political base. At least two of the groups that had encouraged the establishment of the Resurgence Party in late 1974 made separate presentations in late 1977. Houshang Nahavandi's "study group," which was to emerge as a separate faction of the Resurgence Party several months later, told the Shah that only by allowing the party to have real power would his countrymen support it. Otherwise, the masses would be drawn away by the appeals of the dissidents, who were being allowed to harangue without responsibility. The second delegation was led by one of the Shah's brothers-in-law, Minister of Arts and Culture Mehrdad Pahlbod. Included with him were leading sociologist Ehsan Naraghi, future Minister of Education Gholamreza Afkhami, and prominent university and Resurgence Party figures Ahmad Qoreishi and Amin Alimard. All of them urged that the Shah bring moderate opposition politicians such as National Front members Karim Sanjabi and Gholam Hossein Sadiqi into a broadened political process. Both factions advocated liberalizing the electoral laws to permit any group to run candidates in parliamentary elections. They were confident that the government could beat back a challenge by the religious reactionaries in open debate and campaigns.

These appeals were sound, but too late. There is no evidence that the Shah ever accepted their basic thesis: compromise with the moderates to isolate the extremists. In fact, the Shah's mind-set throughout the continuously escalating confrontation is difficult to understand. In retrospect, he appears to have flirted with some generally fuzzy ideas about liberalizing the political system. The Shah vacillated between encouraging the dissidents to participate in politics—but always within what they considered the unacceptable framework of the Resurgence Party—and condemning them as traitors. He never developed a definite strategy to meet the difficult problems created by increased political activity that had been stimulated by his own half-hearted decision to allow more freedom.

One example of this approach would be the Shah's reaction to disturbances at two political rallies. On October 16, 1978, the monarch branded the dissidents as "men who would set back the country 1,500 years." The theme of "red" (communist) and "black" (reactionary mullah) traitors was trumpeted by the press at the behest of the government on several occasions, most notably at the December 4, 1977, and January 3 and 4, 1978, Resurgence Party conferences. Government speakers explicitly linked Iran's economic advances to the existing system of government, cautioning that the opposition wanted to destroy modern Iran. In effect, this forced the opposition to operate outside the accepted framework. As a number of intellectuals pointed out privately, however, if the Shah had encouraged the Resurgence Party at that time to address questions of corruption in government, political participation in decision making, resource allocation for development, and the granting of more civil and political rights, it would have found a very receptive audience among the growing middle class. It would also have severely undercut the arguments of the opposition.

Instead of the Shah forcing the dissidents to play the game his way, the opposition increased its prestige by scheduling meetings that would spread its ideas and provoke a reaction from the government. Political assemblies, ostensibly for thinly disguised purposes such as the "poetry readings" that took place at Tehran's German Club the week of October 12 to 19, 1977, featured libertarian, anti-government speakers. Such gatherings were always monitored by SAVAK or military intelligence. From time to time, such meetings were broken up, either by security forces, the police, or mobs gathered for the occasion, but it was not a consistent policy. When the unrest was beginning, in late 1977, orders to police and security forces were continually changed. SAVAK was directed to "control" public gatherings but not to "disrupt" them, after several major opposition meetings had been vandalized. Police, security forces, and even the counterterrorism committees were told to "monitor" dissident activity, but not to move against known perpetrators of violence unless they were caught in "illegal acts." This ambiguity noticeably affected police performance. The security forces were steadily overworked and frequently involved in life-threatening situations. Many military officers, enlisted men, and SAVAK agents were killed in the line of duty. Some were deliberately assassinated. All chafed under what they felt to be self-defeating restrictions.

Despite the inconsistency of government behavior, the opposition did not see it as ambivalent. The release of political prisoners would be followed by attacks on dissident meetings. Talk of judicial reform would be offset by physical attacks on dissident lawyers. As a result, Liberation Movement and National Front leaders believed the government, at the Shah's direction, was engaging in calculated repressive activities to drive them underground. The nuances of "control" and "monitor" were lost on those who were being beaten, shot at, and occasionally killed.

On the other hand, it was fairly clear to government and Resurgence Party officials that the opposition was not being intimidated. After the Tabriz riots, Amouzegar and some of the deputy secretaries-general of the Resurgence Party realized that the center of political activity had shifted from the party to the conflict between dissidents (students, religious leaders, and the old-line opposition) and the whole monarchical power structure. Despite modestly successful efforts to stage party rallies to back the administration in April, there was no ground swell of popular support for the Resurgence Party—which had been emasculated by then in any case—or for the regime itself. There was, however, considerable desire to return the country to law and order, and the government stressed this theme to its advantage as spring turned into summer. The average Iranian supported calls to go quietly about his business and to pay less attention to opposition exhortations.

However, many of those around the throne were doing some serious soul-searching. The steadily increasing drumbeat of rioting throughout April had convinced the Shah and his closest advisors, particularly Hoveyda and longtime royal confidants General Hossein Fardust, chief of the Imperial Inspectorate, and General Nasratollah Moinian, director of the Special Bureau, that a serious challenge was afoot. Despite pronouncements from the government that unrest was being fueled by foreign sources, they suspected that the real key to restoring peace was for the Shah to gain and build up support for the regime among at least some of the Islamic hierarchy. According to persons present at many of the discussions, a major effort was made to work out a compromise with the more moderate religious leaders, particularly Ayatollah Shariatmadari.

Sometime in early May the Shah decided to explore directly with these leaders the possibility of an agreement. Those who watched overtures to the ayatollahs in Qom develop were appalled by the Imperial Court's lack of finesse. The initial emissary chosen was a court functionary with some family ties to the religious movement. His behavior was described as "unbelievably arrogant and uninformed." Besides, his mandate did not include any flexibility to meet the religious leaders' political need to show concessions from the throne in turn for their support. The meeting was a total failure.

Despite some personal antipathy between the two men, Ayatollahs Khomeini and Shariatmadari were cooperating with each other to avoid splitting the religious movement and to maintain a show of unity. With Khomeini in Najaf, Iraq, and Shariatmadari in Qom, Iran, this arrangement worked fairly well, since each had the advantage of his position. Khomeini was unwilling to compromise unless the Shah offered concessions substantial enough that they would eventually lead to the monarch's political demise. Shariatmadari was more willing to consider an arrangement providing an evolutionary solution to the political unrest. He was convinced Khomeini did not understand the pressures in Iran. Khomeini thought the in-country ayatollahs were "insufficiently Islamic."

The Shah's tentative feelers were ineffective because his own rigidity kept him from encouraging direct negotiations with Khomeini's religious rivals. After the failure of the mission to Qom, the monarch decided to approach the problem of political unrest indirectly by making some high-level personnel changes. Ostensibly he did this in order to improve the government's ability to deal with the disturbances, but he was also trying to hint of his willingness to accommodate the moderate dissidents. First to go was Minister of Interior Nasser Esfahani on May 21, allegedly for his failure to quiet the country down. A few days later, the Shah posted SAVAK chief General Nematollah Nassiri to Pakistan as ambassador and replaced him with General Nasser Moghaddam, chief of military intelligence. Nassiri's deputy was also sent away, to Syria as ambassador. This attempt to reshape SAVAK's image achieved the desired effect, at least in the short run. Moghaddam was regarded by the leaders of the Liberation Movement and the National Front as a reasonable man who understood politics.

Unfortunately, simultaneous with these changes came the complete collapse of the Resurgence Party. In early June Resurgence Party wing leaders Abdul Magid Magidi and Houshang Ansari resigned out of disgust over their lack of freedom to act, and by mid-month the already weak party was in even greater shambles. Establishment politicians hoped one of the wings might be made strong enough to survive anyway. It didn't happen. At the same time, former Tehran University Chancellor Houshang Nahavandi announced that he was converting his study group into a "third wing" of the Resurgence Party to offer a loyal alternative to those who wished to support the Shah's modernizing program. The group remained small, and only partially effective. Some of its members were to become ministers in the cabinet of the truncated government of Sharif-Emami.

Partly in reaction to changes at the top in SAVAK and the decimation of the Resurgence Party, the potential for political agitation in Tehran had reached the point where, as an emergency measure, troops were called in on June 3. The mourning day called for June 5 (the anniversary of Khomeini's exile) passed relatively quietly and a second day scheduled for June 17 was also uneventful. Parliament went into summer recess. Calm returned to Iran, but the situation still remained tense and unstable. However, the Shah felt confident enough to leave for a vacation at the Caspian Sea.

The monarch as well as Tehran's political elite thought that the crisis had passed. The vast majority of those closely watching events—government officials, the opposition, foreign diplomats, and ordinary citizens—agreed with his assessment, misled by the apparent calm. They assumed "the people" were less dissatisfied than they had been earlier. It was wishful thinking. Opposition groups, though far from fully unified, had established their ability to cause serious trouble and were continuing to build up their organizational strength, even though it was not yet obvious. The Shah had made a first, awkward effort to deal with an important faction of the religious opposition. Some governmental changes had been instituted and the powerful General Nassiri ousted. The opposition was mildly encouraged that it was having some effect, but feared some wily, tricky political move by the Shah. The government response to the opposition challenge had thus far neither intimidated it nor produced the hint of an accommodation. Regime supporters, on the other hand, were dismayed by the changes. Seeing major unrest ahead, they feared the Shah planned to appease his critics by dumping his friends.

The Foreign Factor

The foreign factor—like Sherlock Holmes' famous dog that wasn't there in *The Hound of the Baskervilles*—was conspicuous by its lack of noticeable impact on the course of events throughout 1977. There are those who believe, however, that it was President Carter's failure to publicly acknowledge the efforts of the dissidents demanding that the Shah improve civil and human rights in Iran that stimulated the events of 1978. Although human rights pronouncements from members of his administration encouraged the opposition, the results of the Shah's visit to Washington in November and of Carter's New Year's Eve and New Year's Day trip to Iran six weeks later convinced anti-Shah leaders that they could expect little direct assistance from the United States.

One international factor did boost the growing opposition movement. The B.B.C.'s Persian service, for three decades considered by both the establishment and the opposition as "must" listening for international news and juicy Iranian items, began reporting extensively on dissident activities in the fall of 1977. By December the government was referring to the B.B.C. as "Public Enemy Number One" and protesting the broadcast of so much "inflamatory material" by the external service of a longtime ally. It also increased the Shah's suspicions of Britain and, by extension, the United States. There is no doubt that expatriate Iranians sympathetic to the revolution effectively "captured" the Persian service of the B.B.C. While wrapping themselves in the flag of freedom of speech, they proceeded to turn their broadcasts into an extension of the opposition's communications network. This gave the opposition movement pronouncements and version of events international legitimacy, and the British government a migraine headache.

The U.S.S.R. would remain committed to the Shah's regime until November 1978, convinced that their own interests would be better served by a stable regime that could honor the various Soviet-Iranian economic agreements. Some Soviet money and weapons probably worked their way to the Mujahidin and Fedayeen through Libya, but it was insignificant compared to that from other sources, including a dribble of material and logistical support from various Arab groups, particularly the Palestine Liberation Organization and Al-Fatah. Another source of weapons was direct purchase from the arms market in Beirut. Even supplies from this open source were negligible. Later on, arms salesmen would note that Iranian purchases in October and November 1978 drove up prices of simple automatic weapons and ammunition to triple their summer levels.

The country's growing tendency toward disorder was a homegrown operation, a testimony to the increasing organizational effectiveness and the hit-and-run tactics of the dissidents. Their emphasis on non-violent political action such as speeches, mass demonstrations, and later strikes gave security and police forces little reason to attack them. The opposition had chosen a very subtle and effective style of confrontation.

Chapter Six

A Misleading Interlude

June-September 1978

After the nervousness in early June, a misleading calm descended upon Tehran and the rest of the country when the Shah left the capital near the end of the month for a six week vacation at his palatial estate on the Caspian Sea. Seeking relief from the heat, both thermal and political, he was determined to remain away from the capital for some time in order to relax and take a fresh look at the situation from a new perspective. Unknown to all but a very few of his closest confidants, there was also a medical reason for the trip. The Shah's lymphomatous cancer had become worse. While he was at the Caspian, many rumors circulated that the monarch was ill, or that there had been an unsuccessful assassination attempt and he was recovering from gunshot wounds. Even so, the U.S. government had no positive confirmation of the ongoing battle with cancer until enlightened by French intelligence in October 1978—a startling lapse on such a vital point. Doctors in France had been treating the Shah since the mid 1970s, from the beginning of the illness. When the political climate in Tehran grew demonstrably worse, as a precautionary measure the French government took the initiative to inform the United States about the monarch's condition.

Although the Shah hoped the passions of his countrymen had cooled, opposition groups were no more reconciled to the government than before. However, overt challenges to the regime ceased while the various factions assessed their positions. The subsurface political maneuvering would continue until the third week in July, when disturbances instigated by the opposition provoked demonstrations in several cities, beginning anew the escalating cycle of violence. In the meantime, the Shah developed some initiatives of his own. After returning to Tehran

104

early in August, in several public speeches he suggested that participation in the political system be opened up to include dissident groups.

Then, in mid-August, the burning of the Rex Cinema in Abadan with the loss of over 400 lives triggered a major government crisis. This disaster, coupled with the regime's continued failure to curtail the demonstrations and the breakdown of law and order, pushed the Shah to change prime ministers for the second time within a year. The competent technocrat, Jamshid Amouzegar, was replaced by the veteran political warhorse, Jaffar Sharif-Emami. More importantly, the sense of unity Iran's political elite had felt for their monarch for decades began breaking up.

The Shah Tries to Compromise

Since his abortive effort to split off the more moderate ayatollahs within Iran from the religious group around Khomeini in Iraq had not produced any significant results, the Shah decided to rely on more visible reforms. On several occasions throughout the summer the monarch stated that he would continue with political liberalization, characterizing those opposed to his policy as "seditious reactionaries" and "agents under foreign influence." Just prior to leaving on his vacation he announced that the next parliamentary elections, scheduled for the following June, would be open to other than Resurgence Party candidates. His initial statement said that "individuals could run, without party affiliation." Immediately after he returned from the Caspian Sea, in a speech he made on Constitution Day, August 5, the Shah repeated his call for the opposition to participate in the next election. He challenged his critics "to test their strength at the ballot box," and warned that "sedition, defiance of and backsliding from the law are not to be tolerated by any country, especially democratic ones." Other changes he mentioned in the Constitution Day speech were revised censorship laws and more freedom of assembly.[1]

Moderate dissidents Karim Sanjabi, Hedayatollah Matin-Daftari, and Rahmatollah Moghadam-Maraghei welcomed these apparent concessions, but they did not believe the Shah would follow through. They had every reason to distrust him if what happened to the new bill was to be a guide. The government presented the legislation to the cabinet for consideration July 17. Drafted by career civil servants in the Ministry of the Interior, it would allow anyone to run for office without regard to party status, but left the Resurgence Party—in contradiction to the Shah's stated plans—as the sole legal political group. It also

prescribed internal Resurgence Party procedures that were less democratic than those currently in use in about 75 percent of the provincial
party organizations; the new law provided for the selection of candidates by committee only, not through primary elections.

The bureaucratic structure had obviously failed to respond in timely
fashion to the monarch's policy guidelines. As presented, the elections
bill offered so little change that, for the opposition, it rekindled suspicions rather than sparked hope. By the same token, when freedom of
assembly and freedom of the press bills were presented to the cabinet in
August and September and published concurrently in the press, their
conservative wording intensified political turmoil rather than eased it. It
appeared as if the bureaucracy was seeking to take back all that the Shah
had promised.

The government's chronic lack of response to the Shah's initiatives
occurred because the changes sought were so important. Not only was
the monarch reversing several decades of basic ruling policy, but his
calls for greater freedom disturbed the majority of the establishment.
They thought opening up the electoral process to "outsiders" would be
too dangerous. Those who had supported the Shah for years began to
feel undercut. As one of the government ministers said at the time:

> Was this to be our reward for faithfully carrying out the monarch's
> policies for years? Are we, the technocrats who built modern Iran, now to
> be sacrificed to its critics? The government has proved incapable of restor-
> ing order — wouldn't the best policy be to tighten up the government? We
> know who these radicals are. They are Mossadeqists, religious fanatics,
> and leftists bent on destroying us. They should be destroyed, not ap-
> peased.

There was also another reason for the elite to feel uneasy. Early in
July word leaked out that the Shah had drafted a "family code of conduct bill" which would keep the extended royal entourage out of business activities. The terms of the directive were never fully published,
but when the Shah's brother and other relatives quietly began leaving
the country in late July and August, this definitely increased uncertainty
among the establishment loyalists.

Under the circumstances, the Shah's efforts to conciliate the dissidents had done more harm than good; he had weakened the morale of
his own supporters and in no way appeased the opposition. In seeking
compromise, the Shah had tried to open up the government without
properly preparing either his supporters or his opponents for the
changes in advance. His poor timing reinforced the growing impression

in Tehran that the monarch had no master strategy for handling the rising dissidence, even though the situation had been gradually deteriorating for several months.

Certainly part of the Shah's ineffectiveness was due to his medical problem. Only a few trusted advisors knew that his condition was worse. Both the expanding cancer and the medicines used to treat it were adversely affecting his general health and alertness. Rumors began circulating in early July that the Shah was terminally ill with (take your choice): leukemia, lung cancer, or irreversible pneumonia. "Medical reports" were for sale to diplomats and newsmen to document different allegations. A humorous interlude occurred in late July when the Tehran newspapers, in an obvious effort to scotch the rumors, published pictures of the Shah and Empress Farah walking along the beach at the Caspian Sea. Stories immediately began to spread that the government had airbrushed out of the picture the two or three people propping up the Shah. The "evidence" was the two pairs of shoes on the beach that the airbrush artist supposedly had missed. They were really the royal couple's beach clogs.

Visitors to the Caspian, including a ranking American embassy official, found the Shah suffering from a mild summer cold and somewhat "down" mentally, but noticed no other visible signs of incapacitation. Senior military leaders who had been seeing the Shah weekly and sometimes daily for years noticed that he was more tired than usual and less aggressive in dealing with matters of state, but they blamed it on his cold and his personally stated need for a real rest.

The other reason the Shah appeared to be indecisive stemmed from the fact that he was beginning to have misgivings about opening up the political system. While he had talked for several years about a transition to a constitutional monarchy (much like Spain had recently become) he was unconvinced that this could occur solely through increased legislative responsibility. Both in 1953 and in 1961–1963, malcontents — including parliamentarians — had effectively interrupted the functioning of the government and come close to causing the Shah's downfall. The monarch and his supporters knew this and feared that if dissidents were allowed to run for parliament, even a few victorious candidates would be enough to block legislative action and disrupt the existing government. The recent crumbling of the Resurgence Party only served to reinforce this fear.

The Opposition Reads the Signals

For the National Front, the various lawyers and writers groups, and other secular organizations the events of July and August were encouraging, but merely a first step. Distrust of the Shah remained deep. No dissidents were willing to cooperate with the government on the basis of the evidence offered thus far. With the Shah vacationing at the Caspian, opposition organizers in Tehran had a field day. Political dialogue revolved around various anti-government solutions, not around the only legal option, the Resurgence Party. During the Shah's sojourn at the Caspian, opposition politicians such as Dr. Nasser Minatchi, director of the Committee for the Defense of Human Rights, National Front Leaders Karim Sanjabi and Dariush Forouhar, and the lawyers Hedayatollah Matin-Daftari and Rahmatollah Moghadam-Maraghei spread their gospels much more openly, drawing more adherents from the heretofore neutral or pro-Shah middle class. Ironically, it was Matin-Daftari, Mossadeq's grandson, who along with Sanjabi continued to urge working within the system in order to institute changes. The others were beginning to talk revolution rather than reform. What was evolving in the Shah's absence was a first-rate political campaign. Each opposition leader promised what he wanted in good electoral style, identifying the issues with popular appeal—corruption, SAVAK brutality, and economic dislocation. The government was under constant attack.

The Liberation Movement and the radical religious activists were even less impressed with what the Shah had done to open up political activity, but they redoubled their organizational efforts. In key provincial towns such as Qom, Mashad, Isfahan, Yazd, Shiraz, Ahwaz, Abadan, and Khorramshahr more direct links were established between various factions of the emerging revolutionary coalition, including putting Mujahidin units into contact with local mullahs and other dissidents.

Moderate religious leaders such as Ayatollah Shariatmadari criticized the regime, but kept their options open. In a broadside issued to the faithful August 14, Shariatmadari blasted the government for attacking religious schools in Mashad and Hamadan and for arresting a leading "political" mullah, Abbas Taheri, in Isfahan on August 1. (This arrest came two days after a bomb went off in the parking lot of the American consulate in Isfahan, amid mounting demonstrations on behalf of religious leaders.) Shariatmadari also condemned "the disastrous and ruthless slaughter of the Moslem people," and proclaimed that the Shiite religious leadership "would continue its rightful and logical campaign until lawful individual and social liberties have been secured, anti-Islamic laws and bills have been abrogated and a just and equitable system has been established in Iran." But there were no cries from him for the overthrow of the Shah. Shariatmadari remained a moderate until the Jaleh Square disaster on September 8. In a major speech just four days before that event he advocated that there be free elections but disavowed any intention to turn the country over to Islamic fundamentalism.[2]

Safe in Iraq, Khomeini called upon his followers "to arm and train" themselves for possible confrontation. In a cassette widely distributed in Tehran in August, he urged continued pressure on the government and insisted on the overthrow of the monarchy in response to the blood shed during nearly a year of riots. Khomeini's strategy as described by a leader in the Liberation Movement was "to build expressions of the popular will, using government violence against the Islamic people to destroy the usurper Shah's legitimacy."[3]

In late July, while the monarch still was vacationing, the religious forces, spearheaded by the Liberation Movement cadres, concentrated their proselytizing and penetrated an organization which normally could be counted on to support the Shah absolutely; the infiltration of the armed forces had begun. Officers and their families were threatened. Parents with sons in the army were urged "to broaden your understanding of your duty to the Moslem peoples of Iran." In any riot situation that should come up from then on, conscripts were urged not to shoot at civilians, especially if they were being led by religious zealots. Propagandizing efforts also concentrated on the social divisions within the armed forces, especially the difference between relatively affluent senior officers and economically less well off junior officers.

Within a month ranking military leaders began hinting of possible trouble because the loyalty of some of the troops was suspect. Renewed violence in Jahrom and Rafsanjan and serious disturbances in Mashad and Isfahan had raised questions about whether enlisted men and draftees would fire on religious demonstrators. Some of the younger troop leaders such as air force General Amir Hossein Rabii and paratroop commander General Manuchehr Khosrowdad advocated that severe military action be taken against the dissidents. Already the army was being pulled two ways. On the one hand, the opposition was urging recruits not to fight. On the other hand the military leaders had been trained to go all out to destroy the dissidents as traitors.

The extensive program to propagandize the military was undertaken because the older mullahs remembered how the army had ended the unrest in 1963 by shooting down the demonstrating mobs. The Liberation Movement agreed that the army, and labor union members and small businessmen as well, should be neutralized or won over. Throughout the summer and fall, the Liberation Movement and the religious dissidents worked together very closely. Their goals were identical: to undermine the Shah through the army and thereby destroy his support.

A Khomeini spokesman spelled out the emerging religious position in an interview published in the Lebanese newspaper *An Nahar* on August 31. He attacked the Shah's land reform program, the country's rapid economic development, and Iran's obsession with Western liberalism. His statement called for the creation of a republican system of government without the monarchy, thereby reorienting Iran's foreign policy and making the country a member of the nonaligned bloc. Other Khomeini supporters, such as Ayatollah Yahya Nouri in Tehran, castigated the Shah for his links with "Zionists." Nouri issued several pamphlets accusing the United States of assisting Zionist imperialism through the sale of Coca-Cola. He claimed that the Tehran franchise was owned by Jewish merchants. (It was not.) Nouri also called upon all Iranians to boycott Coca-Cola, saying to purchase it was "a multilateral contribution to evil."

Beginning with demonstrations in Mashad in July and continuing with troubles in most other cities (except Tehran) through mid-August, SAVAK and the counterterrorist forces would harshly repress riots one day and release their perpetrators the next, reflecting continued indecisive government policy. The arrest of Mullah Taheri in Isfahan and the detention of clerical leaders in Jahrom, however, triggered violent confrontations in both cities, visible evidence that the opposition could react with deadly efficiency when challenged.

Conditions in Isfahan had deteriorated so much by August 11 that a dawn-to-dusk curfew was established, and martial law went into effect 24 hours later. Within two days riots broke out in three satellite towns around Isfahan, and they also were placed under martial law. On August 13 Tehran's Khan Salaar restaurant was bombed. This upper-class eatery catered to Westerners and Westernized Iranians and ten Americans were injured, though none seriously. That same week, in the provincial capital of Khorramabad, the Resurgence Party headquarters was set afire.

The alternating brutal-lenient behavior of the Shah's security forces reinforced rather than destroyed the morale of the opposition. The government's give-and-take strategy failed either to intimidate or to divide the growing dissident movement. Instead, continuing unrest would give opposition leaders practical experience in organizing large numbers of people for parades and mass rallies, training that definitely contributed to the effectiveness of the demonstrations in Tehran in early September, when the Moslem holy month of Ramadan came to an end.

The country was slowly returning to the conditions of semi-anarchy which had prevailed through early June. The opposition resumed the pressure of mass demonstrations that it had withdrawn when direct military confrontation appeared likely. Always, when the armed forces seemed ready to react to provocation, dissidents slowed down their activity, a pattern repeated continuously until the situation would come to a head in early December.

The Abadan Fire Brings Down a Government

What drew the various strands of these political developments together and convinced the Shah he had to change prime ministers was the burning of the Rex Cinema in Abadan. On the evening of August 19 the movie theater, showing a film by a noted Iranian author, was filled with up to 600 people. (Estimates varied considerably, even after several body counts.) Someone set the theater ablaze, killing all those inside but a handful. An official investigation showed the walls had been soaked with gasoline and the fire started with a battery-operated timing device. The one entry and exit door had been locked, and police and fire-fighting equipment were late in arriving. An overwhelming majority of the people inside the burning building died very quickly from suffocation, not from burns. The official number of dead was 377; later this rose to 430.

The opposition claimed the fire had been set by SAVAK to kill Mujahidin members who had fled into the theater. The government story was that Islamic fanatics had started the blaze. Within a few days, ten individuals, five of whom later "confessed" to complicity, were arrested by the Abadan police chief, the same General Reza Razmi who had been in charge in Qom during the riots there on Janurary 9. To add to the confusion, several days later Iraq turned over to the Iranian police a young man they claimed had acknowledged helping start the fire. Events in Iran began to move too swiftly soon thereafter so that a thorough investigation was never completed, though at least one organization, the International League for Human Rights, called for a multinational inquiry.

The facts in the matter were very elusive. The depth of the opposi-

tion's distrust of the Shah and his government was such that many believed the stories of SAVAK complicity. Certainly the official response
was ineffectual. The police station, 300 yards from the theater, had
taken almost an hour to send anyone around to check. Two hours after
the incident was first reported the city fire brigade arrived, and the
more modern fire fighting equipment available through the nearby National Iranian Oil Company refinery was never even requested. To this
day, no one is certain who really started the fire.

The horror of the Abadan tragedy destroyed the last remaining ves-
tiges of the Amouzegar government's credibility. Though the budget
out in mid-August indicated inflation had dropped to 7.9 percent, the
country was in turmoil. The prime minister and his cabinet had practically no popular support. Accordingly, the Shah announced
Amouzegar's resignation August 27 and the appointment of the former
prime minister (in 1961) and then president of the senate, Jaffar Sharif-
Emami, to the prime ministership.

Many date the breakdown of civil government to November 5, when
Sharif-Emami would be replaced by General Gholam Reza Azhari.
However, the visible disintegration of the political apparatus that had
governed Iran for 15 years really began on August 27, when Sharif-
Emami took over. For those seeking stability his appointment, his own
political position, and his cabinet selections all became liabilities rather
than assets.

The Shah turned to Sharif-Emami for essentially the same reason he
had done so in 1961—to conciliate the religious opposition. A politician
who had survived and prospered for two decades, Sharif-Emami was
the son and grandson of prestigious clerics. He had maintained good
contacts with the moderate religious leaders such as Ayatollah Shariatmadari and the leading clergymen in Mashad, Iran's second holiest city.
On the negative side, he was identified in the public mind with the
Shah and his government. More importantly, until his promotion he
had been the executive director of the Pahlavi Foundation, considered
by the opposition to be the principal instrument of corruption in the
royal family. One moderate secular opposition leader put it succinctly a
few days after Sharif-Emami became prime minister. "If you want to
clean out the mess, you don't promote one of the principal culprits.
Sharif-Emami is known to us as the Shah's 'bag man,' a far cry from
our ideas of honest incorruptibility."

In negotiating with the Shah on cabinet appointments, Sharif-Emami
tried to blend the new technocrats and the older loyalist politicians into
one team. If he could have developed a political base of support within

the lower class, both the old and the new elite would have helped the government be more successful. The Shah's promise of free elections, however, had undercut the sense of security within the establishment and called into question the benefits of being a supporter of the monarchy. In the face of the growing dissident challenge, being a cabinet minister was less rewarding and potentially more dangerous. Because Sharif-Emami had no independent base of support within the body politic there was little pressure on the dissidents to come to an accommodation with his government.

The new cabinet gave a no more positive signal to the opposition than it did to the establishment. Though Sharif-Emami tried to appease the fundamentalists by dropping the post of Minister of State for Women's Affairs and elevating the director of the religious endowments organization to a cabinet level position, these were regarded as cosmetic changes. Eight of the twenty-three men in Sharif-Emami's cabinet had strong connections with the Imperial Court, and there was a hodgepodge of personal attachments. Only four were completely loyal to the new prime minister; another two were protégés of Houshang Ansari, a rival for the premiership. Four men were retained from the previous cabinet, but in less important positions. The group did contain substantial new blood—five members of Houshang Nahavandi's "third wing" of the Resurgence Party, including Nahavandi himself. A former Pan Iran Party leader, Mohammad Reza Ameli-Tehrani, and ex-Mardom Party chief Mahmoud Kani were also members. Only four, as opposed to ten in the previous administration, had been educated in the United States. The average age of the new ministers was ten years older than that of their predecessors. Moreover, the cabinet included none of the moderate secular dissidents who might have made it easier to negotiate with the opposition. It is by no means clear that any dissident would have accepted an appointment in the Sharif-Emami cabinet, since all have claimed they would not have done so, though this appears to be the wisdom of hindsight. The new cabinet did adequately represent all factions relevant to the imperial political system, but it could neither coopt nor deal with the emerging forces, especially the religious leadership.

Sharif-Emami's action plan indicated that the Shah was ready to conciliate the opposition. Immediately after his appointment, even before being confirmed by parliament, the prime minister closed the gambling casinos, reinstated the Islamic calendar (replaced for over two years by a Pahlavi dynastic calendar dating back to Cyrus the Great), and pledged a review of legislative acts to ascertain whether they met Islamic standards. At the same time the Shah attempted once again to induce the opposition to participate in his political system. He improved press freedom by informally passing the word to SAVAK to ease censorship regulations. For the first time the monarch called upon parliament to enact specific laws guaranteeing freedom of speech and assembly.[4] Even more important was the fact that the monarch withdrew official support from the Resurgence Party by ending its status as Iran's only legal political organization. To reinforce the Shah's announcement, Sharif-Emami announced that he himself was no longer a member of the Resurgence Party and that his government would not be bound by party discipline.

Showdown at Jaleh Square

The changes in the government's attitude ushered in what came to be known as "Tehran Summer," the most free period in Persian political life since the early 1960s. Long-censored magazines reappeared and parliamentary debates were open to the public and even broadcast over the radio. The governor of Khorasan province, Abdul Aziz Valian, accused of brutally repressing the riots in Mashad in May, was replaced August 28. Several other security officials were publicly dismissed, including 33 SAVAK officers, some of senior rank. Unfortunately, these conciliatory concessions were very much one-sided. There was no effort made to coopt the opposition, and no quid pro quo demanded. So Khomeini repeated his call to the people to overthrow the monarchy. The Liberation Movement, religious groups, and bazaar merchants continued to demonstrate.

Then in early September, the opposition challenged the government directly. The clergy announced a march on September 4 to celebrate the end of Ramadan, the Moslem month of fasting. The government refused to issue parade permits. Opposition factions collaborated to organize demonstrations anyway in all cities and towns of any size. In Tehran over 100,000 people gathered on September 4 and probably 150,000 the following day. The government let the unauthorized marches pass. Religious leaders told the assembled demonstrators that they should keep up the pressure until the constitution of 1906 was strictly enforced, political prisoners were released, corruption ended, and free elections scheduled.

These parade manifestos were the first public calls for government action made at planned demonstrations. They reflected the collective belief of opposition leaders that the Shah's new government was weak, not strong. This estimate encouraged them to escalate their demands to new levels, especially when the government made no attempt to block the marches. The now visible capacity of the religious movement and its secular allies to organize huge demonstrations dismayed the security forces who had been ordered to let the parades take place and to refrain from confrontation.

Sources inside the government said the Shah hoped the upheavals marking the end of Ramadan would subside once religious fervor was spent. It did not happen. Anti-government rallies continued. An Imperial Guard officer had been killed in Tehran on September 3, and seven demonstrators died in Isfahan on September 5. On September 5 the government announced the appointment of new chancellors for Iran's universities, but student groups still threatened revolts. The reopening of the country's universities already had been postponed from August 31 to mid-September, and now it was pushed back to October. On September 6 a bus carrying British civilians was attacked; two passengers were injured. U.S. citizens reported steadily increasing anti-American signs and telephone calls, particularly near the Tajrish section of north Tehran, where two radical clergymen operated out of two flourishing mosques. In a broadside, Ayatollah Shariatmadari asserted that the government had three months to get its house in order and to return to strict adherence to the 1906 constitution. He also asked for the formation of a government "which enjoys the confidence of the Iranian people." Continuing the pressure, the opposition leadership called for a general strike. Many shops closed on September 7. Approximately 7,000 people marched in Tehran's Sepah Square, carrying such slogans as "Monarchy In An Islamic Country Is Nonsense" and "We Will Continue Our Crusade Under Khomeini's Banner."

Faced with a deteriorating situation, Prime Minister Sharif-Emami, with the approval of the Shah, declared martial law in 12 additional cities besides Isfahan: Tehran, Qom, Tabriz, Mashad, Shiraz, Ahwaz, Abadan, Qazvin, Karaj, Kazerun, Jahrom, and Khorramshahr. Ranking military officers had been divided for some time on the wisdom of harsh retaliation against marches by dissidents, but in the wake of increasing anarchy they became convinced that the imposition of martial law was the only way to restore order and to provide time for a political solution to work. Thus a martial law administration was established in each city, headed by senior military officers. It paralleled the civilian government but took over control of the police and the responsibility for maintaining order. A curfew was instituted in each city, usually 9:00 P.M. to 5:00 A.M. Gatherings of more than three persons were prohibited without permission from the martial law administrator for the area. Army units helped police enforce these new rules.[5]

The imposition of martial law was promulgated late in the evening and not fully publicized until the following morning at 6:30, when approximately 20,000 people gathered at Jaleh Square in south Tehran to hear religious leaders. The previous evening a serious debate had raged between the radical and the moderate opposition. Remembering the violence in 1963, Mehdi Bazargan, leader of the Liberation Movement, wanted to reduce the level of the confrontation with the government. He and other moderates feared mass killings by the military if a direct challenge to protest martial law was made the next day. The National Front Leadership did not want confrontation either, but for the first time radical religious leaders—Ayatollahs Mohammad Beheshti, Morteza Motahari, Mohammad Mahdavi-Kani, and Hojatollah Hashemi Rafsanjani—successfully urged over the objection of the others that the confrontation go forward. Buoyed by their success with the Ramadan marches on September 4 and 5, they claimed a mandate from Khomeini to press on.

Friday, September 8, at 7:30 in the morning—following this debate among the dissidents and after an hour of heated argument between government forces and the assembled protesters—the army commander present ordered the crowds to disperse. They refused to do so. The army units at Jaleh Square let loose with several volleys, killing around 100 people in the initial fusillade. By some accounts Mujahidin interspersed among the demonstrators returned the fire. More military units entered the fray; eyewitnesses confirmed that there was shooting from helicopter gunships. The crowd fled, spreading down the side streets and burning banks, stores, and government buildings in their wake. Troops played cat-and-mouse with demonstrators all day, shooting to kill when groups appeared on the south Tehran streets to chant or burn buildings. Gunfire continued sporadically until nightfall, and prudent residents within a mile of Jaleh Square, including approximately 2,000 foreigners, remained under cover.

That evening, after the 9 o'clock curfew, many opposition leaders were taken into custody, including the Liberation Movement's Mehdi Bazargan, several ayatollahs, and moderate lawyer Hedayatollah Matin-Daftari. All were released within two hours. As for the National Front, SAVAK officers who carried out the arrests were directed not to take their leaders into custody because they had not publicly supported the call to demonstrate in violation of martial law.

Casualties began pouring into the three hospitals in the area almost immediately after the confrontation at Jaleh Square began. Medical sources estimated between 200 and 400 dead. Initially the government claimed 58 deaths, but within a week increased this to 122, plus 2,000 to 3,000 wounded. By midday, September 8, opposition figures were set at 400 to 500, but rose to about 1,000 within 24 hours. Other reports mentioned 4,500 bodies; some charged that up to 20,000 people had been killed.

The claims of the radicals were based on their calculations; the government assertions of 122 dead ostensibly came from police figures. Dissidents had taken control of Tehran's Behesht-e-Zara cemetery, the only official burial ground, so there was considerable tampering with the grave registration figures on both sides. Doctors who worked around the clock for 36 hours believe estimates of 300 to 400 dead are reasonable, with another 3,000 to 4,000 treated for injuries in hospitals and makeshift first-aid stations.

The establishment of martial law and the shootings at Jaleh Square had a momentous impact and drastically changed the political landscape in Tehran. The opposition immediately and effectively claimed a massacre and castigated Prime Minister Sharif-Emami for his significant role in the decision to impose military control. His fledgling administration became a hostage to the effectiveness of the military governors and received the blame for their failure to restore order. The Jaleh Square killings were blamed directly on the Shah and the government, and opposition supporters quickly and forcefully spread the dissident view abroad. Liberation Movement and National Front leaders urged their supporters in Washington to take their case directly to the Department of State and the National Security Council. In the U.S., officials of both organizations were pressed by representatives of the dissidents to disavow the Shah.

When word of the telephone calls to the Shah offering support—one from President Carter and the other from National Security Advisor Zbigniew Brzezinski—surfaced in Tehran on September 9 and 10, the religious opposition labeled the United States "an aggressor against the people" along with the Shah. The radical clerics, the Mujahidin, and the left considered the Carter and Brzezinski calls as reconfirmation of their deeply embedded, negative suspicions of anything the U.S. might do, even if it were only to send routine holiday greetings to the government. Far more ominous, however, was the fact that for the first time moderate dissidents—Nasser Minatchi, Mehdi Bazargan, and Karim Sanjabi—began warning their foreign contacts in Tehran that in their view the Jaleh Square events meant their monarch had to go. If the

U.S. continued to stand by the Shah, "America would be tarred with the same brush."

Two days after what the opposition would call the "Black Friday Massacre," a White House statement "reaffirmed the close and friendly relations between Iran and the United States and the importance of Iran's continued alliance with the West." It also "expressed the hope that the movement toward political liberalization would continue within Iran." Privately, Brzezinski had advised the Shah to "do what you have to do" to restore order. The monarch pondered his next move, though Sharif-Emami and his government—but not the Shah—made no secret of the fact that they believed more concessions were necessary.

The public was appalled at the carnage on September 8 and was very anxious to have order restored. Though people were divided as to what measures—conciliatory or coercive—would be appropriate, the advent of a new government, followed so quickly by the imposition of martial law and then a major incident, politicized many who thus far had been only marginally concerned about the mounting violence within Iran. These were the shopkeepers, professional men, and laborers. At first the sense of concern brought needed support for the government, but at the same time it also pushed more of the increasingly affected middle class into sympathy with revolutionary goals. As for the opposition, "Black Friday" hardened its attitudes irrevocably.

Chapter Seven

★

The Shah Vacillates;
The Opposition Mobilizes

September–November 1978

After martial law was imposed in 12 cities on September 7 and the carnage wrought at Jaleh Square on September 8, the political situation deteriorated steadily, with only occasional slight respites. A rash of strikes developed into an epidemic. By mid-October, picketing in the streets had become a way of life; even tourists watched the demonstrations. Though martial law troops often were confronted by gangs of dissidents, the situation was inconvenient but rarely dangerous. On orders from the Shah, the government forces could fire only into the air. Totally frustrated, the military leadership argued among themselves whether or not to countermand the instructions on their own initiative and direct their men to shoot to kill. Meanwhile, downtown businessmen leaving their offices for lunch frequently selected their restaurants according to where the least amount of sporadic gunfire was coming from.

Prime Minister Sharif-Emami pushed hard to get the country on an even keel, attempting to work out a compromise with the opposition and end the strikes. It would prove to be an impossible task. The fundamentalist clergy concluded out of hand that it could not participate in any arrangements backed by the perpetrators of the "massacre" at Jaleh Square. The Ayatollah's coterie became increasingly strident about rejecting any compromise with the Shah and renewed its calls to the people to assist them in replacing the monarchy with an Islamic republic. By November all opposition groups, both religious and secular, were unified for the first time behind Khomeini's no-compromise position.

119

Through it all, the Shah's attitude became increasingly detached from reality and more indecisive. The three-way internal tug-of-war among the Sharif-Emami cabinet, the monarch, and the military leadership concerning how to reverse the disintegration and to minimize fundamentalist religious influence confused an atmosphere already fraught with decaying economic and security conditions.

On November 5 a combination of opposition pressure and intra-government conflict produced by far the worst riots yet in Tehran. Crowds roamed the streets, torching buildings; overturned cars were also set ablaze. Schoolchildren went home through howling mobs. Bus drivers with blond, obviously foreign-born children in their care directed them to lie quietly on the floor and would themselves shout "Long Live Khomeini" out their windows in order to get through the swirling multitudes safely.

The anarchy and tremendous destruction of that day forced the Shah to change the government for the second time in less than three months. In an effort to cow the demonstrators, a general was appointed prime minister. However, Gholam Reza Azhari's cabinet consisted mostly of civilians. Within a week the opposition discovered that following established policy, the Shah forbade the "military" government to allow the army to shoot at the demonstrators. Therefore, since it still was not dangerous to do so, the dissidents became ever more militant, boldly taunting the troops trying to suppress the demonstrations. Meanwhile, in intense under-the-table discussions, the Shah and many elder statesmen tried desperately to coax the opposition into participating in the existing political system. Throughout it all, U.S. support for the monarch remained firm, though the presence of so many foreigners in the country had become a major issue for the opposition. The dissidents began threatening Americans, insisting they leave Iran immediately.

Another Weak Riposte:
The Establishment Reacts Indecisively

Even after the Jaleh Square disaster, Sharif-Emami and his cabinet remained committed to taking conciliatory steps to meet the demands of the more moderate opposition. This became easier to do because direct confrontation between the government and the opposition ceased for several weeks. As before, the press and media remained free and parliamentary debates continued to be broadcast over the radio, but the price was unremitting criticism of the Shah and the governments, past and present, which had supported him. The first new move to pacify the dissidents occurred about ten days after Jaleh Square, when three former ministers were arrested on charges of corruption: Mansur Rouhani (Agriculture), Fereidoun Mahdavi (Commerce), and Shojaeddin Sheikholeslamsadeh (Health). Far from placating the opposition, it merely whetted the appetites of the dissidents while unnerving other former officials.

Further hemorhaging of government authority occurred the third week in September when wildcat strikes erupted in both private business and state-owned companies. The first two unions to break ranks, a factory group in Tehran and hospital workers in Tehran and other cities, received wage settlements "negotiated" by the government which granted between 25 and 30 percent pay increases. By October 1 members of approximately 80 unions had walked off their jobs in defiance of labor laws prohibiting strikes. Included were factory workers, post office personnel, civil servants, bank clerks, shopkeepers, transportation employees, and oil workers. Within two weeks every labor organization with any kind of grievance was talking strike. Many unions simply stopped working, further hampering the country's faltering economy.

Politically, the strikes were a disaster for Sharif-Emami. After Jaleh Square, at first the opposition was fearful that martial law would be vigorously enforced. Instead, employees off their jobs began getting immediate hefty settlements. Moreover, while strikes were illegal, there was no provision in law for withholding pay from rebellious workers. Thus, for example, when Iran Air pilots or the Central Bank tellers refused to show up, they continued to be paid. There were many acrimonious debates within the government, but Sharif-Emami's cabinet, fearful of even more disorder, never withheld salaries and pressured industrial management to continue paying private sector employees. There was no penalty for walking off the job, but there were substantial rewards. The man on the street regarded the strikes as paid holidays. Throughout most of September and all of October work discipline gradually disappeared completely in the cities.[1]

Initially strikers wanted economic gains, but after achieving whopping financial settlements so easily, workers frequently walked off their jobs a second time for political reasons. They would demand that the constitution of 1906 be strictly adhered to, free elections be held immediately, or all political prisoners be freed. By making strikes retribution-free, the government allowed the opposition, particularly the National Front and the Liberation Movement, to press beyond mere economic demands and to politicize the workers to support their aims.

Very quickly organized labor began advocating the same major themes countrywide: that corrupt government officials be punished, martial law be terminated, all political prisoners be freed, SAVAK be dismantled, and full political liberty, including free elections, be instituted immediately. Quite clearly the opposition had defined the major political issues in ways favorable to its prospects, leaving the Sharif-Emami government to cope with increasing disorder and the Shah to seek conciliation. This opposition strategy was effective because the government was so inept, flailing around in its search for a way to alleviate the continuing unrest.

Clashes between the opposition and the army, police, and SAVAK continued. Now demonstrations were increasingly revolutionary in tone rather than expressions of dissatisfaction with a specific issue, such as SAVAK brutality. Rioting had broken out again in several cities by September 20. The bazaars in most cities began closing down, sometimes for days at a time, under pressure from the fundamentalist clergy. On October 10 severe violence marred confrontations in Arak, Ahwaz, and the oil town of Masjed-e-Sulieman. Nine days later the army challenged demonstrators in Mashad; several dissidents were killed or wounded. By October 25 vicious incidents were occurring in Isfahan, and Jewish and Bahai leaders urged their followers to leave that city. Four days later, in Amol, university students joined with town merchants in setting up patrols to prevent SAVAK "provocations." Some of the security officials were arrested by the vigilantes and turned over to local authorities who locked them up. Ordinary citizens stood by, neither helping nor hindering those taking over the city. The army would move into the town three days later, crushing the incipient insurrection. Similar events where the townspeople usurped authority and the army was ordered to regain control occurred that same week in Qazvin, Karaj, and Babol, provoking dissidents of every description into forcing further confrontation.

The martial law administration found itself bound up by the same kind of ambiguous instructions that had hamstrung previous efforts toward effective coercion. Moreover, though the government was taking a conciliatory line politically by arresting corrupt former officials, allowing a wide-open press, and permitting freewheeling political activity, the opposition was responding by continually challenging the army's authority in the streets. Though it had been the Shah himself who had directed the army not to antagonize the demonstrators and who enforced the instructions against indiscriminate shooting, as the disruptive gatherings became more threatening to officers and men, the military shot anyway.

The fine line the Shah was trying to draw between acceptable use of force and unnecessary violence was lost on those who were being attacked. As a result, the administration of martial law was uneven and spotty. In some cities, such as Khorramshahr and Kazerun, the martial law commanders and the opposition worked out truces which allowed some dissident activity to continue as long as there was no violence. These kinds of "accommodations" became more common as conditions deteriorated, especially when the dissidents knew that challenging the army directly would be foolhardy. But in other cities, such as Qazvin, Mashad, and Tabriz, military commanders disobeyed their superiors in Tehran and ordered their men to shoot to kill in self-defense.

An important side effect of the increasing challenge to martial law was continuing and accelerating politicization of the army. Troops, especially recruits, were now more exposed to the mobs. Both regular and noncommissioned officers found themselves involved with political matters. They issued demonstration permits and dealt with the delicate problem of press censorship, particularly in Tehran. The new freedom allowed the media encouraged intense criticism of the government and the Shah, but when the press began to touch on a subject as sensitive as the loyalty of the army, the authorities took over. On October 11 the chief of the martial law administration in Tehran, General Gholam Ali Oveissi, directed material of this nature to be withheld from the newspapers for the following day. Pro-opposition journalists used the opportunity to rally media support for their challenge to censorship. The newspapermen went on strike and the publication of Tehran's five major Persian and foreign language papers stopped. However, Sharif-Emami supported press demands for freedom, and a compromise was worked out with General Oveissi. The constant tension between the Sharif-Emami government and the martial law administration over such issues frustrated both groups; by late October senior military leaders had no confidence in the prime minister.

There were moderately successful pro-government demonstrations in 17 different towns on October 29. Unfortunately, those in Sanandaj, Rezayieh, Gorgon, Kashan, and Hamadan were attacked by opposition cadres. The establishment, obviously, was aghast at the ease with which the Iranian political structure was coming apart. Both public and private initiatives to resolve the impasse proliferated. When Abdollah Riazi, the octogenarian leader of the Majlis, declined to stand for reelection, it gave the government another opportunity to maneuver. Riazi was replaced on October 8 by Javad Saeed, a deputy speaker. Saeed was much more flexible and began to meet regularly with various parliamentary groups, hoping to find some constructive role the Majles could play to settle the crisis. Another establishment figure, former Prime Minister (1961–1962) Ali Amini also played the broker, shuttling between the various political factions to try to piece together a solution to the conflict which would be acceptable to the moderate religious opposition without requiring the Shah's abdication.

Simultaneously, throughout September and October, the Shah was secretly attempting to work out a satisfactory agreement that would bring more moderate members of the opposition into some kind of relationship with the government. He offered groups which had not yet fully disavowed the monarchy, including the National Front and the Liberation Movement, a chance to participate legally, hoping to disrupt Khomeini's growing influence. The Shah's suggestions even included an offer to allow the dissidents to form an opposition cabinet—as long as it was done under the monarch's mandate. These were not major, public initiatives, but private explorations by trusted court officials that could easily be disavowed if word leaked out. At first the dissidents did not believe any of these overtures because of their discreet nature. By late October it made slight difference anyway, since opposition leaders knew they could not compromise. If they disobeyed Khomeini's demand that the "illegal" Shah had to go, they would lose their own influence.

The Ayatollah's absolute intransigence against dealing with the monarch convinced loyalists that something dramatic had to be done. About mid-September a successful plea was made to the government of Iraq to expel Khomeini. The Ayatollah had been living in Najaf for 14 years. On September 23 the police surrounded his home and forbade anyone not of Khomeini's immediate family to enter. Eight days later the Iraqi government formally asked the Ayatollah to leave the country. He went first to Kuwait, where he was refused entry, and then, on October 6, to Paris. The French government admitted Khomeini as a political refugee, but admonished him not to engage in political activity. Should the "Shadow of God" be expected to obey a mere French foreign ministry official? The Ayatollah did what he pleased.

Apparently the Shah's original intention was to have the Ayatollah expelled to Turkey or some other similar country where he would no longer have the Shiite base of support like he did in Iraq. What the monarch got instead was Khomeini's move to Paris, where the Ayatollah quickly became the center of Western media attention, with access to far better communications than he ever had in Najaf. The Shah had correctly identified Khomeini as the principal challenger to himself and his regime, but the monarch's proposed solution merely compounded his problem. Though it is hard to believe now, reliable sources from three different countries have said that the Shah refused to approve assassination attempts on Khomeini's life. At least three intelligence services (including SAVAK, but not the C.I.A.) were pressing him to have the Ayatollah killed. All argued that political compromise might be possible if the immutable Khomeini were removed; surely it would not be otherwise. As for the Shah's closest advisors, they were divided on the question of what to do about the Ayatollah. Some thought Khomeini's assassination would be the ideal solution. Others reasoned that the Shah would be blamed for the Ayatollah's death no matter how it occurred, but that if a murder were linked to the throne, religious opposition would be twice as difficult to control. Iran could explode overnight into bloodshed.[2]

It is a sign of the Shah's lack of will that strong measures to stop the opposition cold—the arrest and internment of all identifiable dissident leaders and a shoot-to-kill policy for curfew and martial law violators—never were given strong consideration. The monarch's desultory attitude had its roots in his increasingly fatalistic view of politics coupled with the disorientation caused by the medication he was taking for his serious (and as yet undisclosed) illness. Court officials knew the Shah was incensed by his countrymen's "ingratitude," but instead of making him more willing to clamp down (as it might have a year earlier), it reinforced the monarch's lethargy. Unlike 1963, the monarch in 1978 simply was not capable of cold-blooded repressive violence.[3] In any case, not until his forced departure did the monarch realize that the mystical "Shah-people" relationship in which he so fervently believed could be destroyed by the political activity of others.

By mid-September authority had deteriorated so much that even many Iranians who had always supported the Shah were beginning to question whether their ruler was as shrewd a politician as his historical reputation suggested. The first to be disillusioned were many in the inner circle. Amir Abbas Hoveyda quietly resigned as court minister just before the Jaleh Square incident. He, as well as former Prime Minister Jamshid Amouzegar and former Finance Minister Houshang Ansari, had become disenchanted primarily because of the Shah's lack of firm leadership in August, when Sharif-Emami took over.

In an effort to pacify the opposition, the monarch speeded up the demoralization of his secret service by dismissing 33 senior SAVAK officers in September. Most of those sacked were from the domestic intelligence section, including its chief, the much-feared Parviz Sabeti.

(Sabeti fled immediately, and now lives in California.) In October the Shah ordered the previous head of SAVAK, Nematollah Nassiri, to leave his job as ambassador to Pakistan and return to Iran. This made the entire organization nervous—with good cause. A month later Nassiri would be formally charged with having tortured SAVAK suspects for years.

For obvious reasons the establishment elite did not feel the Shah was loyally backing those who had served him well. The arrests of senior officials, the gutting of SAVAK, and Sharif-Emami's failure to stop the strikes greatly increased political tension. Even so, as late as October a majority of Iranians supported the Shah, but wanted his wings clipped to the limits of the constitution of 1906. Only the fundamentalist Islamic revolutionaries, growing in strength weekly, already were calling for his demise. But as the government continued to act ineffectively, public opinion began to shift, though not dramatically until massive, sustained civil disorder on November 5 laid waste large parts of Tehran.

The Opposition Consolidates

The two months preceding November 5 were critical for the opposition. After Jaleh Square, the various dissident organizations redoubled their efforts to win adherents to the revolutionary movement, a job made easier because of the disarray within the establishment. Certainly the continuing disintegration of the Resurgence Party did not help the cause of the loyalists. It fell apart completely after Sharif-Emami said that he would no longer be a member and that the party would have no official status. The Resurgence Party announced its dissolution September 30. The breakup was so complete that only 26 of the quorum of 28 executive board members could be mustered to ratify the division of party property. Politics was fractionalizing. By the end of October there were 17 "major" political groups and 103 announced political parties. Many of them would survive the revolution, devoid of influence but supported by a few followers.

With the demise of the Resurgence Party, Shah supporters were left with no formal political structure to help them mobilize support for the monarchy. Party leaders either melted into the general political chaos in Tehran or returned to their hometowns. Many discovered for the first time just how great was the challenge confronting the governing elite when they faced well-organized opposition threats to loyalist control in the areas where they had always before been in charge of the political process themselves—places like Yazd and Mashad. There was no establishment counterweight to the growing effectiveness of the constantly expanding revolutionary coalition. This was particularly true in urban centers where the Liberation Movement, the Fedayeen, and the Mujahidin propagandized striking workers and migrants from the hinterland. The National Front, meanwhile, concentrated on influencing members of the middle class to defect. For the first time, the opposition was becoming a really effective political force in the streets.

Not only were the various secular organizations convincing others to join their cause, but the religious fundamentalists were plotting as well. On September 9 Khomeini's allies issued a bulletin from the seminary in Qom, announcing that martial law was illegal and that the Shah had resorted to it "in order to kill the people." The statement, read in mosques throughout the country, claimed over 1,000 people had been killed at Jaleh Square, "leaving a bloodstain on the so-called national reconciliation government." On tapes and in broadsides Khomeini exhorted the military "to join your brethren who left the Shah to support the people and attack their enemies. . . . Do not let your country be destroyed and your brothers and sisters be killed."

Throughout September messengers constantly passed between Qom and Najaf as Khomeini tried to convince senior clerics in Iran to defy martial law. Ayatollahs Kazem Shariatmadari, Mohammad Reza Golpaygani, Shahab Marieshi, and Abdollah Shirazi feared extensive bloodshed, and resisted. Instead, they moved toward confrontation by degrees. On September 17 Shariatmadari said the religious leadership could not negotiate with the Shah. One week later he issued a broadside stating that it was unacceptable to cooperate with Sharif-Emami's civil administrators as well as officers enforcing martial law "due to the bloodshed perpetrated by the government." In a public statement shortly thereafter, he reiterated the fact that he would automatically reject any Shah-sponsored compromise. However, he never went so far as to advocate shootouts against the military men charged with compelling the populace to obey martial law.

Meanwhile, Khomeini was becoming more obstinate and more defiant. On September 23 he issued a statement from Najaf that said, "U.S. and Soviet agents should be killed if they try to intervene." As the Iraqis began pressuring him to leave, Khomeini was outspokenly hostile to the U.S., and for the first time his taped messages used the phrase "satanic" to describe the United States. The Ayatollah's move to Paris gave him access to Western media and made him an instant, if unusual, celebrity. More importantly, the change in venue brought to prominence revolutionary aides who would become important later—

Ibrahim Yazdi, Sadeq Ghotbzadeh, and Abol Hassan Bani-Sadr. All three acted as spokesmen for Khomeini, part of the inner circle in Paris. They also handled communications with Tehran, largely through phone calls to Ayatollahs Mohammad Behesti, Mahdavi-Kani, and Hojatollah Moussavi Khoeni; Liberation Movement leaders Mehdi Bazargan, Yadollah Sahabi, and Amir Entezam; and activists close to Ayatollah Shariatmadari.

The organizational importance of Khomeini's shift to Paris cannot be overstated. Although he had been prominent in the opposition movement since 1963, his arrival in Europe elevated him above all others as a spokesman for the dissidents now become revolutionaries. Moreover, even as clandestine efforts to work out a compromise between the Shah and the opposition proceeded, Khomeini's obstinate resolve not to negotiate an agreement under any circumstances set the tone of revolutionary activity. On October 19 the Ayatollah urged the overthrow of the Shah, through civil war if necessary, and the establishment of an Islamic republic. He repeated his demands on October 30, exhorting the opposition to intensify the campaign against the monarchy, "even at the price of bloodshed."

The Liberation Movement and the National Front were not quite so eager to take such a confrontational position, though they never publicly disavowed Khomeini's statements. In September the Liberation Movement outlined rough plans for a transitional government that included the establishment of a regency council to rule in the absence of the Shah, as provided for in the constitution of 1906. A month later it contacted the U.S. embassy to propose the idea of an "engineered" transitional regime. It was clear from the initial discussions that the Liberation Movement believed no national government could be formed without Khomeini's approval and that the Ayatollah would accept nothing short of arrangements that included the departure of the monarch, preferably sooner rather than later. According to Liberation Movement projections, the United States would act as the midwife, hopefully guaranteeing that there would be no harsh military reaction. Such a scenario was justified, it thought, because of the growing tendency of the dissidents to favor drastic action. "For two years we have tried to keep nationalist activity non-violent. Events are now reaching a certain point where the masses are leaving us for violent activity."[4]

This approach—a transition from the Shah to a new regime helped along by the United States—would remain the Liberation Movement's basic thesis until after the successful revolutionary takeover four months later. It represented an exaggerated sense of what the U.S. could accomplish as well as the assumption that the Shah would do what the

Carter administration told him to do. It stands in interesting contrast to the growing hostility toward the United States as expressed by the Ayatollah and the religious fundamentalists. Khomeini's anti-American statements contradicted Liberation Movement arguments that by abandoning the Shah the United States could achieve its long-range goals of consistent stability in the Persian Gulf area and continued access to Iranian oil and trade markets. The Liberation Movement did not consider a religious anti-American form of government and continued ties to the West incompatible. It was an unrealistic plan, an appeal deliberately designed for Western ears. Washington never reacted to the idea, even though Ambassador Sullivan prodded the State Department at least to acknowledge the suggestion.

Philosophic divisions representing vast differences of opinion within the opposition would emerge after the revolutionary takeover. At this point, however, the Liberation Movement clearly saw itself as the vanguard of the coalition. For two or three months after the revolutionary victory, it continued to believe it would be the principal interpreter of Khomeini's wishes in ways compatible with the liberal democratic views of Bazargan and Sahabi. Only gradually would they come to realize it was not to be.

The National Front was a more reluctant partner in the opposition coalition and did not definitely exclude the possibility of working within the system until Karim Sanjabi, Mehdi Bazargan, and Nasser Minatchi went to Paris the last week in October. They planned to persuade Khomeini to allow them to cooperate with the Shah and form a government advancing revolutionary objectives, but within the framework of monarchical legitimacy. Under pressure in Paris, their leader, Sanjabi, eventually was forced to agree to a statement rejecting compromise with the Shah. Just two days earlier, in Tehran, Dariush Forouhar had stated in the press that the National Front wanted a referendum on the monarchy. Now the aging Sanjabi had lined up the National Front with Khomeini to insist the Shah had to go. This move upset many of the organization, specifically Shapour Bakhtiar, who had consistently rejected the fundamentalist religious view of an Islamic republic. Sanjabi also was not happy to have been maneuvered into a corner, but he realized that in the turmoil of the autumn Khomeini had emerged as the most significant leader of the opposition. The Ayatollah's henchmen controlled the mobs in Iran; now the coalition leadership was dependent on an alliance with his clerics. The moderate secular dissidents began to fear that the end of the revolutionary process would be a state ruled by Islamic fundamentalists.

Sanjabi's statement from Paris on November 3 that he would not cooperate in a Shah-appointed government foreclosed the possibility of serious compromise with the opposition, including any possibility that the monarch might be able to form a government drawn from respected moderates or prominent nonpolitical citizens. When the National Front accepted Khomeini's leadership the coalition cemented itself to the radical aims of the fundamentalist religious revolutionaries. Now all the dissidents were united under one banner, that of the Islamic movement.[5]

Things Fall Apart

The political situation came to a head early in November. For the previous six weeks, the Shah had been steadily releasing political prisoners. A total of approximately 1,000 were liberated throughout October. More were set free in November, including Tehran's Ayatollah Taleqani, who had been in jail for 15 months. Many of the former prisoners had been Tudeh Party organizers and they immediately linked up with dissident organizations. One result was new impetus to the round of "political" labor strikes. Tehran's newspapers ceased publishing for the second time on October 11. The first of what would become nightly power outages in Tehran began October 16; customs officials walked out a few days later. All the work stoppages were in support of political, not economic, goals that included allowing Khomeini to return to Iran.

The catalyst that would herald the final collapse of the government was the attempt, after several false starts, to open the universities on November 4. Immediately all opposition groups operating on the Tehran University campus—ranging in diversity from the Mujahidin on the right to the Tudeh Party on the left—decided to unite and challenge the security forces on November 3 and 4. On the second day, egged on by professors who had been attacked when their own sit-in had been forcibly broken up less than a week earlier, students tried to topple the 15-foot statue of the Shah near the University. There was shooting. Ten to 12 students were killed and scores were wounded.

Sharif-Emami wanted to discipline the officers and the troops involved. For the military, overworked and underappreciated by the civilian administration, this was the last straw. Unbeknownst to the prime minister, ranking senior officers withdrew their forces and directed them not to interfere in any way with further demonstrations. The next day, November 5, a mob composed of university students, bazaar crowds, and high school pupils mobilized by the teachers' union (which had begun organizing its students October 11) broke out of its Tehran

University stronghold around 9:00 A.M. Because it met no resistance, burning and looting spread almost immediately to all parts of the city, but particularly in south and central Tehran. In a coordinated effort, scores of armed guerrillas attacked 17 police stations, overrunning and capturing two of them. Two of the groups were later identified as Fedayeen; the rest were Mujahidin units. All airline offices except Air France (because Khomeini was living in suburban Paris) were trashed or destroyed. Over 80 banks were broken into, looted, and set afire. Shops that hinted of modernization, particularly those downtown, had their windows smashed and machinery broken up and then were set ablaze. Beauty parlors, liquor stores, office equipment showrooms—all felt the blow. The fire set at the huge B.M.W. dealership on the first floor of an office building one block from the American embassy became so hot from burning gas and oil that the steel girders melted, telescoping five floors into one. The Ministry of Information five blocks from Tehran University was totally destroyed, and several other government buildings were damaged. Prudent citizens retreated into their homes, leaving the streets to the mobs. Committed revolutionaries and the agitated crowds were not totally to blame for the devastation, however— SAVAK detachments, settling old scores with known antagonists, contributed to the destruction and disorder that day.

In an ominous foreshadowing of events to come months later, the British embassy was occupied about noon. First, Iranian troops who had guarded the main gate during the two previous days of rioting just disappeared. Then a Mujahidin unit walked into the large compound on Ferdowsi street and ordered all personnel to leave the chancery immediately. The intruders vandalized the two lower floors, destroying most of the communications equipment, breaking windows, and throwing furniture around. As the invaders withdrew in the late afternoon, after setting the building on fire, they harangued the diplomats and staff watching the violation of their embassy not to interfere with the impending revolution. The troops charged with protecting the embassy reappeared that evening and resumed their duties.

Although the British were convinced the Mujahidin had intended to destroy the building, only the first two of the four stories were fire damaged. Within two days the offices on the second floor were reoccupied by the diplomats and their staff. Within a week the first floor, though badly battered, was back in use as a reception area. Naturally the British protested the incident. They received a standard apology from the government plus an offer to pay the more than $300,000 worth of damages.

Throughout the night of November 5 the Shah met with the entire spectrum of political figures still loyal to the monarchy in varying degrees. The ranking military officers were split into hard-liners—those who would annihilate the opposition—and conciliators. The opinions of other advisors were divided as well. Ex-politicians such as Ali Amini and Gholam Hossein Sadiqi favored a conciliatory approach to the secular dissidents, but they were more ambivalent about what to do with Khomeini. Parliamentarians had similarly diverse attitudes, some urging a tough stance against the religious faction, others favoring conciliation. Although immediate decisive action was mandatory if he were to save his throne, in the face of conflicting suggestions the Shah continued to resist the advice of those who sought a drastic military response. He was determined not to use force.

The British and American ambassadors were called to Niavaran Palace that evening and informed by the monarch that he intended to restore order by establishing a military government. Both Sullivan and Sir Anthony Parsons supported the decision. However, everyone who talked with the Shah the night of November 5 into the morning of November 6—military or civilian, Iranian or foreign—left his presence with qualms of uneasiness. At the very moment when his future as the leader of his country teetered in the balance, the monarch appeared dispirited and listless.

The military government established at Niavaran Palace in the early morning of November 6 was military in name only. Though the prime minister replacing Sharif-Emami, General Gholam Reza Azhari, had been chief of the supreme commander's staff, 5 men in the streamlined cabinet of 11 were civilians. The ministers replaced by military men remained as deputy ministers in order to supervise their former areas of responsibility. Displaying the wiliness even then that would stand him in good stead later, General Abbas Gharabaghi, the Minister of the Interior, was the only officer to actually control his subordinates.

When he presented his military government on nationwide television at midday on November 6, the Shah's speech was remarkably self-effacing. It was a serious attempt, albeit a very belated one, to align himself with the forces of change. Referring to himself as "padeshah" or "king" rather than "shahanshah" or "king of kings," he said, "Your revolutionary message has been heard," then admitted he had failed to persuade the opposition to form a civilian administration. He described the military regime as a "temporary measure." The Shah pledged that the Azhari government would vigorously prosecute the corrupt, continue the development of an open political atmosphere, and reestablish social justice.

Two days later, former Prime Minister (for 14 years) and ex-Court Minister (for one year) Hoveyda and 14 other major figures were arrested. Included were the former chief of SAVAK, Nematollah Nassiri, two former provincial governors (Manuchehr Azmoun and Abdul Aziz Valian) and several former ministers (especially former Minister of Information Dariush Homayoun, the man who had been directed to write the scurrilous story about Khomeini that started the first of the riots in Qom ten months before). In all, warrants were issued for approximately 60 officials from governments going back five years, though over half escaped the net and eventually fled the country. No one currently holding office was apprehended.[6]

The arrests completely destroyed morale among the Shah's remaining supporters in the establishment. From this point on, those who played such an important role in the administration of Iran from 1965 to 1978 were wholly absent from active political life. The remaining civilian ministers were all neophytes.

The military government presented itself to parliament and was duly approved on November 16. There had been some discussion about dissolving the Majles once the new regime was in place, and several deputies thought they had the Shah's agreement to do so. Then the monarch changed his mind, because he wanted parliament to be able to ratify any compromise government that might be negotiated. Perhaps he feared having a military government without a parliamentary counterweight, hoping to use the army to balance off the Majles, and vice versa. In any event, it muddled the question of the authority of the newly installed administration. Normally a military government rules without answering to a parliament. In Iran, theoretically the question of whether government decrees were subject to approval by the Majles remained open. Parliamentary deputies were uneasy. Some were already considering how they might work with the opposition, by either bringing dissident concerns before the Majles or challenging Azhari.

The week before, on November 9, Prime Minister Azhari had directed all strikers to go back to work. The National Front retorted that it would continue using work stoppages as its principal weapon against the regime; the Liberation Movement replied that it would renew its efforts to destroy the monarchy. Still, most employees returned to their jobs, even in the oil fields, though the former Tudeh Party labor officials freed in various amnesties tried hard to make that strike permanent. Street violence died down overnight as the opposition steered clear of challenging Azhari's newly established military government.

It was also on November 9 that the United States finally announced it would sell the Shah police clubs, 25,000 canisters of tear gas, and other riot equipment. This action had been held up by the Bureau (formerly Office) of Human Rights in the State Department since the beginning of the year. The paraphernalia, which would have been considerably more useful if it had arrived several months earlier, came in dribbles. While psychologically helpful, the riot gear was never more than marginally effective in quelling the demonstrations.

Two days later, on November 11 General Oveissi, chief administrator of martial law in Tehran, broke up a scheduled National Front press conference led by Sanjabi and Forouhar and jailed them. Though incarcerated for a month, they were treated like royal guests while negotiations between the Shah and the two prominent dissident politicians continued "under the table." The symbolism of the arrests, coming so soon after the Shah had reiterated during his television speech on November 6 his pledge to continue freedom of assembly, was taken by the opposition as yet more evidence of perfidy. The few dissidents who did not believe the imprisonment represented trickery wondered if the Shah was in full control of all aspects of his military government.

The sense of confusion was legitimate, because from the beginning General Azhari's government was not the strong, hierarchical military regime it needed to be in order to command either respect or fear. Once again the Shah had not changed the operating instructions for forces in the field. Troop commanders were still under orders to fire in the air around demonstrators and to shoot and kill only in self-defense. Armed Fedayeen and Mujahidin retreated, as did other unarmed gangs that had been roaming the city at will before the installation of the military government, because all were afraid they would be killed. When it became obvious that the standard operating procedure was to be business as usual, within a week the revolutionaries were back on the streets, provoking the security forces with cat-and-mouse tactics which would draw fire. Then they would disappear, only to pop up several blocks away to start the process over again. This maneuver put the army and SAVAK in an untenable position. The new prime minister, himself a general, was unable to clarify what the role of the armed forces should be. Thus the opposition became more united than ever. Religious fundamentalists adhering to Khomeini's long distance leadership were setting the rules for all dissident factions, tightening the limits of permissible cooperation with the Shah and his government. As chaos grew more widespread, the organizational abilities of the Mujahidin and Fedayeen became very important to the success of the revolutionary cause. Their job was made easier than it could have been because the military government made no effort to break up the opposition's administrative structure.

Most Iranians expected the Shah to direct Azhari to restore order regardless of how harshly he had to act. His failure to do so immediately was the conclusive disappointment that demolished public respect for the monarch. Until November the Shah had retained substantial support from the urban middle class (though it was rapidly eroding), the peasants (who could have cared less about what was going on in the cities but had grown up with the monarchy and expected it to continue), and large segments of the civil service and the military. When the Azhari government failed to reestablish law-abiding behavior, the fabric of imperial rule was destroyed for good.

The Shah saw the military regime as a stopgap measure until a compromise solution could be negotiated, but the opposition was under no compulsion to comply. It was not even being pressured. Azhari's government was its last barrier to power.

Given Khomeini's unwavering recalcitrance, court politics was full of misperceptions. As the situation developed from August through November, the dissidents united on the sole objective of getting the monarch off his throne. What the Shah should have done months before was to relentlessly fracture the opposition coalition by giving splinter groups an incentive to join the government and vigorously suppressing those who did not. Yet the monarch made no attempt to destroy the fanatically critical opposition and its highly effective "mosque network," and he refused to countenance an attempt on Khomeini's life. Although the more aggressive military leaders, Generals Oveissi, Rabii, and Khosrowdad, pressed for a much more vigorous campaign aimed at undercutting the dissidents' power base and forcing the opposition to be more amenable to compromise, nevertheless both the religious and secular dissidents were allowed to operate without serious hindrance.

The Shah's refusal to accept a "scorched earth" policy stemmed from his oft-overlooked humanitarian impulses. As a successful monarch for 37 years he had no wish "to destroy my people." He sought a political solution to the crisis, though his half-hearted efforts at compromise had united the opposition behind its most extreme leader and decimated the moral and political effectiveness of those who had been his chief lieutenants in building modern Iran. By November the Shah was no longer in a position to negotiate a successful compromise on any terms acceptable to him unless he built up his credibility first by using tremendous military force. The monarch believed then, and continued to insist until his death, that any effort resulting in several thousand political prisoners and perhaps thousands of others dead as well would cause even his supporters to rise against him and alienate the governments of the West. He knew other countries would look with horror at mass violations of civil rights. Without allies, he thought, his son could never hope for an untroubled succession. What his reasoning ignored was the fact that millions of Iranians, loyalists and revolutionaries alike, expected the Shah, with the help of the military, to instigate a decisive, bloody response.

At no time did opposition leaders fear the Shah's political efforts, but until the revolutionary takeover in February they were apprehensive about the potential of the military to destroy them. Khomeini was willing to run such a risk. Starting in October, he called upon his people "to prepare to martyr yourselves in the name of Allah to destroy the brutal tyrant Shah." However, whenever the situation could have led to protracted violence—at Jaleh Square on September 8 and especially after the installation of the military government on November 6—the opposition would pull back from confrontation when the possibility of a military response threatened. The radical leadership had golden opportunities to test the limits of how far it could go without provoking a devastating rebuttal. Since the Shah was constantly trying to find ways to conciliate the dissidents, they always had sufficient freedom to continue agitating aggressively. Thus the opposition never had any difficulty renewing its disruptive activities.

The government never established limits to force the revolutionaries to toe the line. Even the moderates soon realized the Shah had little stomach for harsh measures. By November the one remaining question was whether the collision between the Shah and Khomeini could be avoided short of massive violence, outright civil war, or the Shah's departure. Though the monarch consistently rejected using fully repressive measures, the first days after November 5 were his last opportunity to impose his will militarily. After that his only chance to swing some of his opponents around was to support a solution that included either his own surrender or placing the fate of his dynasty in the hands of the army.

When it became obvious that there would be no harsh military reprisals, support for the revolutionaries burgeoned. The Shah's reluctance to accept a violent solution and the Ayatollah's willingness to force one are interesting contrasts. Khomeini pursued his vendetta against the Shah with impressive single-mindedness. The monarch remained torn between conciliation and coercion, and his alternating policies and awkward timing reinforced the opposition rather than dividing it.

The Foreign Factor

Foreign reaction affected Iranian politics on November 5 and 6 scarcely at all. Except for the United States, there was surprising lack of comment from abroad about the country's internal problems. Washington continued to give the monarch periodic public gestures of support; on October 10 President Carter reaffirmed the country's strategic importance and said that the Shah was moving to establish democratic principles. He repeated this theme to Crown Prince Reza on October 31 during his visit to Washington. There were telephone consultations with Washington on November 3, the first day of the riots instigated by the students at Tehran University that would lead to the installation of General Azhari as prime minister. Brzezinski informed the Shah that the United States would back his efforts to restore order. After the military government was in place, the State Department reiterated its support, indicating U.S. understanding that "military rule is only temporary and he [the Shah] intends as rapidly as possible to move the country toward free elections and a new civilian-directed government." That statement immediately heightened dissident suspicions and convinced both the radical right (the clergy and the Mujahidin) and the radical left (the Fedayeen and Tudeh Party members) that Washington remained committed to the Shah. Though his private talks with Brzezinski—first on September 10 following Jaleh Square and then on November 3 just prior to the devastation in Tehran—may have reinforced the monarch psychologically, they had offered no new advice or magic solutions.

Uneasy because of the growing disorder, dependents of private contractors and other nonofficial Americans began leaving the country in late October. Some companies cut back their personnel or suggested early Christmas vacations. Commercial representatives from other foreign countries began to do likewise, but no other nation had anywhere near as many of its citizens involved in as wide a range of activities. Americans remained the prime targets of harassment, but so far, nothing violent had happened. Many found printed cards on the windshields of their cars, addressed "O cursed Yonky [sic]" inviting them to leave the country because of "your domed [sic] president." Though receiving such a missive was disquieting, it also inspired jokes. Two foreign journalists, for example, offered to open a bar called "The Cursed Yonky."

The fact that the Shah had failed to find opposition leaders willing to cooperate in a compromise solution was obvious to the diplomatic missions in Tehran before the installation of General Azhari's military government. Prior to November 5, however, with the exception of the American, French, Israeli, British, and possibly the Soviet embassies, no country had an in-depth understanding of how badly the trend of events was going against the Shah. Individuals in each of these missions had detected patterns that spelled trouble, but in no case had the decision making process of the country involved assimilated that information and converted it into policy actions. Prescient Western analysts found their home office bureaucracies still convinced that either the Shah or the military or both would prevent a revolution from occurring.[7] Soviet propaganda remained neutral toward the Shah. There is no evidence of significant additional Russian involvement with the various dissident factions, only indirect military aid to guerrilla groups, channeled through the P.L.O. for a decade, and the traditional modest financial assistance to the Tudeh Party.

The Iraqis were loath to see the monarchy fall. They feared repudiation of the three-year-old Iran-Iraq Treaty of Algiers, which had resolved several items of contention between the two countries. Iraq had expelled Khomeini to please the Shah and to eliminate an agitating influence from the midst of the approximately 50 percent of its own population which was Shiite. The Baathist government did not wish Khomeini and his radical followers to seize power next door and thus pose an even bigger threat to it.

The onset of military government jolted interested countries into awareness of the depth of deterioration in the Shah's position that had occurred in a very short time. But no foreign nation significantly affected the Iranian policy and decision making process, which remained mysterious and secretive to the man on the street and confused and complex to those involved.

Chapter Eight

★

Slide to Collapse

November 1978–January 16, 1979

After the Azhari government was installed, the Shah's political fortunes went steadily downhill. First, however, there was a short lull in street violence, a time of retrenchment for both sides. Then the revolutionaries began testing the newly established military regime to see if it would act more decisively against them. When they discovered that the army and police still were forbidden to shoot to kill, the rounds of crippling strikes and violent demonstrations began again. The increased number of average families supporting the opposition swelled revolutionary mobilization to enormous proportions. More significantly, people who had been passively supporting the Shah with little enthusiasm and who wanted public order restored above all began shifting their allegiance to the opposition, because they believed their monarch could never again regain control. Near the end of November the revolutionary coalition renewed its direct challenge; once more Ayatollah Khomeini called for an end to Pahlavi rule. Disorder in the streets soared.

Meanwhile, within the establishment camp, the Shah and his closest advisors frantically searched for a formula that would bring moderate dissidents into the government and prepare the way for a compromise solution. The job was made even more frustrating because many of Iran's most prominent political elite for the past 15 years were in exile (Ansari), discredited (Sharif-Emami), or in jail (Hoveyda). Therefore, sometimes with the Shah's tacit approval and sometimes without it, ex-politicians and respected dissidents worked hard to patch together a compromise to avoid either the total collapse of the government or extensive bloodshed.

Political dialogue in the teahouses and on the streets gradually shifted

139

from the ability of the Azhari government to restore public order to speculation about what kind of government would replace it. Time now was working against the Shah, because after November 5 public opinion had shifted decisively against the monarchy. As far as the Azhari government was concerned, it was considered by the man on the street to be a stopgap measure.

Khomeini continued adamantly to reject any conciliatory solution. By now Western countries, especially the United States, constantly were attacked by the opposition for being the Shah's principal source of support. The harassment of Americans became obvious and many U.S. citizens working for private companies began to leave. Just before the biggest protest marches in Moharram, December 10 and 11, the U.S. government authorized voluntary departure for dependents of official personnel. By the end of January all embassy wives and children and unessential staff were ordered home. Private citizens continued to leave as well, and by late January the number of Americans in Iran was down from a high of 54,000 to 7,000.

Khomeini and his followers planned to use the Islamic holy month of Moharram (December 2 to 30) as the period when they would push "the faithful" into overturning the monarchy. Traditionally, the highest holy days of Moharram are Tassua and Ashura, when Shiite Moslems march in sorrow to commemorate the death of their "patron saint," Imam Hossein, murdered in 680. On Ashura, the second of these days, the ceremonies in Iran always feature phalanxes of chanting males— from the very young to the very old—marching for hours throughout cities and towns and flagellating themselves with objects the size and shape of feather dusters. But instead of using feathers, they are hitting themselves with chains. They do this in rhythm as they march, first over the left shoulder, then the right, in penance for their sins and to scourge themselves for martyrdom. Referred to as "chain-bashing day" by Westerners living in Iran who did not understand this manifestation of religious fervor, even Persians who do not attend mosques regularly participate. For Tassua and Ashura 1978 the Khomeini forces in Tehran not only organized the regular squads of flagellants, but also mobilized women and girls to demonstrate the depth of their opposition to the Shah's regime by joining the parades, though they did not beat themselves.

Over one million people marched each day to Tehran's Shahyad Monument. This edifice is an impressive structure more than 300 feet high built by the Shah in 1971 to commemorate the 2,500 anniversary of the establishment of the Persian monarchy by Cyrus the Great. Iron-ically, it was at the foot of this monument that dissident leaders called a mass meeting each of the two days, exhorting the massive crowd to help them end the monarchy and establish an Islamic republic. According to an agreement worked out just before the first march began, the Iranian armed forces stood by unobtrusively, not immediately involved. Order was maintained by Mujahidin guerrillas who called themselves the Islamic militia. There was no violence either day, only a few minor scuffles.

Contact within the remnants of Iran's establishment, between the Shah and opposition leaders, and among various moderate dissident factions continued virtually around the clock throughout December until mid-January. The revolutionary coalition wanted a solution in which the monarch would turn over power to a regency council and leave the country. It also sought the right to make top-ranking military command appointments, but the Shah was adamant that he would not give up his control over the armed forces. The moderates within the coalition sought compromise to avoid the specter of bloody military repression. Khomeini and the Islamic militants wanted victory, regardless of cost, willing to martyr themselves for the cause. Meanwhile, military leaders were split over whether they should mount a devastating attack against the dissidents-turned-revolutionaries or seek some kind of a compromise with the opposition, either with or without the Shah's approval.

In the end the Shah and his opponents could never come to an accommodation; dissident leaders inside Iran dared not go against Khomeini, who had forbidden any dealings with the "illegitimate" monarch. The Shah ignored advice to crush the revolution; he did not want to order a slaughter of his people. Instead, he opted to try and ride out the storm by appointing a prominent opposition leader as prime minister, National Front spokesman Shapour Bakhtiar. As conditions became even worse under Bakhtiar—government ministries ceased to function and military desertions increased—the Shah finally agreed to a regency council which would supervise the Bakhtiar government while he left the country "on vacation." The departure from Iran of Shah Mohammad Reza Pahlavi on January 16 signaled the total collapse of his structure of government and opened the way for Ayatollah Khomeini to come back from exile as Iran's driving political force.

The Return of Violence and Chaos

For a brief time, it appeared as if General Azhari would restore some order to Iran. On November 12 he ordered all oil workers back to their jobs on pain of dismissal, the first attempt to put economic pressure on any of the strikers. Within three days 75 percent of the 67,000 employees in the oil industry were at work and production resumed. From less than a million barrels a day it went to 4 million by November 20. A high percentage of government employees and those in other industries also came back to work. On November 18 the prime minister added eight nonmilitary men to his cabinet. Now that group consisted of fourteen civilians and only five military officers. Simultaneously he called for public order so that a successor, completely civilian, government could be formed to hold free elections. He did this the day after a very low-key celebration of Iran's Armed Forces Day on November 17. Unlike previous years, there were no parades in major cities, only ceremonies within the barracks.

At a press conference on November 13 President Carter stated "the U.S. would hate to see Iran disrupted by violence," since it regarded a strong, independent Persia as a stabilizing factor in the Middle East. Six days later Soviet Communist Party chairman Leonid Brezhnev cautioned the West that "any interference, especially military interference, in the affairs of Iran would be considered a danger to Soviet interests in the area." The next day, in an interview with *The New York Times*, the Shah said that no friendly country would be permitted to intervene to help him. Carter explained on November 30 that the U.S. would not become involved and "did not approve interference by another country." The President was alluding to evidence that funds from foreign sources were finding their way to the Shah's opponents. Since his retirement, Richard Helms could be more blunt. "The K.G.B. [Russian intelligence] is there. We ought to beef up the C.I.A."[1]

Washington had begun to give Iran special consideration in terms of its own policy and decision making process just about the time Azhari became prime minister. A special coordinating committee was created on November 2, chaired by the President's national security advisor Zbigniew Brzezinski. Other members were Secretary of State Cyrus Vance, Secretary of Defense Harold Brown, and C.I.A. chief Admiral Stansfield Turner. (Secretary of Energy James Schlesinger was a sometime participant beginning in December.) News of President Carter's personal criticism of U.S. intelligence gathering in Iran surfaced on November 23, through letters he wrote to Vance, Brzezinski, Brown, and Turner. For the first time the questions of whether or not and how badly the U.S. had been caught by surprise were in the public domain. Now there was new interest and greater concentration within Washington on the Persian Gulf region, but at the same time heightened fear of being blamed for unfavorable developments in Iran. The Carter letters made cautious bureaucrats even more cautious.[2]

Activity increased; a 6-to-12 man "working group" was set up, chaired by Brzezinski's deputy, David Aaron. It dealt in detail with issues raised in the special coordinating committee. To handle the day-to-day coordination, an interagency working group (State, Defense, C.I.A.) was established December 27 under the third highest person in the Department of State hierarchy, Undersecretary of State for Political Affairs David Newsom.

Events in Iran continued to unfold, little influenced by increasing foreign interest. The lull following Azhari's assumption of power was an artificial one, for the Liberation Movement, the National Front, and the religious leaders all had decided to continue challenging the government by organizing new demonstrations to begin November 20.

Not only did street violence increase, but it spread to cities like Kerman, Rasht, and Zanjan where heretofore there had been only peaceful demonstrations. By November 26 Qom and Masha, Iran's two most holy cities, were in the hands of the Islamic militants. In Qom an Islamic republic was declared. To the surprise of the dissidents, some of the gatherings were confronted with swift, substantial uses of force. For the first time since June tanks rumbled down Tehran's streets on November 22. More demonstrators—approximately 600—were killed in minor incidents throughout the country from November 20 to December 1 than in the previous three months. The level of violence went up sharply because Khomeini stridently exhorted his followers to confront the government. They responded, oblivious to danger.

On November 26 and 28 Khomeini issued manifestos from Paris calling upon Iranians "to go on perpetual strike until the criminal Shah is deposed." Wildcat strikes broke out everywhere. Customs offices closed, oil production dropped below a million barrels per day, banking activities came to almost a complete halt, and air and rail service was sporadic. Revolutionary employees at Iran's Central Bank published a list, allegedly showing 144 ranking government officials who had transferred about $2 billion out of Iran the preceding two months. Many bazaars throughout the country closed down completely or opened only on a random basis. The collapse of public services, oil production, and by implication government authority was impressive.

But this would be only the beginning. Khomeini and his supporters within Iran—particularly the leading clerics Ayatollahs Beheshti, Moussavi, and Lahouti—were gearing up their followers to participate in a dramatic confrontation with the government from December 2 through December 30, the Islamic holy month of Moharram. During this lunar calendar period, Shiite Moslems (and only Shiites) mourn the death of Imam Hossein, grandson of the prophet Mohammad, who was martyred in Iraq in the seventh century. The opposition coalition was primed to force confrontation during the entire month, but especially on the high holy days of Tassua and Ashura, December 10 and 11.[3] The apparent gains in public order in early November were washed away. The Shah found himself more embattled than ever before.

Public anti-American sentiment also increased. As November ended hundreds of U.S. citizens had notes slipped under their gates or their car windshield wipers which said "Death to American's imperialism. If you not go from Iran we will kill you and your family or explode your house and your car. Say this message to all your American Friends." Three journalists, Loren Jenkins and Barry Came of *Newsweek* and Kenneth Clark of the *London Daily Telegraph*, were detained in early December for arguing with soldiers while they were watching a demonstration. Most ominous of all was the manifesto issued December 11 by the University Band for an Islamic Republic calling upon all foreigners and their families whose governments supported the Shah to leave Iran. The French, because they had given refuge to Khomeini in Neuphle-le-Chateau, and all journalists, because the militants wanted all the publicity they could get, "were exempt for the time being."

Even before Thanksgiving, November 23, the American embassy had begun encouraging private companies to withdraw "unessential personnel." As violence accelerated at the end of November and the beginning of the holy month of Moharram, the embassy and Washington discussed via phone and cable the need for a possible evacuation of the wives and children of U.S. government employees. Tension had been growing within the American military community for over a month, particularly after the cars of two families were firebombed, one in the garage and the other in front of the house. Many dependents were particularly unhappy about the briefings provided periodically by ARMISH-MAAG, especially one in mid-November following the destruction of the automobiles, when the spokesman returned all passports. Ostensibly this was because there no longer was room to store them in official safes. No mention was made of the possible need to make a quick getaway. Such efforts to gloss over visibly deteriorating security conditions led to subsequent charges in the U.S. press by some military dependents that American citizens were being kept in Iran for political reasons to show continued U.S. support for the Shah.

There were intense three-way arguments among Ambassador Sullivan, the State Department, and Brzezinski about exactly that—whether withdrawing dependents of official Americans would undercut the monarch. Sullivan was not yet ready to evacuate anyone. Brzezinski and the White House sought to get as many people out as possible. The State Department argued for the phased departure of wives and children beginning immediately. The voluntary evacuation of approximately 1,200 American dependents began December 8, just in time to get them out of the country before the expected confrontations on Tassua and Ashura, December 10 and 11. The departure of American citizens who had lingered in Iran continued throughout the turmoil, and by the end of December about 25,000 had left the country, leaving only 27,441, down from a peak of approximately 54,000 in July.

On November 28 the government banned processions during Moharram. From the evening of December 1 through the evening of December 8, when the Shah rescinded the prohibition on religious demonstrations, chaos filled the streets of Tehran, even in the usually peaceful affluent northern suburbs. The veto had failed to prevent public outbursts against the regime. Almost everyone in the ever-growing group loyal to the revolution began the month of Moharram the night of December 1 by violating the 9 o'clock curfew. Men, women, and children jammed the mosques for evening services which were scheduled to end as the curfew began. Mujahidin units enforced order in principal mosques during these early evening services. In several cases attendance overflowed into the surrounding streets so that loudspeakers had to be set up outside, often blocking traffic. Buoyed by the spirit of Hossein's martyrdom, crowds were whipped into a feverish pitch by speakers who called for confrontation with the "godless Shah" and the "corrupt usurpers of Islam." As the hordes left the mosques after curfew to roam their designated areas (dressed completely in white, thus signifying their willingness to become martyrs) revolutionary organizations signaled those who remained in private homes to get up on their easily accessible flat rooftops and to chant loudly and continuously. Specific homes in each area were designated to play prerecorded slogans that also included bursts of machine gun fire, thus implying that government troops were attacking the multitudes. The incessant chanting of "*Allaho Akbar*" (God Is Great) and "*Khomeini Rahbaranieh*" (Khomeini Is Our Leader) would continue each night from December 1 to December 9 for about two hours, from 9:00 to 11:00.

As the revolutionary organizations proved they could mobilize vast numbers of supporters to flaunt the curfew, troops were sent into the streets, including armored units. There was always a prodigious number of shots fired, but as usual, most went straight into the air. However, the revolutionaries had more sinister activities planned. For the first time, guerrillas were on the offensive, attacking the police and the army in the streets. The evening of December 2 American eyewitnesses watched a small insurgent group decimate a five-man army team patrolling a neighborhood less than a mile and a half from Niavaran Palace, the Shah's home. Casualty estimates in the capital for all confrontations in the nine-day period beginning December 1 range from 100 to 1,000 dead. The most commonly accepted figure is about 700 killed and over 1,000 injured. The city of Tehran gave a very unusual impression—relatively peaceful by day, filled with wild chanting and vicious skirmishes at night.

The revolutionary movement's strategy was to build up the enthusiasm and solidarity of the religious faithful in preparation for the major procession days of Tassua and Ashura. Planning had begun several weeks before to turn these holy days—the most mournfully emotional days in the Shiite year—into an overwhelming show of solidarity with Khomeini and against the Shah. The effectiveness of the Ayatollah's earlier calls for an indefinite strike were gradually grinding Azhari's military-civil government to a halt. The prime minister struck back by blaming "communists, atheists, and saboteurs" for the internal strife. Such claims may have diverted foreign attention from Iran's internal problems, but by the time of the Tassua-Ashura marches it was clear to even the most disinterested urban dweller that there was much more to the dissidence than an active fringe group creating discord. Each week Iranians heard escalating criticism of the Shah and his government at the mosque. The press, which had resumed publishing on a sporadic basis, was completely dominated by radical staff members. Editors and publishers, destroyed by intimidation, had very little control over their own papers. While radio and television remained under firm government control, there was enough counterinformation available to show that civil disorder was a significant, continuing feature of national life. Oil production dropped off again. By December 13 it was about one million barrels a day. By December 30 it had dropped to a 27-year low of 350,000 barrels a day, about half the amount required to meet the country's internal needs. The social and economic fabric of Iranian life was unraveling. Politics was nearing open warfare.

Confidential Attempts at Compromise

Although the Azhari government had been installed to restore order, that goal became entwined with the Shah's other aim—to engineer a coalition regime that would hold elections and restore peace to the country. Starting in mid-November private discussions on several levels began between those for keeping the Shah on the throne and those against it.

Indeed the arrest of Sanjabi and Forouhar in early November was turned into an advantage because the two men could be approached in their prison quarters. On at least three occasions they talked with emissaries of the Shah (usually SAVAK chief Nasser Moghaddam or Chief of the Supreme Commander's Staff Abbas Gharabaghi, who had replaced Azhari in that capacity). The Shah also sought advice from others, including the head of the National Iranian Oil Company Abdollah Entezam (who had taken over in August when Eqbal died of a heart attack), former Prime Minister Ali Amini, and Majles deputy Mohsen Pezeshkpour, as well as old-line politicians who had not been active since the 1960s.

Even the opposition found ways to put their case before the Shah. At the time of Azhari's appointment, at least two serious efforts were made to present the monarch with cabinet lists acceptable to all but the radical opposition. In one instance, the Liberation Movement explored different options through contacts in the Imperial Court. The National Front was approached directly in early November through Sanjabi, after he returned from visiting Khomeini. The Shah hoped to draw Sanjabi away from the extreme position he had endorsed in Paris. He was not successful.

A few days later, emissaries of Ayatollah Shariatmadari also went to Paris, but were unable to develop a proposal acceptable to the Shah that would also gain Khomeini's approval. Shariatmadari's men were probably even more disposed to work out an agreeable compromise than the leaders of the Liberation Movement or the National Front, but they could not pressure Khomeini since Shariatmadari did not want to break ranks with him. Such was the Khomeini charisma that if he did, then Shariatmadari would lose credibility with his own followers.

Under the circumstances, the Committee for the Defense of Human Rights and Freedom became the most important organizational mechanism for preparing and discussing alternate possibilities. All moderate opposition factions were represented on it, and the group was respected and had become well known to the Shah through its criticism of human rights violations. Dr. Nasser Minatchi, its director and a staunch Shariatmadari admirer, and Dr. Haj Seyed Javadi, an opposition lawyer (and first post-revolutionary minister of the interior), prepared several proposals, all suggesting that a regency council be instituted. They said those chosen to serve would be admired non-establishment figures who could take over power when the Shah left the country either "on vacation" or permanently. Their final suggestions, prepared in late November, outlined two options: to establish a regency council which would include senior military officers as members, or to name a regency council and create a separate military council under it.

Attempts to work out a compromise that would be agreeable to both sides foundered on mutually incompatible demands. Efforts to establish a government of opposition leaders under the Shah collapsed on Khomeini's insistence that the monarch had to be replaced. He could not remain even as a figurehead; cooperation with him was "treason," and defiled the purity of the Islamic cause. On the other hand, accommodations which called for some form of a regency council linked to the Shah's departure were always unacceptable to the Imperial Court. In fact, the November negotiations never reached the point where formal proposals were made by one side to the other. Even the proposition that was finally presented to the monarch in early December did not have Khomeini's prior approval. By mid-December various go-betweens were struggling to come up with anything that might avoid a bloody confrontation. Khomeini remained obstinate; things were, after all, going his way. It was the Shah, by his own uncertainty and vacillation, who appeared to be the insincere negotiator.

Under pressure because of the projected confrontations on December 10 and 11, the private discussions intensified in early December. Former Prime Minister Ali Amini approached the Shah on December 2 and 3 (some say this was done through the Shah's chauffeur) to propose a regency council, or alternatively, a national government composed of prominent figures not associated with the regime since 1963, when Khomeini's movement was crushed. One such list included Amini himself, Karim Sanjabi (National Front), Mohsen Pezeshkpour (Pan Iran Party), and Gholam Hossein Sadiqi (minister of post and telegraph under Mossadeq in the early 1950s and on the political sidelines since 1963). For the first time, the Shah tentatively accepted the suggestion. Then, within 24 hours, he rejected the idea of a regency council. He changed his mind when his inner circle of advisors, including his ambassador to the United States, Ardeshir Zahedi, convinced him he could weather the storm. Thus the monarch told them he had decided to continue trying to get the opposition to form a government in the standard constitutional fashion. In a public statement after his release from jail as a goodwill gesture on December 5, Sanjabi immediately rejected the Shah's appeal that the opposition form a national government. From Paris, Khomeini dismissed outright the idea of a regency council.

Negotiations for a compromise solution had foundered on the opposition's demand that the Shah depose himself and the Shah's refusal to do so, plus the monarch's wish to retain a position of dominance regardless of what the future might bring. According to those involved, he was willing to appoint an opposition government, but insisted on retaining control of the military. On November 15 the Shah had commented to a foreign ambassador, "If I can't be commander-in-chief I'll pack my bags and leave." Conversely, opposition leaders seeking a proposal that they could put before Khomeini with some hope of acceptance wanted a guarantee that the Shah would not try to take back with the military control what he apparently was willing to give up to a civilian opposition government. Throughout December and January the feeling of trust between the adversaries was so weak that serious negotiation remained impossible. Moreover, given the needs of the imperial ego, all the discussions remained secret. Despite the difficulty of the Shah's position, the fact that there were talks in progress with the opposition was never made public. The monarch did not want to highlight his own weakness, and the moderate dissidents who participated in these various discussions did not want to undermine their own situation in terms of the radical militants.

Communication between the opposition and the Shah had improved enough, however, that the government could very privately negotiate with it to lift the ban on public demonstrations during Moharram. From November 29 until the day before the major marches were to begin on December 10, Generals Gharabaghi and Moghaddam met with dissident leaders to work out an agreement between the army and the religious movement. The compromise stated that the armed forces would not interfere with the Tassua and Ashura marches as long as the demonstrators were orderly. This agreement had three major consequences: It introduced the military and SAVAK into a direct negotiating role with the opposition. It showed that both sides were willing to give a little, but very little, to avoid a bloody confrontation. It clearly marked a rough equality of force between the government-army and the opposition-mobs. But the failure of all other possibilities reinforced the views of the military hardliners, Generals Oveissi, Rabii, and Khosrowdad, that politics in Iran was rapidly becoming an "either them or us" proposition. They acquiesced most reluctantly in the Tassua-Ashura parade agreement, although privately they were relieved that a showdown had been avoided.

The Legitimacy of the Monarchy
Becomes Illusory

Using the same organizational tactics employed for at least half a dozen major marches since September, the Islamic movement turned out about 1.2 million followers in Tehran for the Tassua commemoration December 10. Supporters converged on the Shahyad Monument near Tehran's Mehrabad International Airport. This graceful modern structure towers over the surrounding countryside, dominating the approaches to the city from the south and west. Signs carried by the marchers were primarily religious, though placards saying "Death To The Shah," "Kill The American Dogs," and "Khomeini Is Our Leader" were intermingled with more traditional slogans. On Ashura, the following day, over five million people turned out in approximately 20 cities—including about 1.5 million in Tehran—for ceremonies which were much more political. The massive crowds heard speakers who attacked the government and asked the people to "approve" a 17-point program, including the following:

—recognition of Khomeini as the imam (leader) of Iran and of the march as "the sincere vote of confidence of the nation"

—abolition of the Shah's regime and the monarchy and the end to all foreign exploitation

—establishment of a "just Islamic state" on the basis of democratic vote

—protection of women and religious minorities under Islamic law

—establishment of social justice and an end to discrimination and exploitation of man through unjust profiteering and economic dominance

—immediate freedom for all political prisoners

—continuation of strikes until the Shah's government collapses

The manifesto also proclaimed that the use of the army against the people was "treasonous," and called upon the armed forces "to protect the country from its foreign enemies and not to fight its own people."[4]

The massive Ashura march on December 11 was remarkably peaceful in Tehran, with only minor problems in other cities. (The exception was Isfahan, where police attacks on demonstrators on December 11 led to major riots on December 12 in which foreign reporters witnessed at least 40 killed and 600 injured.) Ayatollah Khomeini issued a statement from Paris, widely distributed by broadside in Iran, that the two marches were a "referendum against the criminal Shah" and called upon the monarch to accept the will of his people and resign. Opposition leaders within Iran stated that the huge two-day demonstrations clearly indicated the Shah had lost the confidence of his nation.

After Tassua and Ashura, street fighting and more demonstrations started up again on December 14 in 12 cities and over 20 smaller towns. Severe rioting continued in Isfahan. Army troops attacked a mob in the town of Najafabad near Isfahan and several hundred were killed and about 1,000 wounded. Continual unrest began taking a severe toll on military morale, especially after army troops saw the size of the Tassua-Ashura demonstrations and heard the crowd enthusiastically cheer the call of the rally speakers on December 11 to stop firing on the people. By mid-December the Islamic infiltration of the army had been traumatically effective. In Tabriz, on December 18, two army units of approximately 800 men publicly joined the opposition, refusing to fire on rioters. The individual defections of officers and men increased across the country, especially in the larger cities, where the army had been on constant alert and was worn out. Figures from Iranian military intelligence show the desertion rate rose from 3 percent per week to 8 percent in September-December 1978, and by February 1 the rate was up to 20 percent.

The Moharram marches dramatically emphasized the whole question of political legitimacy. The demands of the Islamic movement, quickly spread across the country by the mosque network, appealed to a wide spectrum of dissatisfied Iranians. Certainly the government's performance in November and December did not inspire support even among those inclined toward the Shah. The monarch's continual vacillation, best exemplified by intermittently repressing demonstrations which subjected "the people" to sporadic violence and by permitting the religious marches which completely reversed stated government policy, indicated confusion and weakness. Public opinion had thoroughly shifted. Now for the first time many more Iranians were against the Shah than for him and were willing to say so. The impact on the government's authority was devastating. Many provincial officials throughout the country began making private accommodations with the opposition, usually a mutual agreement to inhibit violence perpetrated by either the demonstrators or the soldiers. Work discipline disappeared completely in the Finance, Commerce, and Justice ministries. Employees would not show up, and would not obey instructions if they did. All these acts further undercut the Shah's military government.

An inadvertent comment by President Carter undoubtedly helped along the disintegration of the sense of legitimacy. At a breakfast press briefing for selected journalists on December 7, the President was asked whether the Shah would survive. He replied: "I don't know. I hope so. This is something in the hands of the Iranian people. . . . We personally prefer that the Shah maintain a major role in the government, but that is a decision for the Iranian people to make."[5] This comment was interpreted in both Iran and the United States as a retreat from Carter's previous policy of total support of the Shah. Although the President emphasized on December 12 that the U.S. backed the monarch, the damage already had been done. Even Iranian government officials were convinced that the United States was prepared to shift away from the Shah. One called Carter's statement "America's second Pearl Harbor," a massive disaster, this time in the Middle East, on the 37th anniversary of the original.

The tense situation in Tehran, the rapidly changing events, and the growing anti-Americanism left few to raise their voices against a simplistic interpretation of Carter's remarks and fewer still who would listen. More questions were raised in Iran the following week with the news of the special report prepared for the President by former Undersecretary of State George Ball. President Carter had asked Ball to review the situation in the Persian Gulf. What surfaced in this private report on December 13 was the former undersecretary's belief that the U.S. should encourage the monarch to broaden the base of his regime by including Iranians opposed to him. Since the Shah had been trying unsuccessfully for months to do that very thing these recommendations were, at best, much too late. Their effect on the U.S. government was minimal. Their impact in Tehran was to add one more piece to the pile of ever-growing evidence, reinforcing the goal of those seeking the Shah's overthrow.[6]

The heart of the matter was political. The revolutionary forces, confident of victory, were holding out for an end to the regime, through a plebiscite on the monarchy, through direct overthrow, or through some compromise such as a regency council. Leaders in the Liberation Movement exuded confidence, bluntly informing foreign diplomats: "Any government under the Shah is no longer possible. The Shah has to go; a council should replace him. If your government wishes to help, it should concentrate its thought on the idea of a means to replace him." Their revolutionary contacts urged American embassy officers "to cooperate with the solution desired by the people." Other moderates, especially those in the National Front and the writers and lawyers groups, hoped for Western help when it came time for a showdown, both to avoid bloodshed and to support the emergence of a government dedicated to democratic ideals and not dominated by either the clergy or the leftist radicals. Members of these organizations urged their Iranian friends in Europe and America to renew their efforts to convince the Shah's allies that it was time for a change.

The Tassua-Ashura demonstrations also affected the Shah. Though violent, open confrontation had been avoided, the size of the marches and the depth of feeling displayed finally convinced him that his political stock had reached an all-time low. In mid-December he intensified his efforts to find a civil government acceptable to the opposition, though he still rejected any formula for installing a regency council. The monarch's attitude was totally unrealistic. After the Ashura march it was clear to all but a handful of the imperial faithful that there was no chance of the Shah remaining on the throne in other than a titular capacity, and precious little chance of that unless he brutally and completely repressed the revolutionaries. Yet the Shah would not consider that option. Repeatedly, he told foreign ambassadors and his trusted advisors that he could not "bring a bloodbath" on his own people.

It is also true that after the two major marches it is doubtful if such a coercive strategy would have worked. By reining in the army the Shah avoided confrontation, but at the cost of conceding the streets to the opposition. The impact on the armed forces was insidious. Aware of the increased desertion rates, the command began to question its own position and to suffer increasing division within its ranks. Top leadership remained committed to the Shah, but junior officers, particularly Western trained men whose promotions had been delayed by what they saw as "deadwood" at the top, began to sense other possibilities. The opposition played on these feelings and publicized Khomeini's injunctions to the military not to kill their brothers. The cumulative impact was fatally debilitating. Officers began to question seriously the reliability of their troops, particularly in the big city garrisons. As for the police, they were overwhelmed by the size of the demonstrations. Many of them were quietly going over to the revolution. Many more were simply opting out—reporting for work, but not actively patrolling.

Old loyalties, under pressure since September, gave way to much more pragmatic (and equally Persian) instincts for survival and accommodation. The Moharram marches had established Khomeini once and for all as the leading charismatic revolutionary figure, even for those who disagreed with him on particulars. Thus everyone's attention was focused on the one goal all segments of the opposition could agree on—ousting the Shah. What was left of the fabric of legitimacy had been stretched very thin in many places, ripped apart in others.

Solution Too Late: The Bakhtiar Option

The weekend immediately following the huge demonstrations on December 10 and 11, the Shah had resumed efforts to create a coalition cabinet. Many of the moderates and even the more rigid Liberation Movement leaders were ready to consider a government consisting of a "council of notables" made up of prominent non-establishment figures—as long as the council controlled military appointments. If ever there was a chance for an agreed-upon compromise, it occurred during discussions the Shah had with Shapour Bakhtiar and others in December. Even the moderate religious leadership, led by Shariat-madari, was prepared to lobby with Khomeini to force his approval of an agreement leading to a coalition government. In one proposal the Shah would turn over power to a regency council consisting of loyalists, opposition leaders, and two or three mutually acceptable neutral "notables" and then leave the country. In the plan advanced by the Committee for the Defense of Human Rights on behalf of clerics and others loyal to Ayatollah Shariatmadari, two current military commanders and one or two retired leaders of the armed forces would represent the opposition on the regency council. Military men they mentioned who could fill the latter positions were Admiral Ahmad Madani (who would become a prominent and eventually disillusioned figure in post-revolutionary politics) and Generals Fereidoun Jam and Hossein Batmangelidj.

With the Shah's blessing, Dr. Gholam Hossein Sadiqi, in his early seventies, had been working behind the scene for some time attempting to form a cabinet. He was rebuffed by all opposition politicians both publicly and privately, when he tried to assemble a government of respected public figures who had been out of politics. Sadiqi quietly gave up in mid-December, just as news of his efforts became common knowledge.

While the political discussions were going on, economic dislocation persisted and public order continued to deteriorate. Food prices soared and rice and sugar were unavailable. Huge lines formed at the small shops selling heating oil and stocks ran low. A major head-knocking occurred in Tehran on December 27. The violence broke out during the funeral procession of a professor who had been shot accidentally by army troops searching for snipers. This time both soldiers and demon-

strators were killed, each side blaming the other for starting the shooting. Qom and Mashad remained under the authority of the Islamic
militants. In some cities, including Isfahan, Khorramshahr, and Tabriz,
the revolutionaries established effective power within parts of the towns
and in other areas only at night. In fact, soldiers patrolling the streets
throughout the country were killing snipers and were being killed.

Gradually, Iranian customs officers and security officials noticed that
dozens of "students" who had formerly been on SAVAK "wanted" lists
for security reasons were returning from the United States and Europe.
In the political confusion, the government made no effort to arrest
them. Many of these "student" leaders immediately took charge of organizing revolutionary units to support the militants. One was
influential Marxist leader Ahmad Behazin, who had arrived on January
17 from somewhere in Europe and promptly became commander of a
Fedayeen unit. By mid-January about 20 young revolutionaries a week
were returning "to be part of the dawn of Iran's new day," as one was
quoted as saying at the Mehrabad airport.

The first American to die in the revolution was Paul Grimm, an oil
company executive, assassinated on December 23 while driving to
work. Within a week all foreign administrators and engineers in the oil
fields were pulling out and petroleum production dropped rapidly. On
December 24 a mob burned a U.S. official car at the gates of the American embassy. Some troops assigned to protect the American embassy
began shouting pro-Khomeini slogans and chanting "Yankee Go
Home" to American and Iranian employees. Though these soldiers
were withdrawn and replaced by others, including ultra-loyal Imperial
Guard units, this was a striking indication of how deeply the infiltration
was undermining the military forces.

Grimm's death emphasized the growing problem of security for foreigners and especially Americans in Iran. Though the embassy was trying to analyze the extremely complex, fast-developing situation,
throughout the last two months of the year it spent most of its man-
hours protecting American citizens and arranging and assisting their
hasty departures. Well before the evacuation of many of its own dependents on December 9, the embassy maintained a 24-hour-a-day telephone watch center to set rumors straight, check on incidents, and
make instant contact with security services when necessary. By the end
of December, Ambassador Sullivan had recommended that all American dependents, both official and private, leave Iran temporarily because
of the growing food and fuel shortages. Mandatory departure of non-
critical official personnel and of all official dependents who had re-

mained after the voluntary evacuation in December began on January 30. It was at this time that Marie Sullivan, the ambassador's wife, left Iran.

With public order collapsing and Sadiqi unable to rally enough support to form a cabinet, the Shah was forced to turn to a well-known opposition figure for help, National Front spokesman Shapour Bakhtiar. Frail-looking, courtly, French-educated, and 62-years-old, Bakhtiar firmly believed in parliamentary democracy along the European social democratic model. He had become increasingly ill at ease with the way the religious fundamentalists were dominating the revolutionary movement. Actually, the Shah had been mulling over the possibility of forming a cabinet with Bakhtiar as early as November 27, though it was never publicized.

Before discussing Bakhtiar's efforts, however, it is worth mentioning another figure whose shadowy influence floated over the Tehran political arena from early November until late December. Ardeshir Zahedi, the ambassador to the United States for a total of 11 years (and the son of the man the Shah had appointed prime minister to succeed Mossadeq when the monarch returned to Iran in triumph in 1953), came back to Tehran, the first time he had set foot in the country in seven years, "to put some backbone in the Old Man," as he reportedly told two of his confidants. Working with establishment figures, ex-politicians, and even some opposition leaders, Zahedi pressed hard to get dissidents and political neutrals into the regime's camp via a coalition government. He also met with the hard-line generals and explored the possibilities of the "Pinochet option." This would have been a military coup, named for the regime instituted in Chile in 1973 by General Augusto Pinochet. Zahedi waxed hot and cold on supporting widespread military action to pacify Iran's continuing unrest, but he pursued the possibility of repressive pacification to the point of serious planning.

The Shah was depressed by the way events were unfolding. He felt Zahedi did not understand what was happening. In the end, Zahedi concluded that his leader had neither the energy nor the will to make such a drastic solution work, and that in the absence of solid royal support to unify the military, he could not do it alone. By the same token, Zahedi urged the Shah in his negotiations with Sadiqi and Bakhtiar to resist the pressure on him to give up control of the army. This was a critical concession Bakhtiar insisted upon, as did other National Front leaders and the moderate religious opposition. So Zahedi's ultimate effect was extremely pernicious. He was unable either to engineer a compromise or to unite the military to strong action, yet he disrupted the only real compromise efforts which might have brought forth a controlled transitional government.

After the Tassua-Ashura demonstrations, Bakhtiar began working in earnest to form a broad-based coalition government. With mandate in hand, the prime minister designate faced his colleagues the evening of December 29, seeking to convince them to go along with him. The rest of the National Front leadership was shocked by Bakhtiar's apparent defection. Sanjabi was jealous; Forouhar was fearful of a split in the opposition and afraid that Bakhtiar might have gotten the jump on him. After three acrimonious hours together, they rejected his overtures and expelled him from the National Front the following morning.

That same day, December 30, despite his formal ouster from the National Front, Bakhtiar continued to talk privately with politicians and dissidents of all persuasions. He announced that the Shah had agreed to leave the country within a month after Bakhtiar took office as the prime minister and further stated that his civilian government would be formed within a week. The Shah's agreement to leave the country "on vacation" and place the affairs of state in the hands of a regency council was considered a major victory, and made Bakhtiar at least minimally credible to other members of the opposition. Although the Liberation Movement rejected Bakhtiar's overtures out of hand, they were fascinated with the possibility that the new prime minister might actually get the monarch to leave. Bazargan and others adopted a wait-and-see attitude. They would not help, but they did not hinder.

Something else Bakhtiar had insisted upon was that the Majles indicate its support before he was formally designated as head of the government. The practice of a vote of confidence had been abandoned by the Shah after 1953 because it gave parliament the opportunity to veto the monarch's selection of prime minister. Reinstatement of this principle was another victory for Bakhtiar, but the National Front, the Liberation Movement, and the major religious factions did not see it that way. Following Khomeini's lead, they rejected the legitimacy of the Majles.

Despite these difficulties, the truly critical aspect of Bakhtiar's continual negotiations with the Shah and the opposition concerned who would be commander-in-chief of the armed forces. When first approached about forming a cabinet, Bakhtiar had insisted upon having the power to veto any military appointments. By late December, as negotiations progressed, Bakhtiar had reduced this demand to insuring that the military would accept his government and that he could name the minister of war. He implied that his minister of war would dismiss the hard-line generals, and other military officers would be appointed to the most important positions. The new appointees, he said, would be widely respected and sympathetic to the constitutional goals of the moderate opposition.

The key to these negotiations was Bakhtiar's choice for war minister, Fereidoun Jam. A former chief of the supreme commander's staff, Jam had been living in London in retirement after being fired for refusing to adopt harsh tactics against dissidents in the mid-1960s. He was admired by all opposition leaders. Bakhtiar announced his appointment as minister of war on January 2, but there was a hitch. Jam would not take the job unless he had complete control over major appointments. This the Shah would not give. Privately, Jam said that the Shah would not allow him a free hand, and was "imperious and arrogant." Iran's monarch regarded Jam as an upstart. The rigidity of their attitudes toward each other is jarring evidence of the ever-increasing perceptual gaps between the Shah and others, even when the Shah was dealing with those trying—in their own ways—to help him. Jam was not there when Bakhtiar's cabinet was presented to the Shah on January 6. Finally, on January 9, the prime minister admitted defeat in his efforts to bring the general into the cabinet. Instead, General Jaafar Shafiqat, who had successfully governed Azarbaijan province following the disastrous riot in Tabriz the previous February, was appointed minister of war.

Bakhtiar's failure to bring Jam or a comparable military figure respected by the opposition into the government ended the prime minister's last hope of collaboration or even tacit support from the moderate opposition, both religious and secular. The plum of a workable transitional government had been dangled, but personal rigidities on both sides obstructed any deal. The Shah had made substantial concessions to Bakhtiar on the issues of parliamentary approval and of leaving the country. The moderate opposition would have seen these compromises as sufficient reasons to allow them to collaborate with Bakhtiar, if the military leadership question could have been resolved successfully. But with Shah loyalists still in control of the armed forces, the fear of a coup remained the paramount worry of the dissidents. Thus the revolutionary coalition was unwilling to stop agitating or to ease up on the strikes until the Shah was gone, and only then if the new regency council was acceptable to the Islamic movement, specifically Ayatollah Khomeini.

The Bakhtiar cabinet was generally an unimpressive lot, consisting of technocrats, relatives, and minor figures who had been out of active politics for years. His most controversial appointment was the selection of a cousin, Abbas Qoli Bakhtiar, as minister of industry and mines.

The minister of foreign affairs was Ahmad Mirfendereski, a second-rank diplomat. The ministry of finance went to a young banker who had been trained in the United States, Rostam Pirasteh. There were no prominent opposition politicians in the cabinet, though Bakhtiar labored hard to tempt them in. His program included complete freedom of press and assembly, an end to martial law within one month, cessation of all oil shipments to South Africa and Israel, removal of political influence from the Ministry of Justice, and free elections as soon as possible. He adopted the foreign policy of the National Front. This meant there would be a more nationalistic, even handed approach with the emphasis on self interest in regional matters and a neutral international stance between East and West. The program was eminently acceptable to the opposition; Bakhtiar's acceptance of the Shah's offer to be his prime minister was not.

Events in the first week in January 1979 favored Bakhtiar. On the economic front, after the Shah indicated he would leave the country for a rest once the Bakhtiar government was installed, employees in the oil fields agreed to meet domestic production needs, but not to produce for export until the Shah had actually left. On the political front, when General Azhari resigned as prime minister he also left his job as chief of staff and departed for the United States for medical treatment. (He had suffered a minor heart attack in December.) General Gharabaghi, who had been acting chief of the supreme commander's staff and was known to be more amenable to nonconfrontation and compromise, was promoted to fill the vacant post. Within three days Generals Oveissi, Rabii, and Khosrowdad had "resigned," fulfilling the Shah's agreement with Bakhtiar to eliminate the hard-line generals from positions of power.

The U.S. announced it would support Bakhtiar, and the State Department said the United States would cooperate with the new government whether or not the Shah remained in Iran. The basic American position, communicated privately to all parties, was that the U.S. "would support any constitutional prime minister named by the Shah."

The opposition groups had been trying to drag the United States into assisting in the dismantling of the monarchy since November. In private discussions with embassy officers, moderate dissidents had urged Washington to pressure the Shah into naming a government acceptable to the opposition as early as the change of government on November 6, when General Azhari took over. In early December the Committee for the Defense of Human Rights made overtures to the U.S. and Britain, requesting that the ambassadors from the two countries present the proposal for a regency council to the Shah. Both countries declined to do so, but discreetly emphasized to the monarch the need for compromise.[7]

Until January, Washington steadfastly refused to get involved in specific initiatives with the various parties to the crisis. The policy changed after Washington announced it supported Bakhtiar's efforts to form a government. A senior American air force officer was dispatched from NATO by the President to consult with Iranian military leaders. Deputy NATO commander General Robert Huyser arrived in Tehran on January 5 and stayed one month. He immediately began talking to the ranking officers, urging them to support a constitutional solution to the crisis. From the viewpoint of the Iranians, the Huyser mission was the first public indication that the United States was more than an interested observer of current events in that country. All the previous appeals by dissidents to the State Department and the National Security Council staff and the continuous talks between embassy officers and opposition leaders had gone unheeded. But Huyser's arrival was different. Within the context of stated U.S. support for Bakhtiar, it was viewed at best with suspicion and at worst with fear of American collusion in a military coup similar to the one that returned the Shah to power in 1953.[8]

At least some of the revolutionaries in contact with the American embassy understood that the United States, through Huyser, was seeking only to steady the Iranian military so that it would support whatever transitional arrangements developed, especially after the Shah announced on January 6 that he would "take a rest" abroad as soon as order was restored. But the opposition was basically split on the U.S. role thus far: On the one hand, the National Front and the Liberation Movement were unhappy that the United States had not been more helpful in engineering an acceptable compromise. On the other, the religious leaders gathered around Ayatollahs Beheshti and Taleqani had no use at all for the United States. Instead, they reiterated the Khomeini line, stating that the Islamic movement opposed the new regime because Bakhtiar had accepted his mandate from the "illegal" Shah.

Khomeini moderated his stance ever so slightly on January 10 when he said Iran could have good relations with the U.S. and Western European countries if they stopped supporting the Shah and ceased interfering in Iranian internal affairs. He also said that he would feel "no hostility" to any country that gave the Shah political asylum.[9] This statement, offered on the advice of key advisors Abol Hassan Bani-Sadr and Ibrahim Yazdi, was meant to encourage the Shah's Western allies, easing the transition to a new government without the Shah. In view of the American hostage crisis later that year which was triggered by the Shah's admission to the United States, Khomeini's statement is an ironic footnote suggesting the degree to which the revolutionaries were willing to deal with even the U.S. in order to gain a nonviolent transition to power. In the context of other American initiatives, failure to capitalize on the Ayatollah's remark must be considered a lost opportunity for the United States to have resolved early the thorny problem of where the Shah's future home would be.

The in-country religious leadership, which coordinated its activities with the Liberation Movement, saw the Bakhtiar government as a bloodless transition arrangement ultimately leading to an Islamic regime. That was the difference between the lay and the clerical leadership of the revolutionary movement. Khomeini and radical Ayatollahs Beheshti, Lahouti, and Moussavi believed that bloodshed was inevitable because it was unlikely that the army could be fully destroyed from within. The Liberation Movement hoped the military could be neutralized without being crushed. Though the Islamic movement had continued to make great headway breaking down resistance in the army and increasing desertion, hoping to wear out the will to fight and thus minimize the "final struggle," not until the very eve of the revolutionary triumph on February 12 did the opposition forces believe they had succeeded.

Farewell to the Shah

The imperial system created by the Shah and his father simply collapsed. With a prime minister in power publicly committed to enforcing the 1906 constitution and privately pledged to ending the Pahlavi dynasty, the Shah had compromised himself by promising to leave the country. Iran's last monarch had achieved neither a stable regime through opposition participation nor military control of street violence. Installing Bakhtiar did not relax tensions. The Shah's only remaining options were to leave or to order the military to fight under circumstances more adverse than at any earlier time. With hard-line commanders already dismissed and the government he had appointed in place, the Shah was boxed in. Even if he had experienced a last minute change of heart, the loyalist command structure had been shattered. Those who knew the Shah well enough to guess his feelings believe he really had given up several weeks earlier, after Azhari's failure to restore order in November and/or after the huge Tassua-Ashura marches on December 10 and 11.

U.S. policy focused on Bakhtiar as the last chance for a "constitutional" (nonviolent) solution to the crisis. After the installation of Bakhtiar, Washington directed Ambassador Sullivan to inform the Shah that the United States believed it would be wise for him to leave the country temporarily. News of this, one of many leaks about U.S. policy, made the press the next day. It did not mean much, however, since all opposition groups already anticipated their monarch's departure.

Bakhtiar presented his government and his program to parliament January 11. He pledged to dissolve SAVAK immediately, to end martial law, and to support Palestinian and Arab causes. On January 13 the fourth prime minister in six months formally announced the formation of a nine-man regency council that would rule in the Shah's absence. It included chief of staff General Gharabaghi, head of the National Iranian Oil Company Abdollah Entezam, former Senator Sayed Jalaledin Tehrani (who became the head of the council), Minister of Court Ali Qoli Ardelan, four obscure representatives of the opposition, and the prime minister. Khomeini countered by denouncing Bakhtiar and declaring from Paris on January 12 that a revolutionary council "to prepare the institutions for an Islamic republic" would be formed. No names were mentioned; Khomeini said they would be announced later.

On January 15 Iran's Senate approved the Bakhtiar government 38–1. A court spokesman announced the Shah would be leaving the next day, at the conclusion of the Majles (lower house) vote of confidence, to visit Egypt and then to go to the United States for an extended stay. That evening, extremists killed American engineer Martin Berkowitz, an ex-army officer working for a private American company in Kerman. He became the second American to die in Iran's revolutionary upheaval.

The Majles approved Bakhtiar's government at noon, January 16, 149–34, with 13 abstentions. Following the vote, the Shah, his wife, three of his four children (the crown prince had been studying in the U.S. for several months), his mother-in-law and many senior officials went to Mehrabad airport. There to see them off were ranking military officers, the regency council, and Prime Minister Bakhtiar (who to the dismay of his revolutionary ex-colleagues kissed the Shah's hand). Shortly thereafter, the air force plane left for Egypt. When Tehran radio broadcast the news, public celebrations broke out all over the city. Revolutionary groups took to the streets without hindrance from the security and military forces. Several thousand gathered at various points throughout Tehran and began pulling down statues of the Shah. Mobs "invited" drivers to turn on their car lights in celebration. American embassy minibuses taking employees home early were equipped, prudently, with pictures of Khomeini. Thus the crowds jamming the streets garlanded the vans with flowers.

The day the Shah left his country public order was maintained in Tehran by the Islamic movement, not the army. The armed forces took the news of the Shah's departure with mixed feelings. Senior commanders in the capital were aware of the unfolding political collapse. Those in the hinterlands were not. In oil-rich Khuzistan province, garrison commanders ordered troops to fire on demonstrators celebrating the departure of the Shah. Foreign journalists in Ahwaz reported that soldiers killed 20 people and injured 200. Troops also killed and injured civilians in Khorramshahr and Abadan, until Bakhtiar ordered the army back to barracks.

In Paris, Khomeini hailed the removal of the Shah and then immediately called for the resignation of Prime Minister Bakhtiar, parliament, and the regency council. He said, "It [the departure] is not the final victory, but the preface to our victory." The next day the Ayatollah issued a manifesto to his followers telling them to avoid violence and to continue their campaign to bring down the Bakhtiar government through demonstrations and mass pressure. He urged the strikes be continued and exhorted his followers to win over the armed forces in support of the Islamic republic. For the first time he also called for the nationalization of the Shah's property. The National Front underlined its solidarity with Khomeini when two of its leaders, Dariush Forouhar and Tehran attorney Hassan Nazih, met with the Ayatollah in Paris immediately after the Shah left Iran.

The Islamic movement in Iran already had started planning for Khomeini's return, and on the day the Shah withdrew made its first overtures on the subject to Bakhtiar and to the embassies of the United States and France. These diplomats suggested that the Islamic movement would be wise not to attempt returning the Ayatollah to Iran without a prearranged deal with the military and the government. The Americans and the French knew, and the British suspected, that Bakhtiar had failed to establish a political base or to split off his former colleagues from Khomeini.

Religious leaders like Shariatmadari, who did not care for Khomeini's style, were in eclipse, afraid to say anything opposing the Ayatollah for fear of retaliation by Islamic fanatics. Though the religious moderates had played the leading role in mobilizing the masses in Iran from 1977 to mid-1978, Khomeini had emerged as the man of the hour. It was his militant followers who now dominated political activity in Tehran and other cities.

In an effort to strike a deal with Khomeini, Bakhtiar dispatched the chairman of the regency council, Sayed Jalaledin Tehrani, to speak with the Ayatollah. After being kept waiting for four days, then hearing harsh words from Khomeini and his chief lieutenants about the illegitimacy of the regency council and the Bakhtiar government, Tehrani acceded to their wishes and resigned from the council, staying on in Paris. This was followed within three days by the departure of two of the four opposition members of the council, Abdul Aliabadi and Mohammad Ali Varasteh, who quit in Tehran. Meanwhile, Bakhtiar's justice minister, the elderly Yayah Vaziri, resigned in protest after a radical group of Islamic supporters broke into his office and harangued him.

The Shah's leavetaking marked the end of an era in Iranian politics. While Bakhtiar and his government kept up the polite fiction that the vacation was "temporary," no one in Iran believed he would ever return as monarch. The absence of the Shah did not take the pressure off the new prime minister; indeed, it intensified his problems. The revolutionary movement remained solidly behind Khomeini and shifted its line of fire to the Bakhtiar administration. Now the goals of the revolutionaries were to destroy the last vestige of the old regime, to bring Khomeini back to Tehran, and to seize political power.

Chapter Nine

Takeover!

January 17–February 18, 1979

As soon as the Shah left his country, political activity accelerated to a frantic pace. A severe earthquake that struck the town of Tabas in southeastern Iran the day the monarch departed killed 25,000 villagers, appearing as a powerful signal that radical change was imminent. Ironically, Tabas would figure in history again 15 months later, when the American hostage rescue mission would come to grief on salt flats near the town.

Because the Shah supposedly had left behind a prime minister loyal to him, Bakhtiar found himself beset on all sides. The government was forced to be defensive immediately, because of the resignation of the chairman of the regency council, and the prime minister never was able to gain the initiative. The revolutionaries staged demonstrations daily throughout the country and encouraged men in the army and SAVAK to desert the Shah's prime minister. Even though both organizations remained loyal to the government, some military leaders began independent maneuvering. Defections to the Islamic opposition increased; the focus of politics had shifted from concern over what the Shah would do to when Khomeini would return. Negotiations between Bakhtiar's representatives and the revolutionaries continued practically up to the minute the Ayatollah was allowed to fly to Iran. Ultimately, the army reluctantly consented to let him come ahead, primarily because there was no one in authority—civilian or military—willing to try and stop him.[1]

From the moment he arrived on an Air France charter February 1, Khomeini betrayed his vague assurances to Bakhtiar to "behave" and intensified his campaign against the remnants of Pahlavi control. On

165

February 5 the Ayatollah named a provisional government and urged civil servants to refuse to work for anyone but Khomeini's fanatically religious appointees to the various ministries. The Ayatollah's men were everywhere, negotiating with supporters of the Bakhtiar regime and building up their own organization. Several of Khomeini's key lieutenants had arrived with him, including the man who would be elected Iran's first president, Abol Hassan Bani-Sadr; he gave up his economic research in Paris to accompany the Ayatollah. Ibrahim Yazdi, deputy prime minister and later foreign minister in the post-revolutionary government, left an American-born wife and four children in Houston, Texas, to do the same. Yazdi never renounced his naturalization in 1962 and even today is an American citizen.

As Islamic pressure on the government increased throughout the first days of February, the situation grew steadily more tense. The flash point came on February 9, when air force warrant officers loyal to Khomeini took over two military bases in Tehran. Eight hundred of the 8,000 man Imperial Guard, crack troops intensely loyal to the monarchy, moved in to put down the rebellion. Instead, they suffered substantial casualties, including the deaths of two of their top officers. The following day, February 10, the military leadership decided to stay out of the fray. The armed forces abruptly collapsed, and along with them the Bakhtiar government. Guerrilla units stormed the remaining military installations in Tehran on February 10 and 11, triggering public jubilation. Bakhtiar disappeared; Khomeini took over on February 12. In the midst of the triumphal celebration, the various revolutionary groups were privately jockeying for preeminence in the newly forming Islamic regime.

Some factions, particularly the Fedayeen, were paranoid with fear that the Shah, with the help of the United States, was plotting a counterstrike. In the wake of the revolution, rumors spread that former officials of the Shah had been encouraged to take refuge inside the American compound and were in the midst of helping execute the coup. The U.S. Marine guards at the embassy were automatically suspected of collusion in the nefarious plan. The marines, normally a 13-man contingent of enlisted men 19 to 25 years old, had been reinforced to 20 after the December unrest. As at U.S. embassies worldwide, they were responsible for nothing more than guarding embassy entrances and maintaining order.

Keying its strategy to the maxim "the best defense is a good offense," one Fedayeen group took over the six-story International Communications Agency (U.S.I.C.A.) building in downtown Tehran on February

13. U.S.I.C.A. had been called the U.S. Information Service (U.S.I.S.) until a few months before, when Washington changed the name of the organization worldwide. The Tehran branch was overrun in the belief that the C.I.A. (U.S.I.C.A.=U.S.C.I.A.) office had been captured. "*Ettela'at*," the Farsi word for information, also means intelligence, and based on this "evidence" of spying in the guise of cultural and information activities, the Fedayeen, aided by some sympathetic Mujahidin, stepped up their plans to attack the American embassy next.

On the morning of February 14, groups of Fedayeen and Mujahidin fought their way over the walls of the embassy compound and beseiged the main building. The marines used only tear gas against the raiders, who eventually cornered most of the American staff on the second floor. In the two-hour struggle for control of the structure, it was so immersed in the fine, white, tear-gas powder that the mess was not fully cleaned up until two months later. Three tear-gas decontamination kits (one is supposed to be sufficient) had to be used and the inside of the entire building repainted. As late as June some offices still were not habitable unless windows were open.

About noon Mujahidin forces loyal to the provisional government and the central revolutionary committee arrived, led by Deputy Prime Minister Yazdi who "set free" the embassy personnel. Mujahidin guards stayed on duty, "protecting" the staff. The confrontation between Yazdi and the leftists who had staged the seizure precipitated general street fighting between the Fedayeen and the Mujahidin the next four nights. The result was a shaky "victory" for the Islamic movement (Mujahidin) and a very fragile "peace" which more closely resembled anarchy than order in the streets.

Faced with this split in the revolutionary coalition, the provisional government encountered several obstacles in trying to consolidate its power. The Fedayeen was suspicious of the religious guerrillas and the Mujahidin did not want to be restrained, not even by the government it professed to back. Serious internal differences between these and other revolutionary factions began to surface, blocking the restoration of authority and foreshadowing future chaos.

The Contending Factions Maneuver for Control

The Islamic movement organized massive demonstrations for January 19, the fortieth day after Ashura. Bakhtiar had no choice but to agree to them since, ostensibly, they were ritual celebrations. Almost a million people paraded in the capital city that day. The declaration read at the march called for the abolition of the Pahlavi monarchy and urged the army, the government, and the parliament to join the revolution. The next day Khomeini announced from Paris that he would return to Iran "within a few days." In a public speech Bakhtiar countered by urging Khomeini to postpone his arrival. The mood nationwide was tense and electric as everyone waited to see what the next move would be. Something had to give.

The beginning of the end for Bakhtiar started on January 22. About 800 air force warrant officers (homafars) declared themselves loyal to Khomeini and revolted against their officers at air bases in Dezful, Hamadan, Mashad, and Isfahan. This was the first large military group not only to shift its loyalties but also to take over government installations. The homafars were educated technicians who never were given the status of commissioned officers. Therefore they had less to lose and perhaps much to gain by supporting Khomeini.

The military closed Mehrabad airport on January 24 and blocked the runways with tanks and troops in order to prevent Khomeini's arrival. This made it clear the armed services planned to be a force to be reckoned with. That same day and the next, moderates around Bakhtiar organized demonstrations supporting the legal government. They proclaimed loyalty to the 1906 constitution—not the Shah—and drew about 50,000 people to Baharestan Square. Liberation Movement leader Bazargan and the National Front's Sanjabi warned on the second day of the pro-government marches that failure to let Khomeini into the country would ensure continued violence. Stepping up the pressure even more, mullahs led another round of exhortations demanding the prime minister resign. Bakhtiar offered to hold a plebiscite on the monarchy and then quit if Khomeini would remain in Paris.

The Islamic movement and the Fedayeen countered that proposal with even larger demonstrations. On January 29 revolutionaries attending a rally at Tehran University issued a statement that "all U.S. advisors must leave Iran within one month or face death." In view of the deteriorating security conditions, the embassy declared itself in phase II of its emergency evacuation plan. The following morning all dependents and nonessential personnel began leaving Iran permanently by U.S. Air Force C-5 jets. Because of the chaotic conditions at Mehrabad airport, embassy officers also began coordinating evacuation flights for private citizens who had not yet departed. About 12,000 Americans flew out of Tehran between January 31 and the revolutionary takeover on February 11 and 12. (An additional 6,600 foreigners, the majority of them U.S. citizens, would be evacuated between February 18 and 25, after the embassy was overrun by revolutionaries on February 14.) While many Americans left in an orderly fashion, others were forced to leave behind their personal belongings. Some of the abandoned property was turned over to the embassy later and sent to the families; much was not. There was significant looting from the empty houses of U.S. officials, including the homes of those officers still in Tehran who, for security reasons, now lived in furnished apartments close to the embassy compound rather than in their all-Iranian neighborhoods. The household goods of these Americans were "requisitioned" by revolutionary gangs who ransacked houses. Public order had broken down completely.

While popular discussion centered on the prospects for Khomeini's return and the pressure upon the Bakhtiar government to resign, private talks began within hours of the Shah's departure between Bakhtiar and his intermediaries on the one hand and Bazargan and representatives of the Liberation Movement, the National Front, and the Islamic movement on the other. There were two critical questions. How would the military react to Khomeini's return? Could the conflict between Bakhtiar's administration and Khomeini's vague "Islamic government" be reconciled?

The hard-line revolutionaries insisted that Khomeini be allowed to come back and made every effort to neutralize the armed forces and induce them to accept his return. Bakhtiar wanted to keep the Ayatollah out of the country. He implored the Islamic militants to give him a chance to stabilize Iran and avoid the bloodshed which would almost certainly occur if Khomeini arrived before the Islamic movement and the government could agree on what to do. The military, represented in the talks by chief of staff Gharabaghi and SAVAK's Moghaddam, found itself caught in the middle under the worst possible circumstances. The armed forces had sworn an oath to the Shah and the constitution, but the Shah was gone. Already at loose ends, the generals were holding fast to the idea of protecting the constitution, if only because it was the one political concept left which carried any shred of governmental legitimacy.

Each of the three parties involved in this deep-rooted political struggle faced a dilemma. First of all, Bakhtiar headed a foundering government that had received the Shah's approval, the kiss of death. The prime minister's foremost accomplishment had been to get the monarch to leave the country, but he had failed in his attempts to bring any of his moderate dissident colleagues into the government with him. Bakhtiar desperately needed to expand his political base. On the other hand, the revolutionary coalition did not yet have full control, nor was its legitimacy recognized by the only military force that could block its rise to power. The opposition leadership believed the army could make the dissidents-turned-revolutionaries pay a very high price in any direct and violent confrontation. Thus the political stance of the armed forces suddenly became the central issue. With the Shah gone, only the military stood against the armed guerrilla movements of the left and right as the guardian of the government which remained.

Discussions between the various groups began before the Shah's plane had left Iranian airspace. On behalf of the Liberation Movement, Bazargan contacted Bakhtiar to arrange for the triumphal return of Khomeini, hopefully within a few days. He was disconcerted to discover that Bakhtiar—since the military, though shaky, was behind the prime minister—meant to make a go of his government. On January 22 Nasser Minatchi, the moderate closest to Ayatollah Shariatmadari, arranged to meet with General Gharabaghi to determine whether Khomeini could return without military interference. The answer was ambiguous. The government and the army were willing to talk with Islamic leaders, but not yet ready to make a deal.

By January 25 the Committee for the Defense of Human Rights, under Minatchi's leadership, was proposing the amalgamation of the truncated regency council and Khomeini's Islamic council. The opposition believed that joining the two groups into one would lead to the eventual takeover of the government by revolutionary forces under an umbrella of legitimacy. Then, during the final days of January, the Liberation Movement tried another tack. It proposed to Bakhtiar that he resign as the Shah's prime minister and be reappointed immediately by Khomeini. The possibility of a compromise along these lines was the reason that Khomeini initially agreed to receive Bakhtiar when the latter announced on January 27 that he would come to Paris to talk with the Ayatollah. That same day, 15 people were killed in Tehran rioting. The next morning more violence broke out, and when the day was over 35 additional people had been killed in the capital and about 50 others elsewhere in the country. That evening Khomeini reversed himself, saying Bakhtiar would have to resign first if he were to be received. Bakhtiar dismissed Khomeini's demand, but neither did he travel to Paris. The result was a stalemate.

As the negotiating continued, Islamic militants beseeched the military leadership to desert Bakhtiar and join the revolutionaries. Though General Gharabaghi and his colleagues held fast, there was considerable dissension within the ranks. Several, including Generals Ali Neshat, commander of the Imperial Guard, Manuchehr Khosrowdad of the air force, and Abbas Ali Badrii, commander of the ground forces, wanted to attempt a coup, ending the Bakhtiar government. They were ready to impose the repressive hard-line solution that the Shah had resisted for so long. A number of other generals believed the army should stay neutral between the government and the revolutionaries. A few thought the leaders of the military should bow to the inevitable and bring the army over to the side of the opposition intact, thus preserving both the military command structure and order within the country. As for the revolutionary leadership, they knew that conscripts were not wedded to the institution of the military. Therefore they continued to play on the fears of senior officers and worked diligently to undermine the authority of the commanders with their own troops.

It was obvious that the central question for the armed forces was whether and under what circumstances Khomeini should be allowed into the country. Faced with divided opinion among the military, General Gharabaghi insisted that the Ayatollah could not come back if he was advocating disloyalty to the constitutional government. Liberation Movement negotiators, on the other hand, focused on what differences in the existing governing arrangements the armed forces would be willing to accept. Eventually the military agreed to a formula for change, but only if it was carried out constitutionally. The generals insisted that alterations in Bakhtiar's government had to be made by constitutional amendment. Final plans concerning Khomeini's return were worked out on January 28 in a meeting between Generals Gharabaghi and Moghaddam for the military and SAVAK on the one hand and Bazargan and his deputy, Yadollah Sahabi, for the Liberation Movement on the other. Although the arrangements for Khomeini's arrival were complete, the argument persisted over whether the Regency Council, incomplete because three of its members (including the chairman) had resigned, would continue as is or be modified.

The army had implied it would accept changes in the cabinet, but insisted on retaining its growing independence. Gharabaghi warned that if Khomeini tried arbitrarily to appoint a rival government there would be military trouble. He also stated that the armed forces would no longer tolerate revolutionary speakers' "calls to treason" and the advocating of desertion. To make the point, several of the more hotheaded dissident stump speakers were detained by the military in early February under the existing martial law regulations. They were not released until after the revolution a week later.

Bakhtiar was not happy about Khomeini's impending return. The prime minister's influence was already shrinking, so there was little he could do unless he was prepared to take on the Islamic mobs and the various well organized revolutionary groups. The army was loath to support such a confrontation in any case. When Khomeini aides gave some vague assurances that the Ayatollah would not proclaim an Islamic government, it seemed easier, and certainly less provoking to the revolutionary mobs, to allow him to return.

The United States supported Bakhtiar's efforts to stabilize the political situation. President Carter endorsed the prime minister's government at his press conference on January 17 and urged Khomeini to give it a chance to succeed. On January 24 the U.S. agreed to ship the Bakhtiar government 200,000 barrels of diesel fuel and gasoline so that essential government and military transportation could function. This undercut the effects of the strikers at the oil fields and the refinery and greatly annoyed the Islamic movement, but did give Bakhtiar some breathing space. When the airlift shipments began, feelings of anti-American xenophobia surged again, in demonstrations and personal unpleasantness on the streets. On February 6 State Department spokesman Hodding Carter outlined the U.S. position. "What we are doing is to support the government and the constitutional process. We recognize Bakhtiar as the head of the government of Iran. We continue to deal with that government on an official basis."[2]

But U.S. pronouncements were not nearly as important to the situation as U.S. actions. Supplying oil to Iran made it clear where Washington's sympathies lay as far as the revolutionaries were concerned, particularly since they continued to believe that the United States had influence with Iran's armed forces. They knew that American General Robert Huyser had arrived in Iran on January 5. By the end of the month it was widely believed among upper-class Iranians that Huyser had kept the army from violently repressing unrest and establishing a military government, while the Islamic movement feared he was promoting a coup. Huyser had been sent to Iran by the President to assess the future of U.S. military programs in the country. Of special concern were sensitive American electronic equipment and aircraft, not to mention $12 billion of undelivered aircraft, ships, and missiles previously ordered by the Shah.

However, the Islamic militants who were to overrun the American embassy eight months later have published copies of cables allegedly written by Huyser which claim to show he advocated a military takeover of key sectors of the economy suffering from chronic strikes—the oil fields, the customs offices, the banks. Certainly Huyser influenced the generals not to carry out a coup against Bakhtiar, either before the Shah left Iran or later. Beyond that, since his instructions from Washington were put together by the Defense Department, the White House, the State Department, and the National Security Council, they were vague. Although the military remained divided about what to do, Huyser obviously stressed to them the need to remain united behind the constitutional government. Unfortunately, his instructions contained no guidance on what to say if that government disappeared.

It is worth noting that the military continued to back Bakhtiar until February 10, six days after General Huyser left the country. Huyser, who was not a specialist on Iran and did not speak the language, was influenced by what the ranking generals told him about the loyalty of the army. Aware of the political negotiating between Bakhtiar, the generals, and the opposition, he began to suspect near the end of his mission that some of the generals, particularly Gharabaghi, might be negotiating for a transfer of military loyalties to the revolutionaries, not a standfast attitude behind Bakhtiar. Huyser was basically upbeat about the ability of the armed forces to hold, but he was in a poor position to assess the continuing disintegration of authority and the impact this was having on the attitudes of senior officers.[3] In his final book, *Answer to History*, published just a few months before his death in 1980, the Shah suggests that Huyser arranged some kind of a deal between the revolutionaries and the military, and was the middleman getting the Liberation Movement's Bazargan together with General Gharabaghi. His assertion that the United States prevented the army from acting to protect Iran from the revolutionaries is part of the liturgy of Iranian exiles as well.[4]

The assumptions of both the Shah and the establishment figures now out of the country were wrong. Huyser's instructions were neither to rally the generals behind the monarch nor to arrange for an orderly Khomeini takeover. He was a professional army man assigned, like Diogenes, to search for "truth," but in an unfamiliar environment with a very dim light. Military leaders within the country already differed greatly on what the army should do. Each general heard what he wanted to hear from the American. Undoubtedly, the mission of the U.S. general will loom larger in historic legend than its importance to the political dynamic of the revolution justifies. Huyser's observations and conclusions about possible outcomes to the Iranian crisis, for example, may have caused policy and decision makers in Washington to overestimate the cohesiveness of the military, but that is a separate issue. In the months since the revolution, surviving generals and politicians have found the Huyser mission a convenient scapegoat when rationalizing their own roles in the debacle.

The Return of the Charismatic Ayatollah

Eventually the finishing touches to the final agreement on Khomeini's return were arranged. The airport and area leading up to Freedom Monument (renamed by the Islamic movement from the original Shahyad Monument) were to be controlled by the Mujahidin, its first formal introduction into the political process. The military and SAVAK were to guard the route from Freedom Monument to Tehran's main cemetery, where Khomeini's first act upon his return after 15 years in exile would be to pay tribute to the revolutionary martyrs.

The Ayatollah arrived at 9:15 A.M. on February 1. His entourage of about 50 included his advisors Abol Hassan Bani-Sadr, Ibrahim Yazdi, and Sadeq Ghotbzadeh. The event was covered live on Iranian television and beamed worldwide. About two million of his countrymen turned out to meet the Ayatollah, who proceeded in triumph to Behesht-e-Zahra cemetery, where he spoke to his followers. Then he went to his new residence at the Alavi School in south Tehran, a few blocks from parliament. Moving immediately to the offensive, Khomeini called for the arrest of Bakhtiar and his "illegal" government saying, "I shall shut their mouths." He called for the expulsion of all foreigners from Iran, especially Americans. The next day, February 2, in a statement read at Friday prayer services throughout the country, he reiterated all these points.

From the moment of his arrival Khomeini overshadowed Bakhtiar and Islamic forces controlled the streets. Earlier, armed guerrillas had military patrols to attack, but beginning on February 3 the army progressively decreased its presence in Tehran in order to diminish the prospect of confrontation with the militants. Amid the escalating street violence, there was also a growing number of army and air force detachments changing their allegiance and joining the revolutionaries. To add to the troubles of the military, on February 1 the Islamic movement made public a tape recording, allegedly of the Shah briefing his ranking commanders and calling for the armed forces to instigate prolonged civil war. Though it was analyzed later as a forgery by voice experts in the United States and Britain, the Mujahidin used it effectively in its program to discredit the military, particularly its senior leadership.

One Country, Two Governments

As soon as Khomeini returned to Iran, talks resumed between the Liberation Movement, which was representing Khomeini, and Bakhtiar. The prime minister was prepared to let Khomeini name some cabinet ministers, hoping thereby to placate the Ayatollah into accepting the legitimacy of the Bakhtiar government. Instead, Khomeini insisted the prime minister acknowledge the legitimacy of the revolution. The negotiations played with variants of the demands of each. February 3 and 4 were the critical days. During on-again, off-again talks about a joint government or some other form of transfer of power, both sides made concessions. Bakhtiar allowed a series of religious demonstrations and Khomeini's aide, Ibrahim Yazdi, announced that a transfer of power could be carried out "within the framework of the constitution." One possibility had Bakhtiar becoming minister of defense in a Khomeini-dominated government. But Bakhtiar absolutely refused to resign, so the Ayatollah decided to announce the formation of his own Islamic government. The prime minister offered no objection "as long as it is considered merely a shadow cabinet."[5] The generals followed Bakhtiar's line.

Late on the afternoon of February 5 Khomeini named as prime minister the leader of the Liberation Movement, Mehdi Bazargan. He also announced five other cabinet appointments, including retired Admiral Ahmad Madani to be minister of the interior. In this same speech Khomeini urged civil servants to stage sit-ins at all government offices and thereby force out Bakhtiar's ministers. The following day the Ayatollah said that Iran's 1906 constitution would remain in effect until his new Islamic constitution would be ready.

It was also on February 5 that Bakhtiar cancelled $7 billion worth of U.S. weapons deliveries, including two destroyers, almost 1,000 air-to-air, surface-to-air, and anti-ship missiles, seven airborne early warning craft, and 176 of the newest jet fighter planes. His foreign minister, Ahmad Mirfendereski, withdrew Iran from the CENTO defense pact the following day. Neither act affected the intentions of the powerful Islamic movement; nothing Bakhtiar could do would mollify the revolutionaries striving for complete control. The next day Khomeini supporters flooded the streets in major cities and engaged in their own version of "throw the rascals out," by establishing "Islamic" governments in Mashad, Isfahan, Shiraz, and several other smaller towns.

The revolutionary coalition had one more constitutional ploy up its sleeve. The evening of February 6 the last pre-revolution speaker of the

Majles, Javad Saeed, called for a no-confidence vote on the legal (Bakh-tiar) regime. If successful, under the constitution the government would have to fall, leaving no legitimate successor. The planned arrangement was ingenious. With the "constitutional" regime dismissed, the speaker would move parliament to "approve" the Bazargan government announced by Khomeini, thus finessing the question of legality. This solution appears to have had at least tacit support within the armed forces. However, after four hours of wild and wooly parliamentary infighting and with some 70 deputies missing through resignations (in conformance with Khomeini's wishes), the speaker was unable to deliver a majority vote on a motion of no confidence. A number of backbench deputies, some loyal to the Shah and all distrustful of the Islamic clergy, coalesced around a medical doctor, Akbar Bahadori, the Majles deputy from Arak. They defeated the speaker by eight votes, probably 92–84. (No recorded tally was ever published.) Though his end-run effort nearly succeeded, it did Majles Speaker Saeed little good. He was executed for "treason" along with Bahadori and many other deputies after Khomeini took power.

Defections from the Bakhtiar camp increased on February 7 and 8. About 20 more parliamentary deputies resigned. (Many had stayed around merely to vote Bakhtiar out.) Meanwhile, the Islamic movement appointed revolutionary committees (*komitehs*) to take over the functions of government. Over one hundred "Islamic" cooperative stores sprang up in Tehran, and large areas of the bazaar passed into committee control. The revolutionaries simply proceeded to establish their authority in helter-skelter fashion throughout Tehran and as much of the rest of Iran for which they could find revolutionary neighborhood komitehs to assume responsibility. The police melted away. Mujahidin and Islamic gangs, operating from the komiteh headquarters, took over responsibility for law and order and in some areas even basic services like trash collection. Authority as well as legitimacy gradually passed into the hands of the Islamic movement.

Both the constitutional forces under Bakhtiar and the Islamic movement under Khomeini gave exclusive attention to establishing or maintaining control over their specific geographic areas. External events had minimal impact. The fact that United States Ambassador to the United Nations Andrew Young commented in New York that Khomeini was "a saint" and that, because of Western influence, "it would be impossible to have a fundamentalist state in Iran," drew little attention and no reaction in Tehran. Neither did the news that Secretary of Defense Harold Brown would leave in a few days for Saudi Arabia, Jordan,

Israel, and Egypt, despite the normal fears of Islamic fundamentalists that such a move might be a prelude to U.S. intervention in Iran.

One Armed Insurrection and the Military Crumbles

With more authority passing into revolutionary hands every day, the position of the military became even more sensitive and critical. Gharabaghi and others who believed in accommodation with the Islamic movement continued to negotiate with Bazargan and his deputies over the means by which the armed forces could transfer their loyalties to the revolutionary shadow government. However, substantial sentiment still existed within the military to crush the revolutionaries. Generals Neshat and Badrii, who led the Imperial Guard and the ground forces respectively, wanted to round up army detachments that had defected and to crush the armed guerrillas. Others argued that this was impossible; the insurgent movement was too strong and had too much popular support. The Supreme Council of the Armed Forces, military men who had been appointed to key command positions by the Shah, met daily after February 1, but could come to no agreement. The divisions remained.

Then events took the possibility of control away from any one group. On February 9, at Farahabad and Doshen Tappeh air bases in Tehran, warrant officers and cadets in formation gave a salute to Khomeini. This was too much for the Shah loyalists. The Imperial Guard's Javadan Brigade ("The Immortals," who were the Shah's personal guards and who had put on an impressive pro-government parade January 23) moved in at Farahabad to break up this show of disloyalty. The position of the Supreme Council of the Armed Forces consistently had been that any direct challenge to the government or the army would be met by force. In the revolutionary confusion, each commander had interpreted this policy in the light of his own situation at any given time. Most were reluctant to shoot. Events during the week since Khomeini's return had shown that some form of "settlement," probably the gradual assumption of power by Bazargan's government, was becoming the most likely option. For this reason commanders generally tended to withhold fire. The Javadan Brigade, however, was spoiling for a fight. Cadets and warrant officers had barricaded themselves inside both Farahabad and Doshen Tappeh and proclaimed their loyalty to the Islamic revolution. The brigade sent officers and men to both locations.

The Islamic movement was fearful about this development. While

Farahabad and Doshen Tappeh were under siege, the head of the provisional government, Mehdi Bazargan, was giving a prearranged speech before 10,000 enthusiastic supporters at Tehran University. He called for Bakhtiar to resign and for the strikes to continue until the prime minister either was ousted or quit. He also urged calm and asked his followers not to take the law into their own hands. Bazargan knew that the revolution was approaching victory, but he also understood that this was the most dangerous time, because the military hard-liners might act on reflex, without government orders. The chain of command was crumbling.

The radical Islamic leadership, also sensing victory on February 9, came to a different conclusion. Now was the time to support actively those military units expressing loyalty to Khomeini. At Farahabad the cadets fought back, and several were killed in a short, intense struggle. Because the rebels were supported by armed Islamic mobs milling around both inside and outside the base, eventually the Javadan Brigade was forced to withdraw and the renegades were able to hold their ground. Opposition sources said 60 insurgents died, but there was no way to verify it. There would be no government reply since there would be no Shah-appointed government after that day. That afternoon, as the fighting at Farahabad died down, an interim decision was made by the radical Islamics to come to the aid of warrant officers and cadets at the Doshen Tappeh air base. Mujahidin and Fedayeen units were rushed there to assist the rebels and to prevent cadets and homafars from being crushed by loyal soldiers.

Around 11:00 P.M. the Javadan Brigade moved in to stop the conversion of Doshen Tappeh into a revolutionary stronghold. It knew already that the disloyal air force homafars and cadets had been reinforced and, just as had happened at Farahabad, weapons from storage magazines were being distributed indiscriminately. The Mujahidin and Fedayeen defenders realized the raid was coming because military supporters of Khomeini tipped them off in advance about the planned movements of the Javadan Brigade. Thus the brigade was attacked even before it arrived at Doshen Tappeh. Fierce fighting broke out over a large area around the base. In a break for the revolutionaries, several key officers in the Javadan Brigade were killed early, including the ranking Imperial Guard commander, General Neshat.

The defecting air cadets had begun distributing automatic weapons to the supporting mob immediately. By midday two days later approximately 300,000 guns and rifles plus ammunition had been handed out from the magazines in Tehran. About 1.5 million weapons from government arsenals were distributed throughout the country in the days that followed, arming every conceivable revolutionary unit plus supporting mobs and stray teenagers. Despite calls later to turn in these weapons, only about six percent were handed back. The existence of so much firepower in the hands of those whose loyalties and sense of discipline were questionable and diverse severely complicated the eventual problem of restoring some semblance of law and order.

The Islamic leadership had authorized the distribution of weapons because it believed that full confrontation with the military was now imminent. On February 10 fighting continued at Doshen Tappeh and spread from there to other areas in Tehran. *Los Angeles Times* correspondent Joe Alex Morris was killed by a stray bullet while observing the struggle at that air base, the third and last American to die as a result of revolutionary violence.

The military ordered a 4:00 P.M. curfew February 10, which was immediately denounced by Khomeini. He pointedly warned that any efforts on the part of the armed forces to resist the Islamic movement would cause him to proclaim a *jihad* (holy war) against army units that did not surrender. Negotiations between military commanders and several different opposition factions began almost immediately. Ayatollah Taleqani, Tehran's leading religious figure, was chosen by Khomeini to be his principal representative. Taleqani insisted that the army withdraw and let the revolution take its course.

Simultaneously, armed guerrillas began moving up to attack the Imperial Guard base on Saltanatabad Avenue in north Tehran, in the process overrunning the nearby "Gulf District," where U.S. facilities were located, including army communications equipment and ARMISH-MAAG offices. By 7:00 P.M. all American military buildings, including the commissary (not actually at Gulf District, but close by) were in the hands of the Fedayeen, who promptly invited its Palestine Liberation Organization allies to establish a guerrilla training camp there. U.S. officers and men had left their work sites as the invasion began and either returned to their homes or went to the homes of friends. They had not been attacked and had offered no resistance.

Evin Prison, in north Tehran, was taken over with the help of a number of former officials jailed since the previous November on corruption and other charges. All prisoners were released when the building was overrun that afternoon by insurgent groups and relatives of prisoners.

About 6:00 P.M. the rumor spread that General Badrii, commander of the ground forces, would lead the army infantry in a coup and that

General Oveissi (who had left for Europe after being relieved of his duties by the Shah when Bakhtiar became prime minister) had returned to mastermind the pro-Shah takeover. Gunfire echoed throughout the night, but there were no unit-sized fights. No coup took place, and hundreds of soldiers, mostly conscripts, quietly deserted.

A coordinated assault on government installations still under Bakhtiar's control began the morning of February 11. Mujahidin and Fedayeen units together rushed police headquarters in Tehran and 17 other regional police stations. By noon, east Tehran was in the hands of forces loyal to the Islamic movement and the insurgents controlled the capital's only radio station and transmitters. Revolutionaries also captured military bases in west Tehran and at Mehrabad airport. Although there was chaos in the capital, there were only minor skirmishes elsewhere in the country.

The Supreme Council of the Armed Forces met in the late morning of February 11. There was a brief but intense discussion about the political situation and Bakhtiar's declining prospects. As usual, some officers argued that they should destroy the guerrillas roaming the streets. Others stated that the armed forces were foolish to fight if the politicians were going to settle matters. Eventually the group concluded that the political leaders soon would agree to establish an effective government. There was a certain air of unreality about this debate, but these were men under pressure. Their influence was unraveling by the hour and forceful military action taken within the previous two days had been less than successful. There was little stomach for fighting. The final decision, to withdraw to barracks, offered psychological support to officers with differing views. It was the basis for agreement between "hawks" and "doves," a professional approach that would take the army out of politics. Those military officers loyal to the constitution convinced themselves they were not abandoning Bakhtiar, though all knew in their hearts that withdrawing to barracks meant the army was neutral in favor of Khomeini. In fact it already was too late to preserve the military establishment, but its conscious decision not to enter the fray certainly saved lives, though not those of the members of the Supreme Council of the Armed Forces. Except for those few who escaped, including General Gharabaghi who went into hiding, all would be executed, including SAVAK chief Moghaddam.

The decision not to fight suited General Gharabaghi's strategy; if the army could not be led into the revolutionary camp, at least it would be kept neutral. Through fortuitous circumstances, the American embassy was able to pass word very swiftly to Bazargan through Assistant (later

Deputy) Prime Minister Amir Entezam about the military's decision to withdraw. Certainly this helped to reduce casualties significantly on both sides. Two hours later, at 2:00 P.M., Tehran radio announced that the military "finds itself being close to the people and will pull back to barracks and not interfere with the political situation." It also said that the armed forces were doing this "to allow the clergy to find a solution" to the crisis, and urged everyone to remain calm.

By evening Khomeini himself had issued a statement calling for peace in the streets and asking the people to return to their homes and to obey the Islamic committees. Ayatollah Taleqani forbade attacks on foreign embassies, but the Mujahidin and the Fedayeen already had taken over the Israeli mission, converting it into a "P.L.O." embassy. Speaker of parliament Javad Saeed announced that the Majles had resigned en masse. Nearly all the Imperial Guard troops retreated to their barracks at Lavisan and Saltanatabad, both near the Shah's Niavaran Palace.

Throughout the night of February 11 the Islamic movement consolidated its position, preparing for the final takeover of what remained of the constitutional government. Supreme military headquarters, in north central Tehran, fell to the insurgents that evening. About 25 U.S. ARMISH-MAAG personnel who were posted there were led to safety at the American embassy by Ayatollah Beheshti, the leader of the Islamic insurgent forces in Tehran. Bakhtiar disappeared, apparently trading a resignation note for shelter and safe conduct. He repudiated his resignation after making his way out of Iran secretly in March with the help of friends, surfacing in Paris in August as one of the self-proclaimed leaders of the anti-Khomeini forces. Though the Islamic movement occupied the office of the prime minister the evening of February 11, Bazargan's provisional government did not begin operating from there until mid-afternoon on February 12, when the new team gradually began extending some control over the chaotic situation.

The Imperial Guard units remained holed up in their barracks at Lavisan and Saltanatabad. An attack on them by revolutionaries began just after 9:00 A.M., February 12, and by noon the insurgents occupied both locations. Many of these crack soldiers died fighting. Many others just disappeared. Three ranking officers, including General Neshat of the Imperial Guard and General Badrii, who was shot by his own troops when he sought to block the revolution, had been killed in the fighting February 9 through 11. Capturing the barracks of the Imperial Guard ended the major violence connected with the transfer of power. By mid-afternoon on February 12 Bazargan had announced his first post-revolution appointments. Ibrahim Yazdi was named deputy prime minister for revolutionary affairs. Amir Entezam became deputy prime minister for public affairs, and Hashem Sabaghian was the deputy prime minister for the transfer of power. Major General Mohammad Vali Gharaneh was named chief of staff of the armed services, and Sadeq Ghotbzadeh became head of National Iranian Radio and Television.

Despite three major appeals from Khomeini beginning at 3:00 p.m. on February 12, only a few hundred people turned in the weapons they had been issued two days previously, when the arsenals were emptied. A week later 90,000 guns and rifles had been returned to the provisional government, leaving about 200,000 weapons in the hands of revolutionary gangs and unsupervised teenagers. Politically, Islamic committees began exercising authority within the various cities and towns. In many cases the transfer of power was relatively peaceful, but in communities such as Isfahan, where there had been severe confrontations between the military and the revolutionaries, it meant more violence. Officers and men who retaliated against the takeover eventually would be executed by revolutionary tribunals.

Islamic committees and individual Mujahidin units began hunting down supporters of the old regime, dragging them to Parliament Square, where the revolutionaries had converted one of the buildings in the Majles complex into a prison. The national television network began showing "interrogations" of prisoners, including SAVAK's General Nassiri, former Prime Minister Hoveyda, General Mehdi Rahimi (who had been the administrator of Tehran when it was under martial law), and commander of the air force, General Hossein Rabii. Revolutionary courts were set up immediately to begin the "trials." The first series of tribunals and summary executions began the night of February 15, a little more than three days after Khomeini and his revolutionary followers took power.

Foreign Governments React by Not Reacting

On February 12, on its state television network, the Soviet Union praised Khomeini for his anti-imperialist views and recognized the new regime. That same day President Carter said the United States "had been in touch with the people in charge of the Iranian government and we expect to work with them," adding his "continued hope for very productive and peaceful cooperation" with the Bazargan regime. One day earlier, Washington had confirmed news reports that 69 marines and 6 helicopters were being sent to the NATO base in Izmir, Turkey, to evacuate the 200 official American personnel still in Tehran, if necessary.[6] When the move became public knowledge through a newspaper leak, the Turks withdrew permission for the helicopters to overfly their country.

Although the Shah had established diplomatic relations with Israel, he insisted that country set up a "trade mission" rather than an embassy, in deference to Moslem sensibilities. After its building was overrun and given to the P.L.O. on February 10, Israel considered its relations with Iran broken. Its diplomats were sent home the week after the revolutionary takeover on a U.S. evacuation plane.

Considering what had happened and the future implications, there had been no major foreign reaction against the ouster of Bakhtiar. Most nations, including the French, British, and West Germans, began doing business with the Bazargan government within days. On February 13 a State Department spokesman confirmed that the new regime in Tehran had accepted President Carter's offer of cooperation and had asked that the United States and Iran continue mutual relations.

Seizing the American Embassy: The First Time

The provisional government had to surmount major administrative problems before it could establish full control. "Victory had come before we were ready to manage it," said one of the deputy prime ministers a week after the revolutionary takeover. For one thing, many different factions had cooperated to overthrow the Shah and then participated in the destruction of the Bakhtiar government. Now each felt it had the right to operate more or less on its own. Two major groups, the Fedayeen (Marxists) and the Mujahidin (leftist Islamics) had opposing views about the course the revolution should take and how power within a future government should be divided up. In fact, the only thing they could agree on was the need to prevent a counterrevolution. Wild rumors circulated about coups, hidden armies, and SAVAK agents-at-large. Both groups wanted to expel all foreigners immediately, particularly Americans. Although U.S. contacts with Bazargan's provisional government remained good, the leftists continued to be deeply suspicious of U.S. intentions. Stories abounded about Shah loyalists and SAVAK officials hiding on the American embassy compound; at least one of these rumors could be traced back directly to the Soviet embassy. Now that immediate revolutionary pressures had eased, reports of the impending visit to the Mideast by U.S. Secretary of Defense Harold Brown further spurred anxiety.

From the moment that government troops were ordered back to barracks, the People's Fedayeen (the most radical Fedayeen group) and one Mujahidin faction began working on a plan to attack the American embassy. When the U.S. decision to send helicopters and marines to Turkey for possible use in Iran became known, the conspirators urged action against the American embassy to forestall what they feared would be a 1953-style effort to return the Shah to power.

The first effort in this direction occurred on February 13. A Fedayeen unit seized the U.S. International Communications Agency (U.S.I.C.A.) building that was four blocks from Tehran University and a half mile from the embassy. No Americans were there. They had left their offices on February 11 when the shooting started in earnest between revolutionaries and those military units willing to fight, and it was still considered imprudent for them to return. The militants who captured the building were under the impression it was C.I.A. headquarters. The prime minister's office apologized for their action, admitting it had no control over some of the armed revolutionary groups. That became obvious when the building was not restored to U.S. control until March 7, 22 days later. This happened not because Bazargan wouldn't allow it, but because the revolutionaries weren't finished with it yet. When the ranking I.C.A. employee returned to investigate, all furniture and files were gone. The building was totally empty. "They even took the cockroaches," Public Affairs Officer Jack Shellenberger told Ambassador Sullivan.

The same day U.S.I.C.A. was taken over, February 13, the embassy was threatened by a guerrilla who came to the main gate and told the locally hired Iranian guards that if the American flag flying by the front door was not pulled down, the compound would be attacked.[7] The Iranian guards gave this message to the U.S. Marine guards, who passed it to Ambassador Sullivan. The flag was left flying. Nothing happened. The next morning, Valentine's Day, began normally enough. However, about 9:30 there was steady gunfire outside the embassy walls and gradually the shooting was concentrated on the building itself. Ambassador Sullivan ordered the 20 marine guards to fire tear gas and to shoot only in self defense, and even then to use only birdshot. Groups of militants began trying to climb over the 9-to-12 feet high brick walls at the front and sides of the 27-acre embassy compound. Snipers appeared on all the surrounding rooftops and poured down gunfire, making it impossible for anyone inside the grounds to move. Gradually, small groups of the attackers worked themselves over the wall. By that time most of the marine guards were in the main embassy building; two were at the ambassador's residence, about 100 yards northeast of the chancery. Two or three others found themselves with about 20 people at the embassy restaurant 100 yards northwest of the main building.

For a time, as the two marines watched and the servants slipped away, the invaders contented themselves with shooting up the ambassador's residence. New attackers concentrated on taking over the restaurant. Seeing the mass of insurgents grow to 200 and then to 400, over the walkie-talkie network Ambassador Sullivan ordered the marines to surrender in order to avoid bloodshed. As the attack on the outlying buildings intensified, Americans in the chancery began locking it up. Sullivan told his staff aide, Ralph Boyce, and another embassy officer, David Patterson, to call for military support and protection. Patterson reached Ayatollah Taleqani's lieutenants promptly, but it took nearly 30 minutes to get through to the government—first because the phone lines were busy and then because no one answered. A call finally reached the prime minister's office around 10:45. Immediate help was promised. But by then marines in the ambassador's residence and the restaurant already had surrendered and the main building was heavily besieged.

The marines continued throwing tear gas canisters at the attackers and clouds of the noxious fumes wafted by. As invaders would be overcome by the gas, a new wave would follow, some wearing gas masks. Eventually a few guerrillas successfully battered down the wooden doors at the front and the steel doors at the side of the chancery. Using only tear gas and occasionally firing shots over the heads of the attackers, the marine defenders forced the insurgents to fight their way up to the second floor. It had been nearly 90 minutes since the assault had begun, but it took only half an hour after the insurgents broke into the building for them to reach the top floor. Approximately 70 Americans had gathered behind the 11-inch thick steel door of the communications vault on the upper level. Everyone pitched in to destroy classified documents and the sensitive communications equipment. Telephone links had been cut off by the revolutionaries about 11:00 A.M., when they entered the switchboard room, but one line, manned by political counselor George Lambrakis, remained open to the State Department until just before the embassy surrendered.

When the attackers reached the barricaded communications center those inside heard faint voices threatening in both English and Farsi to blow the room up or to burn the embassy down around it. (This was not empty talk. When it was all over and the insurgents had left, several five-gallon drums full of gasoline were found on the second floor of the building.) Sensing the seriousness of the situation, Sullivan ordered the vault door opened. The Americans were herded into the ambassador's office 20 feet down the corridor. Meanwhile, the invaders began going through the rooms on the second floor, where all safes and file drawers holding classified material were locked but anything loose was strewn around.

Then several of the Fedayeen guerrillas—identifiable because throughout the revolutionary period they had a predilection to wear ski mask caps at all times—began arguing among themselves about whether or not some of the Americans should be killed. Suddenly a round was fired from outside the building that ricocheted into the room where the Americans had been herded. One of the invaders insisted the shot had been fired from within. In the several tense moments that followed, both the Americans and his own comrades worked to convince the guerrilla that it had been an accident. This was the time that the captured embassy personnel regarded as the most dangerous for them. But, in the midst of it, a flurry of shots heralded the arrival of Deputy Prime Minister Ibrahim Yazdi and his detachment of 50 to 75 Mujahidin. The negotiations between the People's Fedayeen contingent guarding the ambassador and other Americans on the second floor and Yazdi and his group were intense. After approximately 15 minutes the deputy prime minister took control. Part of the deal was that the Fedayeen would be allowed to leave the American embassy compound before the last of the U.S. staff would be released. The Fedayeen feared they would be shot in the back by the Mujahidin.

The transfer of the Americans to the control of the provisional government and its Mujahidin "military" wing took place soon after 12 o'clock. The Americans remained "interned" within their own compound for the rest of the afternoon, first at Ambassador Sullivan's residence, then at the restaurant. British Ambassador Anthony Parsons and Swedish Ambassador Kaj Sundberg were allowed to call on the Americans and report on their condition about 4:00 P.M.

Several U.S. government employees not at the embassy at the time of the attack remained at large. Admiral Frank Collins, head of the ARMISH-MAAG navy section, was at home when he discovered what was happening, so he began contacting other American military personnel. He found two army communications officers holed up with a private ham radio transmitter and ordered them to contact other American embassies in the Persian Gulf area or any European outpost. By noon they had reached a U.S. Army communications center in Germany, telling them that the embassy had been taken over by Iranian revolutionaries.

Elsewhere, about 10:30 that morning, I was approaching the embassy by car. Thinking at first that we had run into merely another street disturbance, the driver tried to circle the compound and come in from another direction. After running three blockades manned jointly by Fedayeen and Mujahidin, we retreated to the apartment of American friends of mine, Lawrence Steadman, who taught at the Iran Center for Management Studies, and his wife Elizabeth. Safely hidden away about two miles from the embassy, I began trying to contact other Americans by telephone. Barbara Schell, an embassy economic officer, was in her apartment three blocks from the compound and I set her to work locating other U.S. government employees who might be free.

By noon I had alerted the American consulates in Shiraz and Isfahan. They had heard nothing about the trouble in Tehran; everything was tense but peaceful in those cities. These consulates radioed the news of the takeover to nearby U.S. embassies in the Persian Gulf. The third consulate, in Tabriz, did not answer its phone; it was under attack as well. By 2:00 P.M., Admiral Collins and I had contacted each other and had a fairly clear picture of what had happened. This was because diplomats in the Swedish embassy, on the fifth floor of one of the buildings overlooking the compound, had told us what they had seen.

Twenty-five to 30 Americans were taken prisoner during the takeover. All of them were returned to the embassy within 24 hours except one. Those captured by Mujahidin forces (not Yazdi's contingent) in the area away from the main building were sent to Khomeini's central committee offices near parliament. The dozen or so seized by the Fedayeen were taken to Tehran University, exhibited at a mass rally, and then turned over to the revolutionary government, which brought them back to the embassy. Five others were seized by Iranians loyal to Ayatollah Taleqani and returned to embassy officer Patterson at his residence. Everyone was accounted for except Kenneth Krause, a marine sergeant who was injured in the head during the capture of the restaurant and taken by his attackers to a nearby hospital.

After his wound was bandaged, Krause was moved from the hospital by Mujahidin guerrillas and thrown with other Iranian prisoners into the central komiteh jail near parliament. The revolutionary prosecutor wanted to try the marine for "murdering" two of the insurgents who had died in the assault on the embassy. Krause had not handled a rifle that day, only tear gas. He was off duty when the attack started and had gone to the restaurant when he heard shooting. After the group he was with had surrendered, one of the guerrillas asked the marine how to shoot an American rifle he had found in the restaurant. There was a scuffle; Krause was wounded. No one, not even the ambassador, knew where Krause had been taken until the evening of February 17, three full days after the takeover. He was not released until February 21, after four more long days of prolonged negotiations and prodding, a personal visit by Sullivan to Bazargan, and a virtual sit-in at Deputy Prime Minister Entezam's office by me. Eventually Khomeini's public affairs officer, Ghassem Salekhou, who was armed with a letter signed by Entezam, went with me to the makeshift prison and pried Krause loose from the guards. After overnighting at Ambassador Sullivan's, the marine left Iran for the United States the following morning. Until the incident that started November 4, 1979, he would have the distinction of being the American held longest by the revolutionaries.

Krause's situation was the most sensitive, but not the most frightening. In Tabriz, American consul Michael Metrinko, in his first foreign service posting overseas, was in the hands of militants who were looking for a place to hang the rope with which they planned to lynch him. The consulate had been taken over at the same time as the Tehran embassy, possibly under a coordinated effort. The group which had seized it and wanted to harm Metrinko, the only official American there, was the most radical of the Mujahidin factions in Tabriz. He was saved by bazaar merchants who knew and liked him and whom Metrinko had quickly called when it was obvious the compound was about to be overrun. After he was rescued, the central komiteh in Tabriz negotiated the dispute by phone with its colleagues in Tehran. Metrinko and three Europeans who had been caught in the city by chance were allowed to fly to the capital a few days later. They were delivered to the embassy against an itemized receipt: "Received: four individuals of the followed alleged names:. . . ." (Metrinko, a Farsi-speaker, was one of a half dozen official Americans then in Iran who was not replaced within a few months by someone else who had never before served at the embassy. He took a month's leave in the United States and then agreed to return to Tehran.)

After the Fall

By nightfall on February 14 another large evacuation of Americans was being planned. The seizure of the embassy compound and its continued occupation by the militants revealed not only the fragility of the U.S. position, but also the shakiness of the provisional government's control over the Tehran political scene. Americans and Europeans from outlying cities converged on Tehran or the Persian Gulf ports of Bander Abbas and Chah Bahar, where British, German, and American ships picked them up. Approximately 6,000 Americans and 600 other foreigners were evacuated between February 17 and 25, 3,800 by chartered Pan American and U.S. government planes, the rest by sea. The last official Americans to leave were 21 U.S. Air Force personnel who were held at their electronic listening post at Kabkan, near Mashad, until arrangements could be made to pay off local employees who refused to let them go. This contingent left Iran on February 28.

The evacuations were successful, since no one was hurt, but the departures were not smooth. Many evacuees were roughly treated at the airport and their belongings taken from them during "customs searches" supervised by revolutionary guards. The provisional government, however, cooperated with the effort to speed the departures along, supplying buses and armed escorts for the daily 4:00 A.M. rides to the airport. Those leaving had to be at the embassy with no more than two suitcases apiece by the previous evening, where they slept on the restaurant floor. Anyone who arrived at the compound in his own car parked it on the grounds and left the keys with embassy personnel never to see his automobile again. After February 28 approximately 80 official Americans, including 20 marine guards and an ARMISH-MAAG contingent of about 30, remained at the embassy. Just two months before, in December, the staff had been 15 times as large.

The consulates in Tabriz, Isfahan, and Shiraz were closed without fanfare in the immediate aftermath of the takeover. Their staffs left Iran, with the exception of two Farsi-speaking officers reassigned to the Tehran embassy, Michael Metrinko from Tabriz and Victor Tomseth from Shiraz. Both would become hostages November 4.

The seizure of the embassy, though short-lived, was a shock for the Americans involved but it also caused some intriguing problems. Unlike the brief sacking of the British embassy on November 5, for the first time ever Islamic forces were in charge of an embassy's security. Not until February 18 did American diplomats regain enough control of the chancery to secure the battered doors and protect the remaining communications equipment. The embassy reestablished non-coded communications with Washington via Athens late in the evening on February 14. By that time there was also telephone communications between the ambassador and the dozen or so official Americans outside the embassy. Direct access to the State Department came on line about 10 days later, when replacement cypher and radio equipment arrived.

After Yazdi took charge of the situation at the embassy, security for the compound was provided by various revolutionary forces. They were on the grounds 24 hours a day for several months and regarded themselves as virtual conquerors. At first there were four groups: a Mujahidin contingent of 30 to 40 which remained until July; a smaller group of 7 to 9 Mujahidin assigned to guard Ambassador Sullivan which was withdrawn in May when its leader was arrested for taking bribes; a group of 15 to 20 air force homafars; and a handful of air force cadets. All four factions were suspicious of their American "hosts." Each group distrusted the others as well. On several occasions Farsi-speaking embassy officers had to mediate disputes which threatened to flare into violence. There were so many "guards" because the provisional government did not have the power to force them out. They stole from the mini-commissary on the grounds, dismantled equipment, and ransacked the warehouse, all in direct violation of the Vienna Convention on diplomatic immunity. Embassy personnel were not masters in their own compound.

Because the situation was so extraordinary, Washington never fully comprehended the degree to which the mission had lost control of its own property. While the Iranian "government" did not authorize the attack, it was obvious that radical forces were just as happy to see this systematic violation of diplomatic rights and security continue. Bazargan's government could not dislodge the insurgents without endangering itself, and the fundamentalist clergy, Mujahidin, and the leftist Fedayeen reasoned that if the embassy was occupied with the problem of evacuating its citizens, it would be unlikely to plot a counterrevolution.

There were forays each evening from mid-February until late May on the mission compound. Sporadic, hit-and-run raids were commonplace. Even when it was the embassy's resident Mujahidin guards who were staging these bombardments (they would find their positions at nightfall and blaze away beginning on the hour at 9 or 10 o'clock), there was always the danger of being hit by a stray shell. At least some of these attacks were instigated by rival Fedayeen and Mujahidin groups who were frankly envious of the opportunity of the "guards" to acquire spoils. Merchandise from the embassy exchange, liquor, and household goods and cars left on the compound by departing Americans disappeared with startling regularity.

U.S. reaction to the attack on the embassy was muted for excellent reasons. Approximately 7,000 Americans remained in Iran prior to February 14, some of whom had no intention of leaving no matter how bad the situation became because they were American women married to Iranian men. In his statement to television networks the evening of February 14, Ambassador Sullivan fuzzed over the question of who had been responsible for the attack. The safety of the remaining Americans and plans for an orderly evacuation depended on Bazargan's cooperation, and until this was accomplished no one wanted to accuse his regime of complicity. Whether or not any senior figure in his government knew about the incursion in advance, it did "come to the rescue" after the Fedayeen captured the Americans, did reestablish "order" of a sort, and did provide security within the limitations of Mujahidin light-fingeredness.

Who really attacked the embassy in February? Farsi-speaking American diplomats who talked to members of all the factions guarding the compound in the months after the raid have concluded that at least two separate groups participated in the takeover. One Mujahidin and one Fedayeen unit planned it together. The Fedayeen actually penetrated the chancery building, and it appears that this was not part of the original Mujahidin instructions. Certainly the hostility displayed by the Fedayeen departing the embassy after Yazdi's Mujahidin had taken over suggests there was little love lost between the two revolutionary groups. Sources close to Fedayeen members believe their original objective was to kill at least some of the Americans during the takeover and thus ruin budding relations between the Bazargan government and the United States.[8]

There was some criticism in the U.S. that the embassy had not resisted attack as forcefully as it might have. Two major reasons convinced Ambassador Sullivan not to shoot to kill. One was an accurate belief that a more vigorous defense would have accomplished nothing except more bloodshed. The embassy staff and the marines who were there had no doubt that a spirited Alamo-type defense would have produced scores of Iranian casualties. But after the original wave of invaders, hundreds more would have followed. The result would have been a massacre of the defenders and almost certainly the killing of other non-official U.S. citizens in Tehran. Several thousand Americans were still in Iran, all of them potential targets for fanatics. Sullivan's instincts were correct. In 1831 a similar attack on the Russian embassy in Tehran was forcefully resisted. The result was the slaughter of all but one of the 37 diplomats inside by a frenzied mob led by religious fanatics. It had happened once; it could have happened again.

The second factor was the state of U.S.-Iranian relations. Sullivan had no reason to doubt that the Bazargan government would protect the embassy if word could get through, which it had. He surmised there were hostile factions seeking to disrupt U.S. links to the new government and guessed rightly that these could be neutralized if there was no, or very little, accidental bloodshed. After the fact, the provisional government admitted that four revolutionaries were killed in the raid. Approximately 20 wounded Iranians were removed from the compound. On the U.S. side, one Iranian employed by the embassy was killed and the relative of another. Three other local employees were wounded. No Americans died and only three were injured, none seriously.

Was there, in fact, Iranian government collusion in the takeover? Mujahidin participated in the attack, but Mujahidin also stopped it. Other Mujahidin besides the actual attacking group, as well as several of the Islamic clergy, probably knew in advance about the plan to storm the embassy and encouraged it, even if they did not want it to go as far as it did. There is no doubt that Prime Minister Bazargan was not told about it before it happened. In view of the many rumors about hidden SAVAK officers, the intense suspicion of U.S. motives virtually required that there be some move against the embassy.

On February 28 Bazargan asserted publicly that Khomeini aides had been involved in the seizure. That same day, Hashem Sabaghian, deputy prime minister for the transfer of power, accused the People's Fedayeen of organizing the attack. Certainly radical Moslem leaders bragged about their roles after the event. The whole affair illustrated just how tenuous was the provisional government's control over the various armed groups.

Unfortunately, the seizure of the U.S. compound made it a chip in the Iranian political poker game. The magnitude of that fact would gradually become ever more obvious, but the problem was not fully appreciated by either Bazargan's government or Washington. For most Iranians the "capture" of the embassy, both in February and later in November, symbolized the destruction of old U.S. ties with Iran and foreshadowed the direction the revolution would take, for better or for worse.

The Left Versus the Right

The takeover of the U.S. compound also marked an important turn in emerging post-revolutionary politics. The Fedayeen's role in the seizure and Yazdi's efforts to remove the insurgents was the first open collision between the left and the Mujahidin. Whether this clash was the trigger for the four-day mini-civil war which followed or merely the opening salvo, starting February 14 there was open conflict between left and right. For four nights after the attack on the American embassy, the

Fedayeen and the Mujahidin fought each other for control of Tehran. The battle began the evening of February 14, when the N.I.R.T. (National Iranian Radio and Television) station and transmitters in north Tehran were attacked about 10:00 P.M. by Fedayeen units. Frantic calls over radio and television by Islamic movement supporters who controlled the station brought help from throughout the city. The attack was repelled, but both Mujahidin and Fedayeen units went from house to house that night seeking their counterparts and shooting at their rivals. Gunshots were heard into the early morning hours of February 15, but at daybreak the anti-Fedayeen forces still controlled the city. The following evening and for two more nights gunfights broke out again as soon as twilight fell. Embassy personnel were no longer incarcerated but kept a very low profile for fear of being caught in the middle of a shootout near the compound. Though some of the firing came from mopping-up action against isolated pockets of pro-Shah resistance, most of it revolved around direct intergroup conflict between the two revolutionary factions.

Bazargan's government ascribed these fights to "resistance by ex-SAVAK agents and fanatic forces loyal to the Shah." Though fear of a counterrevolution remained strong, by February 14 the Mujahidin and the Fedayeen saw themselves as rivals as much as allies. Both the Islamic movement and Bazargan were dismayed by the apparent breakup in the coalition and felt betrayed. There were efforts made to patch up differences between the two factions and to arrange cease fires, but they were only marginally successful. Given the general public disorder and the vast number of weapons in untrained and irresponsible hands, it is remarkable that large-scale organized violence was avoided. Fighting between the two groups died down by the morning of February 18. The easing of tensions occurred because the Fedayeen had taken a beating wherever and whenever they forcefully challenged the Mujahidin and other Islamic movement gangs. It was a conscious decision on the part of the Fedayeen to withdraw from the fray.[9]

In terms of Marxist doctrine, the Fedayeen attacked the Mujahidin because it was trying to keep the revolution moving to the left. On the day of the embassy attack Fedayeen spokesmen at a rally at Tehran University called for the establishment of "radical popular government and a true people's army." Its attempts to gain control of National Iranian Radio and Television and the universities were consistent with its doctrine of "revolution within a revolution."

But the Fedayeen lost the struggle between February 14 and 18 to control Tehran. In the process, its organizational structure was severely damaged. All the members of some cells were killed or the groups broke up of their own accord for safety's sake. The Fedayeen had to spend the next several months rebuilding its organization. Had it not been so impetuous, the leftists would have been in a strong position to attack the Islamic leadership in the late spring. By then other groups within the revolutionary coalition—the National Front, the National Democratic Front, and the moderate religious leaders—were becoming disaffected.

The attack on the American embassy illustrated that little united the Fedayeen and the Mujahidin except a common fear that the Shah might return and their mutual suspicion of the intentions of the United States. It also showed how much the provisional government depended upon the Mujahidin forces in order to maintain its authority after the revolutionary takeover. Disparate groups had been united in a common cause: to overthrow the Shah. But the post-takeover honeymoon lasted only three days.

Chapter Ten

★

The Dawn of the Islamic Era

February–November 1979

The departure of the Shah and the disintegration of the military, followed by the "neutralization" of the American embassy, eliminated the one factor that had joined together the revolutionary coalition: fear of a countercoup supported by the United States. Immediately after the seizing of the compound, each political group jockeyed to establish its own position in post-takeover Iran.

Khomeini and his supporters, including the leftists, had been joined together only in their opposition to the Shah. On other issues, particularly the nature of a future government, there were as many visions of the new Iran as there were groups within the dissident coalition. Visible strains began to appear. The Liberation Movement, for example, wished to continue the policy of modernization, but under a popularly elected government. Bazargan and Sahabi did not want to throw out the United States abruptly, because of the dislocation and hardship this would generate for the country. The clerical leadership of the coalition, however, especially Khomeini, sought the final destruction of the Pahlavi legacy, the creation of an "Islamic" republic, and the demodernization of Iran, including a complete end to a U.S. presence in the country. The Fedayeen, on the other hand, wanted a regime along the lines of the "democratic centralist" models of Qadaffi in Libya or Castro in Cuba. Its followers emphasized the need for social revolution and the creation of a mass society.

Conflicts between these various views had been papered over while the opposition worked hard to defeat the Shah's regime. Under the circumstances, political concepts such as "constitution" and "Islamic republic" developed different connotations for each group. All agreed

195

that corruption must end, free elections must be held, SAVAK must be abolished, and Iran's foreign policy must be reoriented. Beyond these generalities, each faction had different programs to put forth that outlined what ought to be done.

Although a provisional government had been established with Khomeini's blessing, there was no formal link between it and the dissident groups. Coordination was woefully inadequate. As one of Prime Minister Bazargan's aides explained, "We were not prepared for victory; most of us believed it would take much longer. We did not have our government ready to fit into place. Many people want to do many things, and priorities have to be sorted out." Even so, at first Bazargan's administration appeared to be gradually bringing the political situation under some sort of control.

The religious leadership also had problems getting organized. One example of backing and filling was Khomeini's edict announced in March that in public all women would have to wear the chador (the black veil that covers the body, except for the face). Two days later, 20,000 females in Western-style clothing paraded through the center of Tehran protesting such a return to strict Islamic teaching. Men on the street taunted them, but they were not otherwise harmed. The next day, between 150,000 and 200,000 chador-clad women, exhorted by the mosque network, marched north through Tehran to a rally near the television station. Here they cheered Khomeini (and were filmed doing so for international television) and supported his call for "Islamic modesty." Though the chador edict was quietly allowed to lapse, some women were subsequently stoned for appearing in Western dress in south Tehran, where the majority of the population is fundamentalist.

Very quickly Bazargan and his cabinet had to deal with serious problems of disunity. With approximately 200,000 small arms loose in Tehran and more than a million other weapons floating around elsewhere in the country, each dissident organization armed itself and asserted control over its own area. The revolutionaries were itchy for action. Ex-SAVAK and military men, distraught over the ecclesiastical takeover, roamed the streets, especially at night, killing revolutionaries who were guarding government buildings and patrolling the city—or being killed themselves. The revolutionaries also distrusted civil servants, who were automatically branded "lackeys of the Shah and his corrupt system." Another difficulty was the attitude of the Fedayeen toward the Mujahidin and vice versa. Members of both organizations were suspicious since too many of each group had been killed by the other during the four nights of violence from February 14 to 18. Also, the left, particularly the Fedayeen, paid lip service to the Ayatollah but often disobeyed representatives of the revolutionary government trying to exercise power in specific locations.

Disagreements between major groups in the coalition were a direct threat to the survival of each faction, thereby limiting the opportunities for all of them to push forward an ideological or religious point of view. The establishment had disappeared, been executed, gone into hiding, or was in exile in the West. Only anarchy and political warfare prevailed in the streets of the major cities. Moreover, short of Ayatollah Khomeini himself, there was no legitimate authority to which the government or any other group could appeal to resolve differences among former comrades-in-arms. The political infighting has continued to the present, with little likelihood of winding down.

During the first phase of this internal struggle, February to November 1979, the three strongest factions contended for power: the revolutionary moderates, centered at first in the Bazargan government; the Islamic movement, incarnated in the newly established Islamic Republican Party; and a series of leftist and radical factions grouped around the Fedayeen. The Islamic Republican Party would emerge as by far the most powerful organization, particularly after the left, with the help of the Islamic mobs, was driven underground in August.

The Shah's arrival in the United States on October 22 for medical treatment renewed fears of a counterrevolution. Two weeks later radical Moslems, with tacit Fedayeen support, seized the U.S. embassy a second time. This move destroyed the relatively moderate Bazargan government, ushering in a chaotic period of institutionalized crisis.

How Islamic Government Evolved

The emergence of the religious extremists as the dominant political force occurred as much by happenstance as by design. Although Khomeini had already written a book about how an Islamic government should function, neither he nor his colleagues could explain how to establish such a regime initially. However, the Ayatollah was able to move toward his goal by taking excellent advantage of circumstances. The first few months after the takeover Bazargan and the moderates dominated the provisional government. But the fundamentalists controlled the Revolutionary Council and the revolutionary committees set up in each neighborhood and both organizations soon became as powerful as the government. Meanwhile, the newly established Islamic Republican Party, led by Ayatollah Beheshti, pressed for a new constitution to enshrine religious control of the government. In response, the Revolutionary Council organized elections for a constitutional assembly to be held several months later, in August. It would be the duty of the assembly to write the constitution that would guide the Islamic Republic.

Because they had substantial influence over the selection of candidates, from the very beginning there was no doubt that the extremists would control the assembly. It met for nearly four months, from August to December. At first the moderates were strong enough to stymie the radicals; not until the American hostages were seized in November did the cause of the extremists rapidly advance in the Constitutional Assembly. After November 4 it became very easy to whip up potent anti-American feeling and convert it into support for the fundamentalists' conception of Islamic government. The constitution the extremists produced was bitterly opposed by the secular and moderate religious forces but they could do nothing about it.

The Islamic constitution was approved overwhelmingly by a referendum on December 3, 1979. However, the cause of the radicals suffered a setback when Abol Hassan Bani-Sadr was elected president the following month in a landslide vote. Undaunted, the fanatical clergy quickly regrouped, winning a substantial majority of seats in the National Consultative Assembly (parliament). The first of these elections was in March 1980, with the runoffs in May. The Islamic radicals had regained the upper hand within the chaotic Iranian political arena; the comparatively moderate Bani-Sadr faced a solidly fundamentalist parliament. Although as president Bani-Sadr should have had the right to choose his prime minister, the Majles balked at his choice. In return, the president refused to acknowledge the radical candidates for the job that parliament suggested. The protracted stalemate was finally broken when a compromise candidate favoring the fundamentalists was chosen on August 9, 1980, one year after the Constitutional Assembly began its work. The evolution to Islamic government had been very slow and painful.

Islamic Politics in Action

Political jockeying began within days of the takeover. Ayatollah Khomeini announced immediately that his role was to serve as the guiding hand, the chief theologian, and the one who conferred acceptability on those actually chosen to govern. By his own choice he would not actually rule. But the reality was quite different. For one thing the men in Bazargan's cabinet, members of the secular opposition and the majority of whom had close ties with the Liberation Movement, took over existing ministries and installed their own men in second-level slots, attempting to get the pre-existing bureaucracy back to work. However, the government never was able to translate its provisional mandate into exclusive legitimate authority recognized throughout the country. Civil servants who remained on the job and even Bazargan's new cabinet ministers were ignored. The religious radicals dominating Khomeini's central headquarters at Tehran's Alavi School had set up a parallel administrative network reaching out into the cities through the revolutionary komitehs set up in each neighborhood. They shunted aside police and civil servants trying to do their jobs, often replacing them with untrained guerrillas. They also rounded up suspects from the old regime and took over the property of establishment families who had fled. Within all the major cities the komitehs were extremely powerful neighborhood governments.

Coordination between the central komiteh and Bazargan's administration was sporadic, particularly at first. Conflicts between the provisional government and the Islamic committees were resolved by the Revolutionary Council, whose membership remained secret. From January 13 to February 11, when Bazargan displaced Bakhtiar, the Revolutionary Council had six members. Liberation Movement officials Bazargan and Sahabi participated, along with Ayatollah Mohammad Beheshti and two aides who had come from Paris with Khomeini, Yazdi and Ghotbzadeh. The key to the expanding influence of the Revolutionary Council was the rapid increase in the religious membership and the growing influence of the fundamentalist clergy. As the power of that faction multiplied, other religious leaders became members. The ayatollahs involved were Hassan Lahouti, Morteza Motahari, Hussein Ali Montazeri, and Ali Ashgar Moussavi. Hojatollahs Razi Shirazi, Hashemi Rafsanjani, and Sadeq Khalkhali (who promoted himself to ayatollah and would become famous as "Judge Blood" for ordering executions indiscriminately) joined the council in the weeks following the seizure of power. Other clerics were added or dropped from time to time, depending on the issue being discussed and Khomeini's personal wishes. He himself never was a member. As the "Imam," a title which places him above all other ayatollahs spiritually as well as politically, he did not get involved in their discussions. His power derives from his revolutionary charisma. He is the chief guardian of the faith and therefore the council reported to him. After the newly elected parliament chose its officers and approved a prime minister in September 1980, the Revolutionary Council was dissolved.

The religious leaders on the Revolutionary Council supervised day-to-day political activities through the Islamic komitehs. As spring progressed, they combined the fanatic loyalists in the komitehs with the Mujahidin to form the Islamic Republican Party. The organization gradually grew in strength over the summer of 1979 and emerged as the dominant political force after the second U.S. embassy takeover in November and particularly after the Islamic constitution was approved in December. What Beheshti (the emerging leader of the Islamic Republican Party), Rafsanjani, and others did was to convert successfully the most trustworthy workhorses in the old mosque network into the leaders of a political organization strong enough to usurp gradually the power of the formal government.

In early April, to "protect" the revolution, the Revolutionary Council ordered the loosely organized Islamic militia and the most loyal young men in the Mujahidin—about a third of the total—to be transformed into a new military organization, the Revolutionary Guards, or Pasdaran. Mullah Mustafa Chamran was appointed to the joint responsibilities of deputy prime minister and director of the newly established military wing of the Mujahidin. He set up a major training complex midway between Tehran and Qom plus six other smaller bases. Three of these were in Tehran, one of them at the former U.S. ARMISH-MAAG headquarters. Small units, to be organized later into brigades, received army training. In the process, "unreliable" troops were weeded out and better discipline was established.

After Yasser Arafat's visit to Tehran on February 18, the P.L.O. provided about 800 Palestinians to help train the Pasdaran in Tehran, Qom, and Ahwaz. About that time Ayatollah Lahouti joined Chamran as a promoter of the Revolutionary Guards and together they increased the strength of the Pasdaran to 6,000 men. On May 6 the organization was formally incorporated into the Islamic government and given the title "Guardians of the Revolution." It has always remained more loyal to the radical clerics who created it than to the government and constitutes the bedrock military support of the Islamic fundamentalists.

It soon became a major responsibility of the Revolutionary Guards to organize the mob. The hezbollahi, or "Members of God's Party," is composed of young men, often unemployed, whose sole function is to support Islamic fundamentalist doctrine and to intimidate its opponents. The mob can vary in size, depending on what it is scheduled to do, from 500 to 5,000. It is let loose after being instructed when and how to attack Fedayeen or Tudeh Party rallies, specified embassies, newspaper offices, or any other "enemies of the revolution."[1]

Cracks in the Coalition Fractionalize Authority

Working together to achieve the destruction of the monarchy had given a false appearance of unity to the Shah's opponents. Their success allowed divisions and conflicts which had existed for years within the revolutionary coalition to become dramatically obvious. As the revolutionaries destroyed the power of the old ruling system in 1978, they made no effort to organize the coalition by any more than loose arrangements whereby leading dissidents could consult each other. All groups advocated freedom of thought, free elections, and ultimately a new political framework, but the opposition concentrated its energies on only one goal: to oust the Shah. Until the takeover, organizational efforts were focused almost entirely on coalition building, with no thought given to post-revolutionary government. It was assumed that unity in overthrowing the Shah would extend beyond victory as well. Each group believed it would have the key leadership role and win over the others in any disagreements over policy. The first ten months after the political demise of the Shah brought home forcefully to all that the various factions of the coalition were far apart on what they wanted to see emerge from the existing chaos.

From the beginning the Islamic movement and the provisional government faced political, ideological, and power challenges from the left. The fundamentalist clergy always dominated clashes between factions, primarily because they were backed by the Revolutionary Guards and the hezbollahi, thereby hemming in the leftist militants by better tactical use of crowds, effective deployment of their armed units, and barely effective but adequate mobilization of what was left of the armed forces.

Though the Mujahidin as a whole continued to support the radical clerics, several factions remained independent of Revolutionary Council control. On occasion certain units would ally themselves with the Fedayeen, taking a leftist — not a religious — stance. In May and November, for example, some detachments supported the Fedayeen against the Pasdaran when that group was being attacked at political rallies. A Mujahidin-Fedayeen combination was involved in the one-day takeover of the American embassy on February 14, and radical Mujahidin units calling themselves "Followers of the Imam's Line" who took over the embassy on November 4 received assistance from at least one Fedayeen group.

Immediately after the debacle in February against the Mujahidin, the

Fedayeen had begun rebuilding its tattered organization. While inferior to the Mujahidin militarily, especially when the army was brought in on the side of the new government to help maintain order, the Fedayeen and the other leftists clustered around it could make substantial trouble on issues they felt impinged on their political role. For example, they were opposed to the idea that approval by a fundamentalist committee was needed before a candidate could run in the upcoming election for the Islamic Consultative Assembly. On February 21 a rally planned by the leftists at Tehran University was cancelled by the Revolutionary Council. The Fedayeen criticized the arbitrariness of the council for calling off the meeting. Two days later, 75,000 Fedayeen supporters took to the streets despite an order forbidding demonstrations.

Other disputes reinforced the split between the religious fundamentalists and the Marxist left. There was jockeying over who would control various newspapers, the universities, and the radio and television stations. Leftists demonstrated regularly and occasionally fought pitched battles with the Revolutionary Guards and the hezbollahi. There were major clashes in April at rallies in Tehran to condemn excesses of the Islamic komitehs, in late May when the Fedayeen scuffled with the Mujahidin outside the U.S. embassy and at Tehran University, and also in May in the southern port city of Khorramshahr. In the latter incident, Admiral Madani, who went from being minister of the interior to serving as governor of Khuzistan province, called in army reinforcements to maintain public order when the large local Arab population (both Shiite and Sunni Moslems) joined ranks with the Fedayeen. Madani claimed that the Lebanese leader of the Popular Front for the Liberation of Palestine (P.F.L.P.), George Habash, had been in Khuzistan province fomenting trouble among the Arab population. Whether true or not, the P.F.L.P. continued to aid the Fedayeen under the table, supplying arms and training.

During the spring the Tudeh Party played both sides of the fence. It supported Khomeini in its public statements, yet cooperated with the Fedayeen by challenging government efforts to consolidate its position. The party discouraged the collection of weapons or the establishment of civil administrative divisions (the komitehs) under Mujahidin control. The left, as represented by the Tudeh Party, stressed the reactionary features of Khomeini's rule and appealed directly and primarily to the modernized middle class. It wanted an elected parliament that would limit the role of the clergy.

Other cracks in the revolutionary coalition began widening as well.

Foreign Minister Karim Sanjabi resigned on April 15. Though his colleague Dariush Forouhar stayed in the government until November, Sanjabi made it clear he was leaving because of the breakdown in law and order, especially the government's inability to halt the indiscriminate execution of former officials. He also announced that he was returning to active politics immediately, in order to rebuild the National Front.

The lawyers and writers united around Hedayatollah Matin-Daftari formed a new organization in April, the National Democratic Front. More attuned to the mood of the younger professionals than the National Front, it attracted the new middle class, but did not get much other urban or rural support. It spent the summer organizing and participating in protests, occasionally in conjunction with other groups, including the Fedayeen. It was forcefully dismantled in August, however, after it sponsored demonstrations against "Islamic authoritarianism."

With the quiet concurrence of Ayatollah Shariatmadari, the Islamic Peoples' Republican Party was established in April and May to compete with the Islamic Republican Party. It caught on particularly well in northwestern Iran, especially in Azarbaijan, Shariatmadari's home province. It sponsored political rallies in Tabriz, Tehran, and Qom throughout the summer, and Revolutionary Guards clashed with these demonstrators in June and August. After Rahmatollah Moghadam-Maraghei, the governor of Azarbaijan province (and the same man who established the Radical Movement) resigned on May 29 because he disagreed with the religious domination of the provisional government, some Islamic Peoples' Republican Party officials were arrested. Later, party candidates campaigning for seats in the Constitutional Assembly (the elections were scheduled for August 3) were harassed. Khomeini's Islamic Republican Party "enforcers" began beating up Islamic Peoples' Republican Party and National Front candidates at rallies, and the former went underground.

It is one of history's ironies that it was Shariatmadari who headed the group of senior religious figures who conferred ayatollah status on Khomeini following the riots in 1963. Today Shariatmadari remains in Qom, where there have been occasional violent physical struggles between his bodyguards and Khomeini loyalists. Some of both have been slain. Although he is not under arrest, Shariatmadari and his supporters believe he would be forcibly detained if he tried to leave Qom for his native Tabriz. Islamic radicals know he could mount a serious political challenge if he were to escape their "protection." In June similar guardianship was forced upon Sheik Mohammad Taher Al-Shobel Khaghani, spiritual leader of the Sunni Moslems in oil-rich Khuzistan province, after he accused the Khomeini regime of ignoring the rights of the Arab Moslem minority. Khaghani still remains an "honored guest" in Qom.[2]

Probably the most serious threat to Khomeini's domination of the revolution came from Tehran's Ayatollah Mahmoud Taleqani. Taleqani had been in prison often under the Shah and was a true folk hero from the time his last detention ended (in one of the Shah's general amnesties) on November 30, 1978, until his death on September 9, 1979. A former university teacher and an Islamic social theorist, he was idolized by the urban poor and by the young intellectuals in both Mujahidin and Fedayeen circles for his opposition to the Shah. He also commanded the largest and wealthiest local political organization in Tehran. Two of Taleqani's sons and a daughter-in-law who had helped coordinate friendly relations between the Mujahidin and the Fedayeen were arrested on April 14. The ayatollah vanished. His disappearance touched off demonstrations throughout the country. Mujahidin units loyal to him insisted all "truly revolutionary groups" should place themselves under his control. On April 17, while in hiding, Taleqani joined just-resigned Foreign Minister Sanjabi in deploring the return to "dictatorship and despotism" and announced his "retirement" from politics. Finally, five days later he resurfaced, when his sons and daughter-in-law had been released.

After three more days of uncertainty, Taleqani met in Qom with Khomeini and officials in the Bazargan cabinet. The budding confrontation was defused when Taleqani went on television, reiterating his support for Khomeini. Had he wished to continue his challenge, civil war between the followers of the two ayatollahs would have been a real possibility. Having backed down, however, Taleqani henceforth played a secondary role in internal politics. His death on September 9 removed the major independent cleric from politics, the only individual whose personal reputation was impressive enough to defy Khomeini and whose organization continues to be the single religious faction with close ties to the Fedayeen. Even today the followers of Ayatollah Taleqani remain potential components of an anti-Khomeini coalition.

One other organization has played a spoiler's role, the Forghan Group. In ancient Persian, *forghan* is another name for the Koran and means "the true word of God." Laying claim to being an Islamic offshoot, the Forghan Group stressed "the unity of God, the Koran, and its interpretations." It came to public attention with the assassination on April 23 of General Vali Gharaneh, who had retired over a disagreement after six weeks as revolutionary chief of staff. Forghan also claimed credit for the deaths of two Revolutionary Council members, Ayatollah Motahari, also on April 23, and Hojatollah Shirazi on June 15, along with the elimination of six other Khomeini supporters by December. The group asserted it wounded Hojatollah Rafsanjani on May 27 and Qazi Tabatabai on November 2. All were gunned down in broad daylight. Many individuals have been arrested on different occasions, and the group's known activities tapered off in 1980. However, the revolutionary government has remained intensely interested in tracking down gang members.

The Forghan Group may have been an umbrella under which several different factions have operated in order to hide their real identities. At least two gangs within the larger group originally supported the Shah, but became merely anti-Khomeini. The professionalism of the assassinations, the propaganda it distributed, and its vague revolutionary ideology lacking specific prescriptions for political action, suggest it was a fundamentalist Islamic organization with mixed views of how to institute change. It considers the Soviet Union, China, and the United States equally guilty of imperialist aggression against Islam. There is even-handed hatred of both the East and the West. The Forghan Group rejected authority and seeks to destroy its opponents in order to disrupt the basic foundations of any ruling power. Its addiction to violent death as the answer led Western journalists to refer to its political activities as "The Forghan Conclusion."

As Khomeini supporters tightened their grip on revolutionary Iran, those in the coalition who broke away from the Ayatollah and the new "establishment" directed by the Revolutionary Council found themselves increasingly isolated. Several leaders of Shariatmadari's Islamic Peoples' Republican Party were jailed; many others went into hiding. National Front leaders either fled the country or have gone underground. Only the Fedayeen, which commands small but organized armed forces, has been able to resist intimidation as practiced by the Mujahidin, the hezbollahi, and the Revolutionary Guards.

One of the difficulties in determining who exercises authority in contemporary Iran is that no official hierarchy is universally accepted. No government has fully established its legitimacy or even completely organized itself, so revolutionary institutions have not stabilized rapidly. It was eighteen months after the overthrow of the Shah before Iran had a permanent prime minister. There was no prime minister at all from November 1979 until August 1980, though Abol Hassan Bani-Sadr exercised some of these powers after his election as president in January.

Formal authority is diluted. Revolutionary charisma remains with Ayatollah Khomeini, but his word is not fully accepted as law throughout Iran, or even in Tehran. There have continued to be major clashes with the Fedayeen, who ostensibly still are part of the revolutionary coalition, as well as with ethnic minorities in the provinces. Outside opposition from exiles has been insignificant, though there have been signs that those in the establishment who fled the country have partially recovered from the shock of the Shah's fall and have begun nibbling at the edges of revolutionary Iran, attacking the government in speeches abroad and trying, though feebly, to set up their own insurgent forces within the country.

Conflicts between the Bazargan government and the Islamic radicals, between Khomeini and Taleqani, between the religious movement and the National Front and the National Democratic Front evolved into power struggles over the structure of the revolutionary institutions and the policies of the provisional government. The moderates were at a severe disadvantage against the religious fanatics because the clergy had the loyalty of both the hezbollahi and the dominant military force, the Revolutionary Guards. It is hardly surprising that post-Shah government became the politics of drift and ad lib.

Major Policy Differences Develop: "Justice" for All and Reviving the Military

Any violent upheaval on a national level will have its excesses, and Iran was no exception. Two major policy differences soon became obvious. The first dispute within the coalition centered on revolutionary justice for officials of the old regime. After the takeover Ayatollah Mohammad Mahdavi-Kani, head of the central komiteh in Tehran, quickly seized responsibility for law and order in the capital. He organized the first revolutionary courts, which began operating immediately. Mahdavi-Kani refused to allow the trials to take place before the regular legal establishment because all judges and lawyers were tarnished since they had worked under the Shah and "were not familiar with Islamic law." "Justice" began with interrogations on live television February 12, when a team headed by Deputy Prime Minister Yazdi questioned former SAVAK chief Nassiri, former Prime Minister Hoveyda, and several generals about their roles in "the crimes of the Shah." The first executions occurred the evening of February 15. Four generals—Nassiri, plus Reza Qazi and Mehdi Rahimi, the top military men in Tehran and Isfahan when those cities were under martial law, and hard-line commander of the air force, Manuchehr Khosrowdad—were machine-gunned by a firing squad. Executions occurred every night for approximately two weeks and were announced the following day in the press, complete with grisly pictures of the bodies.

By the end of February, amid mounting clamor from international organizations, the liberals in the provisional government—Minister of the Interior Ahmed Haj Seyed Javadi, Minister of National Guidance (Information) Nasser Minatchi, Foreign Minister Karim Sanjabi, and Minister of Labor Dariush Forouhar, plus Prime Minister Bazargan himself—had urged Khomeini and the Revolutionary Council to stop the summary deaths. Under Ayatollah Khalkhali, nicknamed "Judge Blood," or "The Hanging Judge," the tribunals were disposing of dozens of individuals each night. The accused heard charges brought against them for brutality, murder, or the all-purpose allegations, "war against God" and "corruption on earth." They were given one or two minutes to reply, sentenced, and taken to the roof of the Alavi School and shot forthwith.

The provisional government exercised no control over these trials. Bazargan was surprised to learn through the media on February 20 about the execution of several of the military and civilian elite under the Shah. By the end of the month it was obvious that the prime minister's government was not involved in the judicial proceedings. Although only prominent figures were identified in the press, the list of those known to have been executed is well over 1,000. During the first month junior officers in SAVAK and the army and even some enlisted men were killed after the barest vestige of a hearing. There would be three or four executions of nondescript individuals for every VIP killed. Within five months, by midsummer 1979, over 70 percent of the Shah's senior officer corps had been executed as well as nearly all ministers from previous governments who had not had the foresight to flee the country.

Except for one brief period, March 16 to April 5, revolutionary executions continued. Though Bazargan was able to convince Khomeini to halt the killings for three weeks, the provisional government could not prevail permanently against the wishes of the Revolutionary Council, especially Ayatollah Khalkhali. Trials and executions resumed on April 5 and 7, with the killing of three police generals, former Prime Minister Hoveyda, and several other former ministers. Hoveyda was put to death in spite of international concern, including an appeal by letter from United Nations Secretary-General Kurt Waldheim urging that his life be spared. This communique was inspired by Hoveyda's brother, Fereidoun, who had been the Iranian ambassador to the U.N. during the latter years of the Shah's reign. Ironically, Hoveyda had been set free by the revolutionaries who opened the doors of Evin Prison February 9. He refused to escape, saying he had nothing to fear, and turned himself in to the new authorities instead. Since he was well known abroad, the execution of Hoveyda made it dramatically clear that the Islamic fundamentalists would take a hard attitude toward former officials and not be swayed by diplomatic niceties.[3]

The revolutionary courts have never been placed under government control. Individual judges have operated in a free-lance fashion which horrifies the International League of Jurists and Western public opinion. The executions have also become an embarrassment to other Islamic countries. Bazargan, Minatchi, and others who had campaigned so energetically against the Shah for human and civil rights were humiliated, but they were powerless to change anything.

The second area of conflict between the provisional government and the Islamic movement emerged over the question of rebuilding the armed forces. Bazargan and his deputy prime ministers Amir Entezam and Ibrahim Yazdi began almost immediately to select "loyal" (anti-Shah or neutral) officers who could reestablish order. Concurrently, the Islamic movement created committees of men within the military who were loyal to the revolution and who could root out pro-Shah officers. Both efforts went forward slowly, because the radicals were purging known enemies. Though the navy restored its command integrity relatively quickly—by May 1 approximately 90 percent of its personnel were back on duty—discipline had dissolved in the army and the air force. In June army commander and chief of staff General Taghi Riahi reported his forces at only 50 percent of pre-revolutionary strength. The air force was in even worse shape. Warrant officers and cadets at the Doshen Tappeh base who had sparked the uprising in February refused to submit to officers "who had not been in the vanguard of the revolution." Homafars joined with Mujahidin units to be "the guardians of revolutionary purity." Cadets were unwilling to take orders from anyone other than members of the Mujahidin and sometimes not even from them. Many pilots were either Shah loyalists or neutral. Until the war with Iraq erupted in September 1980, air force planes were not allowed to fly without authorization from Khomeini headquarters for fear "unscreened" pilots would bomb Qom and flee the country. Approximately 200 of them were jailed after an alleged military coup attempt in July 1980. Some were released two months later, when Iraq attacked Iran, in order to fly combat missions.

Regular members of the armed forces who survived the purges were intimidated by the Mujahidin and the Revolutionary Guards. Officers had seen what happened to generals who obeyed commands in defense of the previous regime—they were shot. Therefore the Pasdaran and Mujahidin would order military units to do what religious leaders wished, often countermanding senior officers. One example of this occurred at the U.S. embassy, where Islamic guards had been ensconced since February 14. On two occasions, in April and May, regular army units were sent to the compound by the government to replace the Islamic militiamen. Both times the commander of the men "protecting" the embassy abruptly ordered the army detachment to leave. Direct orders from Khomeini had brought the guards to the compound, and they refused to depart unless the same source directed them to do so. Each time the military detachment withdrew and the Bazargan administration did not press the matter with the clergy.

Civil Uprisings Cause a Problem

Violence never subsided; profound political unrest continued. The most serious incidents involved the Kurds, a large ethnic group in northwest Iran. In March, under tribal leadership calling itself the Kurdish Democratic Party, the Kurds revolted against the central government and attempted to establish an autonomous Kurdish province within Iran. The Fedayeen allied itself with the Kurds and assisted the rebels by supplying them with arms and supporting their demands for more autonomy. Major fighting flared up in August, October, and December, as the government tried to put down the "rebellion," claiming the Kurds wanted to secede. About 3,000 government troops have died trying to reestablish central control. For the most part, however, the army has been reluctant to move against them. At least 12 officers were executed in September for refusing to fire at the dissidents. Perhaps 5,000 Kurds were killed in the uprising, including at least 150 executed by the army as "instigators." Photographs showing slumped bodies tied to stakes appeared in the Western press, provoking a furor and further alienating public opinion from the revolutionary government. By December 1979 the Kurds controlled their own affairs, at least in fact, if not formally. Government authority in Kurdestan remains minimal.

In March there were also major clashes in eastern Iran between the army and Revolutionary Guards against Turkoman tribesmen. The center of resistance was at Gonbad-e-Qabus, a medium-sized town in Khorassan Province north of Mashad. Other outbreaks, less than rebellions but more than demonstrations, occurred in Ahwaz, Khorram-shahr, and Abadan in the spring and summer. There, the Arab minority protested discrimination and ill treatment, especially by the Revolutionary Guards. Over a dozen Pasdaran and around 100 Arabs died in a series of outbreaks. In other major riots 17 demonstrating Azarbaijanis were killed on December 8 in Tabriz.

From March 1 to December 31, 1979, over 600 deaths because of civil disturbances were acknowledged by the government, with approximately four times that number wounded. From January 1 to July 30, 1980, over 400 more were killed and about triple that figure injured. If anything, these numbers understate the casualties. Deaths and injuries in the smaller towns are underreported.

Such turmoil led to continued political chaos as the authority of the central government slowly weakened. All the tribal groups have watched this struggle with interest. While none has broken away yet (the Kurds have come the closest), Iran's revolution has clearly reversed the process of unifying the tribes into one nation, a policy first imposed by Reza Shah and continued by his son. Clan leaders now look to their own interests and distinguish them from those of the government—whatever government—in Tehran. The war with Iraq that erupted in September 1980 interrupted this process because loyalty to the country against the invaders prevailed. But it did not halt it.

The Clergy and the Constitution

The declared mission of the provisional government was to hold a referendum on the monarchy and to prepare for the Islamic Republic that would surely be voted in. Seven weeks after the revolutionary takeover, on March 30 and 31, 97 percent of the electorate decided to do away with the monarchy and make Iran an Islamic Republic. Although the Shah died without ever having abdicated, this referendum legally marked the end of the Pahlavi dynasty.

The next thing on the agenda was to draft a new constitution. Differences in philosophy among the various revolutionary leaders emerged very quickly. The "intellectuals"—Bazargan, Sanjabi, Sahabi, and the liberals such as Matin-Daftari—sought a Western-style constitution in which the clergy would be content to minister to the nation's moral and spiritual needs, leaving the business of running the country to secular leaders. However, mullahs imbued with the spirit of the Islamic movement appealed to Khomeini's teachings, insisting instead that religion be enshrined in the constitution above politics in teh form of the *velayat-e-faghih*, or the "religious guardian," of Islamic laws. This would mean institutionalized supreme political as well as spiritual authority for the recognized leader of Iran's Shiites, Ayatollah Khomeini. Previously, a major element of Shiite doctrine had been that constitutional power would be a secular responsibility. A religious person could exercise such authority only when the Twelfth Imam returned to earth. Yet the cornerstone of Khomeini's political philosophy is that the clergy should dominate the government for political as well as moral reasons.[4] If carried out in practice, this doctrine would most likely lead to a regime resembling that which ruled Persia in the eighth century. Little is known about the 22-year period from 719 to 741 except that the clerical institutions eventually disintegrated because they could not govern effectively.

Controversy over the secular versus the religious understanding of power continued from April to December, throughout the constitutional struggle. At mass rallies on June 22 leftists strongly criticized the rumors about what the proposed constitution would include, saying it was going to be too religiously oriented. Followers of a moderate policy agreed, especially members of Ayatollah Shariatmadari's Islamic Peoples' Republican Party. They challenged rather than approved of the political sovereignty of the Khomeini wing of Shiite Islam. In mid-July a draft document prepared by concerned moderate revolutionaries and embodying the basic Western precepts of an elected president and an appointed prime minister responsible to a national assembly was forwarded to Khomeini. It was rejected, on the advice of the newly formed Islamic Republican Party, especially its chairman Ayatollah Beheshti and his colleagues Ayatollahs Lahouti and Mahdavi-Kani, because it did not allow for religious absolutism. This would be the first visible emergence of the fundamentalist ecclesiastical faction as a major political force and would signify the corresponding decrease in power for the secular revolutionaries grouped around Bazargan's Liberation Movement and Sanjabi's National Front.

By mid-June the non-radical clergy and the secular leaders found themselves on the periphery, while Beheshti and his allies, increasing their influence, manipulated the constitutional process. The Revolutionary Council called for a constitutional assembly to be established. Its job would be to write the constitution that would direct the Islamic Republic. The balloting was scheduled to be August 3. To insure the election of an overwhelming majority of representatives sympathetic to Khomeini's constitutional views and to freeze out revolutionaries who were not fully loyal to the Ayatollah, Islamic hard-liners rigged the electoral process, forcing opponents off the ballot and intimidating voters. The tampering was so blatant that members of the Islamic Peoples' Republican Party, the National Front, and the National Democratic Front boycotted the polls. Seventy-three "elected" officials took office. The Khomeini forces refused to seat Abdul Rahman Qassemlou, who had won a seat from Kurdestan, because he was "not sufficiently faithful" to the Islamic Republic. At least one other delegate was also denied his place. Exclusive control of the Constitutional Assembly by the fundamentalists was assured.

Just prior to the voting on August 3, faced with the threatened resignations of 11 of his 17 cabinet members and unable to fire military Chief of Police Amir Rahimi because of obstruction from the clergy, Prime Minister Bazargan warned he would quit. The threat was taken seriously, and the cabinet quickly negotiated an agreement with the Revolutionary Council that had been desultorily discussed since May. It said there would be improved coordination between the government, the council, and the neighborhood komitehs. Now five cabinet members would sit on the Revolutionary Council, but more importantly, five men on the Revolutionary Council would be ministers or deputy ministers. Ayatollah Mahdavi-Kani and Rafsanjani became deputy ministers of the interior (Rafsanjani also took over the Revolutionary Guards' portfolio from Chamran, who had led them since May). Abol Hassan Bani-Sadr emerged as deputy minister of the economy, in charge of banking, and Ayatollah Hassan Bahonar was named deputy minister of education. Mustafa Chamran moved laterally to be deputy minister of defense as well as a deputy prime minister.

While these changes brought the membership of the Revolutionary Council at least partially out into the open and linked it more directly to the government, the practical impact of the proposal was to increase greatly the strength and influence of the pro-Khomeini clergy loyal to the Islamic Republican Party. Within seven weeks Chamran took over the Ministry of Defense completely. The job opened up September 12, because General Riahi resigned as both chief of staff and acting minister of defense in disgust over meddling by the clergy. Though the alterations increased the effectiveness of the government just in time for the Constitutional Assembly elections, the price was high. Hard-line religious representation was now entrenched in Bazargan's own cabinet. As Bazargan commented to Italian journalist Oriana Fallaci in late October, "Everyone wants to be prime minister."[5] Having failed to establish his government's control over the Islamic fundamentalists at the outset of the revolution, he was now forced to give their leaders a part in running his administration.

Post-Revolutionary Political Dynamics

After the "guided" Constitutional Assembly elections religious moderates, secular leaders, and leftists all felt betrayed. The Fedayeen demonstrated, demanding a "popular" government, an end to bullying by the hezbollahi, and the revision of the repressive press code enacted in late July which restricted both reportorial and editorial freedom "for the good of the Islamic nation." The fundamentalists retaliated by destroying some Fedayeen offices and closing down the leading leftist newspaper, *Ayandegan.* On August 21 Khomeini issued instructions to shut down 22 more opposition publications throughout the country and ordered all organizations opposing clerical rule to turn in their weapons. The hezbollahi attacked the headquarters of all major political groups—the Islamic Peoples' Republican Party, the National Front, the Tudeh Party, the National Democratic Front, and the Pan Iran Party. A warrant was issued for the arrest of the leader of the National Democratic Front, Matin-Daftari, and he slipped out of the country, surfacing in Paris. Those men hounded underground or forced to leave had not been even lukewarm supporters of the Shah's regime, but independent nationalists of considerable standing. Two months earlier Khomeini had declared an amnesty for all who had worked with the former government except for SAVAK and military personnel who had "tortured and killed Iranians." Now he was reversing himself, vehemently attacking his disillusioned allies.

The events of the summer of 1979, especially the rigged Constitutional Assembly election, mark the ascendance of the fundamentalist religious movement over its former sympathizers, the secular revolutionaries. The Bazargan government did not disintegrate completely until after the American hostages were seized November 4, but the process began with the selection of a "tame" assembly. Until then, all the groups in the revolutionary coalition had believed that they would have a fair chance at power in the Islamic Republic, whatever their conflicts with individual clergy or Mujahidin units. Now they knew this was not to be. Increasingly, moderates and leftists referred to Khomeini as a dictator. The Fedayeen talked of the "Fascist mullahs." Secular leaders bemoaned the loss of civil liberties as represented by the restrictions on the press and the intimidation and outright violence of the hezbollahi. The National Front and the National Democratic Front were damaged most because they had no independent paramilitary force to protect them. In fact, the National Democratic Front had no influence after Matin-Daftari fled, and the Pan Iran Party disappeared without a trace, though its leader, Forouhar, remained in the cabinet until Bazargan resigned as prime minister in November. The Fedayeen, on the other hand, decided to go underground and accelerate the rebuilding of its clandestine organization.

Islamic radicals wanted to overcome their opponents decisively by writing a constitution that would give them preeminence. On September 13 the newly formed Constitutional Assembly approved a clause giving supreme power to Khomeini as the country's chief religious leader. (He was formally recognized as such on October 19.) September 18 the Islamic Republican Party charged that Bazargan's government was falling apart and called for his dismissal. Within two weeks the prime minister was forced to fire Hassan Nazih, prominent revolutionary lawyer and head of the National Iranian Oil Company since the revolution. Nazih had been close to Matin-Daftari and other liberals. By May he had begun criticizing Khomeini. Eventually, the Ayatollah would take it no more. Nazih was not only sacked, but Khomeini suggested he be tried for treason. He fled the country, however, reemerging in the spring of 1980 as another dissident living in Paris.

Two primary themes form the basis of Iranian revolutionary political passions and action—anti-Shah and anti-modernization, as well as anti-Western sentiment amounting to hatred. These issues unite the Marxist left and the religious fundamentalist right. When domestic affairs or foreign policy can be linked to these feelings, the fundamentalists force political activity, policy making, and decision making along channels agreeable to them. Otherwise, disagreements between factions have inhibited decisive action. Since its shaky inception the revolutionary system has had a dreadful time coping whenever the unifying anti-Shah and anti-capitalist themes cannot be used to bolster official policies.

A loathing for the Shah and his grand design was the cement that united old-line nationalists, both moderates and radicals. The older, more traditional left as represented by the Tudeh Party was always anti-Shah, but came late to revolutionary participation, doing little to aid its more radical brethren until October 1978. Radical Marxists like the various Fedayeen groups were anti-Shah because his regime repressed their subversive activities and because of his clase indentification with U.S. policies in the Middle East, especially on the Arab-Israeli question. Oil shipments to Israel during the 1973 war did more than any single act to stimulate the P.L.O., P.F.L.P., and Libya into giving additional support to the radical Marxists.

The anti-Western aspect of leftist ideology was echoed by the fundamentalist right. Khomeini had tied his hatred of the Shah to the monarch's efforts to modernize his country. Moslem clerics strongly opposed the regime for its continuous efforts to diminish the clergy's role by taking control of the religious foundations and by distributing its property among the peasants as part of land reform. As long as the Shah controlled Iran, it was easy for both left and right to be unified, especially against the corruption and brutality that were by-products of official efforts to control social-political stress.

Differences lie dormant in this left-right alliance. The Fedayeen does not want clerical rule and religious fundamentalism. It does want modernization, if it can be carried out by leftist leadership in the name of collectivism or "Islamic socialism." Therefore, the key issues between left and right revolve around the extent of clerical control of social and economic life. The Fedayeen and the Islamic fundamentalists have clashed over constitutional arrangements for the distribution of power, economic control of industry, the future status of the armed forces, freedom for open political activity, and women's rights. The left has effectively challenged the clergy over Revolutionary Council efforts to control the press, manipulate the Constitutional Assembly, and dominate the government. Other groups, specifically what is left of the National Front and the National Democratic Front, have supported the Fedayeen. While Shariatmadari's Islamic Peoples' Party has not lined up with the Fedayeen on any major issues, it opposes religious supremacy and restrictions on political freedom.

If anti-modernization inhibits left-right rapprochement, anti-Americanism strengthens it. The Islamic movement considers the United States the main foreign supporter of the Shah for 30 years and a major cause of the "corruption" of Iranian society. The U.S., along with the Shah, has been blamed for everything from high rents to excessive urban traffic congestion. In his cassette messages in 1978, Khomeini railed against America's "satanic influence over the minds of Islamic youth." This extreme anti-American view, if not the quaint language, is fully shared by the Fedayeen and other leftists. Despite the benign American attitude during the triumph of his movement, Khomeini and the radical clerics remained extremely skeptical of the United States. When General Gharaneh was assassinated, the Ayatollah accused the United States of "being behind the Forghan Group" and of "wanting to destroy our revolution."

In mid-May the U.S. Senate passed a relatively mild resolution sponsored by Senator Jacob Javits, which criticized the summary executions and called upon the revolutionary government to allow due process in court trials and to respect other religions. After a noted Jewish millionaire and close friend of the Shah, Habib Elghanian, was sentenced to death for "corruption on earth," Javits had pressed the Senate to act, hoping to curtail further outbursts against Jews. At the same time, the Senate approved the nomination of Walter Cutler, ambassador to Zaire, to be America's first envoy to Iran since the revolutionary takeover. When Khomeini and the radical clerics heard of the Javits resolution, they exploded. The Ayatollah accused the U.S. of interference in Iranian internal affairs and sarcastically labeled Javits "a puppet of the Shah," because his wife had received payments from Iran Air for public relations work on its behalf. America was accused of great hypocrisy—excessive moralizing while itself sinning. To the radical fundamentalists, the United States had become "the great Satan . . . the moral corrupter of the world."

To underline its point, the Revolutionary Council directed Bazargan to suggest that Cutler "postpone" his arrival until relations between the two governments were "clarified." Two weeks later, the government abruptly cancelled its previous decision to accept him as ambassador. In the meantime, the Islamic movement searched for other ways to show its displeasure. On May 24 about 80,000 hezbollahi paraded past the U.S. mission chanting anti-American slogans. There were scuffles in the crowd between the Mujahidin and the one Fedayeen unit that joined the march. A group of militants broke through the reinforced line of Islamic sentries guarding the embassy. Though the latter stood their ground, the invaders pressed forward to the flagpole, tore down the American flag, and ripped it up, passing pieces to the crowd. But when it became clear that the Islamic forces were resisting the incursion, the militants retreated.

The following day the chargé d'affaires, Charles Naas, directed the majority of his staff to attend the semiannual tennis match between the British and American embassies. It was to be at the British "summer compound" in north Tehran, seven miles away. Only the marine guards, security officials, and a few political officers remained at the U.S. embassy during the match. The marines put up a new flag, tied off the halyards 20 feet above the ground, and smeared the pole with pig fat. Approximately 100,000 demonstrators arrived, chanting slogans, and shouting speeches, and then dispersed, never rising to the challenge of capturing the flag. Again the Islamic guards had held the line. (Let history record an unexpected side benefit. Imbued with the excitement of the occasion and despite having lost two top players in the evacuations in December and January, the U.S. embassy tennis team's patchwork lineup scored a surprising 7–2 victory over its British counterpart to take home "The Crash of '79" cup, christened after the Paul Erdman novel about Iran of the same name.) The next day was anticlimactic. Only about 10,000 people paraded, and the atmosphere was more festive than hostile. By May 27 overt manifestations of anti-American sentiment had greatly diminished.

There had been no direct takeover attempt, though few doubted that if the guards had not indicated their determination to resist the invasion of the compound by fighting, if necessary, then the militants would have continued moving in and would have captured the mission. Thus the second successful takeover might have occurred in May rather than six months later. (On the latter occasion, the embassy's government-supplied guards would quietly leave at the first sign of trouble.) Oddly enough, this tense three-day period received little publicity in the United States. It was overshadowed in the media by the tragic crash in Chicago on May 25 of a DC-10 which killed 273 people.

Antagonism toward America was not shared by more moderate members of Khomeini's own coalition. Liberation Movement leaders recognized the Western contribution to Iran's development. The National Front and the National Democratic Front felt even more strongly that they did not support the Islamic revolution to bring about the destruction of their country's economic development, but should reform it and humanize it. Although they criticized what they saw as America's excessive influence, they spoke of "new relationships of mutual respect," not cessation of trade and communication. These differences within the coalition were particularly apparent in two areas—foreign policy toward the West and the reconstruction of the armed forces.

The post-revolutionary turning away from the West was reflected immediately in the reception given Yasser Arafat in Tehran and Qom during his five-day visit to Iran in February. He was treated as a head of state. The provisional government immediately announced the termination of both diplomatic relations with and oil shipments to Israel. On March 3 Bazargan also broke diplomatic (but not consular) ties with another international pariah, South Africa. Vituperative attacks on the United States for "plundering the lifeblood of Iran" were standard, particularly after Khomeini aide Ibrahim Yazdi became foreign minister on April 24, following Sanjabi's resignation nine days earlier. Within a few weeks the anti-Western tilt became pronounced. In May the Foreign Ministry announced that it had officially asked to join the Nonaligned Movement. The request was quickly accepted.

But the Bazargan government had no plans to reject the West completely, particularly the United States. The prime minister wanted Iran to continue trade with the U.S. and Europe in order to speed up the rebuilding process and to avoid further economic deterioration. At least minimal ties were also necessary to keep the military operable, especially in regard to supplies and equipment. The cabinet did agree, however, that the purchase of "unneeded" arms should be stopped. Therefore on March 15 the United States and Iran announced simultaneously that of the $11.6 billion of filled orders $7 billion would not be delivered. Bazargan had reviewed the arrangements Bakhtiar had already negotiated and confirmed the former prime minister's original intentions.[6]

From March to May relations between the two countries concentrated on sorting out financial arrangements and untangling reciprocal liabilities in previous business dealings. The provisional government attempted to work out an acceptable agreement concerning a continued but reduced U.S. military presence. Bazargan wanted to reestablish certain arrangements so that American hardware already delivered — advanced Phoenix missles and sensitive F-14 jet aircraft—would remain usable. The U.S. sought to protect its investment and the security of its equipment. At the time Bazargan, his aides, embassy personnel, and the State Department all failed to understand just how much suspicion this willingness to cooperate fomented among other members of the revolutionary movement, specifically the left and the fundamentalist right. The Fedayeen decried absolutely any relationship with "the degenerate capitalists who kept Iran in slavery for decades." The reactionary clergy feared the United States was trying to block Khomeini's plans for comprehensive social change or perhaps even planning to restore the former monarch or his son to the throne.

As the Shah lingered in Egypt, then moved on to Morocco before flying to the Bahamas on March 30, the fears of the radical ayatollahs increased. They were convinced the Americans would attempt to repeat their successful adventure of 1953. This apprehension festered throughout the summer. When the Shah was admitted to the United States for medical treatment on October 22, fear was transformed into paranoia that they were correct in their assumption. Both Islamic militants and the Fedayeen have claimed subsequently that the second American embassy takeover, on November 4, 1979, had been planned for months, because if the Shah ever moved to the U.S. they were prepared to take drastic action.[7] Whether just the Shah's arrival in New York for an extended stay triggered the takeover is conjectural; certainly the combination of his coming to the United States plus the meeting of

Brzezinski, Bazargan, and Yazdi in Algiers on November 1 was enough to do so. Islamic and leftist militants, exhorted by those close to Khomeini who wanted to humiliate the U.S., invaded the embassy.

The Foreign Factor

The Soviets gained tremendously when America's regional position all but collapsed. They recognized the new regime immediately. Vladimir Vinogradov, the ambassador, called on Khomeini February 24 and regularly every two months thereafter. During his first meeting he was lectured on Soviet interventionism, informed that Iran's foreign policy would be nonaligned, and cautioned not to interfere in internal politics. There was nothing secret about this session. An account was front page news in Tehran the next day. Vinogradov fared no better other times. In June he was again chastized; an accusation that the U.S.S.R. was suppressing the Islamic movement in Afghanistan was included. Exasperated, the ambassador told his colleagues in other embassies that the Kremlin "was a damn fool to keep sending me down to Qom for regular beatings."

The important thing, however, was that the American position had all but disappeared. Furthermore, the increasing disorder was made to order for covert meddling. Though the Soviet embassy, like its American counterpart, sent its dependents home in December and January of 1978–1979, the number of Russian diplomats assigned to Tehran increased steadily throughout 1979. By the time of the second seizure of the U.S. embassy, Western diplomats had identified approximately 70 political and economic specialists in the country in contrast to 8 for the Americans. The Tudeh Party and the Fedayeen stayed clear of other Soviet contacts, but undoubtedly they exchanged views since both they and the Soviets supported Khomeini as a nationalist hero leading his people away from imperialism. However, Moscow would become disapproving in August because the Kremlin did not like it when the Islamic movement began managing the electoral process in order to squeeze the left out of politics. At that time Soviet radio began criticizing the provisional government and the Revolutionary Council alike for being "reactionary" and "anti-progressive" and for attacking leftist newspapers. Khomeini never has had any use for communism, and he frequently equates it to U.S. imperialism as a "satanic force." Nevertheless, from a Russian point of view, Iran's descent into chaos opens up excellent prospects of a Marxist regime in the future, much like that which came to power in Afghanistan in April 1978. But the Soviet approach has remained basically low key, waiting, preparing for the right moment.

Other countries made their peace with the new regime. The British and West Germans quietly resumed normal ties in the shadow of the Iranian fixation on the United States. France was unable to capitalize on having given Khomeini refuge while he was in exile. In fact the French suffered almost as much from the cancellation of joint economic projects as the U.S. The construction of two atomic generating plants was terminated when the new energy chief, Feridoun Sahabi (son of Bazargan confidant, Yadollah Sahabi), declared Iran would not continue to develop nuclear power. Revolutionary officials reviewing the $7 billion contract to build a subway in Tehran decided to cancel that as well.

As for the neighboring conservative Arab monarchies, Ayatollah Sadegh Rouhani announced in October that if the Emir of Bahrain "does not want to stop oppressing the people and restore Islamic laws, we will call upon the people of Bahrain to demand annexation to the Islamic government of Iran." The preceding month Ayatollah Montazeri had announced, "We will export our Islamic revolution to all the Moslem countries of the world."[8] The rulers of Abu Dhabi, Oman, Kuwait, Bahrain, and the United Arab Emirates were understandably nervous about speeches calling upon Persian Gulf Shiites to rally to the revolution and to overthrow their leaders. Saudi Arabia was also uneasy about Iranian intentions, but kept relations with the new leaders correct, if cool. Foreign Minister Yazdi denied expansionist aims at the United Nations in mid-October, but it hardly assuaged the concern of the other Arab nations.

The biggest problem was Iran's rapidly deteriorating relations with its immediate neighbor to the West, Iraq. With its nearly 50 percent Shiite minority, it was the country most wary of Khomeini's militant Islamic stance. Iraq had maintained good relations with the Shah's regime since March 1975, when the monarch stopped arming Kurdish guerrillas in Iraq and the two countries agreed to settle a century old dispute along their common border, especially the Shat-el-Arab Waterway (called the Avand Rud by Iranians). When unrest broke out in Khuzistan province in May, Iraq aided the Arab Moslems who were revolting against the Shiite government. Iran charged Iraqi planes strafed a village on June 6. Several other incidents punctuated their bilateral relations throughout 1979, erupting into war on September 22, 1980.

The inability of the revolutionaries to establish a strong, stable government, the increasing internal conflicts between factions within the revolutionary coalition, and the expansionist dreams of the radical clerics made the international community uncertain and uneasy. Iran's neighbors worried about that country interfering in their internal affairs. Its more distant traditional trading partners in the West hoped for the best and sought to adjust old alliances to new conditions. Then, on November 4, 1979, relations between Iran and the United States plummeted to new depths. Radical militants invaded the American embassy, this time to stay.

Chapter Eleven

★

Institutionalized Crisis

November 1979–April 1980

The seizure of the American embassy on November 4 by a group of 500 militants calling themselves "students" and "Followers of the Imam's Line" was a repeat performance of the February takeover until the invaders refused to leve the compound when the Bazargan government asked them to turn over their prize to government forces. Before that day, the political dynamics of the post-revolutionary period had centered around hatred of the Shah and the manipulation of anti-Western and anti-modernization sentiments. Though the radical clerics controlled the Revolutionary Guards and the Mujahidin, they could only influence—not dominate—the militants occupying the embassy.

Differences over what relations with the United States should be, particularly concerning the American captives, accelerated conflict among the various groups within the revolutionary coalition. Anti-American attitudes became the dominant emotion in Persian politics, and holding the hostages became inextricably intertwined with the domestic struggle for power. The militants used classified cables found in the invaded compound as "evidence" of "spying" and justification for making the fate of the prisoners the most important political issue in the country. By late November the trespassers had displayed a Belgian passport on international television with the picture on it of Thomas Ahearn, one of the imprisoned Americans, but made out to a different identity. This, plus other documents in their possession allegedly "proved" that he and two other captives were C.I.A. agents. The taking of hostages placed Iran and the United States squarely in confrontation, with no visible way for either country to back off, despite the fact that the conflict was definitely not in the long-range interest of either nation.

At first, everyone assumed that the crisis would be resolved quickly. As the months dragged by, it became clear that there would be no easy solution. Fortunately many of the 53 captives, who ranged in age from 19 to 63, were able to kill at least some of the monotony of their incarceration by reading for hours on end. At the time of the invasion, the library books and sophisticated electronic learning equipment of the Tehran American School (3,000 students, kindergarten-through-twelfth grade) were being packed up by the former superintendent, William Keough. The shipment was to be made available to administrators of American schools overseas, meeting on the Greek island of Rhodes during the Christmas break. All of it was to be sold at bargain prices. Unfortunately, in overseeing the move Keough picked the wrong day to be away from his new job as superintendent of the American school in Islamabad, Pakistan. Similarly unlucky was the oldest hostage, Robert Ode. A consular officer, he had agreed to come out of retirement to help in Tehran for six weeks. He was scheduled to be home before Thanksgiving.

Prime Minister Bazargan's resignation, two days after the capture of the embassy, triggered the final round of the constitutional struggle. The Revolutionary Council assumed control, and the radical forces around Khomeini used the opportunity to ram an Islamic fundamentalist constitution through the assembly and thus gain complete power.

The hostage issue riveted worldwide attention for several months. Tehran became a mecca for media personnel, who focused on the plight of the captives. Even after American journalists were expelled in January, European tapes sold to U.S. networks kept the situation visible on stateside television sets. Almost immediately the United Nations became involved in efforts to free the captive Americans. First the Security Council and then Secretary-General Waldheim tried to mediate the dispute. After months of negotiations and false starts, in April a U.N.-sponsored arrangement appeared on the verge of success when it fell victim to Khomeini's intransigence.

The overwhelming majority of countries opposed the seizing of the embassy, with only Albania, North Korea, Laos, and Vietnam officially supporting the Iranians. Moslem states, like Pakistan, remained silent or, like Saudi Arabia, limited their criticism to Iran's violation of diplomatic rights. Although the U.S.S.R. initially played a double game of public criticism coupled with modest private support of the Revolutionary Council, that country's invasion of Afghanistan on December 26 heightened Iranian suspicions of ultimate Soviet intentions toward their country. Meanwhile, Iran found itself an isolated outlaw because of its willful violation of diplomatic law.

The Politics of Seizing an Embassy

Until the embassy takeover Iranian-American relations had been one issue among many in Iranian domestic politics. On November 4 they became the central focus of the internal struggle. The more moderate, street-wise cabinet members like Abol Hassan Bani-Sadr, Sadeq Ghotbzadeh, and Mehdi Bazargan knew from the beginning that resolving the hostage issue was a necessary precondition for carrying out thoroughgoing social reform and reshaping society. For the Islamic clergy it was a different story. Immediately following the capture, they were thrown into a quandary. Although all wanted to expunge Western influence, radicals such as Ayatollah Morteza Montazeri and Hojatollah Hashemi Rafsanjani favored the militants. Others such as Ayatollahs Mohammad Beheshti and Hassan Mahdavi-Kani feared a U.S. riposte. It was the way the embassy had been taken over that led to the divided opinions.

The attack began about noon on Sunday, November 4. As in all Moslem countries, Friday is the holy day in Iran, so Sunday was the first day of the embassy's work week. About 500 young men and women paraded by the compound, as they had done several times before, ever since the Shah's admittance to the United States two weeks previously. Suddenly they rushed the embassy's main gate. Islamic guards who were supposed to protect the mission stood aside and allowed those trespassing to occupy the grounds and besiege the buildings. Several of the invaders, apparently unarmed, forced themselves inside the front door of the largest structure, ostensibly to deliver a "protest." Once inside, guns materialized. They moved quickly to take over the chancery. Collusion between those actually responsible for the seizure and the radical clergy was strongly suggested when Hojatollah Mohammad Moussavi Khoeini, representing Khomeini's office in Qom, prayed with the insurgents the evening of November 4 on the grounds of the compound.

In all, about 150 captives were taken. Sixty-three Americans, including 27 military men—14 marine guards and 13 others attached to the remains of the once massive ARMISH-MAAG contingent—were overwhelmed. All were employees of the U.S. government in Tehran except William Keough, former superintendent of the Tehran American school, and Jerry Plotkin, a Los Angeles businessman seeking letters of introduction from the commercial section of the embassy, both trapped by unlucky accident. Others seized were embassy employees who were nationals of Iran, Vietnam, Laos, the Philippines, Thailand, or Pakistan, plus the Italian chef attached to the ambassador's residence. The Iranians were turned loose immediately, and other non–Americans were gradually released during the following three weeks. The chef and his Pakistani assistant volunteered to stay and cook Western-style food for the hostages. Not until May, six months later, did they give up their voluntary servitude.

Three American diplomats were transacting business at the foreign ministry 15 blocks away at the time of the takeover. Chargé d'affaires Bruce Laingen, political counselor Victor Tomseth, and security officer Michael Howland had been on an official call when they received word of what had happened. The men would remain together as "guests" for all but the last few weeks of their incarceration in the largest of the elegant protocol reception rooms, despite pleas by the militants to ministry officials that they should join the other hostages at the embassy. In December Foreign Minister Ghotbzadeh (he had just been promoted to his new job from his previous post as head of the National Iranian Radio and Television Service) offhandedly commented that the three captives "were free to leave." In the next breath, the foreign minister said that the government "could not guarantee their safety," not even to the airport, if they left the foreign ministry. The three men stayed where they were. Until they joined the other hostages on January 4, 1981, Laingen was the senior American in direct conact with the revolutionary government. He also remained in occasional touch with the State Department in Washington by telephone.

The Ayatollah's son, Ahmad Khomeini, arrived at the compound the second day, November 5, and in his father's name endorsed the capture of the "nest of spies." He warned the Bazargan government that if it protested the takeover, it "opposed the will of the Iranian people." "Little K," as he was called, also supported the five-hour seizure of the British embassy the day before. The objective had been to force England to turn over the Shah's last prime minister, Shapour Bakhtiar. When the hezbollahi learned Bakhtiar was not living in Britain, but in France, they left the mission grounds without pressing the issue.

From the beginning to the end of the prolonged hostage ordeal, contradictory statements by the various factions were made at every point. A month after the takeover, several revolutionary leaders, including Khomeini himself, said that the students invaded the embassy "as a 'game' because America had the Shah." The most militant of the Mujahidin units truly believed that the monarch's arrival in the United States was the first step in a counterrevolutionary plot to overthrow the

Khomeini regime. It had been encouraged to reach this conclusion by its P.L.O. allies and trainers, some of whom helped plan the takeover.[1] These feelings were strongly reinforced by events in Algiers on November 1 when Bazargan and his foreign minister, Ibrahim Yazdi, joined with Zbigniew Brzezinski, President Carter's assistant for national security affairs, in a prearranged meeting. The two Iranians and the American were attending the celebration honoring the beginning of the Algerian revolution 25 years before. The combination of the Shah's arrival in the United States and of Bazargan's meeting with Brzezinski was more than enough to activate plans which had been on the drawing board since the spring.

After the takeover Bazargan immediately issued a statement saying that his government would fulfill its responsibilities under international law. Very quickly it became apparent that the militants and the fundamentalists would not allow the prime minister the authority to hand over the hostages. Bazargan resigned on November 6, provoking the first of many government crises. An unperturbed Khomeini immediately ordered the Revolutionary Council to assume supreme authority, hold a referendum on the new Islamic constitution, and prepare for a presidential election. He made absolutely no mention of the hostages.

Bazargan left office when it became clear that his government could not obtain the speedy release of the detained diplomats. In the February takeover Yazdi had led the Revolutionary Guards to the embassy and set the Americans free. This time both Yazdi and Bazargan were suspect because of their meeting with Brzezinski. The prime minister had tried to quit at least four times previously, the first attempt less than a month after the revolutionary takeover in February, because he felt the clergy never supported his efforts to run the country. Each time the Ayatollah had refused to accept his resignation, urging Bazargan to remain prime minister and saying he would "speak" to the clergy. Apparently, through a slipup, Khomeini was not aware in advance of the proposed meeting between Bazargan and Brzezinski.[2] Thus, this time he was inclined to accept the resignation of his prime minister. Even after he left that office, however, Bazargan retained his membership on the Revolutionary Council.

Cabinet ministers were unaffected except for Yazdi, sacked because he participated in the meeting with Brzezinski. Bani-Sadr replaced Yazdi at the foreign ministry. Since no new prime minister was appointed, the new foreign minister became spokesman by default, but he was not to remain on the job long. Within a month, Khomeini fired him, because the Ayatollah did not think his foreign minister should argue Iran's case before the United Nations. The country did not have a formal government leader for about two months, until Bani-Sadr was elected president on January 25.

The clerics on the Revolutionary Council were caught between their own desire to hold out for the terms first mentioned by the militants on November 5—the return of the Shah—and their temptation to use the crises to fully consolidate their authority within the country. The latter urge won. Matters were complicated by the fact that the group actually controlling the embassy and the hostages was oblivious to the potential international dangers of keeping diplomats captive. Through their comments to the ubiquitous press, they quickly established themselves as a separate bargaining force capable of taking an independent line from the radical clergy, something they continued to do. Though several factions with different perspectives were holding the Americans, they could agree on one thing—that they, not the government, keep custody of the hostages.

On November 16 the Fedayeen surfaced publicly for the first time since being driven underground in August. At least one group in the organization had been involved in the original planning and occupation of the compound, and now the entire Fedayeen adamantly supported the militants. Throughout the crisis it advocated that the captives stay under the control of the militants. It also supported initiatives to try the hostages in court in order to "reveal the sordid truth of America's crimes in Iran." The ultimate goal was to ruin any hope of a U.S.-Iran rapprochement in the future that might prevent the Fedayeen's eventual ascension to power.

Like most Iranians, in the first few days after the takeover the American government thought the matter would be resolved quickly. Unaware that Bazargan's moderate government was crumbling, on November 5 Secretary of State Cyrus Vance called upon the prime minister to fulfill Iran's responsibilities under international law and free the captives. Two special envoys, former Attorney General Ramsey Clark, who had met Khomeini in Paris the previous December, and William Miller, who had served as a foreign service officer in Iran in the early 1960s and now was on the staff of the Senate Select Committee on Intelligence, left for Tehran the evening of November 6. The following day Khomeini rejected this effort to resolve the impasse, largely because the Revolutionary Council could not make up its mind what to do. Clark and Miller were forced to land in Istanbul, where they remained until directed to return to Washington on November 15. While in Turkey waiting for the permission to enter Iran that never materialized, they met with low-level representatives of the Palestine Liberation Organization. Together, they discussed P.L.O. initiatives to free the hostages, but nothing came of it because by this time the Palestinians had very little influence on the Iranian internal debates then in progress about what to do.

Move followed countermove: As soon as the embassy was overrun, the Iran Working Group of the State Department, a desk manned by Middle Eastern specialists 24-hours-a-day, was reactivated. (It had been formed the first time during the February takeover and dissolved three weeks later.) On November 10 the Immigration and Naturalization Service was directed by President Carter to review all Iranian visas and deport individuals who had violated the legal terms of their stay in the United States. To do this would cause the Iranians substantial hardship, since U.S. officials already had estimated that approximately 20 percent of the more than 40,000 students studying in America had overstayed their visas or were working, making them subject to deportation. (It is illegal for any alien in the United States on a student visa to be employed while attending school.) On November 12 Carter halted oil trade with Iran, though this involved but five percent of U.S. imports and hardly inconvenienced either country. Two days later he froze Iranian money and gold on deposit in the United States and in branches of American banks overseas—between $7 and $8 billion. The President did this just hours before the Revolutionary Council ordered that all that country's funds be transferred out of American banks. Freezing these financial assets had the effect of blocking any direct trade between the two countries, as well as crippling Iran's ability to trade with other nations. Though not surprised by Carter's move, Revolutionary Council members were outraged that the American President had beaten them to the punch.

On November 13 the Revolutionary Council outlined its demands to gain the hostages' release: admit the Shah is a criminal and should be extradited, give back all the money the Shah stole from the Iranian people, and stop interfering in Iranian internal affairs. Before the United States could comment on these proposals or explore privately the possibility of room for maneuvering, the militants holding the embassy publicly denounced the Revolutionary Council's terms and insisted that the hostages be put on trial if the Shah did not return to Iran. Khomeini went along with the idea and on November 20 said the captives would have to be judged in court.

That same day a White House statement, echoed by State Department spokesman Hodding Carter, replied that the U.S. would have to consider "other remedies" if a peaceful solution to the difficulty could not be found. The State Department went on to suggest that the United States might have to resort to Article 51 of the United Nations charter, which recognizes "the inherent right of individual or collective self-defense if an armed attack occurs against a member of the United Nations, until the Security Council has taken measures to maintain international peace and security." The militants retorted that the hostages would be killed if the U.S. attacked Iran. On November 22 Khomeini endorsed their statement, saying "we cannot restrain the students, who are very emotional now, from blowing up the embassy."

The invaders released 13 black and female captives that same day, in time to spend Thanksgiving with their families in the United States. They announced it was a goodwill gesture, "to show Iran's sympathy with America's oppressed minorities." For all their talk, one black and two women still remained hostages. Both the former prisoners and the American officials who debriefed them declined to comment extensively about their ordeal, in deference to those still incarcerated.

The United States announced its support for U.N. Secretary-General Kurt Waldheim's call for a meeting of the Security Council on November 25. The possibility of action in the United Nations brought on the second government crisis in less than three weeks. Should Iran attend the session or shouldn't it? Foreign Minister Bani-Sadr wanted to go to New York, but after intense infighting he was outvoted by the radical clergy on the Revolutionary Council. Khomeini promptly removed him from his post and Sadeq Ghotbzadeh replaced him. Ghotbzadeh announced that he would not go to New York and that his country would not participate in any way in the U.N. debate. After three days of discussion, with Iranian input provided only by Mansur Farhang, its ranking delegate to the United Nations, on December 4 the Security Council passed Resolution 457. It called for the hostages to be set free and for the United States and Iran to settle their differences peacefully. The U.N. deliberately postponed any discussion of economic sanctions, something President Carter was pushing for, since it preferred to seek a diplomatic solution. The Khomeini government ignored Resolution 457. Its only public comment was that the United Nations "had followed the U.S. imperialist line."

The previous week, on November 29, the U.S. tried one more ploy. It filed suit with the International Court of Justice in The Hague, charging Iran with violations of basic international law and seeking an immediate hearing on a preliminary motion directing that country to release the hostages. To emphasize the importance the United States attached to the matter, Attorney General Benjamin Civiletti presented the case. Iran refused to participate in the proceedings. When the court ruled in favor of the motion on December 15 and ordered the prisoners released, the government in Tehran made no comment and the press carried no news of the verdict for three days. Even then it limited itself to calling the court "a tool of the West."

On December 4, almost six weeks after the successful operation to remove a stone from his bile duct, the Shah left New York's Cornell Medical Center Hospital. While the world waited to hear where Iran's former ruler would go next, he recuperated for two more weeks at Kelly Air Force Base in San Antonio. The whereabouts of the Shah's future permanent domicile quite unexpectedly had become an international hot potato. On November 30 Mexico had refused to renew his earlier visa, preventing him from returning to that country. The constant pressure to extradite him immediately coming from militants at the embassy and the religious fundamentalists meant that the Shah remained a serious political problem for the United States. It was in the best interest of the American government to assist him in finding a place to go as quickly as possible.

The U.S. approached several countries, including Switzerland, South Africa, and two or three Latin American nations, but none was eager to involve itself in the hornet's nest. Eventually, after ten days of intense negotiation, including two trips to Panama by Hamilton Jordan, special assistant to the President, an arrangement was worked out with the government of that Central American country. The Shah and his entourage flew to the island of Contadora on December 15. The militants holding the embassy immediately protested the former monarch's "escape" from the U.S., but the Revolutionary Council showed its tacit approval of what the Carter administration had done by remaining silent. Foreign Minister Ghotbzadeh claimed the Shah's departure from the United States was a "victory" for Iran. Once again, the Iranian inhabitants of the embassy and the members of the Revolutionary Council were at odds.

Beginning on December 10 the Carter administration had started to step up pressure verbally, alluding once more to the possibility of military action. It also announced a drastic cut in the number of persons that would be allowed to work in the embassy in Washington and the consulates in San Francisco, Houston, Chicago, and New York. The number of diplomats represented in the United States went from approximately 160 to 35, with five employees allowed at each consulate and 20 at the embassy. Although the Iranian mission at the United Nations was not affected, its personnel were restricted to within 25 miles of the U.N. building unless they had written permission from the State Department.

The Internal Struggle Intensifies

Meanwhile, within Iran the Islamic fundamentalists were pressing toward their goal—the ratification of a new constitution and the consolidation of their power. In the frenzied wake of the embassy seizure and over the protests of their secular allies in the revolutionary coalition, Shiite radicals ramrodded a strict Islamic document through the Constitutional Assembly. The Revolutionary Council scheduled a referendum for the people to vote their approval within a month. Because the final draft provided for the even greater ascendancy of religion in politics than had earlier, much-criticized versions, secular politicians such as Kurdish leader Abdul Qassemlou and Karim Sanjabi of the National Front were dismayed. So were moderate clerics like Ayatollahs Kazem Shariatmadari and Mohammad Reza Golpaygani.

In a few urban areas the fundamentalist clergy pressured their constituents to approve the constitution by forcing them to go to the polls and use non-secret ballots, but Qassemlou urged the Kurds to boycott the referendum and they did. Shariatmadari directed members of his Islamic Peoples' Republican Party to ignore the election and pro-Khomeini forces delivered a very modest vote throughout Azarbaijan province. Followers of the National Front and the National Democratic Front, who had refused to vote in the elections to form a constitutional assembly in August, also ignored the plebiscite.

Despite the light turnout on December 1 and 2, the year anniversary on the Islamic lunar calendar of the Tassua and Ashura marches which had been major milestones in the destruction of the Shah's regime, the results of the voting were overwhelmingly favorable. Over 97 percent of the approximately 70 percent of those eligible who voted endorsed the Islamic constitution. Among other things the referendum confirmed that Khomeini would be the all-powerful *faghih* or Religious Guardian. It gave him the power to dismiss the elected president and to name the Council of Guardians, six religious leaders and six lawyers who would supervise legislation to ensure it was "in harmony" with Islamic doctrine and law. The constitution provided for the prime minister and his cabinet to be nominated by the president and approved by the National Consultative Assembly (parliament) to be elected to replace the Constitutional Assembly. As in the 1906 constitution, Shiite Islam was the state religion, but other faiths whose doctrines were "of the book"—the Old and New Testaments and the Avestas—were to be tolerated. This included Jews, Christians, and Zoroastrians, but not members of the Bahai faith (less than one half of one percent of the population), considered to be an heretical offshoot of Islam. The Religious Guardian, like the Shah before him, would appoint the highest ranking military commanders and the head of the supreme court.

The principal difference between the new document and the old is the vastly increased importance of Islam in political affairs. The monarchy is eliminated and the Religious Guardian becomes the overriding authority, superior to the president, who is head of state. In contrast to the old constitution, specific functions are not attributed to major offices, forcing the Religious Guardian, the president, and the prime minister to struggle over what their areas of responsibility should be. Parliament is unicameral, as opposed to the previously bicameral Senate and Majles. The 1906 document provided a framework that could be used by either a strong monarch or a more democratically inclined leader. The constitution of 1980 enshrines absolutist leadership in the name of Islam. While still prime minister, Bazargan told Khomeini that the new arrangements would not outlast the Ayatollah. The Islamic constitution is not a neutral document, and it is closely tied to Khomeini's personal version of Shiite doctrine.

The tribal minorities were especially upset by the new state document, particularly the two million Sunni Moslems living in Khuzistan province. Faithful Moslems in the rural areas who never have been as fanatically religious as their more urban brethren—the five million Azarbaijanis, the four million Kurds, the one million Baluchis and Turkomans, and the smaller Lur, Bakhtiari, and Qashqai ethnic groups—were alarmed at the status being given a narrowly fundamentalist view of their faith.

Feelings of unrest increased, especially in Azarbaijan province, where Ayatollah Shariatmadari's supporters were clustered. On December 5 Shariatmadari loyalists took over Tabriz for two days, forcing the Pasdaran to abandon the center of the city. After a pitched battle, the reinforced Revolutionary Guards recaptured major installations on December 9. In Qom that same day, still under surveillance amounting to house arrest, Shariatmadari claimed that the agreements he had made with the revolutionary leaders were being broken and that he would not be responsible for what happened in Azarbaijan province. (He never specified what these "understandings" were, and neither side mentioned them again.) On December 11 he criticized the constitution at a mid-week mosque service, bluntly announcing that he had not voted for it. There were other outbreaks of violence in Khorramshahr, Hamadan, and Ahwaz the rest of the month. They subsided only as the campaign to elect a president heated up in early January and dissatisfied Iranians turned their attention toward that contest.

The Mixing of Domestic and International Politics

Beginning in December domestic political conflicts and the international wrangling over the hostages became hopelessly bound up with each other. "Intermestic" politics became the norm. After the constitutional referendum, statements about the American prisoners would be ever more erratic and contradictory. For example, on December 5 Bani-Sadr said Iran should release the hostages. The militants holding the embassy reiterated their opposing view, that the Shah should be returned to Iran or else the hostages should be put on trial as spies.

Meanwhile, throughout December the United States pushed for the United Nations to approve economic sanctions. Specifically, this would block Iran's ability to sell oil in exchange for badly needed machinery and raw materials to keep its industries running. The Soviets used parliamentary tactics to delay the discussion. From the beginning of the crisis they took positions on both sides of the issue. The U.S.S.R. rejected the taking of diplomatic hostages as contrary to international law, but quietly provided economic support and encouraged its COMECOM (Eastern European Bloc) trading partners to do likewise. The Soviet invasion of Afghanistan on December 26 abruptly halted the budding of any potential Russian-Iranian reconciliation. Iranians of all persuasions were universally opposed to this aggression against their neighbor to the east. There were many who feared Iran might be the next Soviet target.

After the U.S.S.R. threatened to veto sanctions in the Security Council, President Carter settled instead for a January visit to Tehran by U.N. Secretary-General Waldheim. Backroom debate between the Revolutionary Council and the militants intensified. As with the hostage issue itself, there was deadlock on how to handle the Waldheim visit. Because of the unresolved controversy, the secretary-general's reception when he arrived on January 1 was cool. When it became apparent that he would not have an audience with Ayatollah Khomeini, Waldheim cut his visit short, staying only four days. After his return, the Security Council took up the question of economic sanctions. The motion was defeated by the expected Soviet veto on January 14.

As the hostage crisis stretched out, more people began to get into the act. American Congressman George Hansen, a Republican from Idaho, flew to Tehran twice in an attempt to break the controversy. On his first visit, from November 22 to 26, he talked briefly with a majority of the hostages and several Iranian officials, including Foreign Minister Ghotbzadeh. Neither that trip nor his second, in April 1980, accomplished anything.

During the Christmas holidays, with Khomeini's approval three American clergymen arrived at the embassy to preside over church services for the hostages. The ministers talked briefly with 43 of the 50 captives plus the three men incarcerated at the foreign ministry. At first the Iranians said the seven men not seen did not want to participate in the services. Later the story changed; they were "unavailable." Since this group included those identified earlier as "spies," the evasiveness sparked fears that some of the captives had been harmed. This concern would not be fully assuaged for four more months, when the State Department was finally able to account for all the hostages in late April.

The embassy invaders used the media to good effect, focusing worldwide attention on the plight of the hostages through extensive television interviews. Though they were getting excellent access to U.S. audiences, the militants seriously misjudged American reaction to their cause. It was overwhelmingly negative. On January 14 the Revolutionary Council decided it had had enough, that the pressure brought to bear by the media was complicating its job. It ordered all U.S. journalists out of the country within three days, including foreigners who worked for American publications and television networks. About 90 individuals departed, 60 of them U.S. citizens. But stateside on-the-spot coverage did not stop, since the networks and major newspapers could still buy material from European news agencies such as Reuters or from independent television companies based in Britain or France.

On both sides of the dilemma, feelings of frustration had been building up for some time. The militants and the members of the Revolutionary Council prodded the media to focus on the Shah's crimes, not on the hostages. Western newsmen were annoyed by sporadic censorship and government exhortations to speak well of the Islamic Republic. Within two months some of the expelled journalists were allowed to return by "special permission." The ultimatum was not completely rescinded until November 1980, when the Revolutionary Council sought sympathetic Western coverage of the Iraqi invasion. Nevertheless, the government was very restrictive when issuing visas to journalists. It wanted American newsmen to write about the war, but was not eager to have veteran Middle East correspondents like William Branigan of *The Washington Post* or Eric Page of *The New York Times* on the scene to report the chaos spreading throughout Iran.

Concurrently, the Revolutionary Council proceeded with its plans to establish a govrnment. The presidential election was scheduled for January 25. When 109 candidates applied for the job, Khomeini asked Hojatollah Asghar Moussavi Khoeini (no relation to Mohammad Moussavi Khoeini) to regulate the procedure and limit the number of hopefuls allowed to present their programs on television. Unhappiness with the constitution was clearly reflected in the campaign.

Opponents of the Islamic fundamentalists received an unexpected boost when the candidate of the powerful Islamic Republican Party, Jalaladin Farsi, was disqualified ten days prior to the balloting because he did not meet the proviso that the parents of any aspirant be "Iranian by origin." (Farsi's father held Afghani citizenship.) Throughout, the operation was marred by confusion, charges, and countercharges. The contest was won by Abol Hassan Bani-Sadr. His victory came as a surprise, but the margin was truly shocking. He received 76 percent of the vote to 15 percent for his nearest rival, Admiral Ahmad Madani, the governor of Khuzistan province from February to August 1979. In addition to receiving a large amount of Islamic support, Bani-Sadr captured the overwhelming majority of votes cast by those Iranians dissatisfied with the constitution and fearful of "government by mullah."

Bani-Sadr's win cleared the way for another effort to negotiate freedom for the hostages. In a speech on February 2, the new president minimized the importance of the captives. He referred to the militants as "children," and said the Shah need not be returned to Iran in order for the crisis to be resolved. Those occupying the embassy immediately denied Bani-Sadr's statement most vehemently, but on February 12 they conceded that they would follow Khomeini's wishes if he directed that the Americans be released. The Ayatollah remained silent for the moment, apparently unprepared for the militants' comments. Throughout February and March Bani-Sadr's influence grew because he controlled access to Khomeini. This was reflected in a more forthcoming attitude in Iran over a multitude of details concerning the hostage negotiations. Specifically, there were ongoing discussions concerning a package arrangement involving the establishment of a United Nations commission to investigate the "crimes" of the Shah and U.S. involvement in Iran in exchange for the freedom of the 53 captives. Although President Carter had told Waldheim earlier that the United States would reject such a proposal, the landslide election of a president who had stated the need to settle the hostage question quickly led to a change in American policy in favor of the intricate maneuver.

In his State of the Union message on January 22, Carter said America would cooperate with Iran once the Americans were released. After

Bani-Sadr's election three days later, a series of shadowy private conversations began between U.S. officials and a Parisian lawyer. The firm
of Bourget, Cheron, and Vallette had been working with the revolutionary government for several months. One of the partners, Christian
Bourget, and a close friend of his, Hector Villalon, a politically active
Argentine businessman, approached Washington offering to mediate the
controversy. Bourget and Villalon were in close contact with President
Bani-Sadr, and would serve as significant intermediaries starting in February. They met several times with presidential assistant Hamilton Jordan, and together they tried to develop a formula that Bani-Sadr could
use to persuade the fundamentalist clerics to let the Americans go. In
early April Khomeini rejected yet another of their initiatives to free the
hostages. The pair continued to try to arrange a deal, but their lack of
influence with the real power—the Moslem fundamentalists—caused
U.S. attempts to resolve the impasse to shift elsewhere.

The "Paris connection" was supplanted over the course of the summer by the government of Algeria. Abdelkarim Gharaib, the Algerian
ambassador to Tehran, had gradually gained the confidence of Beheshti
and other clerical figures. Eventually they were willing to let him inter-
cede for the Americans. Algerian diplomats, with Gharaib in the forefront, would emerge as the primary go-betweens, especially after
November 1980. To them belongs much of the credit for working out
the arrangements that would finally lead to the release of the hostages.

On January 28 a difficult, hidden problem with respect to any
negotiated settlement was removed, and American morale received a
sharp boost besides. Six potential hostages were whisked out of Iran in
secret. They were five consular officials, three men and two women,
who escaped during the embassy takeover by walking out the back
door of the small building they were in, and the agricultural attaché,
whose office was across the street from the compound in the same
building as the Swedish embassy. These Americans hid out for nearly
three months, protected by Canadian diplomats. Never listed as hostages, they used specially prepared Canadian passports and departed on
January 28 as diplomats or their spouses on a regularly scheduled flight
to Europe. The embassy had already announced it was closing its doors
for the time being and all the legitimate envoys also left.

The reason given the Ministry of Foreign Affairs for the mass evacuation was that the continued unrest in Iran had slowed business between
the two countries to a trickle. Ambassador Kenneth Taylor chose his
moment well—the country was in the midst of the presidential election
and attention was focused elsewhere. "The Canadian Caper" not only
enhanced relations between the U.S. and its neighbor to the north,

causing a nationwide outpouring of appreciation, but it also erased the sticky dilemma of what to say about the missing six in any talks with the revolutionaries. There was no reaction to the incident in the Iranian press, and the only public comment came several days later when the militants holding the embassy criticized the government for allowing the escape to occur. Foreign Minister Ghotbzadeh appeared on television to lambaste the Canadian government for violating international law. Nobody in Canada and few people in any other nation were repentant.

After several weeks of delicate discussions, on February 18 the United Nations announced the establishment of an international commission to explore and hopefully to resolve the hostage problem. The members were Muhammad Bedjaoudi, an Algerian delegate to the United Nations; Andres Aguilar, a former Venezuelan ambassador to the U.N.; Louis Pettiti, a French lawyer; Adib Davood, a foreign affairs advisor to the president of Syria; and Hector Wilfred Jayewardene, a lawyer from Sri Lanka. They were expected to spend about two weeks in Iran gathering information, after which a report would be submitted to the United Nations and the hostages would be released.

Though it appeared there had been agreement in principle between the United States, the United Nations, and Iran on the proposed scenario, it was never clear that the conception of each entity participating concerning the purpose of the visit matched that of the others. On February 20 the White House stated that the establishment of the commission would give the United States an opportunity to air its grievances concerning the unprecedented violation of its diplomatic rights. Waldheim described the group as a fact-finding body. Bani-Sadr referred to it in his acceptance telegram as a court of inquiry. The religious hard-liners had not even agreed to that definition, preferring one which focused solely on an investigation of alleged U.S. "crimes" as they related to American support of the Shah.

From the beginning Khomeini and Beheshti (who still led the religious contingent on the Revolutionary Council, though he had automatically been replaced by Bani-Sadr as chairman when the latter was elected president) explicitly disavowed a link between the commission and freedom for the captives. The five men arrived in Tehran on February 23. That same day, Khomeini issued a statement saying the Consultative Assembly (to be elected on May) would determine conditions for the release of the Americans. Beheshti reiterated the point on February 27, adding "it will be ten weeks or more before the Majles can even address the hostage question."

One important element of this "package deal" was a commitment from Iran to allow the commission members to see the captives. This simple request precipitated yet another internal crisis. On March 6 the militants agreed to turn the hostages over to the Revolutionary Council for a short time so that they could meet with the U.N. visitors. However, two days later, when the transfer was to occur, the captors refused to go through with it. A public argument by press statement ensued between Foreign Minister Ghotbzadeh and the jailers, each accusing the other of lying about the terms under which the commission would meet with the prisoners.

On March 10 Khomeini said the only thing the commission could do was question the captives about "U.S. crimes in Iran." In effect, he was siding publicly with those holding the embassy. Speaking on television, the young radicals praised their "support from the true Islamic clergy and the Ayatollah." Then they reversed themselves, denying that they had ever said they would surrender the hostages to the government. It was a devastating defeat for Bani-Sadr and Ghotbzadeh, for once the Americans were under the control of those loyal to the Revolutionary Council the militants could have been squeezed out of negotiations and the more moderate voices in the government would have controlled the discussion. This incident also marked the first time since Bani-Sadr's election as president that Khomeini had not backed him in an internal political struggle. It was to mark the beginning of Bani-Sadr's decline from preeminence.

The events from March 6 to 11 illustrated all too graphically the deadlocked dynamics of the hostage crisis from the Iranian perspective. When the militant captors felt Khomeini's support was wavering, they had begun to fear for their safety. They resisted the request of the Revolutionary Council to turn over the hostages. Their wariness received unexpected reinforcement from Khomeini when he sided with them by insisting that parliament have the final say on the fate of the captives. After that the militants felt certain they could continue to defy the government as long as Khomeini supported them. By refusing to encourage the Revolutionary Council's initiative, Khomeini was accommodating the country's most unyielding faction and thereby increasing its power.

The Shah again became a factor in any negotiations toward the end of March, when he accepted President Anwar Sadat's long-standing invitation to establish himself in Egypt. The former monarch's hasty departure from the island of Contadora had a whiff of intrigue about it. In December, shortly after he had arrived in Panama, the Revolutionary Council requested their former leader be extradited. Aristides Royo, the president of Panama, indicated that the Islamic Republic would have to file formal papers, meanwhile assuring the Shah that he could not be handed over to the revolutionaries since Panamanian law prohibits extradition for crimes carrying the death penalty. By the time Iran was prepared to present its case in mid-March, the exiled ruler had become very uneasy about his future prospects in Panama. Simultaneously, he had been advised that he needed another operation, this time to remove a cancerous spleen. Complications developed when the authorities in Panama insisted that a local surgeon would perform the operation. The Shah wanted his medical team to be headed by Dr. Michael DeBakey of Houston. A hurried trip to Contadora by White House aide Hamilton Jordan for the express purpose of convincing the former monarch he should remain where he was only increased royal suspicions that the Carter administration was using him as a pawn to induce the return of the hostages by dangling the hope of extradition. Thus when Iran announced it would file the papers on March 24, the Shah found it expedient to leave Panama on March 23. He said that he was accepting Sadat's offer because he desired "to be among friends" in a Moslem setting closer to Iran and because he wanted "to avoid medical problems."

Almost Free . . . But Not Quite

Another intractable dispute between the militants and Revolutionary Council members that involved the hostages ended on April 1. Amidst stories in the American press about economic sanctions soon to be enacted against Iran, the government in Tehran made public the text of a letter Ayatollah Khomeini allegedly had recently received from President Carter. It admitted "past mistakes" in U.S. policy and agreed to the establishment of a joint American-Iranian commission to review relations between the two countries once the hostages were transferred to government control. White House spokesman Jody Powell denied such a letter had been sent. A day later he indicated " . . . messages may or may not have been transmitted. . . . This is a period of some ferment." Actually there were three letters, two to President Bani-Sadr and one to Khomeini. The administration was extremely upset by the cavalier treatment given what was supposed to have been a serious, confidential effort to end the impasse. Chargé d'affaires Bruce Laingen, languishing in the foreign ministry, always had been more or less in steady communication with both Washington and some officials in the Iranian government. He had heard optimistic comments from foreign ministry personnel who visited the three captives periodically. In fact, Bani-Sadr's government was so sure a breakthrough was imminent that enough mattresses for all the hostages were deposited at the Foreign Ministry. Even as events were still evolving, however, Laingen concluded that the Islamic fundamentalists were intent on blocking any potential deal.

The possibility of a release fizzled out on April 1. About 3:00 A.M. Washington time Bani-Sadr released an announcement:

> If America issues an official statement that until such time as the Majles is formed and the proper decision is taken, America will refrain from resorting to any propaganda or making any claim or saying anything or making any provocation, then the Revolutionary Council agrees to take the hostages under its care and control.[3]

About 6:00 A.M., speaking for President Carter, Press Secretary Powell replied:

> The announcement by President Bani-Sadr that the hostages will be transferred to the care and protection of the Iranian government is a positive step. Accordingly, we will defer imposing further sanctions at this time. The Iranian government has said that the hostage issue will be resolved when the new parliament convenes. We will continue to work for the earliest possible release of all the hostages.

By 4:00 P.M. Washington time Bani-Sadr had announced that the Carter statement transmitted by Powell "failed to meet Tehran's demands for transfer of the American hostages to Iranian government control." A message from Khomeini issued about the same time advised his countrymen to "ignore the U.S. words," and assured them "the hostages will not be transferred to government control, but parliament will make the decision on the conditions for their release."

The Ayatollah's comment, repeated on April 7 in a major bulletin so that it could be circulated the next day in the mosques during Friday prayers, put an end to Bani-Sadr's initiative to free the hostages, stripping him of power on this important issue and weakening him on all others. He had failed to get not only Khomeini's approval for his proposal, but even his neutrality.[4] Thus there was no way the government could either crush or outmaneuver the militants. Islamic Republican Party leaders rejoiced and urged the fanatics in the embassy to stand firm.

In the final vote of the Revolutionary Council in the last few days of

March about who would take control of the captives, only 5 of the 18 members declared themselves against the proposal that the government take charge.[5] All were fundamentalist clerics loyal to Beheshti. Outvoted, they insisted the situation be discussed with the Religious Guardian in Qom. The other members of the Revolutionary Council had no choice but to acquiesce. Khomeini, whose sentiments had always been with the militants, claimed the "pure" revolutionaries were not ready to give up the Americans and sided with the hard-liners. After coming so close to a settlement, both the Iranian moderates and the U.S. administration felt frazzled and let down.

Chapter Twelve

★

Deadlock and Frustration

April 1980–January 1981

With both the United Nations' mediation effort and Bani-Sadr's attempt to end the crisis in ruins, the U.S. imposed an economic blockade that was just as unsuccessful a ploy as the others in inducing the militants to release the hostages. As a last resort, the President attempted to free the captives by military means. The daring helicopter raid started on April 24 and ended in failure the next day. It was called off because of equipment malfunction less than 300 miles from Tehran, but eight commandos died during the withdrawal. Barbara Timms, mother of hostage marine Sergeant Kevin Hermening, had flown to Tehran with great hoopla—and against President Carter's ban on American travel to Iran—to plead for her son just before the military strike. Had it succeeded, Hermening would have wound up free in the United States while his mother extricated herself from Tehran.

Within days of the ineffectual assault, the United States returned to the diplomatic arena and by mid-May had successfully prevailed upon its European allies and Japan to join America's economic boycott. Iran finished electing its legislative assembly (Majles) about the same time. Fierce squabbling between President Bani-Sadr and the Islamic fundamentalists dominating the new parliament surfaced once again, this time over who would be appointed prime minister. Locked in a domestic struggle, the assembly put the hostage issue aside until a compromise candidate, a former primary teacher named Mohammad Rajai, was finally chosen prime minister in August.

Before the cabinet Rajai appointed was even in operation, Iraq, fearful of the politically dangerous spread of Shiite fundamentalism, invaded the southern province of Khuzistan. It was on September 22, ten-and-a-half months after the hostages had been seized. The Baghdad regime sought to capture Khorramshahr and Abadan—the first the principal port and the second the home of the world's largest oil refinery—and to regain land ceded to Iran under the 1975 Algiers Accords. In the wake of the Iraqi attack, for the first time the religious militants were ready to make an earnest effort to settle the hostage affair, but only because Iran needed U.S. spare parts for military equipment, especially aircraft. Hoping to press its case and therefore profit from the strains on Carter caused by the American presidential elections, the Consultative Assembly laid down formal conditions for the release of the hostages just two days before the balloting on November 4—which also happened to be the first anniversary of the Americans' incarceration. But there was to be no quick solution, just an endless exchange of diplomatic notes between the two nations, using Algeria as an intermediary. In a moment of comic relief on October 31, Iran complained of the capture and continued detention of its oil minister when he was visiting the war front, calling it a violation of international law. The reply from Baghdad said, "it seems a strange complaint for a country holding 52 diplomats hostage."

Finally, in the waning days of the Carter administration, a complicated arrangement was worked out to exchange the hostages for the Iranian assets in the U.S. and Europe frozen by President Carter more than a year before. Disdainful of the President to the last, the militants held up the departure of the Algerian aircraft that would whisk away the 52 Americans until a half hour after the office of the American presidency had been transferred from Jimmy Carter to Ronald Reagan.

The release of the hostages did not end internal strife. With oil production slowed to a trickle, trade disrupted, and the effects of the harsh blasts of winter weather not offset by an adequate supply of heating oil, the country's infrastructure was slowly coming apart. The battle with Iraq remained stalemated; the major offensive attempted January 4 demonstrated quite vividly how much Iran's military position had deteriorated. Though the Khomeini regime received patriotic support for the war, even from its internal rivals, this was not enough to reverse the disintegration of the country's political and economic structure or to bring about national unity on any issue. The country wallowed in dissension, foreshadowing chaos.

Sanctions and the April Raid

The continued national public humiliation connected with the vain endeavors to obtain the release of the hostages forced President Carter to order top-secret moves that would retrieve the captives by military means. Because of his strong natural bias toward the use of persuasion rather than armed force, he also continued to wage the battle for the return of the Americans by peaceful means. Two weeks prior to the furtive mission Carter got tougher with Iran. The U.S. government broke diplomatic relations completely, invalidated all Iranian visas for future travel to the United States, implemented an economic embargo, and urged all American companies and private citizens with claims to file them against the assets frozen in November. The interdiction of trade on everything except food and medical supplies was the same plan presented by the United States in the United Nations in January and vetoed by the Soviet Union. In practice, the ban made little difference since trade between the two countries had all but dried up when the assets were frozen. Even so, the United States urged other nations, particularly its Western allies and Japan, to follow suit.

On April 21 foreign ministers of the ten countries in the European Economic Community agreed to reduce their diplomatic representation in Tehran and to consider implementing an economic boycott similar to that of the U.S. The Islamic fundamentalists, both the militants at the embassy and the radical clerics, reacted positively to the prohibition on imported goods, saying it would break Iran's dependence on the West. Just as they had done when the Americans were first seized, the militants threatened to kill their prisoners if there was any attempt to free them by force. This came in reaction to a White House press statement on April 7 suggesting that perhaps the time was drawing near when some kind of military response would have to be considered. In a lull in the battle of words, the day before—Easter Sunday—three American clergymen were allowed to perform religious services for the hostages, drawing on the precedent of the Christmas visits three-and-a-half months earlier.

On April 22, members of four hostage families left on a one-week trip to Europe, visiting Britain, France, Germany, Italy, and Luxembourg. Wives Louisa Kennedy and Barbara Rosen, and mothers Jeanne Queen and Pearl Golacinski split up their itineraries, encouraging national leaders they met with in each country to enforce sanctions. They also talked with the foreign ministers attending the meeting of the European Economic Community April 23 through 26 in Luxembourg. Their purpose was to rally the ministers to compel their respective governments to increase the international pressure on Iran through an economic boycott. All four women were still abroad when the failed attempt to retrieve the hostages took place. Mrs. Kennedy, then in London, echoed the thoughts of the entire group when she described herself as "flabbergasted" upon hearing about the effort. Like the majority of Americans everywhere, she regretted only that it had not succeeded.

The assault occurred on April 24 and 25.[1] The mission involved 90 special forces commandos chosen from all four services, eight navy helicopters, and six air force C-130 combination transport-tanker planes. It was cancelled in the first stage of execution after penetrating 670 miles inside Iran to within 300 miles west southwest of Tehran. Equipment failure forced the President to abort the effort. At least six helicopters were needed in order to carry out the second phase of the rescue; one was forced to turn back early, one had to make an emergency landing in the desert and could not go on, and a third reached the original landing site, but could not take off without repairs for which there were no available extra parts because they were in the first helicopter to founder. That left only five helicopters fully operational. While maneuvering to withdraw from the staging area, an abandoned airfield near Tabas, eight men were killed when one of the helicopters lifting off crashed into a C-130 tanker still on the ground. The retreat became a hasty one. All remaining personnel loaded aboard one C-130 and departed, leaving eight dead commandos, four other sabotaged helicopters and a pillar of fire behind them.

In a television speech the next day Secretary of Defense Harold Brown explained in general terms what had happened, but he would offer no explanation how the mission would have continued if it had been successful. He also emphasized the fact that one aborted mission did not mean that the United States had permanently given up the possibility of using force if necessary to resolve the matter. Two days later Secretary of State Vance resigned, giving as the reason his long-standing opinion that force should never have been used to settle the problem. Senator Edmund Muskie of Maine was quickly named to replace him.

The Iranians refused to believe the American military had penetrated their borders. They first learned of it when a correspondent with the British Broadcasting Corporation telephoned Foreign Minister Ghotbzadeh in the early hours of April 25 to say that President Carter had announced through the media at 1:15 A.M. Washington time that an assault to get the hostages back had failed. By mid-morning Iranian government officials had visited the site and seen the wreckage. There was exultation in Tehran, mixed with relief. Khomeini claimed "God kept Iran from harm." Ghotbzadeh and Bani-Sadr were more subdued in their comments. The foreign minister, for example, complained only that "the raid showed no consideration for the hostages or the Iranian people."

Bani-Sadr's government pledged to return the bodies of the eight servicemen, and eventually it did so. First, however, television audiences worldwide were treated to the macabre spectacle of the remains in plastic bags, on display in the courtyard of the embassy. Ayatollah ("Judge Blood") Khalkhali, who had directed the summary trials immediately after the revolutionary takeover, presided over the grisly viewing, picking up parts of the bodies to give journalists a better look and poking other bags with a long stick.

Three days after the unsuccessful incursion the embassy militants announced plans to move some of the hostages to other locations. Within ten days, over half of the captives were no longer living on the compound, though the three diplomats at the Foreign Ministry would remain there. The militants constantly announced lists of towns where the hostages were being detained—a total of 17—but after the attempted raid the revolutionary government always treated the exact locations and the number of captives in each place as a state secret. Most, but not all, of the hostages were moved out of the embassy. One enterprising newsman tracked down the house in Isfahan where a few prisoners were kept, and a British pilot who suddenly found himself charged with carrying several blindfolded and bound hostages on a scheduled Iran Air flight to Mashad refused to take off until the masks were removed. Though the militants lacked the manpower to keep 50 prisoners on the move and still maintain their power base at the embassy, they knew a "traveling road show" of several hostages moving from place to place would be enough to stymie any future attempts to rescue all the hostages at once.

With Khomeini's blessing the Revolutionary Guards began a witch hunt for Iranians who might have collaborated with the U.S. government on the ill-fated rescue attempt. Several individuals were jailed. The accused were never put on public trial except for one U.S. citizen, Cynthia Dwyer. A 49-year-old free-lance journalist from Buffalo, New York, she had arrived in the country about two weeks before the raid. She intended to paint a sympathetic picture of the revolution for U.S. audiences. One of the few Americans in the country after the assault, she was accused of "spying," specifically of being involved in the rescue attempt. Dwyer was summarily hauled off to jail, but no formal charges were filed until her "trial" began in February 1981, two and a half weeks after the hostages were released.

The captives had become pawns not only in the international scene but also in the conflicts between the various members of the militant coalition. On several occasions one faction or another would take a few hostages out of the embassy compound and keep them at its headquarters as "insurance" that the unit would not be expelled from the militant coalition or otherwise denied its right to participate in guarding the compound and the Americans. In early November, when parliament announced its terms for their release and the end of the ordeal appeared (mistakenly) to be in sight, all the prisoners were brought back to Tehran.

Post-Raid International Maneuvering

With the rescue fiasco behind it, the United States began anew to apply diplomatic pressure. Initial annoyance in the European Economic Community and Japan at not having been consulted in advance about the assault gave way to privately expressed regrets that the attempt had not succeeded. The need for an embargo was now very apparent. On May 18 the European Economic Community approved limited economic sanctions, including a clause cancelling all contracts signed after November 4, 1979. In the only exception, the British Parliament reneged a day later and made the ban applicable to future contracts only. British-sponsored construction projects amounting to between $3 and $5 million were allowed to continue.

Though somewhat less aggressively implemented than the United States had hoped it would be, on the whole the European response was very supportive. From November 1979 until the Iran-Iraq conflict terminated all oil shipments to Western countries 10 months later, these nations greatly reduced their dependence on Iranian petroleum, eventually importing only about 16 percent of the pre-crisis amount. For the first two months after the invasion of the embassy Japan bought substantially more oil from Iran than it had in the past, preparing for the worst. Then, under U.S. pressure, it refused to pay a price increase of $4 per barrel announced by Iran in April. A few weeks later, in May, Japan stated it would coordinate sanctions policy with the European Economic Community and buy no more oil from Iran. Eastern European countries, plus India, took up some of the slack in trade caused by the boycott, but none of these nations could supply the spare parts so critical for the rebuilding of the oil industry or the military.

To emphasize yet again its displeasure with the United States, the Iranian government staged an international "conference" in Tehran, June 2–6, to discuss America's alleged "crimes." Former Attorney

General Ramsey Clark led a renegade delegation of ten Americans in defiance of the presidential ban on travel to Iran. The U.S. press excoriated Clark for lending even a seedy air of respectibility to a meeting with no official delegates (though the P.L.O. and other radical organizations sent observers.) Upon his return to the United States the Justice Department announced it was considering prosecuting Clark. Although the case was dropped in January, three weeks before President Carter left office, to the vast majority of Americans the former attorney general remained a symbol of appeasement and misguided efforts to sympathize with the Iranian point of view. In spite of his good intentions, the Fedayeen spoke for many Iranians when they labeled Clark a "C.I.A. agent."

Although many feared that the raid and sanctions would thrust Iran into the hands of the Soviets, Khomeini and those around him remained cool to Russian overtures to increase trade or to extend military assistance. On July 2 the U.S.S.R. was told to close its consulates in Rasht and Isfahan and reduce its staff at the embassy to nine, the number of people in the Iranian embassy in Moscow. Nevertheless, the Russians have continued their attempts to deepen the rift between Iran and the United States in order to position themselves better should the chaos continue and accelerate. The Soviets see Iran as having taken merely the first step on the road toward a full Marxist revolution. While supporting Khomeini's efforts to destroy the old social and economic structure of "capitalist" Iran, they have provided covert aid to "progressive" Fedayeen and Tudeh organizations who share their Marxist outlook and who would be sensitive to their wishes and responsive to their concerns. In particular, they have sought resumed deliveries of natural gas. If the present governing structure disintegrates completely the Kremlin has stated that it would counter any American use of force. The Soviets want to be the "protectors" of the revolution, thus allowing the fundamentalist clergy to continue focusing on Western sins.

Internal Bickering Continues

After the abortive rescue attempt, Beheshti and his cohorts reiterated their demands that the hostages be put on trial. As campaign strategy for the second round of parliamentary elections on May 9 and 10, it was very successful. The Islamic Republican Party captured 130 of the 210 seats, giving it a solid working majority. Approximately 60 places went unfilled because both the elections in March and the subsequent runoffs in May were marred by irregularities and the preemptory disqualification of candidates. For example, using documentation found in the American embassy, the Islamic Republican Party declared Admiral Madani, a Bani-Sadr sympathizer, an "illegal participant" because he had allegedly "worked with the C.I.A." They reached this conclusion after the militants holding the compound supplied party leaders with documents showing the admiral had talked with an American official prior to the revolution.

In another instance, after winning overwhelmingly in his district, Qashqai tribal chief Khosrow Qashqai was barred from taking his seat. His constituents were outraged, but could do little about it. These tactics were perfectly understandable in terms of the goal of the Islamic Republican Party to gain full power and control. In the process, however, the extremists were alienating moderate religious figures who had supported some of the candidates attacked. Secular politicians also saw themselves being shunted aside.

Prior to the May elections, campaigning reached such a fever pitch that supporters of the Fedayeen and the Tudeh Party battled Islamic mobs in the streets. Throughout the summer this conflict between religious and leftist factions intensified. Simmering unrest in the cities was fueled by vague rumors of "subversion" instigated by exile groups. Persian outcasts sought to wean the discontented away from Khomeini's influence. They were only modestly successful.

In late July, 60 army and air force officers were arrested for allegedly plotting to overthrow the Khomeini government. About 30 were executed after summary trials in revolutionary courts. Religious minorities, traditionally tolerated, also occasionally fell victim to the chaos. Though Khomeini called for goodwill toward all faiths, there have been exceptions. Individuals have been executed for specific "crimes" or involvement with the Shah's regime, but suspicions linger that they were killed at least in part because they were not Moslem. Many prominent non-Islamic Iranians died in the heat of revolutionary fervor immediately following the takeover, and religious prejudice against individuals and groups has continued to smolder. On December 16, 1980, Simon Farzami, the Jewish former editor of Tehran's French-language newspaper, was executed after being charged with "passing information to the U.S. embassy."

One blemish on the general record of live-and-let-live has been the intermittent but systematic campaign against the Bahais. During 1977 and 1978 they were attacked in several cities, notably Shiraz, Gorgon, and Tabriz. Their homes were burned and their property and assets confiscated. In the final weeks of the Shah's rule, Bahais were eased out of government to appease the Islamic opposition. The most prominent victim was the Shah's personal physician, General Mohammad Ayadi, fired from his court job in September 1978. Untrue rumors also spread that the father of former Prime Minister Hoveyda had been of that faith, probably because he had been friendly with many prominent Bahais. Seven months after the revolution, on September 8, the Shrine in Shiraz commemorating the birthplace of The Bab, who founded the Bahai sect in 1862, was destroyed. Revolutionary Guards assigned to protect the temple were unable to do so because of the massive anti-Bahai crowd. Although Bani-Sadr's government has tried to guarantee their physical safety, individuals continue to be persecuted, most obviously by being pressured to leave their jobs.

The other significant exception to the general pattern of tolerance has been a campaign waged by a small group of rabid Moslems from Isfahan against Iranian and foreign members of the Anglican communion. Arastu Sayahar, the Episcopal priest in Shiraz, was brutally murdered in his home within a week after the revolutionary takeover. The attempted assassination in his bed of Bishop Hassan Deqani-Tafti on October 26, 1979, narrowly misfired. He and his wife, who was wounded in the abortive fracas, fled to Cyprus. Their Oxford-educated 24-year-old son stayed behind to continue working as a driver and interpreter for Western journalists and was gunned down in his car in Tehran on May 6, 1980. Jean Waddell, an elderly British woman who had served as church secretary for many years, was badly wounded at her home about the same time. She and two missionary doctors, John and Audrey Coleman, plus a British businessman, remained imprisoned in Isfahan. Four months earlier, a Mujahidin group had charged the Anglicans with "taking money from foreign intelligence groups," and a warrant had been sworn out for the arrest of the one remaining English priest and his wife, who promptly went into hiding and eventually escaped to England. The six church-run schools and hospitals were confiscated by the Islamic authorities in the summer and fall of 1980.

All the unrest and confusion delayed the opening of the new parliament, the Consultative Assembly, which finally convened on May 28. The elder statesman of the Liberation Movement, Yadollah Sahabi, was chosen acting speaker. On July 20, after two months of haggling, Islamic Republican Party member Hojatollah Hashemi Rafsanjani was elected speaker, winning 146 of the 196 votes cast. During June and July the parliament continually postponed discussing the hostage problem, concentrating on its own internal difficulties. Khomeini was not pleased by the constant bickering. On June 10, in a speech in Qom, he warned against factional infighting. Two weeks later he sharply criticized Bani-Sadr's administration and for the first time made wrathful comments about the "indecision" within the Revolutionary Council. He even threatened to call upon the people to overthrow the regime if it could not function more competently. Within two days Bani-Sadr counterattacked, calling upon the Ayatollah "to give me the tools to govern effectively," echoing the pleas of former Prime Minister Bazargan. By mid-July Khomeini was talking of the failures of the revolution and publicly despairing of fulfilling his dream of a government based on Moslem principles. The Islamic Republic seemed no closer to political stability than it had at the outset, 16 months earlier.

In the midst of the internal squabbling, there was one interesting development in the hostage situation. On July 11 Richard Queen, a consular officer on his first assignment abroad, was released by the revolutionary government and flown to Europe. The numbness in Queen's left hand that had developed within two months after he became a prisoner grew progressively worse, affecting his left side from his eye to his toes. By May his right hand was also without feeling; by June he was deaf in his right ear. He started losing his balance and had to lie flat on his back all day because of nausea and vomiting. Queen was moved to a hospital, and on July 8, the physicians there told the militants that they feared he was suffering from a brain tumor. The revolutionary government moved quickly to hand him over to U.S. officials in Germany. Within a few days, doctors who treated him at the U.S. Air Force hospital at Wiesbaden had determined he was suffering from multiple sclerosis. Although he could never be fully cured, with proper care—and the removal of the stress of captivity—the disease was quickly forced into remission. Two months later, following the Labor Day holiday, Queen returned to work at the State Department. The only physical aftereffects of his incarceration were numbness in his left hand and a slight case of vertigo.

It was obvious by the way Richard Queen was swiftly whisked away that the militants did not want any of the hostages to die while they were in custody. Some Americans had false hopes that after seven months the Iranians were ready to resolve the crisis, but political deadlock continued to block a settlement. Bani-Sadr and the radical clerics representing the Islamic Republican Party still were at odds over who should be prime minister. Late in July the president proposed Mostafa Mir-Salim, the deputy minister of the interior and chief of the national police. Mir-Salim was a member of the Islamic Republican Party but was not close to the fundamentalist clergy. Bani-Sadr's attempt to split the party failed; parliament refused to approve Mir-Salim because he was the president's nominee. Instead, the assembly tried to induce Bani-Sadr to appoint its choice, Jalaladin Farsi, the presidential candidate who had been disqualified just days before the election. For the same reason that parliament had been obstinate, Bani-Sadr refused to comply. Recriminations flew. Khomeini would not allow himself to be drawn into the controversy, but he obviously favored Beheshti and his allies when he called for a new cabinet that was "100 percent revolutionary," rejecting "the rotten brains . . . gentlemen whose minds have been trained in Europe." This was a direct slap at Bani-Sadr and the Western-educated men around him. The president also came under fire from the ideologist and parliamentary leader in the Islamic Republican Party, Hassan Ayat. In the Majles on July 25 he reminded Bani-Sadr that Article 110 of the Islamic constitution made it legally possible for the Religious Guardian to remove him as president.

In the midst of this domestic dissension the Shah died in Egypt on July 27, the spreading cancer finally overwhelming him. His passing was officially applauded in Tehran and scarcely interrupted the political quarreling. Both government and militant spokesmen stated unequivocally that the former monarch's death changed nothing concerning the hostages. In fact, Islamic Republican Party leaders continued to call for trials. Beheshti himself asked parliament to arrange a tribunal and Speaker Rafsanjani, acknowledging the justice of bringing the prisoners to court, said it would be some time before parliament could take up the matter of the prisoners' release. By now the fate of the Americans was firmly tied to the ebb and flow of the struggle between the Islamic Republican Party and President Bani-Sadr. The goal of Beheshti and his cohorts was to reduce the president to a figurehead while vesting real power in the new prime minister of their choice.

Bani-Sadr understood this and rejected all the suggested candidates of the Islamic Republicans, yet the party refused to accept the president's nominees. Finally, after two months of feuding and under pressure from Khomeini, Bani-Sadr named a "compromise" candidate on August 9. Mohammad Ali Rajai, a member of the Islamic Republican Party, is a former teacher with little political and administrative experience and no international background. He is a true fundamentalist on social issues, advocating no drinking and no dancing, and a hardliner by inclination on the hostage issue. Though the president had forced the Islamic Republicans to abandon their principal candidates, when Bani-Sadr had to accept Rajai, Bani-Sadr was the ultimate loser. Rajai named a cabinet composed exclusively of Islamic radicals. Bani-Sadr retaliated by refusing to accept 4 of Rajai's 15 choices. The skirmishing continued until a full cabinet was approved in mid-September. The prime minister and his cabinet scarcely had time to begin considering what to do about the captives when the country suffered a traumatic calamity. Iran was attacked by Iraq and suddenly the two countries were at war.

The War with Iraq

On September 22 Iraq invaded Khuzistan province in southern Iran, sending an armored column toward Khorramshahr and Abadan.[2] Ever since the call had gone out more than a year before for Shiite Moslems in the Persian Gulf states to rally to Khomeini's banner, the possibility of some kind of retaliation had been building up. Although the small Gulf sheikdoms could do nothing, they carefully watched to see what the outcome would be in the seemingly endless internal struggle among the revolutionary factions. At first Iraq, Iran's powerful neighbor to the west, limited its response to aiding the Arabic-speaking minorities in Khuzistan. It supplied arms and refuge to the Kurdish rebels, and retaliated by radio in the same manner as the propaganda spewing forth from Tehran. In the war of words Khomeini's followers urged Iraqi Shiites to revolt against their president, referring to his rule as "the bloody dictatorship of Saddam Hussein." The Iraqis' countercharge said Khomeini and his allies were "fanatical tyrants" murdering innocent Iranians.

When it became apparent with Rajai's appointment as prime minister that the hard-liners were gaining the upper hand in Tehran, Baghdad took matters into its own hands. Iraq sought the return of territory ceded to Iran in the 1975 Algiers Accords and hoped for a quick decisive military victory that would, if not destroy the Ayatollah, at least severely tarnish Khomeini's charismatic image. The invasion caught Iran completely by surprise. An army unit supposedly guarding the approaches to Khorramshahr was in the hills 200 miles away trying to pacify the restless Bakhtiaris, unhappy ever since Shapour Bakhtiar's unseemly leave-taking. When the invasion began the Revolutionary Guards bore the brunt of the fighting, and not successfully. Suddenly it became terribly important for Iran to have an effective armed force. Khomeini decreed that 90 American-trained pilots jailed for months because of suspected disloyalty should be released and returned to duty. It was obvious that the Pasdaran needed help so badly that the Islamic leadership was eager for the military to begin rebuilding as quickly as possible.

The pilots were immediately sent into action against Iraqi aircraft. Both sides flew numerous air raids during the first two weeks of the war. Iraq damaged the Abadan refinery and 15 military airfields, including Tehran's Mehrabad International Airport. The refinery in Tabriz was immobilized, though damage to the Tehran plant was repaired in two weeks. Iranian pilots acquitted themselves well, bombing the largest Iraqi refinery, at Basra just across the river from Khorramshahr. They also interrupted the pipeline to Syria and Turkey at Kirkuk and attacked Baghdad daily, though the raids on the Iraqi capital did little damage. Near the end of October, bombing runs became sporadic as both sides began to conserve fuel.

Concern about the effectiveness of the armed forces brought Bani-Sadr back into favor and heightened the conflict between him and Rajai. The new prime minister barely had his cabinet in place when, in the interest of effective national defense, the fundamentalist clerics decided to let Bani-Sadr operate more freely. Thus it was easy for the president to continue directing the government (what little of it there was), something he had been doing since his election in January in any case. A new surge of patriotic unity superseded the disputes of the recent past. Even so, internal conflict led the Revolutionary Council to send Prime Minister Rajai rather than the more experienced (and more conciliatory) Bani-Sadr to New York to present Iran's case against Iraq to the United Nations Security Council.

An unkempt Rajai arrived in New York on October 16 for a two-day visit. At the outset, he refused to meet with any American officials and insisted that during his sojourn he would deal exclusively with discussions about Iraq's aggression. To his dismay he found concern for the prisoners as great as that for the Iran-Iraq war. U.N. representatives had a bigger stake than most in resolving the hostage crisis, since they, too, were diplomats. Rajai did consent to a private meeting with Catherine Keough, wife of one of the captives and president of F.L.A.G. (Family Liaison Action Group), an organization established by the hostage families. He reassured her about the health of the incarcerated Americans but said little more. As for the United Nations itself, it took no formal action, instead urging both parties to settle their dispute peacefully.

An October 31, his twentieth birthday and the age of majority in Iran, Crown Prince Reza announced from exile in Cairo that he was "ready to accept full responsibility as the lawful king of Iran." In the low-key ceremony he proclaimed himself Reza Shah II, naming himself after his grandfather. No country recognized his claim to the throne and no exile groups rallied to his support, but he had put himself on record as the royal successor to his father.

During the first six weeks of the war, patriotic fervor overwhelmed nagging doubts about the ability of the Islamic movement to manage the country. Although the economic boycott and Iraqi naval sorties in the Persian Gulf kept the country from getting needed military supplies and spare parts, eventually North Korea airlifted some ammunition and the Soviet Union delivered some food.

After recovering from the initial military thrust that forced them back into the suburbs of Abadan and Khorramshahr, the Revolutionary Guards and supporting army units held their ground much more effectively than most observers thought would be possible. Although army officers admitted they would not be able to carry out sustained offensive action, despite a lack of spare parts, shaky military morale, and inadequate logistical support the Iranians defended their country well. Even so, by November Iraq occupied about 300 square miles of Khuzistan, including most of Khorramshahr and all of the approaches to the Abadan refinery. As winter approached, the military effort degenerated into an inconclusive struggle sapping both sides. The Iraqis said they would gladly accept a cease fire and outlined a settlement that would give them full control of the disputed Shat-al-Arab waterway and the 150 square miles of territory ceded to Iran in the Algiers Accords. Iran dismissed the offer out-of-hand.

Despite having stabilized the military situation, Iran's strategic position remained grim. By late December, mud and water covered the battlefields of Khuzistan, where Iraqi forces had dug in for the winter along natural defense lines formed by two rivers. Khorramshahr and Susangerd were the only towns of any size within the perimeter, but the Iraqi army surrounded Abadan and remained within artillery distance of Dezful and Ahwaz. The main roads connecting these cities with central Iran remained in Persian hands. Iraqi forces occupied the oil field just south of the border town of Qasr-e-Shirin and three small salients near the Iraq-Iran frontier north of Khuzistan province. Army officers states that they had advanced as far as President Hussein desired and were prepared to stay put and keep pressure on the Iranians all winter.

On January 4 an Iranian armored unit attacked Iraqi positions near Susangerd, the only offensive effort undertaken during the winter. The Iranians penetrated a few miles into the enemy lines before being forced back to their old positions. In the process they lost a substantial number of their British-built Chieftain tanks (estimates range from 88 to 200). In fact, the only benefit the Iranians gained from the military thrust was an opportunity to parade several hundred Iraqi prisoners of war through the streets of Tehran. After the one midwinter attempt to change the military status quo, quiet reigned once again.

Politically there were other ominous signs. In mid-December Iraq set up a civilian administration for the part of Khuzistan province under its control. On December 23, authorities in Baghdad sponsored a press conference with two members of the Arab Popular Movement of Arabistan, Iraq's name for Khuzistan. They praised the Iraqis as "Arab Liberators," and promised to continue the fight for self-rule of this strategic area. Such maneuvers suggest that Baghdad was preparing the way to deny Iran direct control of occupied Khuzistan after the war.

By December Iran's economic condition had deteriorated further, beyond its already low levels. Industries were operating at between 25 and 40 percent of normal. Three to four million laborers remained out of work and, in the final two months of 1980, inflation went from a pre-war 40 percent to between 60 and 70 percent. Food shortages became obvious and rationing went into effect on two staples, sugar and rice. As the war turned into a stalemate and winter brought cold weather and discomfort, anti-Khomeini demonstrations broke out in Tehran, Qom, Mashad, Isfahan, and Tabriz.

Oil deliveries to other nations had been reduced to almost nothing. From November 14 through 16, Iraqi forces attacked the main road out of Khuzistan leading to Tehran and disrupted the pipeline junction at Susangerd, south of Ahwaz. Simultanteously Arab workers in Khuzistan interrupted production in the largest oil fields, first by striking and then by industrial sabotage, including shutting down machinery. With access to the primary producing centers limited to the output from one small pipeline to Isfahan and production from a tiny field at Livan, 400 miles southeast of Khorramshahr, Iran could manage only half of its pre-war production of about a million barrels per day and one-sixth of its pre-revolutionary output. Because the oil at Livan could not be refined, approximately 200,000 barrels per day were exported, though Iran itself was in desperate need of them.

By January production had improved to between 1.0 to 1.4 million barrels per day, but use of the refineries was still restricted. The increase was sold to countries in Eastern Europe, India, Turkey, and North and South Korea. Iran itself used 300,000 barrels per day, barely enough to cover military needs plus drastically rationed civilian consumption. By December owners of private vehicles were allowed only six gallons of gas per month and forbidden to drive between the hours of 8:00 A.M. and 8:00 P.M., leaving just buses, taxis, and government vehicles on the streets during the day. The greatest difficulty, however, was that bombing damage to the country's refineries, compounded by the lack of spare parts, made it impossible to refine enough crude into kerosene for heating oil. Winter had arrived, and the lack of fuel for household use posed a serious problem, since the overwhelming majority of urban families use room heaters run on kerosene. The heating oil deficiency strengthened the cause of the leftist forces, who accused the religious leaders of incompetence.

The End of the Tunnel—But With No Light

It was the military setbacks coupled with the dreadful economic prospects that reversed long-standing fundamentalist attitudes about the utility of holding the American captives indefinitely. Even Beheshti and Rajai, consistent hard-liners, realized that the isolation Iran had been forced to endure since taking the hostages was a hardship. After the war started, the problem was greatly aggravated. Therefore, as soon as Rajai's government was in place, parliament tackled the hostage issue. On September 12, ten days before the invasion, Khomeini delivered a major address outlining four conditions the United States had to meet if Iran were to release the Americans: return the Shah's assets, pledge non-interference in Iran's affairs, unfreeze Iranian assets, and cancel all U.S. claims, including private ones, against the revolutionary government. Working from this speech, the Majles began formulating terms. The usual conflicts between various factions within the Consultative Assembly surfaced immediately. The Islamic Republicans in parliament insisted on a verbatim adherence to Khomeini's terms. Bazargan (who had been elected to the Majles in March and also was still on the Revolutionary Council) and other members of the Liberation Movement knew the United States could not and would not agree to such demands. Leftist deputies, who did not want the dispute resolved in any case, insisted that the only answer was to try the hostages rather than to work out a deal to release them.

To show their willingness to act, however, the clerical faction allowed the West German ambassador to Iran, Gerhardt Reitzel, to arrange a meeting between U.S. Deputy Secretary of State Warren Christopher and Khomeini confidant Sadegh Tabatabai, a former deputy prime minister under Bazargan and son-in-law of the Ayatollah. The Iranians had passed the text of the Khomeini speech outlining the four conditions for the hostages' release to the Carter administration three days before the Ayatollah was to deliver it, thereby indicating they wanted to resolve the hostage matter as soon as possible. Christopher met secretly with Tabatabai in Bonn on September 16 and 18. The two men appeared to be making headway in narrowing the differences between Iran and the United States.[3] Then the Iran-Iraq War broke out September 22. There would be no further meetings.

The radical clergy, still by far the most powerful political group, seriously misled themselves about the willingness of the American government to accept the terms as set by the Ayatollah. From the very beginning the fundamentalist clerics in the Majles were convinced President Carter would consent to anything in order to get the hostages released.[4] Thus the Islamic Republicans who controlled parliament were not concerned that haggling over wording prevented the speedy delivery of the final conditions to Washington. After six weeks of bickering, the Consultative Assembly finally forwarded its pronouncement on November 2, 48 hours before the American presidential election. Except for the embroidered language, the terms were exactly the same as those stated by the Ayatollah in September. The revolutionary government called for an immediate, public response. The White House said it would give a considered, private answer.

Iran's ultimatum as well as the peremptory demand for an answer reminded most Americans that the hostage business was a Carter problem. After months of stalling, the revolutionary government's action so close to election day—the first anniversary of the incarceration of 52 Americans guilty of no crime other than being in the wrong place at the wrong time—destroyed the President's reelection chances. By Wednesday morning the magnitude of Ronald Reagan's 51–41 percent landslide victory was apparent in Tehran. Islamic fundamentalists were stunned; it had never occurred to Beheshti and the other radical clerics that Carter would not be reelected, despite warnings to that effect from the more sophisticated Ghotbzadeh and Bani-Sadr. Such a resounding shock stimulated extensive soul-searching. Ali Nobari, president of the Central Bank, best expressed the fears of many in high places:

> On the level of foreign diplomacy we have failed completely. We could have had direct and very positive influence on the U.S. presidential elections, but alas, due to our own failings, we let the chance slip by.
>   What we have done . . . is play a part in changing that [the Carter administration] psychology of nonintervention to an aggressive sort of fascist psychology.[5]

Tempers flared. On November 7 Sadeq Ghotbzadeh (who had been dismissed as foreign minister when Rajai selected his cabinet) was arrested by revolutionary militants for his unflattering comments on Iranian television about the clerical leadership. His case became a rallying point for secular and leftist politicians, whose heavy critism put the Islamic Republican Party on the defensive and temporarily strengthened Bani-Sadr. Iran's president repeated his view that seizing the Americans had been a mistake, that it was Iran which was now being held hostage. After five days, under heavy pressure from all sides, Tehran Prosecutor Assadollah Lajevardi withdrew the warrant for Ghotbzadeh's arrest and the former foreign minister was set free.

The Carter administration studied the Iranian proposals for a week. On November 9 Deputy Secretary of State Warren Christopher and a team of four experts — Assistant Secretary of State for Near Eastern and South Asian Affairs Harold Saunders, Treasury Deputy Secretary Robert Carswell, State Department Legal Advisor Robert Owen, and Arnold Raphel, a special assistant to Secretary of State Muskie — flew to Algiers to discuss the American reply with Algerian Foreign Minister Mohammad Benyahia and his ambassador to Tehran, Abdelkarim Gharaib. It was Gharaib who transmitted the American reply to Iran. In general, the U.S. response was positive. It said the United States would pledge non-interference and would try to meet the other conditions, but it raised serious questions about the ability of the U.S. to meet the full demands precisely as specified. The team explained that it would be legally impossible (not to mention politically suicidal) for the U.S. government to return Iran's assets while unadjudicated claims were still pending against them. With respect to the Shah's wealth, the U.S. indicated it would help the Persians locate any assets and assist them to institute legal action in the United States to get them back, but it could not just hand over an unspecified sum.

The Iranians were not pleased. They were sure President Carter was holding out on them. Why could he not just order the terms fulfilled, as the Ayatollah (or the Shah before him) could do in Iran? They sent a return message, seeking further clarification. Christopher and his team returned to Algiers on December 1, delivering the latest, more detailed American response.

Iran's reply on December 19 to the American proposals was a disheartening shocker. The latest message, personally approved by Khomeini, asked for $24 billion in U.S. "guarantees." Iran considered $14 billion of that amount to be the frozen assets (at least $6 billion more than Carter thought he was dealing with in November 1979) and $10 billion that the revolutionaries said had belonged to the Shah's family. What was being asked for went well beyond Iran's previous demands. American outrage was universal and substantial. Administration officials indicated publicly that there was little hope of an accord before

President Carter left office. Over Christmas, President-elect Reagan responded emphatically and negatively to suggestions that he might give Iran a better deal, capping his statement with a description of the Iranians as "barbarians." The hardening American attitude, plus the failure of the offensive against the Iraqi invaders in early January, induced the revolutionaries to soften their terms almost immediately. The Christopher team had made it clear that, unless an agreement was reached by January 20, the incoming Reagan administration would not feel bound by the parameters of previous discussions.[6]

On January 15, one day before the self-imposed deadline for an agreement to be implemented before Carter left office, Iran scaled down its financial demands to around $8 billion and agreed to pay off all its outstanding loans to U.S. banks. Five days of feverish, nonstop negotiations ensued. The parties involved in the principal discussion, in Algiers, were the original American negotiating team headed by Warren Christopher and the Algerian diplomats. Banking teams representing Iran, Britain, Algeria, and the United States also stood by in New York, Tehran, London, and Algiers. There was a "false dawn" on January 19, when an initial transfer of funds to an escrow account in London was scheduled. It didn't materialize because the Iranian Central Bank had not filed the proper papers. Bank officials in Tehran were too busy wrangling among themselves to do the work involved. After that delay there was no longer any hope of a hostage release before the next day, when Ronald Reagan would be inaugurated. Finally, at 9:00 A.M. on January 20, the first transfer of Iranian assets went to the Algerian-controlled escrow account in the Bank of England. The hostages were taken to Mehrabad airport. As a last slap at President Carter, the takeoff was delayed until a half hour after President Reagan finished his inaugural address. To make sure the Carter administration and the American people got the point, the militants released film showing revolutionaries listening to Reagan's speech over the Voice of America as the hostages were being prepared for departure. Finally, the prisoners — after 444 days in captivity — boarded an Algerian jet, but not until after they had run a gauntlet of jeering militants who lined the way from the buses on the runway to the plane.

The hostages went first to Algiers, where they were transferred to two American medical evacuation planes. From there they flew to Germany, where they spent four days at the U.S. Air Force hospital at Wiesbaden undergoing physical and psychological examinations. At President Reagan's invitation, former President Carter flew to Germany to greet the hostages as the new President's special emissary. On January 25 the group was flown to West Point, New York, for private reunions with their families. Two days later came the "Welcome Home to Freedom" parade in Washington, ending at the White House and a speech by President Reagan honoring the former captives.

Beyond the universal national jubilation over the hostage release there remained nagging problems. The frantic, last minute negotiations had left both sides in some confusion. After the initial transfer of $7.9 billion—$3.7 billion to the U.S. Federal Reserve Bank to pay off outstanding loans, $1.4 billion to the London escrow account to be used to settle other American claims, and another $2.8 billion to go to Iran via the Algerian Central Bank—the Reagan administration announced it would review all the agreements signed during the last hours of the Carter administration. The major items under study were the intention to appoint a commission to adjudicate outstanding claims against the escrow account and the disposition of the remaining $4 billion in Iranian assets still in U.S. banks.

The aftermath of the hostage crisis was anticlimactic. The United States was not particularly eager to resume any trade, let alone "normal" commerce. Many Iranian corporations made tentative offers to start buying again from U.S. companies, but in the first month after the hostages' release over two-thirds of the American firms turned the Iranians down. Most companies bluntly stated that they were not prepared to deal with Iran in the future on anything other than a cash basis. That country's banking system was in shambles, and only a few daring suppliers resumed business. The Iranians fared little better with their European trading partners. The French, while willing to ship food, would not supply 12 high-speed patrol boats until the government adjudicated $11 billion in claims by French businessmen over lost civilian and military contracts. Britain held up the sale of new Chieftain tanks and spare parts for old ones—desperately needed after the fiasco on the battlefield January 4—because four of its citizens still were being held by the Iranians. The two missionaries and the bishop's secretary were released on February 28 after an Iranian court declared evidence against them had been forged. British businessman Andrew Pyke remained in jail, under renewed threats of being put on trial for espionage.

Questioned January 28—during his first press conference—about America's future relations with Iran, Secretary of State Alexander Haig said there would be no further sale or delivery of military goods on any terms. He also indicated that the way Iran handled the cases of the three non-hostage American citizens who remained in Iranian prisons would be a factor in determining the U.S. attitude toward Iran in the future.

Willing to make a gesture, on February 4 the Iranian government released naturalized American Mohi Sobhani, a Rockwell International employee who had been arrested on September 6, 1980, as he was about to leave Iran. A few days later the "trial" of free-lance journalist Cynthia Dwyer began. She was convicted of "spying," sentenced to time already served, and expelled from the country on February 10. Zia Nassiri, an Afghan-born naturalized American, remained in jail. Although he had gone to Iran in mid-1980 to assist those Afghan guerrillas who had been fighting the Soviet-backed regime in Kabul and who had come to Iran as refugees, Nassiri was arrested for "subversive" activities.

The release of the hostages did not miraculously solve Iran's internal problems. President Bani-Sadr immediately attacked the religious fundamentalists, particularly Prime Minister Rajai, saying the deal with the Americans was much less favorable than anything the moderates could have worked out much earlier. Anti-Khomeini demonstrations broke out in several cities. On February 4 the Ayatollah appealed to all factions to stop squabbling and threatened to fire government leaders if they did not learn to cooperate. A week later Khomeini rebuked radical clergymen for "interfering in matters beyond their competence." Bani-Sadr and the fundamentalists still appeared incapable of agreeing on a common approach to solve the country's myriad problems. Iran continued to face dreary economic prospects, social dissension, and political chaos.

Chapter Thirteen

★

Choice and Change: Iran

One of the more common traps to get caught in when analyzing a revolutionary situation is to look at the trend of events and by describing what happened assume that what actually occurred was foreordained. Khomeini's victory was not inevitable. The Shah was never doomed. The outcome of the revolution depended on a series of choices made by both sides. Events were triggered and outcomes determined by explicit or implicit decisions of the Shah, Khomeini, the military, the religious fundamentalists, the moderate opposition, the left, and even (though to a lesser degree than many suppose) the United States government.

Choices within the Iranian environment can be divided into broad strategic decisions that shaped events and narrower, tactical options that indirectly influenced the outcome of particular incidents. Politics, particularly in a situation so uncertain that the legitimacy of the entire system is called into question, is an essentially unpredictable art. In a tense situation basic trends direct policy and decision making less than in more normal times. Iran is no exception. Its political evolution was not a well-defined process, but a panorama of individuals and groups trying to affect one another's behavior and being themselves changed by it. Whether to select one course of action rather than another depended largely upon the individual personalities of the various participants.

Their strategies as well as their perceptions of events guided their decisions and their reactions to what was happening. Of everyone involved, the Shah stands above all others as the person who made the most critical choices. Ayatollah Khomeini, though striving single-mindedly toward his goal, made key decisions only after he left Iraq in September 1978. The Shah's actions set the stage for the finale of the revolutionary drama, while Khomeini's views determined opposition

263

reactions and strategies. Other groups had important bit parts but none dominated like the monarch and the Ayatollah. One person was trying to hold on to power while the other was attempting to seize it.

The Broad Choices: The Shah

Three choices the Shah made set the context for what followed. The first of these was his inclination to liberalize the political system, which led to the rebirth of the revolutionary movement. When the monarch quietly advised SAVAK to ease up on the dissidents, he opened the way for the opposition to "go public," and therefore influence future events more directly. He made this decision in response to pleas that the growing complexity of modern Iran could not be managed in the older, authoritarian pattern. Having done this, however, he failed to work out a strategy to move from a Shah-centered government to a more pluralistic, decentralized pattern. Now far greater, less controlled change became possible.

The Shah assumed that pro-regime political forces would keep control of events but he did nothing to assure this would happen, either by closely monitoring the process or by coopting opposition leaders. He depended on SAVAK to keep dissidents in line, not realizing that such pressure was inconsistent with his desire to promote a loyal opposition. Because he insisted the Resurgence Party was the only acceptable vehicle for political action, the opposition was forced to operate outside the system. As a result the dissidents established their own organizational base, expanding their interconnections through the mosque network. It was the first time since 1963 that an extensive and cohesive movement had challenged the regime. The guerrillas, active since the early 1970s, had nuisance value but could not rally enough support to seriously threaten the government until bolstered by the bazaar merchants and the mullahs late in 1977.

Uncertainty kept those close to the Shah from developing a comprehensive strategy for maintaining control. There is little doubt that a substantial majority of his people was willing to go along with the regime until the autumn of 1978, but the Shah never capitalized on this support. He allowed those offering an illegal alternative to gain a significant foothold within society without paying a price for it. Both the moderate secular dissidents and the radical clerics built up support for their cause with only sporadic, halfhearted hindrance from SAVAK and the military.

A second important move, in this case, a "non-decision," made the establishment alternative, the Resurgence Party, an unattractive option. After deciding to liberalize, the Shah was unwilling to allow the Resurgence Party any real authority independent of the throne. Not only was party membership no guarantee for political advancement, but individuals and groups could not use it to influence the way the government affected their lives. Iranians of all persuasions had participated in the Resurgence Party for the first two and a half years and many had taken it seriously. They became doubly discouraged when the Shah manipulated party officials and eliminated anyone who showed some independence, such as Secretary-General Baheri. The monarch rejected entreaties from the more perceptive around him that liberalization and political decentralization had to include real power sharing if either was to be taken seriously. The Resurgence Party was ineffectual because of this basic conflict over what its role should be. Based on the Shah's perceptions the Resurgence Party was to concentrate on mobilizing the masses and educating them to be loyal citizens of the regime, a conception providing minimum participation in decision making and absolutely no gradual assumption of power. Ceremony overpowered substance. The overwhelming majority of his people correctly deduced that the Shah was unwilling to allow any political freedom. This policy simply was no longer acceptable, especially during the severe economic recession in 1977. The Shah was seeking mutually contradictory objectives: civic participation and authoritarian control.

Having failed to induce cooperation on his terms, the Shah eventually faced his third major quandary — what to do about the growing number of dissidents who refused to play by his rules. Without a comprehensive strategy to direct his moves, the monarch was continually torn between repressing the opposition and attempting to conciliate it. He tried both, buy the arrest of Ayatollah Taleqani in August 1977, followed by the frequent attacks on opposition meetings and the harassment of many revolutionary leaders in November 1977, convinced the dissidents instead that the monarch was endeavoring to crush them. The jumbled signals they received did not encourage the opposition to work out a compromise. Instead, it remained absolutely firm. The Shah's refusal to annihilate or at least systematically incarcerate those opposed to his regime was not considered evidence of his willingness to find an accommodation, but an indication of either his personal weakness or the inability of the government to act effectively against the opposition. Throughout 1978 the Shah had made threatening pronouncements, but whenever the Islamic fundamentalists directly challenged the power of the military, most obviously at Jaleh Square in September 1978, the army was allowed to use but minimal force and then only to solve the immediate problem. Continuing to vacillate, the Shah reversed his initial decision to arrest opposition leaders following the Jaleh Square rioting. Within 24 hours these dissidents were back on the streets.

The Shah never could distinguish between those malcontents who wanted political freedom and would settle for a fair chance at power within the existing structure, and those such as Khomeini who were committed from the first to the destruction of the monarchy. Lacking a strategy to bring the former into the political system, the monarch forced the moderates into an alliance with uncompromising revolutionaries. The Shah's attempts at conciliation in the spring of 1978 were so awkward as to be worse than no attempts at all. Royal imperiousness disgusted those who sought fundamental reform and meant to negotiate or fight until they got it.

Efforts to placate the opposition after Jaleh Square faltered because of a similar feeling of distrust. The government of Prime Minister Sharif-Emami lacked credibility despite his support of press freedom, wage increases for the workers, open parliamentary debates, and rejection of the Resurgence Party. The Shah's attempt to impose a military government on November 6, 1978, yet still leave the door open for compromise was the ultimate expression of the monarch's desire to have his cake and eat it too. By November the revolutionaries suspected an all-out military assault against them would never be ordered. Thus their self-perceived task became one of gradually assuming power without provoking either the armed forces or the Shah into doing something rash.

The monarch's understanding of the seriousness of his dilemma was totally inadequate, primarily because he did not know what was going on in his own country. Since he had no overall plan, he never imposed a "bottom line" beyond which he would not budge, so no dissident action ever provoked a firm riposte. As a result the revolutionary movement gradually pushed him away from his position of power, and eventually from his inherent status as the legitimate ruler of Iran. Ayatollah Khomeini's claim that the Tassua and Ashura marches on December 10 and 11, 1978, represented a plebiscite against the regime sounded believable in the wake of the temporizing which had gone on since midsummer. By November that fear of authority which had kept fractious Persians in line for 25 centuries had disappeared. The father figure had failed completely to establish new arrangements which would be at least tacitly acceptable to the revolutionaries and eliminate the need to insure minimal political obedience by force.

The Shah had lost his ability to conceive that broader view of government that must motivate a leader, particularly an activist monarch, if he is to enforce his will or develop effective institutions. He had shown such vision in 1963, when he promulgated the Shah-People Revolution. Now the heady combination of his newly acquired world position and his own authoritarian vanity, plus the debilitating effect of his terminal illness, prevented the monarch from developing a comparable blueprint for Iran's political evolution. Instead, he fumbled his choices, underlining in the waning days of his rule the absence of a sense of bold leadership.[1] Lacking inner confidence and a comprehensive plan, he allowed his people to fall under the spell of another leader.

The Broad Choices: The Ayatollah

The only other individual with the capacity to affect events significantly through broad strategic choices was Ayatollah Khomeini. His ability to impose his will was due both to circumstances and his own political acumen. From the beginning Khomeini was recognized by the religious and secular dissidents as one individual who never had compromised with the Shah. Arrested in 1963, he was eventually expelled from Iran for refusing to cease his anti-regime diatribes. The Ayatollah based his supremacy on religious principles, including the moral duty of senior clerics to exercise political leadership. He took this conviction to its logical extreme—victory or death. Some of Khomeini's power came from his known willingness to martyr himself for the Islamic revolution. He was not afraid to die if it would help bring about the Shah's downfall.

The Ayatollah's lifelong decision not to compromise with the monarchy eventually brought him to the forefront of the revolutionary movement as its charismatic leader and the source of legitimacy for today's revolutionary regime. Politicians in the governments after the takeover have prospered or fallen, based on their willingness "to follow the line of the Imam." Once Khomeini grasped the mantle of leadership upon his arrival in Paris in October 1978, no opposition leader dared compromise for fear of destroying his own position within the dissident movement. On the eve of the Shah's imposition of military rule, Karim Sanjabi toyed with and then turned down an offer to join the establishment and form a government. When Shapour Bakhtiar accepted the Shah's proposal to become prime minister in January 1979, he was promptly disowned by his own National Front as well as the other opposition groups. The Liberation Movement's Mehdi Bazargan remained utterly faithful to Khomeini, never yielding to the temptation of compromise, so it was he who became the Ayatollah's first prime minister.

Constant reaffirmation of support for the Khomeini line remained necessary for continued acceptance within the inner circle. Ibrahim Yazdi, and his boss, Prime Minister Bazargan, were shunted aside in November 1979, after meeting with the "untrustworthy" Zbigniew Brzezinski in Algiers. Yazdi's successor as foreign minister, Sadeq Ghotbzadeh, lost his job in the August 1980 cabinet shuffle because he no longer favored holding the American prisoners. After criticizing the power of the Islamic Republican Party on national television in November, he also was jailed briefly in Evin Prison.

Though Khomeini has reversed himself occasionally on tactical questions, for example, rescinding the order that all women wear chadors, he never has been pressed hard to compromise. In December 1978, in an effort to avoid bloodshed, the Shah and in-country dissidents selected a Regency Council. As part of this arrangement, opposition leaders agreed to convince Khomeini to accept the deal. They were relieved of their obligation to do so when the Shah rejected to plan within 24 hours after he had accepted it. Had Khomeini refused to abide by such an accommodation, the revolutionaries would have been in considerable disarray. Then the Shah and Ardeshir Zahedi might have regained the initiative long enough to offer Bakhtiar's compromise government at least a chance to generate popular support.

Symbols were critical to revolutionary perceptions. In the eyes of the masses Khomeini remained a man of principle. He used unwavering obstinance to reach the front rank of politics. No one ever successfully challenged him—not the Shah, not the establishment, not the moderate opposition, and not the other religious leaders, though Ayatollah Taleqani tried to in April 1979. A different mix of revolutionary forces might have emerged if the onus for refusing a workable compromise had been placed on the Ayatollah. Then moderate dissidents would have considered him a cantankerous obstacle to the peaceful achievement of political freedom in Iran.

The first time there was serious pressure from within the Islamic movement to compromise on an issue occurred after the Iran-Iraq war had begun. By then Iraq had already badly battered Iran and controlled the two major cities involved with the oil industry, Abadan and Khorramshahr. Some leaders begged the Ayatollah to bend enough so that the government could free the hostages, end its economic isolation, and acquire desperately needed U.S. military spare parts already bought and paid for. Still convinced of his righteousness, the Ayatollah encouraged parliament to outline settlement terms, but he would not go so far as to order the captives released. The internal conflict between those who wanted the Americans set free and those who would continue holding them tested the Ayatollah's ability to back down from a matter of principle in the interest of the survival of his regime. Indecision on the issue of what to do with the hostages was always endemic to his government.

Khomeini's other major contribution to setting the course of the revolution stems from his narrow conception of Islamic purity. After Bazargan was installed as prime minister, the Ayatollah took an elitist view of leadership, an attitude he refined in succeeding months. Instead of calling on the people to unite and to build the new regime together, he restricted the government's organizational base to "true" Islamic revolutionaries. At first he rejected only the establishment, those who had participated in or collaborated with the old regime. Because it totally rejected Khomeini's brand of Islamic fundamentalism from the start, however, the Fedayeen challenged Khomeini as early as February 14, was restless by March, and had been hounded almost to invisibility by August. In May the Ayatollah began castigating the moderate opposition because it did not fully support his idea of an Islamic Republic. By December he was after dissenting religious leaders and had two senior rival religious leaders, Ayatollah Shariatmadari and Sheik Khaghani, under house arrest in Qom.

Khomeini's view of Islamic orthodoxy as manifested in the Islamic Republican Party is exclusionary, not inclusive. The result has been predictable: simmering rebellion in Kurdestan, defections within the revolutionary coalition, the sabotage of the oil fields by the Arab minority in Khuzistan, disagreements with many countries, and a major rift with Iraq that erupted into war. To an unprecedented degree Khomeini's personal beliefs have dominated political dialogue and turned other groups away from supporting the country's new Islamic structure. Ayatollah Shariatmadari's break with Khomeini over his insistence on a fundamentalist constitution is a clear example of this. Shariatmadari's deliberate disavowal of the radical position, even while under house arrest in Qom, clearly sets him apart as a potential religious alternative to Khomeini or his successors.

This exclusionary view of politics was not shared by the first postrevolutionary government. Bazargan and the rest of the Liberation Movement wanted to maintain and expand the support of the broad revolutionary coalition. They accepted, even desired, Islamic influence, but not at the expense of civil rights and free political expression, principles they had fought for over many years. Bazargan's conflicts with the radical clerics culminated in his resignation after the hostages were seized. His move paved the way for Khomeini's Islamic Republican Party to take total political control after the Consultative Assembly organized itself and forced President Bani-Sadr to accept a hard-liner as his prime minister.

Ayatollah Khomeini has been the major factor shaping the revolution, first by setting Iran on the road to total change rather than reform, then by insisting on narrow Islamic control of the political system rather than on a broad effort to reconcile all factions in a more representative government. Like the Shah, the Ayatollah has suffered from ill health, plus the burden of old age. Yet he still imposes his will on the dominant political force, the Islamic Republican Party.

The Military Consideration

One more series of important choices shaped the Iranian environment. As the Shah lost his battle for political support from September to November 1978, the army and SAVAK gradually became the sole institutions supporting the regime. The cumulative effect of the military's inclination—first to obey their monarch and not carry out a violent repression and then to go back to barracks rather than defend the Bakhtiar government—removed it from the political struggle and precipitated its collapse. There were many reasons why the Shah's military juggernaut was weaker than generally supposed even before the climax of the revolution. For one thing, some of the senior leadership developed ambivalent feelings as the Pahlavi system disintegrated, despite the fact that it had been a pampered class, with selection for the higher ranks based on loyalty to the Shah. One of the most effective efforts during the revolutionary period was the work done with officers and troops taunting them to desert and direct their loyalties to the Islamic movement and the speedy disintegration of the armed forces.

For months, within the top military leadership, there had been vastly conflicting opinions about what to do. Generals like Khosrowdad, Rabii, and Oveissi felt to the end that decisive action was the only way to turn the tide of events. But there was little they could change since the Shah, General Azhari, and Azhari's successor as chief of the supreme commander's staff, General Gharabaghi, did not think force would solve Iran's political problems. The tradition of obedience to the wishes of the Shah was a strong deterrent to any plotting to act in the name of the monarch without his approval. The unhappy generals could not generate the support necessary to act without orders, and these were never forthcoming.

In view of the traditional cohesion in military organizations elsewhere, it is surprising that the armed forces did not eventually pull together and take matters into their own hands, particularly after Jaleh Square. However, with the exception of those very few senior officers who clearly saw potential danger to themselves if there was a change in government or who, like Gharabaghi, began to shift their loyalty away from the Shah, most of the generals were ill tuned to the possible political consequences of their actions. When the military had to decide whether or not to support Bakhtiar after the air force cadets revolted at Doshen Tappeh and Farahabad air bases, the hard-line generals had already been dismissed as part of the Shah's agreement with Bakhtiar. Those who commanded troops and wished to retaliate could find no senior leadership in Tehran to coordinate a decisive rejoinder. Without cooperation they were unwilling to act on their own.

The Shah's inability to build a political base that matched the original strength of his military one as well as his unwillingness to effectively destroy the opposition left the leadership of the armed forces open to the steady erosion of their feelings of confidence and capability. When the crisis came to a head on February 10–11, 1979, pro-Shah generals died in battle, already had been retired, or were in exile. Others, less committed, were looking for ways to accommodate themselves to the new order. The Shah's proud army died not with a bang but a whimper.

Lesser Possibilities: The Establishment

Three major decisions of the Shah already have been mentioned—his refusal to repress the revolutionaries after the Jaleh Square uprising in September 1978, his rejection of the Regency Council formula worked out in December, and his general vacillation throughout when considering the use of force versus political compromise. There were other less important choices of his which affected the outcome of the upheaval. Had some of these been different, the course the revolution took could have been substantially changed.

For one thing, the Shah's casual approach to the problem of maintaining political support meant he did not pay as much attention to popular attitudes as he should have. To the end of his life the monarch was puzzled by the fact that Iranians were not more grateful to him for the economic advances he had brought to his country. The ultimate decision maker himself, he could not understand why others insisted on having a voice in their own destiny.

Later on, the monarch's conclusion that he should leave Iran rather than to stay and tough it out with military backing reflected his assessment that by removing himself from the immediate political scene, as he had done in 1953, his supporters would rally and reestablish order. He did not realize that he had gradually lost nearly all support, with even many establishment Iranians eventually eschewing him. Undoubtedly, when he left the country in January 1979, in the back of his mind was the thought that even if the armed forces eventually were involved in a forceful, bloody repression, he or his son would be able to step back in at some future point. The Shah greatly contributed to his own downfall. Because he lacked a clear picture of where he wanted to go, he failed to develop any solutions to the growing problems. It was his decisions, or more precisely, the lack of them, that precipitated the chaos which would envelop Iran.

In two other situations the monarch exhibited an unusual mixture of concern coupled with indifference or ambivalence. Though always interested in what SAVAK and military intelligence were doing, the Shah did not prod them to improve their technique when times were good in the early 1970s. For years SAVAK had been coasting. Take, for example, its failure to anticipate the vehemence of the riots in Tabriz in February 1978. Also, despite the monarch's decision to open up the political system and his knowledge that this could lead to potential disturbance, security forces throughout the county had no advance training in riot control. Even as the need for it became glaringly obvious, there was precious little advance preparation. It appeared as if the Shah expected the government to take care of itself.

The Shah's attitude toward his principal ally, the United States, was also curiously tangled. From 1973 to 1976 he righteously expounded many times about the Western sin of permissiveness; by the end of 1978 the monarch was pleading for American support. Never the most approachable of sovereigns, even by those he respected, he was convinced the U.S. was trying to undercut him, since he kept getting disconcerting signals on human rights from the Carter administration. In spite of this, or maybe because of it, he withheld very important information about his health and, in contrast to his earlier years, rarely discussed the development strategy he was pursuing. In the early 1970s, when the United States lost the economic leverage it had enjoyed previously, this was not replaced by joint planning or Iranian self-imposed restraint on

spending. The result was the 1974 budget which accelerated development expenditure so dramatically and led to drastic economic dislocation.

Deep in the wings was the old establishment, which found itself with
no real choices except acquiescence to Islamic rule or emigration. Rebuffed by the Shah and diverted into the Resurgence Party, it had deserted active politics when that party collapsed. The establishment did
not make common cause with the secular opposition or try to join the
moderate religious groups to form a coalition which might have
stymied the plans of the radical clerics. Years of overdependence on the
Shah and overconfidence about their own position left the modernizers
unable to act when their "protector" could not lead them. Like elites in
other societies beset by revolution, they were blind to the dangers
threatening their own status. Most of them misunderstood the Islamic
challenge and what it portended should it be victorious. As a group, its
distinctive feature was the calm assumption that it would be indispens-
able. Too late, the establishment understood that it was not as necessary
as it thought. Some elites made their peace with the new order; those
who could afford it fled to societies more consistent with their own
values. Since September 1978 approximately 1.5 to 2.0 million Persians
have left permanently, with most gravitating to the United States and
Europe. Thousands already were either resident aliens or held citizenship in the countries to which they traveled. Some had children in
school abroad whom they joined—there were approximately 40,000
Iranian students in America at that time, and about half that number in
various Western European countries.

Only a handful of those who chose exile have become enmeshed in
opposition politics. Still, there are at least three separate factions: One is
led by Shapour Bakhtiar, the last pre-revolutionary prime minister, and
is based in Paris and London. Another group in France is concentrated
around Hassan Nazih, chosen by Khomeini to run the National Iranian
Oil Company until he broke with the Islamic movement and fled late in
1979. A third is headed by General Gholam Ali Oveissi, the last commander of the Imperial Army and the only senior general who urged
the Shah to destroy the burgeoning revolution with military force who
still survives. None of these groups has much following within Iran
now, but all have sufficient contacts at home to act if the Khomeini
government collapses. Around Oveissi, particularly, are other military
men who escaped, giving his movement more potential strength.

One establishment figure, Hossein Fardust, is a special case. The
Shah's confidant since childhood and chief of the Imperial Inspectorate,

he defected before Khomeini took over and surfaced as an important figure in the revolutionary government's intelligence organization, SAVAMA. It is hard to overestimate the value of having a "mole" in the inner councils of the Shah. Fardust is a very private person and he may have cooperated with the religious leadership for the good of the country when he saw his leader's increasingly inadequate grasp of polit- ical realities.[2] Princess Ashraf has hinted that he was responsible for the failure of SAVAK to alert the regime to the potential danger of the Islamic fundamentalists. This seems unlikely, more a comment de- signed to lift the load of defeat off her twin brother's shoulders.[3] In the normal course of his work, Fardust would have had contact with the ayatollahs. And as someone close to the Shah, he would have been among the first to learn about the monarch's serious illness and its ef- fects on his firmness and judgment. He was the only member of the Shah's inner circle to desert him and work for the opposition.

Lesser Possibilities: The Opposition

Like the Shah and his followers, the opposition groups also had op- portunities to make less critical choices that contributed to the shaping of the final outcome of the revolution. At first, how the dissidents acted and reacted was thrust upon them, particularly since those who dis- agreed with the regime were forced to unite in order to make them- selves effective. Throughout 1977 both the religious and the secular op- position harped on issues that appealed to the masses—SAVAK brutal- ity, corruption, and economic dislocation. The National Front, the Liberation Movement, and the various professional groups consciously packaged their complaints under the rubric of "human rights" in order to attract more support both at home and abroad. In addition, in the fall of 1977 the moderate dissidents successfully convinced the guerrillas to cease violent activity, stimulating more revolutionary unity. This paid off a few months later, after the shootings in Qom and the riots in Tabriz, when religious moderate Ayatollah Shariatmadari allied himself with the radical fundamentalists. Those who gained most from the growing cohesion of the opposition were the Liberation Movement and the fundamentalist Shiite clergy, numerically the largest factions.

The National Front and the liberals who formed the National Democratic Front under Hedayatollah Matin-Daftari were in the weakest position, lacking either military cadres to protect them or the advantage of numbers. Nevertheless, they maintained the hope of being in the forefront of political leadership until they were rudely disabused of this conceit after the Khomeini takeover in February. They could not argue with the fundamentalists who controlled the Mujahidin, the country's only effective military force.

The Shah made it easy for the dissidents to select revolution rather than reform. The secular liberals refused to consider cooperating, even after the monarch pledged free elections in his Constitution Day speech in August 1978, because they simply did not trust the man. Their suspicions were based on his 35-year record of resorting to authoritarian measures rather than conciliatory policies of participation. They can hardly be blamed for feeling uneasy, but it is puzzling that they did not push the monarch harder to make good on his public commitment. The secular liberals also appeared startlingly unconcerned about the divergent attitudes of their fellow revolutionaries, despite the fact that real differences of opinion between the various coalition groups were evident as early as mid-1978.

In the same vein, the Shah's very tentative initiatives to the religious moderates in April and May 1978 were so inadequate the overtures were rebuffed. Even so, in view of the rivalries between the various ayatollahs, it is surprising that the moderate religious leaders did not explore more thoroughly the possibility of accommodation.

Starting in the spring of 1978, each component of the revolutionary coalition had a chance to opt for a more conciliatory rather than a combative approach to change. With the exception of National Front renegade Shapour Bakhtiar, none made that choice, then or later. Later on, when the most serious confrontation up to that time played itself out in September and October, certainly the National Front and to a lesser extent the Liberation Movement had second thoughts and were more willing to work out some kind of adjustment either with the Shah or directly with the army. The moderate secular leaders were faced with the dilemma of all middle-of-the-road forces caught up in a revolutionary situation. How much revolution is enough? After aligning themselves with the Mujahidin, a larger, more radical militant faction within the coalition, at first the moderates were unwilling, then unable later, to put the brakes on the disintegrative process they had helped set in motion that was destroying the Shah's authority and legitimacy. They had been outsmarted by their less sophisticated but shrewder colleagues.

The only other organized group with military strength of its own was the Fedayeen, itself fragmented. At least two, possibly three separate but large Fedayeen groups cooperated with each other most of the time. In the mid-1970s they needed aid, both monetary and training, and received it from Palestinian groups, the Libyans, and particularly the Mujahidin. While the Fedayeen has fewer followers than the Mujahidin, it is superbly organized. It consistently harassed the regime, suffering many casualties from 1970 to 1978 when the prospects for ousting the monarch were dim.

In the months prior to the overthrow of the Shah the Fedayeen spearheaded raids on police stations, enhancing its prestige within the coalition. Flushed with its success as a "revolutionary vanguard," it decided to control Tehran by taking over key parts of the city. A Fedayeen unit led the attack on the United States embassy on February 14 and united with other Fedayeen to attack the television station that evening. Regardless of previous differences, for the next three nights all Fedayeen factions engaged in shootouts against members of the ubiquitous neighborhood Islamic committees. The result was a decimated Fedayeen organizational structure and vastly heightened fundamentalist suspicions of the ultimate intentions of the left. Undoubtedly, this impetuous adventure cost the organization a more prominent role in post-revolutionary takeover politics.

Threatened with destruction by its religious compatriots, the Fedayeen retreated from its posture of extreme militancy. From March to August it concentrated on converting itself from a mere paramilitary force into a political movement that concentrated on economic issues — the need for labor participation in management through the full nationalization of industry and banking and the value of collectivization in agriculture. It has always sought a classless society, including the complete destruction of the army and its replacement by a "people's militia." Under its plan, all foreign workers, particularly European and American professionals, would be expelled. Its heavy emphasis on freedom of the press, speech, and assembly is intended to insure its continued access to the political arena.

The Fedayeen opposed the creation of an Islamic Republic, which enraged Khomeini loyalists and eventually drove the group underground. After that, once again the Fedayeen reverted to opposition tactics, concentrating on expanding and strengthening its organization and preparing for what it calls "Iran's second revolution," which would complete the radical transformation of society begun in 1979. The organization was in full agreement with the Mujahidin on the necessity of keeping the American hostages and urged that they be put on trial for spying, not so much to humiliate the United States, but to keep Iran in constant turmoil and to better its own chance of coming to power. From this perspective the United States played into its hands by freezing Iran's assets, imposing sanctions, and forcing an economic blockade. The Iran-Iraq war was also a godsend, for it enabled the Fedayeen to picture itself as truly patriotic defenders of the country, to blame defeats and economic hardships on the inadequacy of the Khomeini regime, and to discredit the military effectiveness of the Revolutionary Guards. Since the revolutionary takeover the Fedayeen has continually been confronted with the dilemma of whether to work within the Islamic political system or to challenge it from without.

The Tudeh Party shares Fedayeen views on domestic policy, but it is much more sympathetic to the U.S.S.R. in foreign affairs. In an effort to make itself more acceptable to the majority and to shuck the onus of being a Soviet puppet, the party accepted the Islamic Republic, though Tudeh leaders regard the present government as merely the first step in a true socialist revolution. The Soviet connection provides the advantages of funds, modest protection, and psychological support, but it also means the party is deeply distrusted by the Fedayeen. In fact, since the revolutionary takeover the fragmentation of the left has continued. Several miniscule Marxist and Maoist parties—the People's Labor Party, the Iranian Socialist Party, and the Socialist Workers' Party—are too busy trying to establish themselves to consider joining with the others.

The left is biding its time, waiting to make a serious bid for power when conditions are right. The Fedayeen's premature attempt to capture all the marbles in February 1979 set it back significantly. Now its leadership is much more cautious about confrontation. Both the Fedayeen and the Tudeh Party oppose any measures that strengthen clerical domination and encourage political choices that maximize their own freedom to maneuver, such as advocating strikes and supporting the demands of tribal minorities for autonomy. If these policies also multiply the government's economic difficulties, so much the better.

The various ethnic groups—the Kurds, the Azarbaijanis, the Bakhtiaris, the Baluchis, and the Khuzistan Arabs—are also carefully monitoring events, waiting for the moment to strike. Two minorities already have attempted to break away. The Kurds maintain a rough form of independence within Iranian Kurdestan, but the Azarbaijani mini-revolt was put down, though without destroying the base of the movement, which remains loyal to Ayatollah Shariatmadari.

"What If . . ."

Often a choice with broad consequences is narrowly made, based on nothing more than a personality quirk or even random accident. To speculate on different choices that might have been made or different lines of behavior that might have been followed demonstrates the variety of possibilities. There is no doubt, for example, that the Shah's decision to speed up economic development dramatically set up the conditions for social disturbance leading to turmoil. His failure to explore the pitfalls of political liberalization before changing the way his regime operated opened the way for a revived challenge from those who had opposed him for years but who had been reduced to impotence by the success of the country's economic development. What if the Shah had developed a strategy to increase participation by tying the opposition into a reshaped political system?

He could have done so. There were enough competent establishment individuals urging him to use the Resurgence Party to mobilize the masses. The critical time came when the Shah was being pressed to allow the party to exercise real, if limited, power—something that had already started to a modest degree at the provincial and local levels. While he talked favorably about a full transition to a constitutional monarchy under his son, the Shah was a captive of his own inflexibility and past success at repressing dissent. Had he been willing to trust the confident establishment, the radical political demands of the left and the Islamic fundamentalists most probably would have been sidetracked and he would have remained in power.

Until the Jaleh Square riots in September 1978, the religious fundamentalists could have been kept away from the center of authority and power. If the political system had been freer, natural competitive instincts favoring skilled politicians wanting to compete in the electoral marketplace would have brought the modernizing secular opposition, rather than the radical clergy, to preeminence. Had the monarch not concealed his decision to liberalize, allowing the opposition to believe it had wrested a major concession from him, had he convened representatives from all the factions to discuss reform, the Shah could have guided political evolution while encouraging the dissidents to participate. In any absolutely free parliamentary election before Jaleh Square, nongovernment opposition would have won no more than 20 to 30 percent of the seats.

Such a policy would have worked if the Shah had been willing to set forth a clear program leading to a more liberal political system and then been willing to forcefully repress those who sought extra-constitutional change. The problem was partly one of timing—the last two years of his reign Iran's monarch never thought far enough ahead of immediate public fears and expectations to dominate events. Not just the dissidents, but also many others perceived the Shah as being reluctantly dragged into reforms from weakness, not intelligent foresight and strength. Political alterations carried out under controlled conditions would have changed attitudes of all the revolutionary factions. For example, when Bakhtiar finally accepted the Shah's mandate, the opposition was jolted by the prospect that one of their own had found the magic key to power. What if the Shah had offered even more liberal activists like Bazargan and Sanjabi a chance to participate before they had become completely tied to Khomeini? But to emphasize open, electoral political skills rather than conspiratorial, violent ones would have meant the Shah no longer would have had control over day-to-day politics. Mohammad Reza Pahlavi did not see the need to take such action until it was too late.

There has been speculation about two other avenues the Shah might have explored. One would have been a fully repressive response by the summer of 1978 to the revolutionary violence which had begun the preceding January. The second is whether the outcome of the revolutionary struggle would have been different if the monarch had accepted the proposals for a regency council, which he approved in December 1978 and then rejected almost immediately. In the first instance, there is little doubt that if the Shah had shown a willingness early on to stamp out any violent challenge to civil order with massive force, including the execution or long-term imprisonment of the perpetrators, the result would have been quite different. Had he ordered the army and SAVAK to quash those organizations which opted for violence while simultaneously opening up the political system, this act would have placed the "carrot and the stick" in proper relationship to each other. After Jaleh Square, if the monarch had ordered the security forces to take into custody all those involved in this direct challenge to authority, it would have reinforced the power of the moderate secular dissidents at the expense of the radicals.

Probably the last chance the Shah had to grasp firm control of events occurred after the massive riots two months later on November 5, which nearly gutted the British embassy and large areas of downtown Tehran. That night, if he had imposed a truly forceful martial law administration, including the authority to shoot to kill, it would have made clear the preconditions for restoring enough order to make meaningful compromise possible. The vast majority of the population was expecting a swift, decisive official reaction to the continuing public disorder. When the Shah failed to respond vigorously, his people thought he was abdicating his responsibilities as a national leader.

The Shah felt that the wrath of his Western allies, particularly the

United States, would cascade upon him if he enforced such action. Whether true or not, self-preservation would seem to be a higher goal than solidarity with an ally, however important. In fact, the United States did nothing more specific than indicate to the monarch that he should do what he had to in order to maintain public tranquility. In his phone call to the Shah after Jaleh Square, President Carter expressed the hope that political liberalization would still continue, but this was never linked to whether or not force should be used to protect the integrity of the country. The real problem was that by September the monarch had only a disintegrating political system that was becoming unacceptable to a sizable minority of his countrymen to protect, and no guidelines to show when to draw the line against violent activity. When the president of a neighboring country visited the Shah in December 1978, he advised the monarch: "Shoot 700 mullahs and end this business." By that time, however, the Shah was physically weak and profoundly depressed. Mohammad Reza Pahlavi suspected that his cause was already lost and passed over the remark without comment.

What if the Shah had accepted a regency council? By December 1978 this would have been a real compromise effort, credible to both secular and religious moderates as well as to many of the elite. The pressure would have been on Khomeini to abandon his stubborn insistence on eliminating the Shah or else risk breaking up revolutionary unity. If the Shah had not only accepted the regency council but made it clear that he was prepared to crush opponents of the idea, this shift in position would have changed everyone's calculations. At a minimum, it would have strengthened the hand of the Liberation Movement vis-à-vis its Islamic fundamentalist allies with respect to differences in revolutionary policy.

Then there is the haunting memory of supposed military capabilities. What if it had taken over, in either September or November 1978 or January 1979? If the armed forces had perpetrated a coup against Prime Minister Sharif-Emami after Jaleh Square and crushed the resistance which followed, rough order would have been restored but the political challenge to the regime would not have been eliminated. If the new government leaders the military would have installed could have followed up with a reform program offering the dissidents ample access to the political system, such a coup might have eventually led to stability. If not carried out until November, the cost would have been substantially higher, but if pushed with vigor such a takeover would have checked the revolutionaries' rush to confrontation and bought time. By December the possibility of using stiff repression successfully was disappearing. Attempting to dismantle the Tassua and Ashura marches would have produced tens of thousands of casualties and triggered a prolonged and messy civil war.

There is one other "might have been" for the military. Khomeini and the revolutionaries carefully refrained from directly attacking the armed forces as an institution right up to the eve of victory. Had General Gharabaghi been able to convince the army to support Bazargan against Bakhtiar in February 1979, the destruction of the military probably could have been avoided. The Shah's generals would have been summarily retired or left the country voluntarily. Thus the armed forces would have remained strong enough as an institution to have prevented dismemberment and would have provided Bazargan the leverage he desperately needed when dealing with his more radical religious allies.

What if the Shah had executed Khomeini in 1963 rather than exiling him, or had allowed those who wished to kill him in 1978 to proceed? Had Khomeini died in 1963, he would have been an honored martyr, but little more. In 1978, only if Khomeini's death had gone hand-in-hand with a decisive effort on the part of the Shah to recapture the political initiative would the outcome have changed significantly. Given the Shah's other weaknesses, the Ayatollah's demise in 1978 might not have changed the fact of the revolution, but more moderate leaders would have emerged triumphant.

Other "what ifs . . ." are more problematical. Had the secular dissidents and moderate religious leaders joined together and pressed the Shah for reform in mid-1978, the worst excesses of the Islamic Republic might have been prevented. But this would have been difficult, requiring the monarch to indicate publicly his willingness to make serious compromises and to behave less autocratically. For the secular moderates, to overcome solidly grounded fears that the Shah was not to be trusted on the hopeful supposition that things might turn out badly for their radical allies would have required extraordinary prescience.

When Bakhtiar became prime minister, the chances for the moderate secular dissidents to ally themselves with the military improved. There were some efforts in that direction on both sides, but little awareness of how important such ties might become. What if the moderates had cooperated with the military? If they had done so, they could have avoided their slow fall from power. Ultimately, the moderate secular opposition wound up on the outside looking in, even though in the beginning Bazargan, Sanjabi, and the other leaders of the Liberation Movement in the cabinet tried hard to govern the country without reference to Khomeini and the Mujahidin. The evisceration of Bazargan's power, well under way by late March, and the departure of Sanjabi on April 15 marked the failure of the moderates to reestablish governmental control. The seizure of the hostages in November merely ratified Bazargan's political impotence and brought about his rapid departure as prime minister.

The remaining "what if . . ." from an Iranian perspective concerns the left. What if the Fedayeen had not tried to seize power the nights of February 14 through 18? Would it have been more successful in the long run if it had worked within the revolutionary coalition instead, husbanding its strength and extending its influence and control? In any case, a clash between the Mujahidin and the Fedayeen would have eventually taken place. Fedayeen doctrine is too fundamentally opposed to clerical rule for this uncomfortable alliance to have lasted very long. Had the Fedayeen been more patient, had the leftist leadership been more farsighted generally, it could have been the dominant power in Iran today. It may yet be. Its organizational capacities have steadily improved and its military wing, if not equal to the Revolutionary Guards, is certainly not far behind it. Nor is it burdened with the official responsibilities of maintaining public order and fighting the war with Iraq, as the Mujahidin has had to be.

At the time of the Fedayeen-Mujahidin confrontation in February 1979, the Islamic leaders had the entire remaining revolutionary coalition and the vast majority of the population on their side. Within 18 months after they took over the government, the Fedayeen, the National Front, the National Democratic Front, and Ayatollah Shariatmadari's Islamic Peoples' Republican Party all found themselves outside the fence, under consistently vicious attack from members of Khomeini's Islamic Republican Party.

In reviewing the choices made which shaped events, it is hard to avoid noticing the naïveté of all concerned, particularly the Shah. Only the Islamic fundamentalists have fulfilled their expectations of power, though they are still groping for the way to govern effectively. The radical clerics understand the political uses of power better than their opponents. The weakness in their decision making process is their near ignorance of modern economics and administration coupled with their desire to hew to eight-century ecclesiastical practice.

One other set of decisions had an important, though secondary, impact on the Iranian saga. The American policy and decision making process also affected the evolution of the revolution.

Chapter Fourteen

★

Choice and Change:
The United States

"No one covered himself in glory." These words, uttered by a frustrated participant, go a long way toward explaining the American policy and decision making process before, during, and after the revolutionary crisis. Given longstanding U.S. involvement in that country, and especially because of deep-seated Iranian perceptions of its role, the United States greatly influenced internal developments between 1953 and the present. Well before the hostages were taken, America's proclivity to get involved in what Iranians considered domestic struggles, plus U.S. positions on issues such as human rights, had affected how Persians viewed their own situation.

Starting with the Carter administration particularly, various Washington officials espoused many different conceptions of what American objectives in Iran should be. The advocates jostled to have their prospective policies receive prime consideration at the top. Because of this internecine struggling, recognizing and defining a constantly changing situation like the turmoil before the revolutionary takeover led to even greater controversy, which inhibited policy and decision making. Under the circumstances, obtaining adequate information and especially analyzing it quickly enough to be useful became a major difficulty. Also present were the problems inherent in dealing with any foreign policy organization: fragmentation of control, the isolation of key policy and decision makers, debilitating intra-bureaucratic conflict, plus the more traditional theme of the field reporter (embassy) versus the home office (Department of State). All in all, particularly from 1970 to the present, the American policy and decision process in action was less than adequate. "The responsibility for failure seems widely enough shared to encourage some general sense of humility."[1]

283

Recognizing the Problem

The conundrum that became revolutionary Iran emerged swiftly, but with little clear warning. Events outran the ability of those involved to keep abreast of them. Even the opposition, which maintained greater control over the pace than any other participants, found itself caught up and pushed along by the onrushing accidents of history—the Abadan fire, the Jaleh Square shootings, and the Tabriz riot. It was even more true for policy makers in Washington, under time pressure, as always, to deal with competing problems. The President and his advisors were concerned with what appeared to be much more important problems, particularly the SALT II negotiations. In the crucial time frame of August to December 1978, there was an additional worry—the outcome of the Egyptian-Israeli peace talks at Camp David preoccupied policy and decision makers. In retrospect, it is easy to suggest more attention should have been paid to the highly volatile situation in Iran. One can sympathize with Assistant Secretary of State for Near Eastern and South Asian Affairs, Harold Saunders, who mused less than 48 hours after the Shah's permanent departure that the real need was for a crystal ball to identify in advance which of several concurrent problems require instant attention.[2]

The accelerating press of events also overran the organizational capacities of the foreign affairs bureaucracy—the State Department, the National Security Council, the C.I.A., and the Pentagon—to handle the unique questions posed by the Iranian crisis. In the best of circumstances it takes time to galvanize behemoths to act. This was particularly true concerning Iran, where conflicting views on human rights, military sales, and regional security frequently clashed. Different participants identified with different outlooks. Liberals on the National Security Council staff and in the State Department's Bureau of Human Rights and Humanitarian Affairs dwelt on Iran's inadequate concept of civil rights and the country's authoritarian political system. Presidential assistant Brzezinski, Defense Department officials, and most State Department bureaucrats were primarily concerned about continued stability in the Persian Gulf and America's regional defense needs. Private U.S. corporations wanted to maintain their profitable business connections, yet organized opposition movements within the United States castigated Washington for dealing with the Shah's regime at all. These divergent perspectives, plus the open style of the Carter administration which encouraged multiple advocacy of different policy options—some diametrically opposed—increased policy and decision making complexities, if they did not actually deadlock the decision making process.[3]

The U.S. also found itself without the leverage it had formerly enjoyed either to exert pressure on the Shah or to begin a dialogue with him on the larger issues of where Iran was headed. In the post-Vietnam period, when the thrust of American foreign policy shifted away from extensive involvement abroad, the ability of the United States to force the monarch to face important considerations disappeared. It became much more difficult to propose and advocate a "maximalist" strategy of engagement either to shape social development in Iran or to induce the Shah to do so.

The deadlock over what to do produced resistance to doing anything at all. In the past the U.S. foreign policy establishment has been accused of being too action-oriented. Take, for example, President Ford's decision to send marines to free the crew of the U.S.S. *Mayaguez* after the ship was seized by the Cambodians in May 1975. In the case of Iran the reverse was true. Because of the intense controversy over what choices should be made, the President adopted a different approach. Carter's caution reinforced the tendency to avoid setting firm policy guidelines that might foreclose an option before sufficient information could indicate a clear, acceptable course. Reduced to its essentials, President Carter decided to leave the crisis to the Shah to handle. He hoped for the best and got the worst.

Having decided that "the Shah knows best," the administration drifted into a "minimalist" strategy of as little direct involvement as possible. Only tactical choices within that framework could be made: whether to try and stiffen the Shah's spine with words, whether or not to encourage him to avoid bloodshed, and eventually what kind of relations to seek with the takeover government.[4] What creates uneasiness is the strong suspicion that, given its historic assets, the United States should have been able to do much more than it did to help shape the outcome. There were points at which America could have strongly influenced, if not decisively altered, the consequences of specific events. After the January 1978 riots in Qom and the destruction in Tabriz in February, or even as late as April when continuous demonstrations became the norm, the administration had enough evidence to call for a serious review of the broadest aspects of Iranian policy, not merely to supply tear gas and other riot gear. The U.S. foreign affairs bureaucracy tends to focus on the here-and-now (as it did in this case) with alacrity and skill, but there is much room for improvement when dealing with broader trends over time and relating them to potential policy options in incipient revolutionary situations.

Defining the Situation

A congressional staff study has identified one of the problems with intelligence gathering about the Iranian situation as a lack of timely upper echelon guidance to those at lower organizational levels. There is always a dynamic interplay between what senior officials think they want and what they are likely to get, and any confusion is quickly reflected at the top.[5] In November 1978 the President himself opened the debate on the adequacy of U.S. intelligence and analysis by sending identical letters to Vance, Brzezinski, Brown, and Turner complaining that American information about developments in Iran had ineffectually predicted the Shah's burgeoning problems. Controversy centered around whether the embassy had adequate contacts with the opposition and whether State Department and C.I.A. analyses were sufficiently perspicacious.[6] Congressional hearings dealt with this situation in January 1979, just after the Shah departed and the triumph of the revolutionaries. At these sessions Assistant Secretary of State Saunders suggested that to focus only on raw intelligence was a mistake:

> On your first question, Mr. Chairman, the issue of whether our intelligence was adequate, let me say this: I don't believe it is accurate or indeed fair to the intelligence community to attribute the problem of American perceptions of events in Iran to a failure of intelligence. I think the problem is a much broader one than that.
> Analysts in the governmental community, in the academic community, over the years have pointed to the potential vulnerabilities in the Iranian political and social evolution.
> The problem is not to have identified what could go wrong in Iran. A lot of people did that. The problem that we did not deal with adequately—and, indeed, maybe can not be dealt with adequately—is the problem of predicting that certain events will come together at a particular time to produce a particular result. For instance, I was the director of [the Bureau of] Intelligence and Research before coming to this job, and during my tenure there we had on several occasions members of the academic community come into the government—as we do from time to time—to sit down and talk about Iran; and we all agreed there were problems in Iran, and we identified the problems, much as I have described them in my statement. But almost no one in that group, I think, could honestly claim today that he could have forseen that Iran would be in January of 1979 where Iran is today.[7]

From the standpoint of intelligence gathering, there never is enough information to eliminate all ambiguity. In the case of Iran, however, despite the general decrease in reporting capability since 1967 because of the reduced number of officers assigned to monitor political affairs, there was sufficient information sent to Washington to suggest problems were developing. Complaints to the contrary, the embassy was continually improving contacts with the opposition. As the political pace quickened in 1977, the mission picked up hints that the dissidents were growing more powerful and began early to cultivate the organizers. Ambassador Sullivan supported this endeavor from the beginning of his tour, as did the White House. The embassy diversified its sources, and by September 1978 Farsi-speaking officers knew personally at least one leader of all the dissident groups except the communists behind the Tudeh Party and the most radical Fedayeen faction. By mid-1978 even the Shah understood the merit of this policy. Given the reluctance of the opposition to deal with "the hated imperialist agents," the number of contacts made was impressive.

There were the inevitable bare spots in overall coverage, but only one worth mentioning. Until March 1978 there were no direct encounters between embassy officers and religious leaders. The first face-to-face discussion with influential Khomeini protégés did not occur until January 1979, when Stanley Escudero, a Farsi-speaking officer with good religious contacts who had served in Tehran from 1971 to 1975 and who came back to Iran on temporary duty just prior to the revolutionary takeover, called on Ayatollah Beheshti. Ambassador Sullivan and I met with Ayatollah Moussavi that same month. Actually, lack of contact with Khomeini followers was less a problem than it might seem. Until the takeover, even the most negative ayatollahs were in close agreement with Liberation Movement policies. In response to American overtures, these clerics indicated that U.S. exchanges with Liberation Movement officials would be sufficient liaison for them. Their attitude was not unusual, since both religious and secular radicals were extremely reluctant to have even a minimal connection with any Western mission, especially the U.S. embassy. As for the more moderate religious figures and their supporters, it took time and careful preparation to induce them to talk to embassy officers, let alone engage in full and honest discussion. Abol Hassan Bani-Sadr met with U.S. officials while he was in Paris with Ayatollah Khomeini but declined or cancelled at least three luncheon invitations in the first months after his return to Iran. Leftist extremists like the most radical Fedayeen faction also consistently rejected any overtures.

The only roadblock to meeting the members of the opposition was imposed by Washington after the Shah's regime began to disintegrate.

Ambassador Sullivan suggested in general terms by cable on November 11, 1978, and specifically by phone December 15, that an emissary meet with Khomeini in Paris. Former Ambassador to Afghanistan Theodore Eliot, a Farsi-speaking specialist in Iranian affairs, was selected to meet with the Ayatollah. His trip was abruptly cancelled, reportedly by Brzezinski, after Carter had met with European leaders on January 5 and 6 at the "summit" on the Caribbean island of Guadeloupe. While there, the President was assured by the French that they had excellent contacts in the Khomeini entourage and further American overtures would be unnecessary. By this time even the Shah was appalled by the U.S. refusal to meet with Khomeini. Bewildered, he told Sullivan, "How can you expect to have any influence with these people if you won't meet with them?"[8]

It is important to remember that until the Shah instituted his policy of liberalization in 1977, the opposition was weak, divided, and unimportant. Given the constraints on manpower and time at the embassy, it would have been imprudent to waste limited resources meeting with dissidents before then. This does not negate accurate criticism of American inability to commit adequate resources to reporting and to shift personnel quickly to wherever they are needed. It does suggest that the responsibility must be more widely shared, since the State Department does not have the last word on funds available for resource allocation. The congressional budget process can delay major changes requiring additional monies for as much as a year under the best of circumstances and even prevent them entirely if the legislators do not share the perceptions of the State Department. In the case of the oil-producing states in the Middle East, the U.S. has been very slow to shift its overall emphasis to take into account their increased importance. Such adjustments go beyond the mere reassignment of a few more junior officers abroad, or the dispatch of additional temporary personnel to the beleaguered country. In the heat of a fast-moving crisis, brand new relationships can be nurtured but not fully exploited.

At the peak of the revolution the embassy and therefore Washington were receiving adequate information, but how it was being used was not impressive. Both the diplomatic mission and the Bureau of Intelligence and Research in Washington had signaled that trouble was ahead. A ten-page analysis of the opposition written by the embassy's political section in July 1977 correctly identified Bakhtiar, Bazargan, Khomeini, and Beheshti as the major actors in the drama that would begin unfolding a year later. While one C.I.A. report completed in August 1978 is often cited because it said, "Iran is not in a revolutionary or even a pre-revolutionary situation," there were other studies that did recognize growing economic unrest, religious discontent, rampant corruption, and SAVAK brutality as increasingly important destabilizing influences. The difficulty was in assessing the relative importance of these factors and ascertaining how circumstances could combine to make the situation extremely volatile. In retrospect, though it is clear now how each event fed upon the next, in November 1978 the situation remained ambiguous. Up until that time it was still possible for the Shah, or the military acting in his name, to negotiate a meaningful compromise with opposition leaders or to repress the revolution by force. The problem was that timely reaction to the fast-changing situation was impeded by unresolved conflict within the administration on what U.S. goals ought to be.

Two aspects of the developing crisis were undiscovered or underreported until too late. These were legitimate deficiencies in intelligence gathering. The first was the news of the Shah's lymphomatous cancer. Policy and decision makers would have been more alert to potential problems in 1977 or earlier if they had known that the monarch was being treated with debilitating medicines for a terminal disease. Not until October 1978 were they fully aware of this change in the Shah's potential ability to manage his country. When they finally knew about it, whether Washington clearly understood the seriousness of the monarch's ill health and diminished capacity and adequately considered this factor is an issue of judgment. Who is to blame for this lapse in vital information? The Shah? The C.I.A.? The embassy? The French government?

The second consideration involves more judgmental factors. As the Shah became depressed and retreated within himself, the question of his survival turned on whether and when he would use force against his antagonists. After the unrestrained rampage in Tehran November 5, Ambassador Sullivan concluded that the Shah had no stomach for repressive confrontation. Therefore he advocated that prominent U.S. officials should contact Khomeini and act as "honest brokers" between the monarch and the revolutionaries. Unfortunately, Brzezinski already had convinced President Carter that the Shah, or at the very least the military without him, could forestall a revolutionary takeover.[9] In view of Brzezinski's attitude and the advice Carter received from the French at the meeting in Guadeloupe, the President was unsympathetic to Sullivan's idea.

The monarch himself had harsh words for the United States, saying he did not receive support when he needed it most. He spoke disparagingly of Ambassador Sullivan, who asked him point-blank in January 1979 when he would be leaving the country. Perhaps the Shah might have reacted differently and been more open with his ally if the Carter administration had not harped continuously on the lack of human rights in his country. He also might have been more forceful in the fall of 1978 if the American government had hinted more strongly that he use military force to repress the opposition. On the other hand, the Shah firmly believed that if the incipient revolution was violently suppressed with many casualties, the Carter administration would turn its back on him.

Whether it was consistent or not with American values to advocate such drastic measures or whether it was true that Carter would have washed his hands of the Shah if he had attempted a serious counterthrust, the monarch's conviction that this was so merely underlined the absence of bold leadership as his kingship was coming to an end. Only the Shah himself is to blame. He cannot escape final responsibility for his own behavior despite his uncertainties about America. If he did not have the sense of destiny and the iron will to impose himself on history in a manner similar to Cuba's Castro, Algeria's Boumedienne, or Chile's Pinochet, he cannot fault the United States, which supported him to its own disadvantage until and beyond his downfall. Perhaps his ungracious attempt to gloss over his own flaws by criticizing his friends is the final legacy of America's intimate relationship with Iran during the reign of Mohammad Reza Pahlavi.

Choosing Between Alternatives

Given the structural limitations on intelligence gathering and the ambiguity of the situation, the American government compiled surprisingly accurate information and reasonable analysis about major events, but three factors prevented translating raw data into 20/20 hindsight and perfect decisions. First was the difficulty in diagnosing the potential of religion as a political weapon. Westerners, even those living in Iran, were unaware that stress and anxiety caused by frustration over economic dislocation and corruption could be channeled into a popular movement using Islamic symbolism to generate explosive power. Second, the rapid development of the revolutionary organization in 1978 from rudimentary demonstrators in January and February to well-disciplined cadres by September exceeded the capacity of foreign decision makers to outline a problem, resolve uncertainties, argue possible solutions, and propose and carry out timely action. Third, ambiguity, weak conceptualization, and the pace of events all combined to multiply organizational problems within the U.S. bureaucracy and to magnify existing conflicts between different decision making groups maintaining divergent basic beliefs. There was no watershed event to unify perceptions, such as Pearl Harbor did for World War II. Nor was there any dramatic revelation, such as the satellite photographs that forced President Kennedy's decision to confront the U.S.S.R. in October 1962 over its placement of offensive missiles in Cuba.

The most difficult of these three elements to understand is the political ramifications of a religious movement such as Khomeini's. Insights into the deeper recesses of the Shiite Islamic political-religious structure did not come easily. What the embassy was sending back to Washington was certainly no worse and may have been better than what other experts in Persian and Middle Eastern politics were thinking, since no one fully comprehended the dynamics of what was happening. One reason is because the Islamic movement took pains to mask its ultimate intentions so that its secular allies would not break away prematurely.[10] For that matter, most of Iran's middle class also did not really understand what was happening to their country. Many of those who are now exiles remain as mystified about what went on as the boxer punched on his blind side.

Even many experts who made an effort to understand the dynamics of the Khomeini movement were misled concerning what the Ayatollah's attitude would be after he gained power. For example, Princeton political science professor Richard Falk, who visited Khomeini in Paris and wrote and spoke out extensively before, during, and after the revolutionary takeover, argued that the Ayatollah's theocracy would not necessarily be anti-West, and would be a moderate government based on social justice.[11] Falk stopped speaking out about the situation in Iran only after the hostage seizure. In another example, despite the obviously expanding anti-American ecclesiastical authoritarianism, Henry Precht, who had served in the Tehran embassy from 1972 to 1976 and was now director of the Iran Working Group in the State Department, advocated policies based on the belief that Khomeini was a moderate. Even in the face of countless rejections of U.S. and U.N. overtures to resolve the hostage crisis, the State Department's basic policy thrust was to meet Iranian demands in order to get the captives back. It was precisely the kind of approach guaranteed to encourage holding up the U.S. to ransom, and that is what the revolutionary government's insistence on $24 billion in exchange for the Americans amounted to. Such faulty perceptions were based on the inability of knowledgeable Westerners to place Khomeini's unique conception of politics and its relationship to his religion in proper perspective.

Problems of understanding were not one-sided. Though the West had difficulty comprehending fundamentalist thought, the Islamic radicals were also guilty of completely misinterpreting American signals. The "Followers of the Imam's Line" who occupied the embassy truly believed that America would force the Shah to return to Iran. Not until the former monarch moved to Egypt—three months after he actually left the United States—did they finally discard this notion. The radical clerics were no less misguided. Over the months they convinced themselves that President Carter would accept any deal to get the hostages back, no matter how humiliating. Iran's demand in December 1980 for $24 billion in "guarantees" was presented as the "final offer." Yet faced with a unanimous negative reaction in America, from Secretary of State Muskie and President-elect Reagan down to the man in the street, Prime Minister Rajai let it be known within three days that his government would listen to counterproposals. After the revolutionary takeover in February 1979, mutual feelings of mistrust between the United States and Iran grew so pervasive that normal diplomatic negotiations proved progressively more impossible to carry out.

As events began moving faster, particularly throughout 1978, the rapidity of change multiplied the difficulty in accurately educating the official community. As early as 1976 a C.I.A. study had predicted trouble, but the time frame was uncertain. Because the U.S. had come to depend on Iran as a valuable ally in the Persian Gulf, short-range optimism prevailed. "Fragmentary tactical indicators of success tend to override more cautious strategic estimates."[12] Long-term warnings made good background reading, but faded into insignificance when the latest cable from Tehran or the consulates was being digested.

As the Shah's regime was collapsing, particularly after the Abadan fire on August 19, 1978, there was continued uncertainty concerning the depth of change and the possible reaction. Events piled one on top of another—the installation of the Sharif-Emami government, the attempts to appease strikers, the expansion of economic paralysis to the whole country, and the gradual shift of opinion against the Shah because he did not act decisively. By the time Washington was setting up special committees in November, the monarch had been trying for some time to negotiate with the opposition. George Ball's recommendation that the Shah move to a broader based government was given to the President in early December, an analysis months behind events. In another example, as Brzezinski sought to rally the military in January—a reasonable option only until November—the disintegration of the Iranian armed forces was already terminal.

There is a natural bureaucratic drag factor in accepting new information about changing conditions, especially if the intelligence conflicts with previous data. The single cataclysmic event that might have galvanized policy and decision makers and short-circuited the time-consuming process of bureaucratic consensus-building never took place. There were, of course, many important bench-marks in 1978—the riots in Qom in January, the major disturbance in February in Tabriz, arson in the Abadan movie house in August, the shootings at Jaleh Square in September, the burning of substantial parts of Tehran in November, and the massive Tassua and Ashura marches in December. Each in and of itself was not enough to penetrate the attention threshold of high-level officials serving in Washington's foreign affairs bureaucracy.

Those closer to the scene foresaw the danger earlier, though warnings from the embassy and the media were not sufficient to change things. Secretary of State Vance and Assistant Secretary Saunders were preoccupied with the Camp David talks from September to December 1978, and the President always has too little time for anything unless it poses a visible, immediate crisis or is forcefully drawn to his attention. Bluntly stated, information from Iran simply did not justify presidential-level attention until too late. Had unequivocal knowledge of the Shah's deteriorating physical and mental condition been available earlier, the equation would have been different. Policy and decision makers at all levels undoubtedly would have revised their estimates of the monarch's capacity to act and moved more expeditiously to review matters at a high enough level to insure the results would be looked at. As it happened, America's historical connection with Iran, particularly its close ties with the Shah, weighed heavily on the side of inertia in the early phases of the revolutionary upheaval. When senior officials finally became more concerned in November 1978, the revolutionaries already had made an issue of the American presence in Iran and consistent U.S. support of the Shah. Washington found itself on the defensive, and also increasingly more worried about the safety of its citizens in Iran, adding another complicating factor to the policy and decision making process.

In the absence of any event or information compelling policy and decision makers to agree, the views of officials tend toward basic stereotypes. "Groupthink" sets in, a situation in which those with like-minded opinions form a coterie nearly impervious to challenge.[13] When the U.S. government was dealing with Iran, such a syndrome developed several times between 1972 and 1979. It became a serious problem soon after Carter took office in January 1977, particularly in terms of the relationship between the advocates for improved human rights in Iran and the proponents of expanded military security in the

Persian Gulf region. David Aaron, Jessica Tuchman, and Robert Hunter, presidential appointees to the National Security Council staff, urged that the United States shift its attitude toward Iran and "rough the Shah up a bit" on civil and political rights issues. These individuals insisted that the United States could not afford to be associated with the excesses of the regime and should distance itself from the political practices of the Iranian government.[14]

Within the State Department the newly established Office of Human Rights, under political appointee Patt Derian, welcomed these views. There is no evidence that the anti-Shah faction wished to cause the monarch's political demise. Nor did that attitude permeate the foreign affairs establishment, since at no time did the State Department's Bureau of Near Eastern and South Asian Affairs agree with the analyses of the National Security Council and the Office of Human Rights. The problem continued to fester because there was no formal policy review to assimilate the new ideas or at least to harmonize thinking on the subject, let alone to change existing policy. The embassy, for example, was not asked to comment on whether it would be better for the U.S. if the Shah were replaced until January 1979. By then, from the American standpoint, a viable alternative no longer existed.

What bureaucrats focus on, however, can change the content of policy, if not its form. Ambassador Sullivan and the Shah had many conversations about human rights in Iran. Embassy officers broached these concerns to other officials in the government and to Resurgence Party leaders. The talks were always general in nature and did not include the broader questions of political stability. Nevertheless, the Shah responded to these overtures and similar ones from private organizations such as Amnesty International and the International Commission of Jurists and began liberalizing opportunities for political activity. Even so, negative evaluations of the regime by individuals and groups concentrating exclusively on human rights continued up to the time the monarch was overthrown. Yet no civil rights advocates ever questioned whether Khomeini's policy on the same subject might be antediluvian. That rude awakening would come later.

Opinions on human rights espoused by many policy and decision makers were more a function of their emotional stereotype and their subsequent bureaucratic struggles than the result of rational policy decision. Those whose main concerns were Iran's value as an ally and its strategic position—the Defense Department, State Department Middle East specialists, and C.I.A. analysts—argued the necessity of supporting the Shah to enhance U.S. aspirations for regional stability and to maximize American access to sites allowing effective surveillance of the Soviet Union by electronic means. Aggressive advocacy by one group immediately triggered a reflex response in the other. The dynamics of the conflict over human rights inhibited widespread recognition of rapidly changing conditions. The sharp criticism the old-line bureaucrats endured from the newcomers emphasizing humanitarian policies retarded the mental process of adjusting to change. Instead of leading to a reanalysis, differences of opinion became conflicts between true believers—the one side lauding the opposition, the other defending the Shah's value to the United States. Neither side focused on the consequences of a possible revolutionary process.

In December 1978 one counterview to the embassy and press assertions that the regime was on the verge of collapse was Brzezinski's strongly held belief that the Shah or the military without the Shah could hold firm, by coup if necessary. Although Ambassador Sullivan had told Washington repeatedly that the armed forces were disintegrating and that chaos was coming, the President's national security advisor persisted in his view even as ARMISH-MAAG headquarters was being overrun by guerrillas. Part of the problem was that General Huyser's reports were more optimistic than what Sullivan was saying and that Ambassador Zahedi was working hard to convince Brzezinski and President Carter that the Shah would hold. Thus it was very late in the game, about the third week in December—too late to be really effective—that the National Security Council staff swung to favoring Bakhtiar, the prime minister appointed by the Shah. Although the embassy and the C.I.A. both warned that a scenario including Bakhtiar had little chance of succeeding, it remained the keystone of U.S. policy.[15] What should have been happening by then was the administration's acknowledgment of the inevitability of a post-Shah regime. Hope obscured reality.

Inaccurate assumptions also influenced American post-revolutionary takeover choices, particularly with respect to the Bazargan government. The size and importance of U.S. military programs in Iran, the need to protect the safety of sensitive equipment, and the desire to continue an American presence dictated that there be immediate reconciliation between the leaders in Washington and Tehran. Prime Minister Bazargan's positive response to a U.S. willingness to forget the past, respect Iran's independence, and cooperate with the new government helped the U.S. to misconstrue how weak that government actually was, as well as the depth of anti-U.S. sentiment among the radical clerics and the Mujahidin that controlled the now feeble military. The decisions of the U.S.

government to begin reissuing visas in Tehran in June 1979 (operations had been suspended after the mini-takeover of the embassy on February 14), to resume shipping military spare parts, and especially to allow the Shah into the United States for medical treatment were all based on the assumption that the United States could deal with Khomeini by working with the revolutionary moderates.

Farsi-speaking embassy officers who had recently returned to Washington warned of the dangers of moving too fast to suit the Islamic radicals and the left, but they were discounted as being either soured by the revolution or insufficiently sympathetic to the tribulations of Iran's new government. For the Carter administration to back the moderates uncritically had become an article of faith. Such an attitude was helpful in dealing with the Bazargan government, but those who supported the policy of maximum accommodation with the new Iran used it as an excuse to downplay signs of looming difficulties. Both analysis and policy and decision making suffered. This syndrome was reinforced not only by Washington's bias, but by the decision made in late February to gradually replace all American diplomats who had been posted to Tehran during the Shah's regime. The result was that in the months before the hostages would be seized in November only two State Department political officers remained who had been through the revolutionary takeover in February, and both of them had served in the consulates, not in the capital.

The belief that the United States could deal with the revolutionaries in terms of traditional diplomacy continued to underlie policy even after the Americans were captured. The State Department was committed to obtaining the release of the prisoners through either formal or informal diplomatic channels. Some unusual venues were used, including dispatching former Attorney General Ramsey Clark to Tehran two days after the hostages were seized only to have the mission be aborted in Istanbul when the Revolutionary Council refused to allow Clark's plane into the country. In another case involving presidential assistant Hamilton Jordan, director of the Iran Working Group Henry Precht, and the French lawyer Christian Bourget and his associate Hector Villalon, there were several meetings to arrange a deal. By April all efforts to deal directly with the Iranians through channels both normal and abnormal had fallen through, not to be reopened again until the Algerian diplomats would become successful intermediaries months later. A plausible argument can be made for the fact that the State Department could leave no stone unturned in seeking the hostages' immediate release. The emotional commitment of the President and Secretary of

State Vance to that position, however, severely minimized the influence of Farsi-speaking State Department officials who had served in Tehran and were knowledgeable about Shiite politics in discussions about whether pressing to negotiate a settlement might be impossible or inappropriate.

How the Bureaucratic Structure Affected Choice

The prolonged revolutionary crisis shows how institutional arrangements and strong personal beliefs can badly skew otherwise accurate information and inhibit successful policy and decision making. The problems connected with the Iranian situation developed not because of specific intelligence failures, but because of the way the available data was used. In any bureaucracy, centralization and specialization and how these concepts fit within the hierarchy distinguish the institutional process from individual decision making. In an organization, leaders expand their ability to get information and prepare for action by directing others to respond to their needs. Specialization allows individuals to become in-depth experts and improve the overall knowledge of the organization. Centralization permits senior leadership to direct work, minimize unintended conflict, and coordinate the efforts of diverse work units. Using these principles, the foreign policy bureaucracy expands its ability to deal with diverse data, to establish rules (policies), to guide decisions, and to minimize uncertainty.[16]

America's foreign policy machinery encountered several traditional problems with respect to Iran. At critical times it had difficulty resolving uncertainty, the hierarchical system broke down to the point of fragmentation, and the senior leadership could not minimize conflict and resolve differences that impeded the development of a coherent, flexible policy in a fast-changing environment. As a result, too often the United States sent out murky diplomatic signals. Policy and decision makers found themselves responding to a series of specific situations in a pragmatic fashion not based on a comprehensive strategy. In every aspect of the seemingly unending crisis, doubts about what would be the correct course of action inhibited the President, Vance, and Saunders from exercising firmer leadership, reinforcing the difficulty in reducing confusion. One senior participant put it this way in the spring of 1980: "We certainly located an awful lot of trees, but some of us are still looking for the forest."

Organizational problems and the difficulty in assessing intelligence properly interacted to make the situation worse. Within the U.S. government, individuals and groups clung to their personal views or those of their organizational unit rather than evolving a unified policy outlook. Divisions within the National Security Council as well as differences between the embassy in Tehran and policy and decision makers in Washington dramatically illustrate this problem of fragmentation. Within the National Security Council, the group led by David Aaron, a protégé of Vice President Mondale, had taken a hard line against the Shah, favoring the dissidents. By December 1978 Brzezinski also considered the Shah a liability, but he wanted to ease out the monarch not by accommodating the Khomeini forces but by a military coup. At the very moment that the Iranian armed forces had all but collapsed and ARMISH-MAAG advisors were pinned down in the headquarters of the Supreme Commander's Staff, Deputy Secretary of State Warren Christopher called Ambassador Sullivan. Upon hearing that the army had fallen apart, Christopher asked for a "second opinion" and requested that he be connected to the head of ARMISH-MAAG, General Phillip Gast. The ambassador replied that the U.S. military group was cut off, unreachable. Christopher insisted on being put through. In exasperation, Sullivan replied, "Do you want me to give it to you in Polish [a reference to Brzezinski's interest in the matter]?"[17] Until the last minute (or beyond), the President's foreign affairs advisor believed that the army was capable of a coup, accepting the more optimistic reports of Huyser, who had warned that the army could restore order but not carry out a full political solution, rather than the pessimistic but more accurate reporting of the embassy and the C.I.A.

The special pleading of the State Department's Office of Human Rights, which gained additional power and prestige when it became a bureau in 1978, posed problems for the embassy all along. The diplomats knew that the more extreme positions of the human rights advocates at home were not geared to reality abroad. On the other hand, Derian and the committed ideologists around her considered the embassy officers "hopelessly stuffy" and "retrogressive fascists." A spirit of confrontation rather than cooperation dominated too much of the dialogue between Washington and Tehran.

The differences of opinion concerning human rights were relatively unimportant in themselves, but the opposing attitudes they engendered lingered, poisoning policy planning at other critical times—September and December 1978 and January and February 1979:

[General Robert] Huyser's reports were almost completely misleading and the real picture was that being painted by Ambassador Sullivan. . . . but this was a message that policymakers did not want to believe. . . . Sullivan had systematically underestimated the strength of the religious leaders in the spring and summer, why should Washington now listen to his alarms?[18]

In the ultimate insult, the embassy had been completely cut out of George Ball's policy review in December 1979, first hearing of his recommendations in the Paris edition of *The International Herald-Tribune.*

The revolution was coming to a head about the time the Ball report was made public and different organizational units developed two distinct options for handling the situation. One, advocated by Ambassador Sullivan and his staff, was based on their estimates of the Shah's decreased capacity to govern. They wanted the United States to become the honest broker and play the midwife to a deal between the opposition and the remnants of the regime, specifically the military. Such an effort would have made a smooth transition of power possible, preserving the basic structure of the armed forces, thus serving the vital interests of the U.S. as well as Iran. Implementing such a solution would have more likely favored the moderates in the revolutionary coalition rather than the extremists.

In the other scenario, worked out in rudimentary fashion by Brzezinski with help from the Pentagon, the U.S. would back the Iranian armed forces to defeat the revolutionaries. By the time Washington had developed this proposal, the opportunity had passed beyond the time (no later than November 1978) when it could have been successfully implemented.

Different elements of the foreign affairs bureaucracy advocated and planned for the contingencies they favored, at the same time trying to keep all options open as long as possible. As policy inconsistencies came to the attention of both the establishment and the opposition, they questioned America's sincerity and ultimate intentions. To quote Shapour Bakhtiar:

> When I was prime minister, the Americans at first supported my government, but after two or three weeks they began flirting with Khomeini. They were undecided about what to do, they changed opinions and tactics repeatedly, and in moments like those, hesitation is disastrous.[19]

Ambiguous Actions Make a Bad Situation Worse

As far back as the beginning of the revolutionary period, contradictory U.S. moves reinforced the ambiguities in American policy. The long delay in appointing a new ambassador in 1977 was read in Tehran as an insult. Simultaneously, Iran's human rights record, a sensitive point with the Shah, was heavily criticized on the one hand, while Iran's value as a regional ally was praised on the other. The monarch convinced himself that the new administration was behaving very much like that of President Kennedy, trying to push Iran toward significant political change.[20] Given the Shah's ego, he considered laudatory praise his due. Although President Carter himself was always extremely cordial, the monarch took any criticism unnecessarily hard, raising his level of insecurity. The dissidents, on the other hand, took heart from U.S. displeasure at conditions in Iran but reacted angrily to public praise of their country as a stable regional ally. Both American policies, though diametrically opposed, reinforced the growing strength of the opposition.

Many other American moves were interpreted two ways, depending on the proclivities of the observer. The Shah perceived the Carter-Brzezinski phone calls after the Jaleh Square riots as evidence of support, but when he asked Ambassador Sullivan to confirm their thrust, Sullivan could not get instructions from Washington to do so. This stimulated, rather than assuaged, the Shah's uneasiness. The revolutionaries thought the calls sent a different message: the U.S. was abandoning its concern for human rights in favor of all-out support for the Pahlavi dictatorship.

In other examples, neither the opposition nor the establishment elite understood what the U.S. was thinking in November and December 1978. Both sides made overtures for American support of their position, but none was forthcoming. Subsequent U.S. pressure for the Shah's quiet departure was widely regarded by the few remaining loyalists as rank betrayal. The opposition suspected some sort of a trick, particularly after General Huyser arrived. Once again, the U.S. got no credit for its efforts from either quarter.

An especially poignant example of the missed opportunities caused by the lack of communication between the U.S. government and the Khomeini forces occurred when the Ayatollah announced from Paris on January 10 that any country which accepted the Shah into exile would not be penalized by the revolutionaries. Without direct contact, there was no reliable way to exploit this opening in a timely fashion, yet it should have been possible to prepare for the arrival of the Shah into the United States on terms acceptable to the fundamentalist clergy. Unfortunately, Khomeini's statement was made when internal bureaucratic conflict was sharpest over whether to back the military in Iran or to act as a mediator between the revolutionaries and the collapsing government. Both the Iranian establishment (what remained of it) and the dissidents felt besieged. Given America's past involvement, leaders on both sides of the struggle expected a U.S. initiative to help ease Iran through some kind of transition. At this point an accommodation with Khomeini was not out of the question. Washington would have been able to take a major step toward its overriding objective, to bring the military through the revolutionary transition with continued capability and some influence, preventing the total dominance of the fundamentalist radicals.

What was missing in the policy and decision making process was a willingness on the part of the President to choose and then to make his decisions known to all the government officials affected. By late December lower level organizational conflict had worked its way up to the highest level, with no possibility of resolution in sight. Despite embassy misgivings, the President remained publicly positive until his breakfast press conference on December 7, when he expressed doubts for the first time about the Shah's ability to survive politically. Later that month the U.S. government officially supported the monarch's decision to leave his country. (In his memoirs, the Shah barely conceals the belief that he was pushed out.)[21] When Bakhtiar became prime minister, the U.S. supported him immediately, despite embassy warnings that unrestrained American backing would be "a kiss of death." The President rejected the Sullivan thesis that the U.S. should take advantage of its historical position and mediate the revolutionary turmoil, orchestrating an outcome more consistent with American interests in regional stability.

There was some advantage to playing both sides of the policy fence as long as possible, hoping that the situation would change or that new information would make the choice easy. But by January Sullivan saw the opportunity for effective decision making slipping away and continually pleaded with Washington via the telephone and telegrams to act decisively. The replies were always temporizing answers, causing him to remark, "We keep asking for strategic guidance and they keep giving us tactical suggestions." Eventually Sullivan received what he describes as a "rude" telegram, inviting him to stop questioning Washington and to do what he was told. He decided to resign from the foreign service as soon as practicable. Sullivan left within two weeks of his recall to Washington on April 5, 1979. The correctness of his analysis was apparently appreciated by the President and Secretary Vance, though belatedly, and he was offered a plum ambassadorship. Sullivan declined it in favor of the presidency of the American Assembly, which is connected with Columbia University and sponsors conferences on major foreign and domestic issues.

The Result: One Failed American Foreign Policy

Differences of opinion are common in policy and decision making, but what was lacking in terms of Iran was a sense of direction. Only administration insiders can tell who was ultimately at fault—the President himself or his senior political appointees, Brzezinski at the National Security Council, Vance and Christopher at the State Department, or Admiral Turner at the C.I.A. Without more firm control from the top, conflict within the policy process, reinforced by glaring uncertainty, impeded both rapid, in-depth analysis and choice itself. In a fast-moving crisis such as this one, obvious differences of opinion also delayed carrying out policies and decisions that already had been made. Emotional commitments reached such a fever pitch after the revolutionary victory in February 1979 that some State Department and National Security Council employees were not speaking to each other.

Arguments over "who blew it" in Iran continued to hobble effective policy and decision making after the revolutionary takeover. The State Department became enamored of the post-Shah government. After all, the embassy had good ties with Prime Minister Bazargan and his key lieutenants. Urged on by both American and Iranian contacts within the United States who had supported the revolution, Washington encouraged establishing a working relationship with the new government immediately. To facilitate the smooth transfer of allegiances, the U.S. government did not formally protest the takeover of the embassy in February 1979, except for those complaints made while the capture was actually in progress and its formal request for compensation for damages. As relations between the two governments slowly improved, the embassy staff, which had been drastically reduced after the February incident to a low of about 30, was back up to 70-plus by the summer. The rebuilding was based on a number of hopeful signs that the United States and Iran were moving toward a standard diplomatic relationship.

Too little attention, however, was being paid to the less benign members of the revolutionary coalition. How increasing the embassy staff would be perceived by radical Islamic groups and the hard-core left was discounted. Consequently, when President Carter was faced with the decision whether to allow the Shah into the United States for medical treatment, he based his choice primarily on the fact that it was the morally correct thing to do. Another consideration, according to press reports, was pressure from the Shah's American friends, specifically Chase Manhattan Bank President David Rockefeller and former Secretary of State Henry Kissinger. They urged Carter to admit the monarch to the U.S. for health reasons. Kissinger has stingingly denied the charge.[22] If the two men did influence the President, what they said was not decisive but only reinforced Carter's natural inclination.

Although the State Department protested the President's wish, based on well-documented embassy objections, Vance agreed with the President that to admit the former monarch on humanitarian grounds would be possible. The opinion of on-the-scene diplomats was overridden, even though they had specifically mentioned in cables that allowing the Shah into the United States could lead to another seizure of the embassy. Carter, Vance, and others on the National Security Council thought the Bazargan government could ride out the storm, particularly since the prime minister himself had promised that the embassy would be protected against demonstrators. Two days before the Shah arrived in the United States, Henry Precht was dispatched to Tehran to reassure the revolutionary moderates that America was not abandoning its improving relationship with the provisional government but meeting a humanitarian need. While Bazargan and his foreign minister, Ibrahim Yazdi, accepted those assurances, the Mujahidin and the Fedayeen did not, especially after Bazargan talked with Brzezinski in Algiers. Exactly two weeks after the Shah arrived in the United States, the embassy was seized once more.

There have been debates over whether it was the Shah's arrival in the U.S. or Bazargan's meeting with Brzezinski that precipitated the takeover. Such an argument misses the point. The haste with which the United States sought to normalize relations with the revolutionaries created a climate that heightened already neurotic Iranian suspicions about American intentions. Under the circumstances some kind of show of force against the U.S. embassy in Tehran was almost certain to occur eventually. Even if the Shah had not come to New York and Bazargan had not met with Brzezinski, some event would have provided the excuse the radicals needed. Permitting the Shah to enter the U.S. set the stage for converting a nasty demonstration into an occupation. Brzezinski's meeting with Bazargan agitated the radicals even further, insuring that the unstable Iranian government would almost certainly be unable to control the volatile situation.

Given Carter's decision to seek swift normalization of relations with the new regime, it made little sense to exacerbate tensions by sending the Shah to a New York hospital. After the first attack on the American embassy following the revolutionary takeover, if Washington had adopted a more coolly correct posture and cut the size of the official U.S. presence in Iran—and kept it small, thus indicating its unwillingness to do business as usual in the face of outrageous provocation—a more realistic relationship between the two nations most probably would have evolved.[23]

Once the die was cast, the revolutionaries rejected all U.S. efforts to negotiate the freedom of the hostages largely because of a fierce sense of righteousness and because of a rapidly expanding political deadlock within the country. Those holding the captives sought different objectives at various times, but major demands included the repatriation of the Shah, the return of his wealth, an apology for past U.S. involvement, the unfreezing of Iranian assets, cancellation of U.S. claims against that country, and a huge financial payment.

In the months following the takeover, the State Department focused almost exclusively on meeting the shifting sets of conditions. Other methods of dealing with the situation were given short shrift and deliberately downplayed. Consequently, when a rescue attempt was considered, a very small group from the Defense Department and the C.I.A. planned and carried out the abortive raid to pluck the captives out of central Tehran. With the exception of Vance (who vehemently opposed the action) and his deputy, Warren Christopher, no one from the State Department was involved. Carter limited discussions about a possible military solution to a coterie in the armed services and the C.I.A., leaving the State Department on the sidelines. Within that framework, when the rescue was attempted, the breadth of perspective was greatly reduced. Vast reservoirs of official expertise were never tapped. The presidential commission appointed to investigate the failed mission concluded that over-restrictive planning greatly inhibited the raid's prospects for success.

First the foreign affairs bureaucracy had sputtered along, then the U.S. military had proved to be a paper tiger. Once again, this time under the disadvantage of a double failure, the Carter administration was compelled to play a waiting game, relying on external pressures to force the resolution of the hostage issue. There were no other organizational assets to draw upon.

The Problems in Perspective

Hindsight is infinitely more accurate than foresight, particularly since more complete information is available. Being aware of the impact of

U.S. choices on the Iranian crisis in terms of the knowledge of policy and decision makers at the time can indicate what to watch for in the future. For example, how might the United States have reacted to avoid the confrontation that developed between the dissidents and the Shah? Paying more attention to the physical condition of the key participant would have helped. If policy makers had been sensitized in 1976 and 1977 to the increasing likelihood of instability, the outcome could have been different. Encouraging a healthy dose of suspicion is another, especially since too many policy and decision makers rejected out of hand analyses opposed to established American policy. Sadly, this planet has become a much more dangerous place in the past five to ten years, and the margin for error that existed from 1945 to the late 1960s is not there anymore. The scarcity of available resources and the greater prevalence of governments devoted to violence has changed all that. The case of Iran is the strongest argument yet for senior policy makers to encourage both more provocative intelligence analysis and active questioning of established assumptions. They must be willing to entertain unwelcome ideas, particularly those which challenge cherished private beliefs. The more dearly held the conviction, the more it deserves reexamination.

In terms of intelligence gathering, American capabilities have been reduced drastically from 1967 to the present on the assumption that more is not needed in terms of money spent. Yet it was far more expensive in the long run to have withdrawn officers stationed in Iran than it will be to replace lost American influence in the area. It is not possible to exercise effective great power diplomacy using minimal resources. If anything, the loss of worldwide strategic superiority the U.S. enjoyed until the early 1970s, as well as the deterioration in the amount of economic and political leverage the country wielded in the 1950s and 1960s, points to the need for more rather than fewer diplomatic resources abroad.

How the American presence in Iran over the years built up the opposition and tore down the Shah suggests that the U.S. needs to take a thoroughgoing look at the impact of a sizable American community on a foreign society. In Iran, pragmatic decision makers moved step-by-step into a situation of overcommitment without looking at the broader trend. At the same time, President Carter was reluctant to exercise U.S. influence, partly from the praiseworthy belief that insiders know what they want better than outsiders do. Unfortunately, this attitude did not take into account the fact that Iranians of all political persuasions were taking their cues from perceived U.S. policy. America could not avoid being influential, even if it did not wish to be. Not to use that leverage to shape the outcome of events in ways more favorable to the United

States, or at least in ways less damaging to its long-term interests, confused Iranians and not a few Americans.

The United States did not attempt to influence events either directly or indirectly until September 1978, after Jaleh Square. America had expressed concern for human rights before that, but had not tried to force the Shah to make specific changes. Until the Huyser mission in January 1979, U.S. "intervention" was limited to positive public statements. However, the very presence of so many Americans in Iran implied support for the Shah and his policies, and was regarded by Islamic revolutionaries who opposed modernization of any kind as meddling in internal politics.

Surprisingly, the revolutionary victory in February 1979 created a situation not wholly unfavorable to U.S. interests. American diplomats exploited their longstanding contacts with the opposition to establish good ties with Bazargan. This continued until unflattering U.S. reactions to the revolutionary executions, expressed most vividly in a Senate resolution in May, triggered livid anger on the part of Khomeini and a rejection of Walter Cutler as the ambassadorial nominee. Despite these obvious and ominously negative signs, the administration pushed ahead on its policy of accommodation by increasing the size of the mission in Tehran, resuming shipments of military spare parts, and pressing for a high-level meeting, which took place when Brzezinski met with Bazargan and Yazdi in Algiers on November 1. Washington's wishful thinking about Khomeini and the radical fundamentalists continued to underlie policy and decision making until it was too late—at least for the hostages.

The futile negotiations to release the incarcerated Americans and the aborted attempt to free them militarily relegated the United States to the role of enemy, while the hostages continued to be poker chips in the Iranian internal political game. For the long-term future beyond Iran, there are more important questions. Under what circumstances does a large U.S. presence in another culture destabilize the very society and government it is there to benefit? What types of military and political support are appropriate? These are very real issues. The current U.S. presence, both official and private, in Egypt and Saudi Arabia is advancing toward 1974–1975 proportions in Iran. Already both countries show signs of strain.

The failure of the hostage raid has raised doubts about U.S. military capabilities in terms of both planning and combat performance. It has weakened the confidence of both friends and foes that America can make good its intentions when the chips are down. Should the United

States have ruled out armed retaliation in the early days of the hostage crisis? Under the circumstances, no. It gave the revolutionary government the wrong signal and encouraged it to prolong holding the hostages and force the Americans to pay a higher penalty for their past "sins." Extremists who had no wish to settle the matter in any case could point to the American President's rejection of the use of force to buttress their views that Iran could only benefit by keeping the hostages. It also undercut the more moderate Iranian officials who argued for a speedy release in order to minimize the potential international damage to their country. When and how to use force takes on a new dimension with the advent of state-sponsored terrorism against diplomats. The response of democratic countries to the problem of political intimidation is important to the future stability of those societies, as Italy, West Germany, and Japan have already discovered.

What happened in Iran has made it clear that there are much higher costs of error than expected. Would the ability to "think big," as opposed to dealing with daily problems, have promoted a more complete understanding of various options and their possible consequences? Probably. In any event, it would have helped policy and decision makers deal with the rapidly changing circumstances more adequately. Given the volatile social and political structures in many areas, there is less reaction time in a crisis situation than there was even a decade ago. The international environment offers greater danger, more swiftly developing, than ever before.

The pace of social and political change demands that policy and decision makers—whether diplomats in the field or the President and the cabinet departments involved or the National Security Council staff—exercise greater flexibility. Accurate intelligence is always necessary, but if the Iran crisis shows anything, it is that better management of analysis and better development of options are the more pressing needs. The organizational diversity of the American foreign policy community is a source of strength, but it is also a source of weakness if it is not handled properly. Otherwise, it breeds different points of view leading to policy immobilization. Coping with increasing complexity and speed of change requires strong organizational leadership, particularly at the highest levels of government. A coherent American philosophy could avoid at least some of the cyclical alternations between too much and too little involvement in world affairs that have marked the past two decades.

Echoes of the Iranian crisis will reverberate for a long time to come. How will America's leaders cope with situations where the prospects for successful positive action are so unpromising, yet U.S. interests are so important? The future of Iranian oil production, the impact of the Khomeini revolution on regional stability (especially countries that supply the United States with oil), the eventual outcome of the struggle between left and right in that country, and the final resolution of the Iran-Iraq war affect American economic prospects, the viability of U.S. alliances, and the prospects for either conflict or cooperation with the Soviet Union.

Chapter Fifteen

★

The Significance of the Revolution

The Iranian revolution is not over. Survivors of the coalition which took power in 1979 presided over the dismantling of the Pahlavi political system and the disintegration of Iran's economic structure, but they could not exhibit consistent administrative skills, let alone build a government capable of giving direction to revolutionary striving and effective prosecution of the war against Iraq. The shaky institutionalized framework that bubbled up intermingled the hostage seizure, the war, and the unending conflict between Islamic extremists and leftists. Thus the more radical Mujahidin factions (about a third of the total) found it convenient to cooperate with the Fedayeen in blocking any rapprochement between the United States and the Khomeini regime, even to the point of holding dozens of diplomats captive for more than a year.

The unorthodox behavior of those in power after the revolutionary takeover sent shock waves through nearly every world capital. Later, Iran's isolation was greatly intensified by the hostage crisis. Even though that albatross has been removed, the country's foreign policy has continued to be in total disarray. It is impossible to take an advance peek at the twists and turns Iran has yet to endure, but future evolution will surely be shaped by past events and reaction to them. What has happened in Iran provides interesting perspectives on how societies cope with upheaval and change and what the consequences for the rest of the international system can be.

Iran in Terms of the Theory and Practice of Revolution

From a theoretical perspective the most important question is whether the Iranian revolution could have been prevented, or at the

309

very least channeled in the direction of less radical and destructive change, if different policy choices had been made on the part of those involved. Everyone in Iran had gained materially during the 15 years of development from 1963 to 1978, some groups much more than others. Psychologically, however, the masses had become alienated from the governing structure. They perceived themselves as either being cut off from an effective voice in politics or becoming worse off relative to others in the country. What happened supports the theory that revolutions do not occur when living conditions are at their worst, but when the situation is getting better but does not keep up with expectations.[1] Although the Shah promised a great deal, the government did not deliver fast enough, no matter how much conditions were improving. Thus when the policy of economic development encountered turbulent times in 1977 and 1978, individuals from all segments of society were much more inclined to ask, "What have you done for me lately?" blaming the Shah for the inevitable shortcomings.

One simplistic theoretical truism must be discarded. It is not true that the people will always back a government which has improved its standard of living. The Shah assumed his subjects would continue to support his regime because of the economic advances he instigated. As conditions got better, their attention turned more and more from matters of minimal well-being to having a say in their own affairs. The desire of individuals to play a meaningful political role, or at least enjoy the effective illusion of it, vastly increased. At the crucial moment, with loyalty to the Pahlavi monarchy in the balance, the Shah favored the devil he knew—authoritarian control—rather than the devil he didn't—unrestricted political participation.

One generally accepted idea about the origin and development of revolution is negated by events in Iran. Nothing occurred there to support standard Marxist and Western theories that to control the rural populace is to hold the key that can unleash violent upheaval.[2] The farmers remained on the sidelines, perceiving the conflict to be a dispute among city dwellers. Three months after Khomeini's forces seized power, the overwhelming majority of villagers in rural towns near Tehran believed the Shah would return to the throne after a deal was worked out with the Islamic leadership! The peasants were flexible. The ones who had migrated to the cities and suffered under the economic depression were eager to follow the discontented mullahs. Until the prospects of the Shah's regime plummeted in November 1978, those still in the villages were equally willing to march in government-sponsored rallies.

Despite the problems, the revolution would not have occurred or could have taken a substantially different direction if no extensive revolutionary underground had been established. But the creation of the mosque network allowed the radical clergy to dominate and then control the evolution of the dissident movement. By mobilizing an effective action group it was easy for Khomeini to become the charismatic leader of the religious fanatics. In the Shah's Iran, from 1963 to 1977 the clergy had been a marginal force increasingly more insulated from power. It is not surprising, therefore, that the fundamentalists rejected the traditional political system to pursue radical, anti-government policies.[3]

Historically, the most important conseqeunce of the revolution may prove to be the rise of religion as a significant political force. Blending theocratic ideology with mob power on a sustained basis offers an alternative revolutionary model to supplement Marxist and other paradigms. It is a way to replace the authority and legitimacy of a monarch or other secular leader with another kind of power based on a different justification. Tactically, it accomplishes its aim without resorting to massive sustained violence. In this case the fundamentalists proved that even a powerful armed force can be destroyed from within. The most disturbing element about Khomeini's Islamic movement is not its doctrine but its effective mobilization of a diverse society into a political organization supporting a religious government. Clerical supremacy as asserted by Khomeini is an implicit standing challenge to secular governments everywhere. If it continues to exist and prosper, a centuries-old Western trend of separation between church and state would be reversed.

Clerical dominance distinguishes Khomeini's movement from that of the Sandinista rebels in Nicaragua, a group it is similar to in many other ways. There, in 1979 a revolutionary movement was spearheaded by an organized elite propounding vague doctrines, but there was no theocratic challenge. In both countries the popular movement was able to mobilize first the disaffected and then a majority of society to the point where the country ceased to function normally, despite the presence of superior power as vested in the armed forces. The result in both instances was the ouster of a supreme leader who had all the traditional levers of the power of the state at his disposal, yet could not bring them to bear. President Somoza and the Shah felt similar frustration when they tried to use the military for political reasons, whether forcefully or not, only to discover that doing so made matters worse, not better. In Nicaragua the Sandinistas established a working government within two months after they took over. In Iran the jury is still out, but the possibility of sustained success for the Khomeini regime looks bleak indeed.

The nationalistic and religious ideology of the Islamic militants who took over legitimacy and power in February 1979 offers neither the organizational capacity to manage Iran nor a philosophical or ideological program that will have long-term appeal to the majority of the population. Today's Islamic leadership has retained the fanatical loyalty of some, the grudging support of others, and the "loyalty of indifference" of many more. As Iran's economy continues to crumble, however, the tribal groups and the leftists are becoming more powerful every day as they win adherents to their respective causes. Khomeini's charisma, the war with Iraq, and the absence of an effective challenger have enabled the Islamic movement to retain control, albeit frayed.

Though the rural inhabitants of Iran were not filled with revolutionary fervor, the opposition managed to take the political initiative away from the Shah because of its good organizational strategy and because of inadequate government reaction to the growing dissatisfaction. Prompt action by the ruling elites to control unrest through reform or to crush it by force or both could have blocked or turned aside total revolt. It was the halfway strategy adopted by the Shah that caused the growth in revolutionary passions, pushing moderates closer to those who would rather overthrow the existing system than compromise with it.

Successful revolutions naturally tend to evolve toward the most fanatical positions advocated. Whether what happened in Iran had to follow the usual pattern is much less certain. Had the Shah seriously attempted to develop the political system in the early 1970s, the outcome surely would have been different. The monarch was hesitant, because he had not been pleased with the consequences when he had tried to loosen things up a bit in 1961 and 1962. Unfortunately, encouraging participation involved risks the Shah was not prepared to take. If he had been more flexible, perhaps the revolution could have been avoided altogether. At the very least the basis for domination of the opposition by the moderates rather than the extremists would have been established. But Mohammad Reza Pahlavi lacked sensitivity and understanding, unable to foresee the outcome of his inability to choose between allowing greater participation or enforcing harsher measures. His temporizing gave him the worst of both worlds.

How a Political System Disintegrates

Many have argued that the Shah should have acted forcefully to maintain the Pahlavi political system, yet the monarch himself ruled out military repression for reasons of his own—his unwillingness to massacre his own people and the fear his son might not be able to succeed him if massive violence were used. Because of the Shah's overwhelming dominance of the decision making process, leaders of the establishment were unwilling to act on their own without assurances from the throne first. From 1963 to 1978 the monarch drew all policy and decision making power into his own hands. Those statesmen who had the prestige and the skill to stand up to the Shah and warn of trouble had either died or been otherwise politically neutralized. When push came to shove, most of the elite decamped for foreign countries, choosing permanent exile in societies whose values they shared rather than trying to fight it out at home, particularly after the triumph of a fundamentalist system negated everything they had helped to build.

The Shah's refusal to share any power with his handpicked followers in the Resurgence Party effectively destroyed that institution as a political force. By focusing military loyalties on himself, at critical junctures from August 1978 to February 1979 senior military leaders were inhibited from acting because the monarch restrained them, even against their better judgment. By September 1978 the Shah's own political skill was very much in question, yet no trusted advisor, old friend, or modern politician stepped forward to make a persuasive enough case for either more firm or more conciliatory measures. The circle of intimates, never large, grew progressively smaller and more divorced from reality as leading politicians were dismissed. By November the Shah had no one left to deal with except the opposition and committed revolutionaries, now lined up together. In the meantime, the dissidents carefully and deliberately chipped away at the sense of authority and legitimacy that had held Iran together under both Pahlavis for 50 years.

Given the nature of Pahlavi politics, the Shah's sense of uncertainty and his policy of vacillation led directly to the nation's political collapse. There were no independent institutions to arrest the breakdown of authority and absorb some of the eroding power. Neither the Shah nor his armed forces were powerful enough to set limits on the demonstrations that were destroying the government. Modest military measures at certain junctures—June 1978 to forestall rioting, September to restore order after Jaleh Square, November to pacify Tehran—halted the disintegration only temporarily. Those with an overall plan for victory were the revolutionaries, not the Shah and his government. By the end of November the dissidents had grown so strong and the pace of events increased so rapidly that any attempt to stop or seriously divert the revolution would have been extremely bloody. Prior to that time the Shah had some room to maneuver, though the possibilities decreased steadily beginning in August.

What could the Shah have done? Some argue that he had no other option except repression once the guerrilla movements began operating in early 1970. Until then the monarch had managed the country by political means — cajoling here, tempting there, bribing another time — and military force had not been used as a tool for controlling the country. As he began to turn his attention to international affairs and the insurgent groups grew more daring, the Shah depended on SAVAK more and more, saying in effect, "take care of the problem and don't bother me." SAVAK pursued its mandate with a heavy hand, and many of those who had been only mildly disaffected were polarized and pushed firmly into the opposition camp. However, it was not until 1977, when the Shah decided to allow more political activity, that the dissidents really gained strength. They capitalized on rising discontent to build a more solid political program that could supplement the hit-and-run exploits of the guerrillas. By converting Iran into a single party political system, Iran's monarch insured that those who supported the regime would be involved in "acceptable" political activity. But instead of bringing the moderate opposition into the fold, isolating the leftists, and immobilizing the religious reactionaries, the creation of a single party forced the outsiders to join together.

The opposition coalition was built on an alliance between the secular dissidents, who provided needed political skills, and both the radical and moderate religious leadership. The disparate groups were united only in the enmity they directed toward the leader of their country. Since the Shah's alternating tactics of coercion and conciliation were consistently awkward, it thrust to the forefront the more extreme faction — the religious reactionaries grouped around the mullahs.[4] The key issue was participation. As the monarch became the symbol of the closed door to politics, what the opposition offered became more appealing, even to the middle class. Until the day he died, the Shah never understood that improving the economic well-being of his subjects was not enough. Once the people reached an acceptable standard of living, they wanted a say in how things were run. The options the Shah had were to allow more political freedom, trick his people into believing they had it whether true or not, or reject their demands and enforce obedience. The tragedy is that he never could make up his mind which alternative to follow.[5]

The Revolutionaries' Rejection of Modernization

The overwhelming majority of Persians backed the revolutionary coalition not to reverse Iran's policy of economic progress but to "purify" it. However, the Islamic fundamentalists around Khomeini reject what they call the "westernization" of Iranian society, seeking to return instead to the old ways and to abandon all efforts to modernize the country. The Islamic Republican Party has the power to reverse the Shah's economic policies, but it has offered few constructive choices to replace them. Rejecting modernization is unlikely to remain a viable policy. The gross national product declined at least 20–25 percent in 1979 and the drop was far greater in 1980. Yet most Iranians see nothing wrong with economic betterment. Their attachment to Islam is modified by practical considerations. After all, one of the reasons they opposed the Shah was because too many of them thought they were getting less than their due. Khomeini's fundamentalism cannot remain an ideology of mass appeal beyond the moment of severe economic dislocation without some sort of hyper-stimulus, such as the Iraqi invasion. It will have great difficulty surviving its own political success.

Islamic fundamentalists are imposing long-ignored Moslem virtues on a rebellious society. Liquor is outlawed; predictably, a thriving black market flourishes. One of the Ayatollah's least successful campaigns has been to ban Western music; "cassette contraband" is everywhere. Revolutionary justice is swift, drastic, and more than occasionally arbitrary. The more antique concepts like stoning adulterers to death and executing alleged homosexuals have provoked outcries from the same human rights organizations that complained of more sophisticated, less terminal punishments inflicted under the Shah. Police brutality has decreased, but has not been eliminated. Random violence has swollen to the point where the average citizen would not consider himself any safer now than under the Shah.

Education has been revamped to stress Islamic principles. In order to minimize the use of institutions of higher learning by leftist organizers, the liberal arts departments of major universities have been closed since June 1980. Only medical schools and science departments remain open. Coeducation has been eliminated. Teachers are not allowed to use dice to illustrate probability in statistics courses because of Islamic prohibitions against gambling. History texts have been rewritten and pages and pictures referring to the Shah's regime have been removed from elementary and high school textbooks. Zealous Islamic officials have been appointed to run all schools and universities. Many of the older, qualified teachers who were in the vanguard of the revolutionary movement have been swept aside by inexperienced but fervent youngsters. Western-trained academics originally in favor of the Shah's overthrow have left the country when given the opportunity, fed up with the abuse heaped upon them because of their "corrupt" ideals. An elderly Islamic philosopher commented from Tehran in mid-1980, "The distance separating today's Iran from the middle ages is very small and shrinking."

A large majority of the peasant farmers and lower class urban poor are wholly disinterested in the doctrinal aspects of Khomeini's campaign against modernization and Western cultural values. They are content with the revival of Islam, the reactivation of Koranic law, and the tightening of restrictions on women, but are uneasy over reports of corruption among the mullahs, specifically rumors that they have sent vast sums of money out of the country. Questions are now being asked why the country was so much better off economically under the Shah if he was stealing from and cheating his people as much as Khomeini and the Islamic radicals say he was. It was the urban poor who provided the manpower for mob demonstrations under the Shah. Eventually they will become susceptible to blandishments by others, particularly the Fedayeen and the Tudeh Party, which advocate radical economic solutions without Islamic fervor.

As the implications of fundamentalist economics become clearer, the middle class also will feel increasingly more alienated, particularly females. Yet the willing participation of this part of society is essential in order to revive Iran's commercial and economic prospects. The middle class possesses the skills the economy needs.

Islamic rule has encouraged the growth of leftist, anti-religious feeling within the body politic as shortages grow, high unemployment continues, patriotism fades, and revolutionary euphoria has given way to internecine bickering. The Islamic constitution has alienated the tribal minorities as well as Khomeini's more moderately inclined religious rivals, both groups being appalled by his particular brand of Shiism. Revolutionary tribunals, operating under Islamic law and condemning former officials to death for "war against God" or "corruption on earth," have had the same unintended consequence for Khomeini that

SAVAK did for the Shah. Families of those killed have become hostile. Relatives of potential victims are filled with hate and fear. While the immediate families of many of those executed have fled Iran, many others remain, deeply committed to revenge and implacably opposed to rule by mullah.

Obviously, the Islamic movement is in trouble. Weakening its opposition to certain aspects of modernization will antagonize its extremist colleagues and Khomeini will lose valuable supporters in the struggle for political legitimacy. On the other hand, if it bends to the ingrained hypocrisy of attacking modernization while trying to make the country work, it will discourage the very talent on whom its effectiveness as a governing force depends—the businessmen, skilled laborers, and trained military officers. Eventually rejecting materialism in favor of Islamic asceticism will bring the Islamic movement to the same choice the Shah faced—to conciliate or to coerce. A militant, moralistic government is likely to turn quickly and decisively to coercion and repression, but in the name of Allah, not the state.[6]

The Impact of the Revolution on Other Nations

Iran's economic and social disintegration was reflected first in the amount of its oil on the world market, lowered to a trickle after September 1980. After producing between 5.0 and 6.1 million barrels per day between 1974 and 1978, the output dropped to between .8 and 1.2 million barrels per day in 1979 and to around 500,000 barrels per day when the war with Iraq began, barely enough to cover the country's own needs. It will be a long time before Iran, once the world's second largest producer, plays the dominant role in international oil policy it once did. Moreover, Iraqi production also has been cut drastically. Originally it pumped about 3.6 million barrels per day. After the war started, production was cut to 1.5 million barrels, and because of damage to pipelines and refineries it was down to less than 700,000 barrels by November. The result has been increased world dependence on the outputs of Saudi Arabia, Kuwait, and Libya.

Strategically, the revolution replaced a stable, pro-Western regional power committed to a policy of development with a regime subject to violent internal change. The Islamic Republic has professed expansionist aims, both ideologically and territorially, in a way much more worrisome to its neighbors than anything the Shah attempted to do. The oil-producing states in the Persian Gulf recoil from the fundamentalist challenge of the Shiite mullahs. There is concern over the desire, if not the capability, of Khomeini or his successors to sharply alter regional power and political patterns.

Actually, revolutionary Iran's involvement with the Arabs has been mixed. The close ties both Fedayeen and Mujahidin leaders had enjoyed with the P.L.O. were forged even before the Shah's overthrow reoriented the foreign policy of the new regime. Instead of the previous discreet cooperation with Israel, now there is unremitting hostility toward the "Zionist enemy." However, the possibility of full rapprochement with Arab Moslems against the Jewish state was first stunted, then eliminated by the growing conflict with Iraq that climaxed in open warfare. Jordan's King Hussein, a long-time personal friend of the Shah, publicly sided with Iraq, and Baghdad considers the regaining of lost "Arab" territories its principal reason for waging the war. The longer the occupation of Khuzistan province continues, the more likely it is that Iraq's President Hussein will insist at a minimum on substantial Iraqi political influence in the area—if not outright control—after the conflict is over. For this reason, in the future the Islamic Republic of Iran is likely to pay little more than lip service to the Arab cause in Palestine.

The Soviet Union, while celebrating the disappearance of a bastion of American influence in a very sensitive area, has not been able to capitalize on Iran's weakness. However, a case can be made that a strong Iran would have inhibited the Russian invasion of Afghanistan, perhaps even forestalled it altogether. The U.S.S.R. is even less comfortable than the West with Iran's doctrine of Islamic fundamentalism because of its potential impact on millions of Moslems living in Soviet central Asia. But the Kremlin does foresee the likelihood of an opportunity in the future to convert the situation into one more amenable to Soviet interests and control. There is always a possibility that a leftist government may eventually come to power and seek Soviet assistance. Also, prolonged instability could provide the Soviet Union with a rare opportunity to gain access to Iran's oil and gas supplies and to year-round ports in the Persian Gulf. The Russians have had to tolerate the unpleasant international consequences of their adventure in Afghanistan, but to control Iran would be worth taking even greater risks.

For the United States, the revolution put past, present, and future strategy and tactics into question. The consequences of what happened in Iran have stimulated serious concern about the adequacy of the American foreign policy and decision making process. Was U.S. intelligence and especially the analysis of that intelligence effective? Which values did the United States choose to promote by its policies? Nonintervention? Steadfast support of allies and like-minded governments? Human rights? How were American intentions perceived by others? Obviously what has occurred there since 1978 has not been in the best interests of the U.S. There is chagrin at the disappearance of one of the "twin pillars" in the Middle East and self-criticism and recriminations over past policy choices. Especially for the next few years, there is bound to be greater instability in the region and chronic shortages of oil for the developed countries. For the future, the United States is faced with assimilating the unpalatable results of the Iranian episode.

The Benefit of Hindsight

When looking at a revolution from the broadest perspective two types of political issues are relevant: those affecting the nation under attack from within and those affecting it from without. The experience in Iran speaks to both. For the besieged state the most important question is "Was this revolution necessary or inevitable?" The Shah made some critical decisions—increasing the pace of economic development, diverting a significant percentage of expanding resources to military expenditure, and delaying political reform by refusing to allow others to participate meaningfully in decision making. The consequences intensified pressures on society. Based on what happened to the Shah, it would seem unwise for rulers to build up tensions in several areas at once lest this irrevocably tilt citizens against the existing political system.

Had the regime gradually allowed greater popular participation and a more open system, the monarch would have had to work harder at his job and forgo at least some of his more grandiose plans. However, his people would have concentrated on electoral and parliamentary politics, not revolutionary activity. If he had opted for gradual rather than ultra-rapid economic development in 1974, social stresses could have been minimized. As late as November 1977 a well-thought-out plan offering dissidents a fair chance to participate in politics, backed by a willingness to use force if they rejected compromise, could have diverted the budding revolutionary coalition from violence to electioneering.

The trick was to block the growth of an effective revolutionary organization, channeling the opposition into activities that reinforced the structure of society, instead of tearing it down. When this is done, it provides the basis for the legitimate use of force, should that become necessary. One example will suffice: At the same time that there was chaos in Tehran on November 5, 1978, there were political riots in several towns in Turkey, which shares its northwest border with Iran. The popularly elected government in Ankara imposed martial law, and 60 curfew violators were subsequently killed while on the streets after hours. Because the overwhelming majority of its people considered the regime legitimate, its actions were accepted even by the opposition party, albeit grudgingly. By contrast, in Iran the government's martial law declaration was rejected out of hand by opposition groups. Not one of them was willing to compromise because all regarded the Shah's rule as illegitimate—unrepresentative of the popular will. Most devastating of all for the prospects of Iran's ruler, he was unwilling or unable to impose any penalty for noncooperation.

The revolution offers scant solace to moderates, both secular and religious. Bakhtiar was swept away by the militant tide despite the fact that it was he who induced the Shah to leave the country. Bazargan and the liberal opposition leaders in his cabinet found themselves dependent on the Mujahidin and later the Revolutionary Guards to enforce their writ, when they could enforce it at all. Since the fundamentalists supported narrow, exclusivist policies, they defied Bazargan's efforts to create an all-embracing revolutionary movement based on national progress through unity and joint effort.

The traditional political elite never really influenced events during 1978. Although important out of proportion to its size at the beginning of the Shah's reign, it gradually was completely dominated by the monarch. Because of 15 years of very individualistic authoritarian rule, the moderates who wished to influence the course of events had neither institutions to join nor models of behavior to emulate—only dependence on royal whim. Even when pro-government demonstrations were organized, the elite and the middle class participated reluctantly, if at all. The establishment, more than any other group, suffered the collective frustration of never having a chance to act independently until it was too late. The Shah created a class of political neuters who supported the regime but who had little inclination and even less practical skill to play an aggressive political role when the system was challenged.

The issues facing those observing a revolutionary situation from outside are different. How does one recognize when political unrest is about to cross the limits within which society can contain and adjust itself? Then there is the subsequent problem of what to do: Is there a need to get involved? Does the observer have the capacity (or the will) to do anything? What are the advantages and/or disadvantages of becoming tied up in the politics of a revolutionary situation?

Reactions to the Iranian experience suggest that no particular kind of political system had any clear superiority in assessing the onset of the revolution. Among Western nations, France can lay some claim to having recognized the problem as it unfolded, but that country as well as Britain made a high level decision to remain detached. This was largely based on the realization that neither could really alter the course of events anyway, especially in the absence of a U.S. decision to intervene more energetically. As for the Communist countries, the Soviets had never had close relations with Pahlavi Iran, but the economic ties were mutually beneficial. There had been no major conflicts between the two countries in the 1970s, and this delayed the Kremlin's acknowledgment that the power of the Shah had deteriorated tremendously. Slowly and cautiously it shifted away from a live-and-let-live attitude toward strong criticism of the monarch and discreet support of his opponents.

The rapid unraveling of the U.S. position raises both practical and philosophical questions about the desirability of close relations with developing, potentially unstable societies. Are Western values, which have motivated most countries to strive for increased economic development, under sustained fundamentalist religious and cultural challenge? Or is Iran's Islamic experiment an exception to, rather than the forerunner of, a tide?

The special relationship the United States enjoyed with Iran did not help that country stave off the fundamentalist threat. In fact it made the regime more vulnerable than it might otherwise have been. Though Washington dealt with Iranian problems in terms of specific cases rather than as part of an overall challenge, from the beginning the Islamic radicals clearly and consistently rejected modernization, seeking a return to Islamic law, customs, and government. Despite this goal the revolutionary regime does not seem so willing to forgo advantages which Westernization provides the country—an economic base, modern weaponry, and instant communication with the rest of the world. Arguing the pros and cons of the various aspects of this issue is the single most disruptive political force the revolutionary coalition deals with today.

Other nations have not rushed to espouse Iran's views. However, traditional as well as dissident forces in all states undergoing the social and economic strains of development are carefully considering whether Khomeini's strategy, carefully followed, will enable them to build an effective opposition coalition in their own societies. It is not in the interest of the United States to make this route to power very attractive. But, since dissident forces begin as outcasts in their own societies, possible Western input into this process is almost always marginal, affecting the nation under attack but exerting little direct influence on the alienated factions. Whether Khomeini's Iran succeeds in holding itself together, supplying at least minimal economic needs while continuing to build a broad national ideology, is what will or will not recommend his ideas and tactics to others.

Iran and the Future

Iran's future prospects are cloudy at best, disastrous at worst. The detention of the 52 Americans, an extraordinary, illegal act which violated the very basis of diplomatic practice, projected the revolutionary takeover and its aftermath onto the world stage. If Iran were a small nation in an out-of-the-way place, this might not have been the case. Unfortunately, the country is at the center of a critical strategic area. The Iranian revolution and the Soviet occupation of Afghanistan have doubly sharpened the world's focus on the Middle East. These two events, followed by Iraq's attack on Iran, have posed the specter of a collision between world powers in the volatile region stretching from Bangladesh to Libya.

Khomeini's particular brand of religious nationalism has both fanatic adherents and more moderate supporters. The Islamic government is struggling to impose a value system that has been fervently supported in the abstract by many, but in the particulars by few. Thus the Fedayeen, the radical Mujahidin, the Tudeh Party, and other leftists know they are leading contenders for power. They are waiting in the wings for Khomeini to die or his movement to falter, and are clustered around the Fedayeen guerrillas, the only well-armed organization capable of mounting a serious military threat to the Islamic regime. As long as President Bani-Sadr and Prime Minister Rajai or their successors continue to disagree adamantly on how the country should be run, the possibility of a total governmental collapse remains strong.

Ethnic minorities—the Kurds, the Khuzistan Arabs, the Turkomans—will continue to revolt, either openly or covertly, against any government likely to emerge in Tehran. Lur, Qashqai, Bakhtiari, and Baluchi tribal leaders are restless, waiting for a propitious moment to break completely with Khomeini's Islamic fundamentalists. Continued chaos and fragmentation are likely. As internal forces struggle for precedence, none will be strong enough to fully consolidate power. Under these circumstances, the prospects for external meddling will increase dramatically. For now, the opposition exiles in Paris are too disorganized to seriously challenge the revolutionaries. If it should become possible, the most likely prospects would be either a regime led by former General Gholam Ali Oveissi, or perhaps a republican government formed by liberals loyal to the factions around either ex-Prime Minister Shapour Bakhtiar or former revolutionary lawyer Hassan Nazih. For any of these options to succeed would require support from the armed forces within Iran. Though Crown Prince Reza announced he was assuming his father's throne in exile, the possibility of the restoration of the Pahlavi dynasty is negligible.

The Soviet Union is publicly waiting, but privately interfering. The media in the U.S.S.R. has made no secret of its feeling that Khomeini's successors are likely to be those who "have most accurately divined the will of the people"—the Tudeh Party or the Fedayeen. Precipitate Soviet action to bring about what it hopes is inevitable is unlikely unless the United States intervenes militarily, or unless energetic pragmatists in the Politburo believe that the opportunity far outweighs the risks. The most dangerous possibility is that Marxist-oriented leaders would take power in Tehran, only to be attacked by the Kurds, other tribal groups, and perhaps scattered anti-communist army units bolstered by the more moderate religious leaders. In an extreme situation even the anti-Soviet leftists might be tempted to ask for Russian assistance to stabilize their position. The call for help, plus the chance to seize Iran's oil fields and warm-water ports, might be too great a temptation for even the present conservative Soviet leadership to resist. This would be particularly true if the Kremlin felt the United States could not or would not counter any thrust the U.S.S.R. might make.

What, for example, would the U.S. do if the Soviets sent tanks into Azarbaijan and Khorasan provinces in the north and west and dispatched air transports for a paratroop drop on the Persian Gulf oil fields in the south? It would truly bring the American government to a moment of decision. Resist, or let Iran's oil and strategic position pass into hostile hands? The Soviet occupation of all or even part of Iran would signal the collapse of the American position in the Middle East. The impact upon other rulers in the area would be equally devastating. Yet too aggressive a policy before an actual Soviet invasion risks forcing the Islamic Republic into the arms of the Russians, despite the fundamentalist clergy's distrust and deep-seated hatred of communism. But the consequences of confrontation would be equally awful; U.S. resistance to an attempted Soviet incursion would bring about an extremely dangerous situation. If the United States occupied the gas and oil fields in southwest Iran, it would be faced with the need to build a political coalition within the country and among its allies to support such a move. Fear of the Soviet Union might bring assistance from unlikely sources (Iraq and Syria) as well as from old friends (Saudi Arabia, Egypt, and the Gulf States). But it could just as easily trigger enmity from many of the same countries, depending on the circumstances.

What sort of internal coalition would emerge is much more difficult to imagine. None of the possibilities is appealing. All reinforce the truth of the adage that real policy and decision making choices are not between good and bad, but between bad and terrible. If the United States remains a strong and determined nation, however, it is unlikely it will have to face such draconian options.

But what of the longer term? Given the inherent weakness of the Islamic government on both organizational and substantive issues, coupled with the potential for foreign intervention, what are Iran's prospects? The most likely possibility is a continuation of the present institutionalized chaos, because of the failure of any faction to firmly establish itself. Forces within Iran will continue to pull the country apart, increasing the power and importance of tribal and ethnic groups whose commitment to a centralized state is less strong than their concern for themselves.

Then, in time-honored Persian fashion—two, five, or seven years ahead—circumstances will favor a new "man on horseback," a new Reza Shah. Whether king or commissar, from the left or from the right, but most likely with some discreet foreign support, he will emerge from Iran's armed forces or from among the array of guerrilla or tribal leaders. Distinguished by his force of personality, the fledgling dictator will reunify as much of present-day Iran as has not already passed under foreign control and destroy the power if not the personages of the religious extremists. He will seek to unite the country against further encroachment, joining with the more moderate religious leaders who will emerge from the shadows to pronounce a final benediction on the wreckage of Iran's clerical authoritarian experiment in the supremacy of mosque over state. Still Iran will be faced with one of the oldest problems in political philosophy: how to reconcile seizing power with attaining legitimacy. It is hoped that the new format will offer more positive prospects than the last.

Notes

Chapter One

1. The best coverage of this early period is in Peter Avery, *Modern Iran* (New York: Frederick A. Praeger, 1965); E.A. Bayne, *Persian Kingship in Transition* (New York: American Universities Field Staff, 1968); George Lenczowski, ed., *Iran Under the Pahlavis* (Stanford: Hoover Institution Press, 1978); Donald N. Wilber, *Riza Shah Pahlavi: The Resurrection and Reconstruction of Iran, 1878–1944* (Hicksville: Exposition Press, 1975); and Nikki Keddie, *Iran: Religion, Politics and Society* (London: Frank Cass, 1980).

2. Iran's foreign relations are covered in Shahram Chubin and Sepehr Zabih, *The Foreign Relations of Iran: A Developing State in a Zone of Great-Power Conflict* (Berkeley: University of California Press, 1974); and Rouhullah K. Ramazani, *Iran's Foreign Policy, 1941–1975* (Charlottesville: University Press of Virginia, 1975).

3. Richard M. Preece, *U.S. Policy Toward Iran, 1942–1979* (Washington: Congressional Research Service, 1979), is a balanced, factual account of what happened. A more exciting rendition of the events in 1953 is offered by Kermit Roosevelt, *Countercoup: The Struggle for Control of Iran* (New York: McGraw-Hill, 1979).

4. The best descriptions of the period from 1953 to 1977 are in Richard W. Cottam, *Nationalism in Iran* (Pittsburgh: University of Pittsburgh Press, 1978); James A. Bill, *The Politics of Iran: Groups, Classes, and Modernization* (Columbus: Charles E. Merrill, 1972); and, from a Marxist viewpoint, Fred Halliday, *Iran: Dictatorship and Development* (New York: Penguin Books, 1979).

5. Robert L. Paarlberg, ed., *Diplomatic Dispute: U.S. Conflict with Iran, Japan, and Mexico* (Cambridge: Harvard Center for International Affairs, 1978), pp. 11–54.

6. Much of the information in this and subsequent chapters was acquired by the author while he was posted to the American embassy in Tehran from July 1975 to June 1979. Where possible and when it would be helpful, corroborating public sources are cited. In some cases, for their own protection Iranian sources are not specifically identified.

7. This period of economic dislocation is outlined in detail in Amin Saikal, *The Rise and Fall of the Shah* (Princeton: Princeton University Press, 1980); and Robert Graham, *Iran: The Illusion of Power* (London: Croom Helm, 1978).

8. For pre-revolutionary analyses see Leonard Binder, *Iran* (Berkeley: University of California Press, 1962); Marvin Zonis, *The Political Elite of Iran* (Princeton: Princeton University Press, 1971); Bill, *The Politics of Iran;* and Keddie, *Iran*, especially chapters 7 and 8.

9. There has been no definitive analysis of the emergent groups which make up Iran's "new elite." The best partial attempts so far are Sepehr Zabih, *Iran's*

Revolutionary Upheaval (San Francisco: Alchemy Books, 1979); and Shahram Chubin, "Leftist Forces in Iran," *Problems of Communism*, XXIX (July-August 1980), 1–25.

Chapter Two

1. His memoir bears this out, Mohammad Reza Pahlavi, *Mission For My Country* (New York: McGraw-Hill, 1961); as does an interview, Oriana Fallaci, "The Shah," *New Republic*, September 1, 1973, pp. 16–21.

2. Quoted to author by a senior Iranian official in the Ministry of Foreign Affairs, September 1978.

3. Graham, *Iran*, pp. 129–189; Saikal, *The Rise and Fall of the Shah*, pp. 53–55, 185–186.

4. This information comes from dozens of personal discussions with the participants spread over a four-year period. In most cases, individuals were able to provide names, dates, and details as well as describe the general atmosphere of tension.

5. Information on the Resurgence Party comes from notes the author made each time after extensive talks with party officials from 1975 to 1978.

6. The hopes of Iranian modernizers for the Resurgence Party are outlined in Jame W. Jacqz, ed., *Iran: Past, Present, and Future* (New York: The Aspen Institute, 1976), pp. 217–266; and Zabih, *Iran's Revolutionary Upheaval*, pp. 5–18.

Chapter Three

1. Zabih, *Iran's Revolutionary Upheaval*, chapter 2, pp. 3–4.

2. James A. Bill, "Iran and the Crisis of 1978," *Foreign Affairs*, 58, no. 2 (Winter 1978–79), 324; and Saikal, *The Rise and Fall of the Shah*, pp. 123–131.

3. *The New York Times*, April 18 and September 10, 1979, recounted Talegani's role in revolutionary politics.

4. Amir Taheri, "The Bazaar," *Kayham International* (Tehran), October 2, 1978.

5. Ruhollah Khomeini, *Islamic Government* (New York: Manor Books, 1979), p. 30. Khomeini's political outlook is also described in Elie Kedourie, "Khomeini's Political Heresy," *Policy Review*, no. 12 (Spring 1980), 133–146; and Lester Ross, "Khomeini's Iran and Mao's China: Crises of Charismatic Authority," *Asian Thought and Society*, 5, no. 14 (September 1980).

6. Oriana Fallaci, "Khomeini," *The New York Times* Magazine, October 7, 1979, p. 29.

7. Translation of speech by Dariush Forouhar; original text in author's possession.

8. The best sources on the guerrilla movement in Iran are Eric Rouleau, "Khomeini's Iran," *Foreign Affairs*, 59, no. 2 (Fall 1980), 1–20; Chubin, "Leftist Forces in Iran"; Halliday, *Iran;* and Sepehr Zabih, *The Communist Movement in Iran* (Berkeley: University of California Press, 1966).

Chapter Four

1. The best source for basic data on U.S. involvement in Iran is Preece, *U.S. Policy*. Documentary evidence of American concern up to 1951 (when the historical series ends) can be found in *Foreign Relations of the United States* (Washington: Department of State), 1940–1951. Good personalized accounts are Arthur C. Millspaugh, *Americans in Persia* (Washington: The Brookings Institution, 1946); and W. Morgan Shuster, *The Strangling of Persia* (New York: Century Co., 1912).

2. Rad 220, Hull to Dreyfus, August 18, 1942, U.S. Department of State, 891.20/165. Quoted in Preece, *U.S. Policy*, p. 12.

3. Avery, *Modern Iran*, chapter 24; and George Lenczowski, *Russia and the West in Iran, 1918–1948* (Ithaca: Cornell University Press, 1949).

4. William E. Warne, *Mission for Peace: Point Four in Iran* (New York: Bobbs-Merrill, 1956); Preece, *U.S. Policy*, pp. 35–46.

5. Roy M. Melbourne, "America and Iran in Perspective: 1953 and 1980," *The Foreign Service Journal*, April 1980, pp. 10–17; Roosevelt, *Countercoup*; Preece, *U.S. Policy*, pp. 37–41; Cottam, *Nationalism*, pp. 224–229. Differing accounts can be found in Allen Dulles, *The Craft of Intelligence* (New York: Harper & Row, 1963), pp. 224ff.; Ray Cline, *Secrets, Spies and Scholars* (Washington: Acropolis Books, 1976), pp. 132–133; Victor Marchetti and John Marks, *The C.I.A. and the Cult of Intelligence* (New York: Alfred A. Knopf, 1974), pp. 28–29; and Thomas Powers, *The Man Who Kept the Secrets* (New York: Alfred A. Knopf, 1979), pp. 85ff.

6. Preece, *U.S. Policy*, pp. 57–59; U.S. Department of State, *Bulletin*, March 23, 1959, pp. 416–417.

7. Bayne, *Persian Kingship*, pp. 192–194.

8. "Foreign Assistance Act of 1968," hearing before the House Committee on Foreign Affairs, U.S. House of Representatives, 90th Congress, March 11, 1968, pp. 251ff.

9. All the information of embassy staffing is from *Foreign Service List* (Washington: U.S. Department of State), May 1, 1967, March 15, 1963, and June 1973; plus personal observation for the years 1975–1979.

10. Robert J. Pranger and Dale R. Tahtinen, "American Policy Options in Iran and the Persian Gulf," *The A.E.I. Foreign Policy and Defense Review*, 1, no. 2 (1979), 2–6.

11. The fiscal data are from U.S. Department of Defense, Defense Security Assistance Agency, Military Assistance Program Data, fiscal year series, 1947–1979; and "U.S. Military Sales to Iran," staff report to the Subcommittee on Foreign Assistance of the Committee on Foreign Relations, U.S. Senate, July 1976.

12. This informal survey was conducted by two U.S. embassy officers.

13. This accusation was repeated most recently on the CBS "Sixty Minutes" television program, April 4, 1980. For the counterview, see Charles F. Doran, *Myth, Oil, and Politics* (New York: The Free Press, 1977), especially pp. 5 and 44–45.

14. Much has been written about this period, but the most incisive description is Abdul Karim Mansur (the pen name of a former senior American State Department official), "The Crisis in Iran: Why the U.S. Ignored a Quarter Century of Warning," *Armed Forces Journal International*, January 1979, pp. 26–33. The best source for the revolutionary period is Herman Nickel, "The U.S. Failure in Iran," *Fortune*, 12 (March 1979), 106. In addition to this book, the best sources to date on U.S. foreign policy during the Iranian episode are Michael Ledeen and William Lewis, *Debacle: The American Failure in Iran* (New York: Alfred A. Knopf, 1981); the Nickel article; and Michael A. Ledeen and William H. Lewis, "Carter and the Fall of the Shah: The Inside Story," *The Washington Quarterly*, 3 (1980), 3–40. For an in-depth view from near the top, see the excellent series on Undersecretary of State for Political Affairs David D. Newsom by Robert Shaplen in *The New Yorker*, June 2, 9, and 16, 1980, especially the June 9 issue. Less has been produced so far about the hostage crisis, but an acceptable discussion can be found in the special issue of *The New York Times Magazine*, May 17, 1981, titled "America in Captivity: Points of Decision in the Hostage Crisis."

Chapter Five

1. *The New York Times*, January 2, February 10, March 1 and 3, 1978.
2. Much of the information in this chapter and in subsequent chapters was acquired by the author while he was in Tehran.
3. *The New York Times*, May 1, July 29, August 1 and 3, 1977.
4. U.S. Department of State, *Bulletin*, 77 (December 27, 1977), 907–912.
5. *Weekly Compilation of Presidential Documents*, 14 (January 23, 1978), 47.
6. *The New York Times*, February 20, 21, 22, and 24, 1978.
7. *The New York Times*, October 26, 1977.
8. Ascertained through interviews.

Chapter Six

1. See *Kayhan International* (Tehran), August 4, 1978, for the text of the Shah's Constitution Day speech and issues of that newspaper from August through mid-September for documentation of the events described in this chapter.
2. Preece, *U.S. Policy*, pp. 109–110; and broadsides quoting Shariatmadari's speech distributed on the streets of Tehran and now in the author's possession.
3. Statement to the author in a discussion with a senior Liberation Movement leader.
4. *Kayhan International* (Tehran), August 25–30, 1978.
5. *The New York Times*, September 5, 9, and 11, 1978.

Chapter Seven

1. Preece, *U.S. Policy*, pp. 109–114; and Zabih, *Iran's Revolutionary Upheaval*, pp. 50–56, cover the events of September and early October, especially the strikes.
2. Interviews with various Iranian government officials.
3. Walter Laqueur, "Why the Shah Fell," *Commentary*, 67, no. 3 (March 1979), pp. 47–55.
4. Discussions with Iranian participants.
5. Zabih, *Iran's Revolutionary Upheaval*, pp. 54–55; and *The New York Times*, October 19 and 31, 1978.
6. *The New York Times*, November 7, 8, 10, and 12, 1978.
7. Ledeen and Lewis, in *Debacle*, pp. 125–135, make much of French and Israeli reports predicting the early political demise of the Shah. At least one British and two U.S. analyses of the period suggested the same thing. The point here is that all of these reports were isolated cries in the wilderness. None of the countries was convinced of the truth of these rumors enough to alter its policy of support for the Shah until after the potential for a stiff military reprisal against the dissidents had gradually dissolved, by the end of December 1978.

Chapter Eight

1. *Time* magazine, December 18, 1978, p. 10.
2. Nickel, "The U.S. Failure in Iran"; and *The New York Times*, November 14 and 23, 1978.
3. *The New York Times*, November 29, 1978; Zabih, *Iran's Revolutionary Upheaval*, pp. 56–59; and the author's own interviews.
4. *The New York Times*, November 12 and 13, 1978, enumerates the basic points. The wording used here is based on the handout, in English, prepared by the opposition press in Tehran.

5. *The Washington Post*, December 8, 1978.

6. Confirmed by *Kayhan International* (Tehran), January 6, 1979.

7. From both Iranian and foreign sources.

8. General Huyser will not comment on his mission. In any case, it was not as clear-cut as two accounts suggest. See Ledeen and Lewis, "Carter and the Fall of the Shah," pp. 33–38; and Richard T. Sale, "Did We Head Off a Bloodbath in Iran?" *The Washington Post*, February 1, 1980.

9. *The New York Times*, January 11, 1979.

Chapter Nine

1. See *The New York Times* and *The Washington Post* for the period from January 1 to February 29, 1979, for descriptive accounts of the events in this chapter.

2. *The New York Times*, February 7, 1979.

3. Sale, "Did We Head Off a Bloodbath in Iran?"; *The Washington Post*, June 3, 1980; and Ledeen and Lewis, "Carter and the Fall of the Shah," pp. 33–38.

4. Dr. Abd al-Rahman, *The Betrayal of Iran* (Denver: n.p., 1980), is the most articulate exile viewpoint. The Shah's point of view is expounded in Mohammad Reza Pahlavi, *Answer to History* (New York: Stein & Day, 1980); and in *Kayhan International* (Tehran), January 14, 1979.

5. *Kayhan International*, Febuary 7, 1979.

6. *The New York Times*, February 13 and 14, 1979.

7. This account of the takeover has been pieced together from the author's own experiences and the stories of others similarly involved. Personal accounts can also be found in *Department of State Newsletter*, no. 210 (March 1979), 12–22.

8. Accounts in *The New York Times*, February 16 and March 1, 1979, address this problem.

9. Reports in the American press in the first days after the revolutionary takeover are sparse, because most correspondents were fleeing the country. *The New York Times* and *The Washington Post*, February 18, 19 and 21, 1979, however, do cover these events.

Chapter Ten

1. *The New York Times*, April 26 and May 27, 1979.

2. *The New York Times*, June 2, August 3 and 8, 1979.

3. Information about the executions can be found in *The New York Times*, February 17 and 27, 1979; and *The Washington Post*, June 19, 1980. A very emotional account of former Prime Minister Hoveyda's death is given in his brother's book, Feridoun Hoveyda, *The Fall of the Shah* (New York: Wyndham Books, 1980), pp. 187–191.

4. Khomeini, *Islamic Government*, pp. 34–75; two articles in *Dissent*, vol. 27, by Sharif Arani, "Iran from the Shah's Dictatorship to Khomeini's Demagogic Theocracy" (Winter 1980), 9–26; and "The Iranian Revolution: Year Zero" (Spring 1980), 144–148; and Kedourie, "Khomeini's Political Heresy."

5. Oriana Fallaci, "Everyone Wants to be Boss," *The New York Times*, October 28, 1979.

6. Preece, *U.S. Policy*, p. 121. See also *The New York Times*, March 16, 1979.

7. *The Washington Post*, November 10, 1979.

8. *The Washington Post*, October 4, 1979.

Chapter Eleven

1. John Kifner, "How a Sit-in Turned into a Siege," *The New York Times Magazine*, May 17, 1981, pp. 54–73, describes accurately the rank-and-file radical students. He is less perceptive about the leadership cadre, which had been trained abroad. This group and its P.L.O. allies were responsible for the effective planning and preparation; their efforts explain why the attack went relatively smoothly. The "foreign involvement" in this case was the fruition of the P.L.O.-Mujahidin-Fedayeen linkage of earlier years, and not a new phenomenon.

2. *The New York Times*, November 7 and 10, 1979.

3. All quotes on this subject are from *The New York Times*, March 29 to April 2, 1980.

4. Unfortunately, President Carter and a few U.S. officials were convinced Khomeini was ready to make a deal at this time. See Terrence Smith, "Putting the Hostages' Lives First," *The New York Times Magazine*, May 17, 1981, pp. 96 and 81. He notes that other State Department officers did not agree at all. They felt Carter should play down the hostage situation by not making such a public issue of it and thus taking some of the pressure off. Smith seems unaware, however, of a "dissident" memo to Vance, which the Secretary discussed with its authors, three concerned Foreign Service specialists on Iran. These officers, of which I was one, suggested that in view of the political deadlock in Tehran, an effective, well-supported military effort to rescue the hostages was the only way to cut the Gordian knot. Since Vance was unalterably opposed to the use of force, he did not pass these opinions on to the President.

5. Knowledgeable Iranian and American sources have confirmed this. Kifner, "How a Sit-in Turned into a Siege," pp. 68–73, provides some interesting insights into the chaotic operation of the Revolutionary Council during this period.

Chapter Twelve

1. The best public account of the raid, because it raises the military issues in their political context, is Drew Middleton, "Going the Military Route," *The New York Times Magazine*, May 17, 1981, pp. 103–112. The unclassified version of the official Defense Department critique of the raid is well covered in the August 24, 1980 editions of *The Washington Post* and *The New York Times*. A devastating unofficial criticism of the military aspects of the raid can be found in Stuart L. Koehl and Stephen P. Glick, "Why the Rescue Failed," *The American Spectator*, 13, no. 7 (July 1980), 23–35.

2. Factual accounts of the war can be found in *The Washington Post* and *The New York Times* since September 23, 1980.

3. Good descriptions of the final hostage negotiations are in *The New York Times*, January 28, 1981; *The Washington Post*, January 25, 1981; and Smith, "Putting the Hostages' Lives First."

4. The dimensions of the gap between the clerics' perceptions and Western views are described in Roy Parviz Mottahedeh, "Iran's Foreign Devils," *Foreign Policy*, no. 38 (Spring 1980), 19–34.

5. *The Washington Post*, November 23, 1980.

6. Carter administration officials agree that Reagan's hard line, though unsolicited, pushed the Iranians into serious negotiations. See Smith, "Putting the Hostages' Lives First," p. 100.

Chapter Thirteen

1. W. Howard Wriggins, *The Ruler's Imperative: Strategies for Political Survival in Asia and Africa* (New York: Columbia University Press, 1969), pp. 1–13, 241–253, outlines basic leadership strategies for both short-term and long-term problems.

2. *The Washington Post*, June 7, 1980; and *The New York Times*, August 15, 1980.

3. Ashraf Pahlavi, *Faces in a Mirror: Memoirs from Exile* (Englewood Cliffs, N.J.: Prentice-Hall, 1980), contains her rationale and explanation of her brother's role.

Chapter Fourteen

1. Nickel, "The U.S. Failure in Iran," p. 106. See also Ledeen and Lewis, "Carter and the Fall of the Shah"; and Mansur, "The Crisis in Iran."

2. "U.S. Policy Toward Iran, January 1979," Hearings before the Subcommittee on Europe and the Middle East of the Committee on Foreign Affairs, U.S. House of Representatives, 96th Congress, pp. 29–33.

3. Ledeen and Lewis, *Debacle*, pp. 134–135, 233–243.

4. Nickel, "The U.S. Failure in Iran," p. 102; and Ledeen and Lewis, "Carter and the Fall of the Shah," p. 39.

5. "Iran: Evaluation of U.S. Intelligence Performance Prior to November 1978," Staff Report for the Subcommittee on Evaluation of the Permanent Select Committee on Intelligence, U.S. House of Representatives, pp. 7–8. This report and Richard K. Betts, "Analysis, War and Decision: Why Intelligence Failures Are Inevitable," *World Politics*, XXXI, no. 1 (October 1978), 61–89, outline the basic dilemmas in intelligence gathering and analysis.

6. Good basic accounts of this controversy are in *The New York Times*, November 23, 1978; and in an article by Henry Trewhitt, "Poor Forecasts on Shah Fire Intense U.S. Debate," *Baltimore Sun*, November 29, 1978.

7. "U.S. Policy Toward Iran, January 1979," p. 32.

8. William Sullivan, *Contacts With the Opposition* (Washington: Georgetown University School of Foreign Service, 1979), p. 4. Sulivan's description of the embassy's work, especially pp. 1–4, belies the claims that the mission had no meaningful contacts within Iran. A particularly egregious article is Jonathan Randal, "Envoy in Iran—U.S. Faith in the Shah Turns into Liability," *The Washington Post*, January 13, 1979.

9. This point is delineated most clearly in Ledeen and Lewis, "Carter and the Fall of the Shah," pp. 35–37; and William Sullivan, "Dateline Iran: The Road Not Taken," *Foreign Policy*, no. 40 (Fall 1980), 175–186. For confirmation of the President's problems in choosing between Brzezinski and Sullivan, see Scott Armstrong, "U.S. Rejects Coup Options," *The Washington Post*, October 30, 1980; and "Interview With Former State Department Press Spokesman Hodding Carter," *Playboy*, February 1981.

10. Mansur, "The Crisis in Iran," pp. 32–33; and "Iran: Evaluation of U.S. Intelligence," pp. 1–2.

11. Richard A. Falk, "Khomeini's Promise," *Foreign Policy*, no. 34 (Spring 1979), 28–34.

12. Betts, "Analysis, War and Decision," p. 53. His basic thesis is that some errors are always inevitable, but it may be possible to protect yourself against certain types of mistakes.

13. Ledeen and Lewis, *Debacle*, p. 133; Nickel, "The U.S. Failure in Iran"; and Walter Guzzardi, Jr., "What To Do About Iran," *Fortune*, June 2, 1980, pp. 44–47. The syndrome is described by its originator, Irving Janis, in *Victims of Groupthink: A Psychological Study of Foreign Policy Decisions and Fiascoes* (Boston: Houghton Mifflin, 1972), pp. 185–225.

14. Accounts of the arguments within the National Security Council differ. What appears here is the most accurate reconstruction possible after discussing the situation with both participants and observers.

15. The general unfolding of events is described in Ledeen and Lewis, "Carter and the Fall of the Shah"; William Branigan, "U.S. Called Too Eager in Wooing the Shah," *The Washington Post*, June 18, 1980; and Sullivan, "Dateline Iran."

16. This process is described in a number of publications about how organizations operate. Its application to foreign policy can be found in John D. Stempel, *Theory and Practice in Foreign Affairs: Why Two Worlds Seldom Meet* (Columbus: The Mershon Center, 1972).

17. Personal interviews with the individuals involved.

18. Ledeen and Lewis, "Carter and the Fall of the Shah," p. 37.

19. *The Christian Science Monitor*, November 12, 1980.

20. Pahlavi, *Answer to History*, pp. 169–174.

21. *Ibid.*

22. *The Washington Post*, November 29, 1979. The alleged Rockefeller involvement is outlined in L.J. Davis, "Hostages for Chase Manhattan," *Penthouse*, December 1980, pp. 70ff.

23. Terrence Smith, "Why Carter Admitted the Shah," *The New York Times Magazine*, May 17, 1981, p. 44, shows that reducing the American presence in Iran was scarcely considered at the presidential level even after the decision to admit the Shah. Debate in the State Department was more lively. On February 27, 1979, for example, the author suggested in a memo to the Iran Working Group that the mission be cut to "three officers and a dog, preferably a hungry German shepherd," as a visible sign of America's displeasure at the attack on the embassy and U.S. willingness to move away from the old relationship with Iran, yet retain modest ties which could be expanded when and if Bazargan's regime could control the revolutionaries.

Chapter Fifteen

1. Crane Brinton, *The Anatomy of Revolution* (New York: Vintage Books, 1952), pp. 34–38.

2. Jack Goldstone, "Theories of Revolution: The Third Generation," *World Politics*, XXXII, no. 4 (April 1980), 426–434.

3. *Ibid.*, pp. 436–437.

4. The result is consistent with one model of revolutionary activity. See Yong Pil Rhee, "A Dynamic Model for the Analysis of System Breakdown in Developing Societies," paper delivered at the American Political Science Annual Meeting, Washington, D.C., August 31, 1980.

5. Imbued with the essence of Islamic fatalism, the Shah ignored the importance of timely, effective action by the elite, as discussed in Chalmers Johnson, *Revolutionary Change* (Boston: Little, Brown, 1965), pp. 12ff.; and in Goldstone, "Theories of Revolution," p. 430.

6. For a review of literature on the meaning of the Iranian revolution, see Jamshid Momeni, "The Roots of Revolution in Iran," *Journal of Political and Military Sociology*, 8, no. 2 (Fall 1980), 287–299.

Index